THE GENOCIDE CO

INTERNATIONAL AND COMPARATIVE CRIMINAL JUSTICE SERIES

Series Editors:

Mark Findlay, *Institute of Criminology, University of Sydney*
Ralph Henham, *Nottingham Law School, Nottingham Trent University*

This series explores the new and rapidly developing field of international and comparative criminal justice and engages with its most important emerging themes and debates. It focuses on three interrelated aspects of scholarship which go to the root of understanding the nature and significance of international criminal justice in the broader context of globalization and global governance. These include: the theoretical and methodological problems posed by the development of international and comparative criminal justice; comparative contextual analysis; the reciprocal relationship between comparative and international criminal justice and contributions which endeavor to build understandings of global justice on foundations of comparative contextual analysis.

Other titles in the series

Punishment and Process in International Criminal Trials
Ralph Henham
ISBN 0 7546 2437 4

A World View of Criminal Justice
Richard Vogler
ISBN 0 7546 2467 6

The Genocide Convention
An International Law Analysis

JOHN QUIGLEY
The Ohio State University, USA

Routledge
Taylor & Francis Group

LONDON AND NEW YORK

First published 2006 by Ashgate Publishing

2 Park Square, Milton Park, Abingdon, Oxon OX14 4RN
711 Third Avenue, New York, NY 10017, USA

Routledge is an imprint of the Taylor & Francis Group, an informa business

First issued in paperback 2016

British Library Cataloguing in Publication Data
Quigley, John B.
    The genocide convention : an international law analysis. -
    (International and comparative criminal justice)
    1. United Nations 2. Convention on the Prevention and
    Punishment of the Crime of Genocide (1948) 3. Genocide
    I. Title
    345'.0251

Library of Congress Cataloging-in-Publication Data
Quigley, John B.
    The Genocide Convention : an international law analysis / by John Quigley.
        p. cm. -- (International and comparative criminal justice)
    Includes bibliographical references and index.
    ISBN 0-7546-4730-7
    1. Genocide. 2. Crimes against humanity. I. Title. II. Series.

    K5302.Q85 2006
    345'.0251--dc22

                                                                2006000103

Transfered to Digital Printing in 2010

ISBN 978-0-7546-4730-0 (hbk)
ISBN 978-1-138-26451-9 (pbk)

Contents

Table of Cases

Note: Texts of cited court cases are typically available on websites of the respective courts. Texts of court cases of Rwanda are available in French from Avocats sans frontières, Brussels, www.asf/be.

International Court of Justice

Preface

The law of genocide dates from the mid-twentieth century. My own acquaintance with the topic dates from 1979, when I served as an expert witness on the law of genocide in the first criminal prosecution charging genocide as defined by the Convention on the Prevention and Punishment of the Crime of Genocide. Two leaders of the recently overthrown Khmer Rouge government of Cambodia stood accused. The trial involved difficult issues of the interpretation of the Genocide Convention. In a statement to the court in Phnom Penh after the close of evidence, I said that the evidence had shown that genocide had been committed: "an intent to use mass killings to wipe out national minorities, religious groups, and the stratum of intellectuals in Kampuchean society. Article 2 of the Genocide Convention also considers it to be genocide if conditions are imposed on a group to bring about its elimination in whole or in part."

A decade after the Khmer Rouge trial, the world watched in horror as atrocities unfolded in Bosnia. Killings and rape were being used to force the Muslim population of Bosnia out of their home areas, and the term "ethnic cleansing" was used as a description. Bosnia sued Yugoslavia in the International Court of Justice, the United Nations court at The Hague. This was the first case in which a state alleged genocide in a lawsuit against another state. It was also the first in which a court injunction was sought, to stop atrocities as they were being committed. The Genocide Convention allows one ratifying state to sue another, but Yugoslavia argued that this meant only for refusing to prosecute or extradite a person who commits genocide. Yugoslavia said that the Genocide Convention did not require it to respond to a suit charging it with committing genocide.

At the invitation of Professor Francis Boyle, co-agent for Bosnia, I served on a team of attorneys for Bosnia that argued issues of first impression in the law of genocide. There was no judicial precedent on "ethnic cleansing" as genocide. Nor was there precedent on the responsibility of a state like Yugoslavia, that was, by Bosnia's allegation, facilitating genocide by others. After hearing arguments at The Hague, the court issued the first injunction against genocide.

Fears heightened that the atrocities seen in Bosnia would be repeated elsewhere in eastern Europe, already in ferment. The US Information Agency asked me to consult with the government of Moldova on ethnic conflict that had led to hostilities. The US State Department and the Organization for Security and Cooperation in Europe asked me to serve as an independent expert to mediate for a political arrangement between Ukraine and Crimea, another potential ethnic trouble spot.

In Africa, members of a recently overthrown government in Ethiopia were being arrested by the hundreds for killing political opponents. A special prosecutor filed charges, including genocide, making this the first instance of genocide prosecutions simultaneously against a large number of persons. The international community pressed Ethiopia to try these cases by due process standards, a difficult feat given the country's poverty and the large numbers of accused. As part of an international effort to assist, I was asked by the US Agency for International Development, through Attorney Libby Cooper, an advisor to the Office of Special Prosecutor in Addis Ababa, to consult with Ethiopian judges about international standards of due process. I had lively dialogues with Ethiopian judges about judicial independence, trials held *in absentia*, and a government's obligation to reveal incriminating evidence to the accused prior to trial.

Soon two special international penal tribunals, one for Yugoslavia and one for Rwanda, began prosecuting for genocide, and to interpret the Genocide Convention, which was ambiguous on key points. These proceedings, as well as my own experiences, convinced me of the need for clarification of the definition of genocide. The intent required for genocide piqued my interest as a teacher of criminal law. The issue of whether a state could be sued for genocide piqued my interest as a teacher of international law.

Lurking behind the technical issues lay that of whether genocide as a legal category is useful. As I surveyed the mass killing in Cambodia, formulated legal arguments against ethnic cleansing in Bosnia, and travelled Africa and eastern Europe, the question in the back of my mind was whether the law, and genocide law in particular, can prevent mass atrocities.

The Genocide Convention: An International Law Analysis is structured around these issues. After three introductory parts, which explain how genocide came to be accepted as a legal norm, the next four parts analyze the intent required for genocide. Part Eight examines suits against states for genocide. Part Nine hazards tentative answers to the question of the utility of genocide as a legal concept. Throughout, I endeavor to show how a document, the Genocide Convention, that was drafted in a specific historical context, namely, the aftermath of World War II, has been applied in circumstances unforeseen by its drafters. That exercise has led to considerable difficulty of interpretation. At some junctures, I argue for a particular possible reading of the Genocide Convention, while at others I find the complexity leaving me grateful that I am not a judge who must resolve it.

A number of colleagues kindly responded to my calls for assistance. Professor Mark A. Drumbl provided materials on prosecutions in Rwanda. Professor Roger Clark provided information on the work of the Preparatory Commission for the International Criminal Court. Professors Jan Perlin and Kelly Askin provided documentation from the Yugoslavia tribunal. Dr Andreas Paulus helped locate German decisional law. Professor Mary Ellen O'Connell and Professor Francis Boyle gave helpful comments on an early partial draft.

The Michael E. Moritz College of Law of the Ohio State University provided a supportive base from which to work, in particular research assistance and research leave. Colleagues at the College contributed valuable insights, Professor Mary Ellen O'Connell on international law, and Professor Joshua Dressler on criminal law. John Wilson, J.D. 2003, checked German language sources. Harry Fogler, J.D. 2004, checked citations and averted a number of errors. The research staff of the Moritz Law Library at the College secured many source items. Amy Beaudreault of the College staff expertly formatted the manuscript for publication.

The literature and statutory law on genocide are written in many languages. Where non-English sources are quoted, the translations are mine. Professor Timothy Jost contributed his expertise on German texts. Professors Daniel Chow and Guohua Wang assisted with Chinese texts.

It is my hope that *The Genocide Convention: An International Law Analysis* will clarify the definition and scope of genocide, and thereby contribute to whatever utility the concept may hold.

John Quigley
Columbus, Ohio

List of Abbreviations

adv.op.	advisory opinion
C.6	Sixth Committee of UN General Assembly
ECOSOC	UN Economic and Social Council
ECOSOCOR	UN Economic and Social Council Official Records
GA	UN General Assembly
GAOR	General Assembly Official Records
ICC	International Criminal Court
ICJ	International Court of Justice
ICJ Rep.	International Court of Justice, Reports of Judgments, Advisory Opinions and Orders
ICTR	International Criminal Tribunal for Rwanda
ILC	International Law Commission
ILR	International Law Reports
IT	International Criminal Tribunal for the Former Yugoslavia
LNTS	League of Nations Treaty Series
PCIJ	Permanent Court of International Justice
PCIJ Rep.	Permanent Court of International Justice: Judgments, Advisory Opinions and Orders, Series A
Res.	Resolution
SC	UN Security Council
SCOR	UN Security Council Official Records
sess.	session
SR	Summary Records (of UN meetings)
Supp.	Supplement
UN	United Nations
UNTS	United Nations Treaty Series
US	United States of America

Note

Format of references: In the footnotes, the numeral following the title of a periodical is the volume number. Where more than one page number is indicated for an article or a book chapter, the first number is the initial page, and subsequent numbers are for the pages being cited. For decisions of courts of the United States, the volume number precedes the name of the court, and the page number follows.

PART ONE
OUTLAWING GENOCIDE

Chapter 1

A Crime Without a Name

The crime of genocide is a result of international efforts to deal with a phenomenon that has plagued the international community. Forcible acts are directed against individual members of a group in a way that threatens the group. In the twentieth century, the first atrocity episode to spur action by governments saw the Armenian population of Turkey as the victims. Numbering nearly two million, the Armenians were viewed as a secession threat by Turkey. In 1915, the onset of war brought the prospect that the Armenians would side with Turkey's enemies. Turkey began deporting its Armenian population to Syria and Mesopotamia. The deportation was carried out with considerable brutality and included mass executions. Several hundred thousand Armenians perished.[1] The historian Arnold Toynbee decried Turkey's conduct, calling it "the murder of a nation."[2] It would be another generation, however, before an international crime would be defined to write into law what Toynbee had in mind.

A commission appointed by the World War I Allies to explore prosecutions for war-related atrocities drew up a suggested list of offenses.[3] For future "international crimes," proposals were aired for an international penal tribunal, either as a self-standing court, or as a function of the Permanent Court of International Justice, which had just been set up by the League of Nations. The French jurist Henri Donnedieu de Vabres described one potential category of offenses as follows: "attacks on humanity that might be perpetrated in a country under the influence of race hatred."[4] The Spanish jurist Quintiliano Saldaña suggested an internationally defined offense for "acts of savagery, such as major political or racial massacres."[5] Saldaña gave as examples then recent atrocities: "the massacres of Christian-Armenians and Russian

1   Dadrian, V.N. (1995), *The History of the Armenian Genocide: Ethnic Conflict from the Balkans to Anatolia to the Caucasus*, Berghahn Books, Providence.

2   Toynbee, A.J. (1915), *Armenian Atrocities: The Murder of a Nation*, Hodder & Stoughton, London & New York.

3   'Commission on the Responsibility of the Authors of the War and on Enforcement of Penalties: Report Presented to the Preliminary Peace Conference, Mar. 29, 1919,' (1920) *American Journal of International Law*, 14, p. 95.

4   Donnedieu de Vabres, H. (1924-1925), 'La Cour Permanente de Justice Internationale et sa Vocation en matière criminelle,' *Revue internationale de droit pénal* 1 (no. 19), p. 186.

5   Saldaña, Q. (1925), 'La Justice pénale internationale,' *Recueil des cours* (Hague Academy of International Law) 10, p. 369.

Jews."[6] The reference to "Christian-Armenians" was to the Armenians killed during the 1915 deportation by Turkey. The reference to "Russian Jews" was to Jews killed in organized mass attacks (pogroms) in Russia around the turn of the century.

There had long been an understanding that atrocities during military hostilities were unlawful and of international concern. Jurists like Donnedieu de Vabres and Saldaña hoped to extend international jurisdiction to atrocities not necessarily connected to a war, and perpetrated within the territory of a single state. These were revolutionary proposals, infringing, as they did, on the traditional prerogative of states in their own territory.

No progress was made during the inter-war period towards defining international offenses or devising any international jurisdiction. Inroads were made, however, during the inter-war years on the domestic domain of states regarding treatment of nationals. A system emerged out of World War I for rights protection for minority groups in certain states of eastern Europe. The League of Nations presided over this system, with an oversight agency to which minorities could appeal.

Nonetheless, it was only after World War II that states began to be held internationally accountable for treatment of their nationals. It was in large measure the atrocities committed by the Third Reich against civilians that galvanized international opinion on rights protection, even though this would mean an international obligation of states regarding treatment of their own citizens. In this context the crime of genocide took shape.

Conception of an Offense of Genocide

The mass killing by the Third Reich served as a catalyst to defining a crime to deal with efforts to wipe out a people. On 24 August 1941, nine weeks after Germany invaded the Soviet Union, Winston Churchill made a radio broadcast in which he lauded the Russians for their resistance to Germany's eastward advance. Said Churchill, "the aggressor ... retaliates by the most frightful cruelties. As his armies advance, whole districts are being exterminated. Scores of thousands—literally scores of thousands—of executions in cold blood are being perpetrated by the German police-troops upon the Russian patriots who defend their native soil. Since the Mongol invasions of Europe in the sixteenth century, there has never been methodical, merciless butchery on such a scale, or approaching such a scale. And this is but the beginning. Famine and pestilence have yet to follow in the bloody ruts of Hitler's tanks. We are in the presence of a crime without a name."[7]

The term "genocide" was invented for the crime that Churchill could not name. The term was the brainchild of Raphael Lemkin, a Polish lawyer who himself

---

6   Saldaña (1925), p. 306.

7   'Atlantic Charter, August 24, 1941, Broadcast, London,' in R.R. James (ed), *Winston S. Churchill: His Complete Speeches 1897-1963*, vol. 6, p. 6474 (1935-1942), R.R. Bowker, New York & London (1974).

narrowly escaped persecution, and who spent the war working in Washington, analyzing Nazi occupation policy. In 1944 Lemkin produced *Axis Rule in Occupied Europe*, which described atrocities in each country occupied by the Third Reich.

Lemkin suggested the term "genocide" to describe Nazi occupation practices. Modeling on such terms as tyrannicide, homicide, and infanticide, Lemkin pieced the term together from the Greek *genos* (a people), and the latin suffix *cida* (kill). "Genocide is effected," Lemkin wrote,

> through a synchronized attack on different aspects of life of the captive peoples: in the political field (by destroying institutions of self-government and imposing a German pattern of administration, and through colonization by Germans); in the social field (by disrupting the social cohesion of the nation involved and killing or removing elements such as the intelligentsia, which provide spiritual leadership—according to Hitler's statement in *Mein Kampf*, "the greatest of spirits can be liquidated if its bearer is beaten to death with a rubber truncheon"); in the cultural field (by prohibiting or destroying cultural institutions and cultural activities; by substituting vocational education for education in the liberal arts, in order to prevent humanistic thinking, which the occupant considers dangerous because it promotes national thinking); in the economic field (by shifting the wealth to Germans and by prohibiting the exercise of trades and occupations by people who do not promote Germanism "without reservations"); in the biological field (by a policy of depopulation and by promoting procreation by Germans in the occupied countries); in the field of physical existence (by introducing a starvation rationing system for non-Germans and by mass killings, mainly of Jews, Poles, Slovenes, and Russians); in the religious field (by interfering with the activities of the Church, which in many countries provides not only spiritual but also national leadership); in the field of morality (by attempts to create an atmosphere of moral debasement through promoting pornographic publications and motion pictures, and the excessive consumption of alcohol).[8]

As we shall see, not all aspects identified by Lemkin would be carried over into the "genocide" that states would accept as an international offense. However, the inspiration for the concept is reflected in Lemkin's analysis.

In August 1945, the World War II Allies decided to hold high Nazi figures accountable through criminal trials. To their written agreement to do so, they appended a document they called the Charter of the International Military Tribunal for the Trial of the Major War Criminals. The Charter identified a category of "crimes against humanity" and defined it as

> murder, extermination, enslavement, deportation, and other inhumane acts committed against any civilian population, before or during the war, or persecutions on political, racial or

---

8   Lemkin, R. (1944), *Axis Rule in Occupied Europe: Laws of Occupation, Analysis of Government, Proposals for Redress*, pp. xi-xii, Carnegie Endowment for International Peace, Washington.

religious grounds in execution of or in connection with any crime within the jurisdiction of the Tribunal, whether or not in violation of the domestic law of the country where perpetrated.[9]

Mass atrocities were individual penal offenses in the documents establishing the post-World War II international tribunals for Germany and Japan under the category "crimes against humanity." One such offense was labeled persecution and involved acts of violence against members of a particular group, when the actor selects them because of their membership in the group. Another crime had been defined as extermination, involving the killing of persons of a particular group. The law on the conduct of warfare already prohibited acts of violence against civilians in wartime. The concept of crimes against humanity, as developed after World War II, brought prohibitions into the realm of atrocities committed in peacetime.

"Crimes against humanity" was as close as the Charter of the International Military Tribunal came to an offense of genocide.[10] Although no one was prosecuted in the post-World War II trials in Germany or Japan for an offense denominated as genocide, the term "genocide" was by then current. When commanders of the killing squads, called "Einsatzgruppen," that accompanied German occupation troops into Poland and Russia were prosecuted for "crimes against humanity," prosecutors used the term "genocide" to describe their conduct.

The Nuremberg indictment, in describing acts of the accused constituting war crimes, recited: "They conducted deliberate and systematic genocide, viz., the extermination of racial and national groups, against the civilian populations of certain occupied territories in order to destroy particular races and classes of people and national, racial, or religious groups, particularly Jews, Poles, and Gypsies and others."[11]

In a prosecution in the US zone in Germany, a US prosecutor characterized Nazi policy as genocide. In his opening statement in the Einsatzgruppen case, Prosecutor Benjamin Ferencz charged that these Nazi units "were to destroy all those denominated Jew, political official, gypsy, and those other thousands called 'asocial' by the self-styled Nazi superman." Ferencz said, "We will show that these deeds of men in uniform were the methodical execution of long-range plans to destroy ethnic, national, political, and religious groups which stood condemned in the Nazi mind.

---

9   Charter of the International Military Tribunal, art. 6(c), appended to Agreement for the Prosecution and Punishment of the Major War Criminals of the European Axis, 8 August 1945, UNTS 82, p. 279.

10   Cassese, A. (2002), 'Genocide,' in A. Cassese, P. Gaeta and J. Jones (eds), *The Rome Statute of the International Criminal Court: A Commentary*, vol. 1, p. 335, Oxford University Press, Oxford.

11   *Trial of the Major War Criminals before the International Military Tribunal: Nuremberg, 14 November 1945 - 1 October 1946*, vol. 1, pp. 43-44, International Military Tribunal, Nuremberg (1947).

Genocide, the extermination of whole categories of human beings, was a foremost instrument of the Nazi doctrine."[12]

Defining Genocide

The UN Charter, adopted in 1945, proclaimed human rights as a goal of the new United Nations Organization and committed member states to work with the UN to promote the observance of rights. One of the first orders of business of the UN was to put rights protection into written form, with the aim of establishing specific obligations for states. The prohibition against genocide developed as part of the entrenchment of the concept of rights of the individual.

In 1947 and 1948, the UN worked along two tracks to protect human rights. One track aimed at getting states to observe rights in their treatment of individuals. This task was complex, since it required defining a broad range of rights. As a preliminary step to an anticipated general treaty on human rights, the UN devised a bill of rights as an aspirational document. This became the Universal Declaration of Human Rights, adopted by the UN General Assembly on 10 December 1948.[13]

The other track was a treaty on major atrocities. Given the horrific nature of the atrocities only recently perpetrated, the attention of the international community focused first on such situations. Whereas a general human rights treaty would take time, it was thought that states would be willing immediately to sign a treaty on major atrocities. This track built on the experience of the Charter of the International Military Tribunal and the prosecutions carried out under it.

In this context, the term "genocide" appeared for the first time in a formal document. The UN General Assembly adopted a resolution asking the UN Economic and Social Council, which was responsible under the UN structure for human rights, to draft a treaty on "the crime of genocide." After the anticipated approval by the General Assembly, the treaty would be offered to states for ratification. In its resolution, the General Assembly affirmed that genocide is a crime under international law for which individuals are punishable, and characterized genocide as "a denial of the right of existence of entire human groups, as homicide is the denial of the right to live of individual human beings."[14]

A crime definition, however, required more than a name. The UN Economic and Social Council undertook to concretize the General Assembly's concept of genocide. It asked the UN Secretary-General to prepare a draft treaty on "the crime of

---

12 USA v. Otto Ohlendorf et al. (Einsatzgruppen case), *Trials of War Criminals before the Nuernberg Military Tribunals under Control Council Law No. 10*, vol. 4, pp. 30-31, US Government Printing Office, Washington (1949).

13 Morsink, J. (1999), *The Universal Declaration of Human Rights: Origins, Drafting, and Intent*, University of Pennsylvania Press, Philadelphia.

14 GA Res. 96, UN GAOR, 1st sess., Part 2, *Resolutions*, p. 188, UN Doc. A/64/Add.1 (1946).

genocide."[15] The Secretary-General in turn sought the preparation of a draft by John Humphrey, Director of the UN Division of Human Rights, and three outside experts, one of whom was Lemkin. From the work of this group a first draft developed, titled Draft Convention on the Crime of Genocide.[16]

In 1947 the UN General Assembly asked the UN Economic and Social Council to move the project of a genocide treaty forward, working from the Secretary-General's draft.[17] The Economic and Social Council appointed a seven-state *ad hoc* committee that by May 1948 produced a new draft treaty.[18] In the fall of 1948, when the General Assembly began its annual session, it referred the *ad hoc* committee's draft to its own standing committee for legal issues, the Sixth Committee of the General Assembly. The Sixth Committee was a committee of the whole, so that each member state of the United Nations was represented. Each member state appointed a person to represent it in the Sixth Committee, and some states added alternate representatives and advisors. Many of these appointees were highly experienced in international law.

The Sixth Committee pored over the definition of genocide with great care through the fall of 1948. The process itself was novel. The international community had no experience at drafting a penal statute. By 2 December, the Sixth Committee produced a new text, which the General Assembly adopted a week later as the Convention on the Prevention and Punishment of the Crime of Genocide.[19] Adoption of the text by the General Assembly opened the treaty for ratification by states. By 1951 the requisite number of states had ratified, and the Convention on the Prevention and Punishment of the Crime of Genocide entered into force.[20]

---

15 ECOSOC Res. 47, UN ECOSOCOR, 4th sess., *Resolutions adopted by the Economic and Social Council during its Fourth Session from 28 February to 29 March 1947*, p. 33, UN Doc. E/437 (1947).

16 UN ECOSOCOR, 2nd sess., *Draft Convention on the Crime of Genocide*, p. 28 (Report of Secretary-General, 26 June 1947), UN Doc. E/447 (1947).

17 Draft convention on genocide, GA Res. 180, UN GAOR, 2nd sess., *Resolutions*, p. 129, UN Doc. A/519 (1948).

18 UN ECOSOCOR, 3rd sess., *Report of the Ad Hoc Committee on Genocide 5 April to 10 May 1948*, Supp. (No. 6), p. 6, UN Doc. E/794 (1948).

19 GA Res. 260, UN GAOR, 3rd sess., Part 1, *Resolutions*, p. 174, UN Doc. A/810 (1948).

20 *Multilateral Treaties Deposited with the Secretary-General: Status as at 31 December 2003*, p. 123, UN Doc. ST/LEG/SER.E/22 (2003).

Chapter 2

The Contours of Genocide

During the drafting, a variety of acts directed against a group were suggested for inclusion in the definition of genocide. Raphael Lemkin conceived the term to include not only an aim of physically destroying a group, but also an aim of forced assimilation. Lemkin wrote,

> genocide does not necessarily mean the immediate destruction of a nation, except when accomplished by mass killings of all members of a nation. It is intended rather to signify a coordinated plan of different actions aiming at the destruction of essential foundations of the life of national groups, with the aim of annihilating the groups themselves. The objectives of such a plan would be disintegration of the political and social institutions, of culture, language, national feelings, religion, and the economic existence of national groups, and the destruction of the personal security, liberty, health, dignity, and even the lives of the individuals belonging to such groups. Genocide is directed against the national group as an entity, and the actions involved are directed against individuals, not in their individual capacity, but as members of the national group.[1]

Forced assimilation and related policies came to be called "cultural genocide." The Secretary-General's 1947 draft included acts of prohibiting use of the national language, systematically destroying books in the national language, and systematically destroying historical or religious monuments.[2] The 1948 draft produced by the Economic and Social Council's *ad hoc* committee followed this approach as well. It defined genocide to include

> any deliberate act committed with the intent to destroy the language, religion or culture of a national, racial or religious group on grounds of national or racial origin or religious belief such as: (1) Prohibiting the use of the language of the group in daily intercourse or in schools, or the printing and circulation of publications in the language of the group; (2) Destroying, or preventing the use of, libraries, museums, schools, historical monuments, places of worship or other cultural institutions and objects of the group.[3]

---

1 Lemkin, R. (1944), *Axis Rule in Occupied Europe: Laws of Occupation, Analysis of Government, Proposals for Redress*, p. 79, Carnegie Endowment for International Peace, Washington.

2 UN ECOSOCOR, 2nd sess., *Draft Convention on the Crime of Genocide*, p. 28 (Report of Secretary-General, 26 June 1947), UN Doc. E/447 (1947).

3 UN ECOSOCOR, 3rd sess., *Report of the Ad Hoc Committee on Genocide 5 April to 10 May 1948*, Supp. (No. 6), p. 6, UN Doc. E/794 (1948).

The Genocide Convention's Definition

Later in 1948, "cultural genocide" was deleted. The Genocide Convention, in its Article II, defined genocide as:

> any of the following acts committed with intent to destroy, in whole or in part, a national, ethnical, racial or religious group, as such:
> (a) Killing members of the group;
> (b) Causing serious bodily or mental harm to members of the group;
> (c) Deliberately inflicting on the group conditions of life calculated to bring about its physical destruction in whole or in part;
> (d) Imposing measures intended to prevent births within the group;
> (e) Forcibly transferring children of the group to another group.

Article III adds four additional categories of punishable acts: conspiracy to commit genocide, direct and public incitement to commit genocide, attempt to commit genocide, and complicity in genocide.

Absent from this definition was one other aspect that had been included in earlier drafts. Political groups had figured as one of the listed categories of protected groups, but this category was omitted in the final text, on the rationale that political groups are less permanent than the others.[4]

The Article II definition of genocide has given rise to difficulty on a number of issues that will be analyzed in succeeding chapters. Half a century on, however, Article II remains the accepted definition of genocide. Article II has not been amended by the state parties. One hundred and thirty-eight states are parties to the Genocide Convention and thus officially adhere to the Article II definition.[5]

Intent Regarding a Group

Genocide is distinguished from other serious offenses by the element of intent. For genocide, victimization of human beings is a necessary, but not the sole element. Acts directed against human beings must be committed with an intent to destroy a group to which the immediate victims belong. No matter how culpable the actor towards these immediate victims, this additional element is required. The act against the immediate victims must reflect a culpable state of mind in regard to the group. Thus, genocide encompasses a dual mental element: one directed against the immediate victims, and a second against the group.[6]

---

4   Jacobs, N. (1969), 'A propos de la définition juridique du génocide,' *Études internationales de psycho-sociologie criminelle*, 16-17, p. 55, p. 56.

5   *Multilateral Treaties Deposited with the Secretary-General: Status as at 31 December 2003*, p. 123, UN Doc. ST/LEG/SER.E/22 (2003).

6   Triffterer, O. (2001), 'Genocide, Its Particular Intent to Destroy in Whole or in Part the Group as Such,' *Leiden Journal of International Law* 14, p. 399, p. 400.

Other ways of defining genocide were considered during the drafting, but this dual-intent formulation carried the day as a device for indicating that the ultimate victim is the group. The problem of protecting groups arises in penal law in other contexts. An offense may require both an act against immediate victims and an intent that the act have an impact on a group.

The UK at one time defined terrorism, for example, as violent acts undertaken for the "purpose of putting the public or any section of the public in fear."[7] By this approach, terrorism involved an act against a specific victim or victims, carried out with purpose to put fear into some larger group.[8]

In the United States, penal statutes prohibiting harm to individuals provide for an increased penalty if the actor selected the victim for membership in a group. Here a type of group is specified. Thus, a Wisconsin statute increases the penalty for any crime directed against individuals if the perpetrator selected the victim on the basis of "race, religion, color, disability, sexual orientation, national origin or ancestry."[9] A New Jersey statute enhances the penalty for weapons possession and certain other offenses if the perpetrator "acted with a purpose to intimidate an individual or a group of individuals because of race, color, gender, handicap, religion, sexual orientation or ethnicity."[10] In federal penal legislation in the United States, an enhanced penalty is provided for any offense if "the defendant intentionally selected any victim or any property as the object of the offense of conviction because of the actual or perceived race, color, religion, national origin, ethnicity, gender, disability or sexual orientation of any person."[11] These domestic statutes are not identical to the Genocide Convention in the manner in which they define the attitude to the group, but they nonetheless include the actor's attitude towards the group as an element of the offense.

Genocide versus Persecution   .

The element of intent to destroy a group distinguishes genocide from internationally defined offenses that fall into the category of "crimes against humanity." One such offense is called "persecution." With persecution, the act prohibited is any deprivation of basic rights of the individual. Thus, with respect to the act, persecution is broader than genocide, although there is some overlap.

---

7   Prevention of Terrorism (Temporary Provisions) Act 1989, §20(1), *Halsbury's Statutes of England and Wales* (4th ed.), vol. 12, p. 1163 (since repealed and replaced).

8   Walker, C. (1992), *The Prevention of Terrorism in British Law*, pp. 7-8, Manchester University Press, Manchester and New York. Dickson, B. (1989), 'The Prevention of Terrorism (Temporary Provisions) Act 1989,' *Northern Ireland Law Quarterly* 40, p. 250, p. 256.

9   Wisconsin Statutes Annotated §939.645, considered in Wisconsin v. Mitchell, USA, Supreme Court, 508 U.S. 476 (1993).

10 New Jersey Statutes Annotated §2C:44-3(e).

11 US Code 18, Appendix §3A1.1.

The two offenses differ in the mental element. With persecution, the actor selects victims because of their group membership, whereas with genocide the actor intends to destroy the group.[12] This distinction may not always be easy to draw. Selecting victims because of their group membership may be difficult to distinguish from harming immediate victims to destroy the group. As will be seen in Chapter 16, some decision-makers have found that destruction of the group is brought about by the action against individual members. On this rationale, victimizing individuals because of their group affiliation constitutes destruction of the group. If this approach is taken to construing "destroy," then the distinction in mental element between persecution and genocide disappears.

Any crime against humanity, including persecution, must be committed in the context of a widespread or systematic attack against a civilian population. In this respect, persecution would require more proof than genocide. It would not suffice that the actor deprived a single individual of rights because of the individual's membership in a group, even while harboring an intent to destroy the group.[13] Finally, with any crime against humanity the victims must be "a civilian population," whereas with genocide, the victims may be military personnel.

Genocide versus Extermination 集体灭绝罪

Genocide differs from another crime against humanity called "extermination." Extermination involves killing, or other actions that seriously affect individuals in a physical sense. The victims must be from a civilian population, rather than military personnel. If the allegation is killing, the actor must have killed at least one person, who can be part of any civilian population.[14] As with persecution, extermination requires that the conduct be part of a widespread or systematic attack against a civilian population. Additionally, the killing must be part of a "mass killing."[15]

Crimes against humanity, including both persecution and extermination, have been charged as indictable offenses by international penal tribunals and thus may be used to prosecute individuals who are subject to their jurisdiction. However,

---

12 Prosecutor v. Krstic, Case No. IT-98-33-T, Judgment, 2 August 2001, para. 553.

13 Preparatory Commission for the International Criminal Court, *Finalized draft text of the Elements of Crimes*, 2 November 2000, art. 7(1)(h) (Crime against humanity of persecution), UN Doc. PCNICC/2000/1/Add.2 (2000).

14 Chesterman, S. (2000), 'An Altogether Different Order: Defining the Elements of Crimes Against Humanity,' *Duke Journal of Comparative & International Law* 10, p. 307, pp. 334-338. Saul, B. (2001), 'Was the Conflict in East Timor "Genocide" and Why Does It Matter?,' *Melbourne Journal of International Law* 2, p. 477, p. 487.

15 Preparatory Commission for the International Criminal Court, *Finalized draft text of the Elements of Crimes*, 2 November 2000, art. 7(1)(b) (Crime against humanity of extermination), UN Doc. PCNICC/2000/1/Add.2 (2000).

crimes against humanity are not the subject of a treaty comparable to the Genocide Convention.

One important difference as regards implementation between genocide and crimes against humanity is that the Genocide Convention gives the ICJ jurisdiction over a state that commits a violation. With crimes against humanity, there being no treaty, there is no similar mechanism to provide for jurisdiction over a state.

Genocide and Crimes against Humanity as Separate Offenses

On given facts, an actor may be charged with both genocide and one or another of the crimes against humanity. Such instances have occurred before international penal tribunals. If the actor kills large numbers of civilians, with an intent to destroy the group of which they are a part, and if the group is one specified in Article II, a prosecutor may be able to prove both offenses. Yet the two differ. As one international penal tribunal said, "where the culpable conduct was part of a widespread and systematic attack specifically against civilians, to record a conviction for genocide alone does not reflect the totality of the accused's culpable conduct."[16] In that circumstance, a genocide conviction would not reflect the large number killed. On the other hand, a conviction for a crime against humanity alone would not reflect the intent to destroy the group of which the victims were members.

In their historical origin, genocide and crimes against humanity have much in common, and some analysts view genocide as a species of crime against humanity. It is sometimes said that genocide is an aggravated form of a crime against humanity, since it includes an intent to destroy a protected group, an element that is lacking in the definition of crimes against humanity. Alternatively, crimes against humanity are sometimes viewed as an aggravated form of genocide, since crimes against humanity require widespread or systematic acts of violence, whereas genocide, as we will see in Chapter 20, can be committed even if harm is inflicted on only a small number, so long as the requisite intent to destroy a group is present.

If one of these offenses were an aggravated form of another, in the sense that the two offenses shared some elements, but one had an element lacking in the other, then a person could not appropriately be convicted of both. However, the special international tribunals established to try crimes relating to events in Rwanda and Yugoslavia have dealt with genocide and crimes against humanity as wholly separate offenses. They have entered convictions for each against the same person for a single course of conduct. Thus, in the case of Radislav Krstic, a trial chamber of the Yugoslavia tribunal convicted for genocide, for crimes against humanity, and for war crimes. It sentenced Krstic to forty-six years imprisonment on the three convictions together, without distinguishing a particular number of years for each.[17]

---

16 Prosecutor v. Rutaganda, Case No. ICTR 96-3-T, Judgment, 6 December 1999, para. 115.

17 Prosecutor v. Krstic, Case No. IT-98-33-T, Judgment, 2 August 2001, para. 727.

The appeals chamber of the Yugoslavia tribunal changed the genocide conviction to one for complicity in genocide and let the other convictions stand. It shortened the sentence to thirty-five years, stating that there is no bar to convicting a person for all three categories of offense, so long as the offenses are differently defined.[18]

By handling genocide and crimes against humanity in this fashion, the tribunals have treated genocide and crimes against humanity as separate offenses. They have not regarded genocide as an aggravated form of crimes against humanity. Nor have they treated crimes against humanity as an aggravated form of genocide. The crime against humanity of murder is characterized by the mass or systematic character of the killing, whereas genocide is characterized by an intent to destroy certain specified types of groups.

---

18 Prosecutor v. Krstic, Case No. IT-98-33-A, Judgment, 19 April 2004, para. 218.

Chapter 3

Genocide in Crime Codes

Under the Genocide Convention, the major route for prosecutions was to be through the penal codes of the ratifying states. Although Article VI of the Convention mentioned the potential creation of an international penal tribunal, the only method of implementation possible as of 1948 was domestic courts. Article VI required states to prosecute if genocide were committed in their territory. Article V required states to penalize genocide in their own law:

> The Contracting Parties undertake to enact, in accordance with their respective Constitutions, the necessary legislation to give effect to the provisions of the present Convention and, in particular, to provide effective penalties for persons guilty of genocide or of any of the other acts enumerated in article III.

Ratifying states would make genocide a local crime.[1] Many of the ratifying states have done so, but by no means all of them.

Article V prescribed no penalty for genocide, leaving that choice to each state. The provisions on penalty vary widely. States typically provide a substantial term of years as the penalty, while some call for capital punishment. Some differentiate the various acts by which genocide can be committed, providing more serious penalties for, say, killing group members, than for transferring children to another group.

Not all the states that have codified genocide have used the same method of adoption. Some have enacted a penalty and refer to Article II as the definition of genocide. The UK took this approach when it first codified genocide: "A person commits an offence of genocide if he commits an act falling within the definition of 'genocide' in Article II of the Genocide Convention."[2] Ireland took the same approach.[3] More commonly, parliaments have written their own text, but many have copied Article II *verbatim*, or with only stylistic modification. This approach has

---

1 Berle, Jr., A.A. (1950), 'Mise hors la loi du génocide,' *Revue international de droit pénal* (no. 2), p. 147, p. 149.

2 Genocide Act 1969, §1, *Halsbury's Statutes of England and Wales* (4th ed.), vol. 12, p. 530.

3 Ireland, Genocide Act, No. 28/1973.

been taken by, among others, Germany,[4] Israel,[5] Hungary,[6] and Austria.[7] The UK later switched to this approach.[8]

A number of states have altered the Article II definition, an approach that creates ambiguity as to whether the state is complying with its obligation to incorporate genocide domestically. To date, no controversy has arisen as a result of such variances. The most common variances have been the addition of additional acts committed against members of a group, and the addition of more types of protected groups.

Statutes Expanding the Qualifying Acts

In Spain, the statutory definition includes two acts not specified in Article II: sexual assault on a member of the group, and "forced removals of the group or of members."[9] The addition of these items was attributed to the fact that Spain's parliament acted shortly after the Bosnian war, in which sexual assault and forced removals against groups were widely practiced.[10]

A number of other states have included forcible deportation: Italy,[11] Estonia,[12] Lithuania,[13] and Yugoslavia.[14] In Russia, the genocide provision includes "forced resettlement or other creation of conditions of life calculated to achieve the physical elimination of members of the group."[15]

---

4   Germany, Strafgesetzbuch §220a, superseded by Code of Crimes Against International Law, sec. 6, Federal Gazette I, p. 2254 (2002), translated in *Criminal Law Forum*, vol. 13, no. 2, p. 214 (2002).

5   Crime of Genocide (Prevention and Punishment) Law, *Laws of the State of Israel* 4, p. 101 (1950).

6   Hungary, Act IV of 1978 on Criminal Code, art. 155 (Ministry of Justice of the Hungarian People's Republic, Budapest, 1983).

7   Austria, Strafgesetzbuch, §321.

8   *Halsbury's Laws of England* (4th ed. 2002 reissue), vol. 11(1), p. 328.

9   Spain, Penal Code, art. 607.

10   Pérez Gonzalez, M., and M.A. Castelos (1995-96), 'Offences Against the International Community According to the Spanish Penal Code,' *Spanish Yearbook of International Law*, p. 3, pp. 26-27. Gil Gil, A. (1999), *Derecho Penal Internacional: Especial Consideración del Delito de Genocidio*, pp. 227-228, Editorial Tecnos, Madrid.

11   Italy, Law of 9 October 1967, no. 962.

12   Estonia, Criminal Code, art. 611, Eriosa, 9 November 1994.

13   Lithuania, Seimas, Law VIII-1968, Valstybes zinios, No. 89-2741, 26 September 2000, codified as Criminal Code, art. 99, *Lietuvos Respublikos Baudziamasis Kodeksas*, Vilnius 2000.

14   Yugoslavia, Criminal Code of 1961, art. 124, *Collection of Yugoslav Laws*, vol. 11, Institute of Comparative Law, Belgrade, 1964. Yugoslavia, Criminal Code of 1977, art. 141, Official Gazette of the Socialist Federal Republic of Yugoslavia no. 44, 8 October 1976.

15   Criminal Code of the Russian Federation, art. 357.

It is unclear when a parliament adds a new term whether it intends to broaden the definition over Article II, or whether it is providing specification of an act that, in the view of the parliament, is already implied by Article II. Russia's formulation for inclusion of "forced resettlement," by virtue of the use of the term "other," appears to deem forced resettlement a sub-category within the category "creation of conditions of life." Spain's parliament may have considered sexual assault a sub-category of "serious bodily or mental harm."

Statutes Adding Other Protected Groups

A number of parliaments have modified the designation of the types of groups listed in Article II. Ethiopia added "political" groups, providing, "Whosoever, with intent to destroy, in whole or in part, a national, ethnic, racial, religious or political group. "[16] Estonia added the category of a group "which is resisting an occupation regime."[17] Estonia,[18] Latvia,[19] Lithuania,[20] and Spain[21] included "social" groups in addition to those listed in Article II. According to a note in the official publication of Spain's penal code, the term was not intended as an addition of a new group but was to be construed in line with Article II.[22] On the other hand, the term could be read far more inclusively. In the Estonian code, it apparently means groups in addition to the others listed, because it appears at the end of the list, with the phrasing "or any other social group." Thus, "social" is used to refer to all the previously listed groups, but presumably to others as well. In later editions of Spain's penal code, the term "social" was deleted from the list by the parliament of Spain.[23]

A few states have devised formulations about groups that are potentially quite expansive. France refers to "the total or partial destruction of a national, ethnic, racial or religious group, or of a group based on any other arbitrary criterion."[24] The term "arbitrary criterion" has yet to be construed by the French courts. Romania describes

---

16 Penal Code of the Empire of Ethiopia, art. 281, Proclamation No. 158 of 1957, Negarit Gazeta, Extraordinary Issue No. 1 of 1957.

17 Estonia, Criminal Code, art. 611, Eriosa, 9 November 1994.

18 Ibid.

19 Latvia, Criminal Code, art. 68-1, as amended 6 April 1993. Criminal Code, art. 71, as adopted in Speka Esoss, 4 January 1999 (Vestnesis, 8 July 1998, no. 199).

20 Lithuania, Seimas, Law VIII-1968, Valstybes zinios, No. 89-2741, 26 September 2000, codified in Criminal Code, art. 99, *Lietuvos Respublikos Baudžiamasis Kodeksas* (2000), Vilnius.

21 Spain, Ley 44/1971, 15 November 1971, adding art. 137bis to Penal Code. Pérez Gonzalez and Castelos (1995-96), p. 22. Gil Gil (1999), p. 204.

22 *Boletin oficial del Estado, Colección Textos Legales: Código penal* (1982), art. 137bis, note at p. 81, Madrid.

23 Spain, Penal Code, art. 607.

24 France, *Penal Code* (1992), art. 211-1, Dalloz, Paris.

the protected groups as "a collectivity or a national, ethnic, racial, or religious group."[25] "Collectivity" is not further defined. Portugal made a potentially even more expansive addition to the Article II language, adding both "community" and "social," thereby describing the protected groups as "a community [una comunidade] or a national, ethnic, racial, religious, or social group."[26] Later, however, Portugal's parliament deleted the words "community" and "social," bringing Portugal's code definition into conformity with Article II.[27]

Canada's genocide definition is atypical in omitting a list of protected groups. Genocide is defined in Canada as

> an act or omission committed with intent to destroy, in whole or in part, an identifiable group of persons, as such, that, at the time and in the place of its commission, constitutes genocide according to customary international law or conventional international law or by virtue of its being criminal according to the general principles of law recognized by the community of nations, whether or not it constitutes a contravention of the law in force at the time and in the place of its commission.[28]

The phrase "an identifiable group of persons" is quite open-ended, referring to the international law of genocide. "Conventional" international law is a reference to the Genocide Convention. The reference to genocide in customary international law may broaden the definition over the Genocide Convention. "General principles of law recognized by the community of nations" refers to norms extracted from domestic law for use by international tribunals. It is unclear how genocide would be used in this fashion.

Statutes Narrowing the Article II Definition

Among states that have modified the Article II definition, some have narrowed its application. In US law, the federal Congress enacted a penal offense based on Article II of the Genocide Convention, defining genocide as follows:

> (a) Basic offense. Whoever, whether in time of peace or in time of war, in a circumstance described in subsection (d) [a jurisdictional clause, which makes the act an offense if committed in the United States, or if the perpetrator is a US national. - J.Q.] and with the specific intent to destroy, in whole or in substantial part, a national, ethnic, racial, or religious group as such:

---

25 *Penal Code of the Romanian Socialist Republic* (1976), art. 357, Fred B. Rothman, Hackensack N.J. and Sweet & Maxwell Ltd., London.

26 Portugal, *Código penal* (1983), art. 189, M. Gonçalves (ed), Livraria Almedina, Coimbra.

27 Portugal, *Código penal* (1995), art. 239, M. Pedrosa Machado (ed), Livraria Arco-Iris, Lisbon.

28 Consolidated Statutes of Canada, S.C. 2000, c.24, §4 & §6.

(1) kills members of that group;

(2) causes serious bodily injury to members of that group;

(3) causes the permanent impairment of the mental faculties of members of the group through drugs, torture, or similar techniques;

(4) subjects the group to conditions of life that are intended to cause the physical destruction of the group in whole or in part;

(5) imposes measures intended to prevent births within the group; or

(6) transfers by force children of the group to another group;

or attempts to do so, shall be punished as provided in subsection (b) [which provides punishments of death, life imprisonment, and a fine up to $1,000,000 - J.Q.].[29]

The US definition of genocide reflects two modifications relevant to the culpability level in genocide. They are found in the introductory phrase; first, the addition of the adjective "specific" modifying "intent," and second, the addition of the adjective "substantial" modifying "part." These modifications reflected interpretation by the United States of Article II in these two respects. The relevance of these modifications will be considered below.

Genocide Definition Used for Non-penal Purposes

Genocide figures in domestic law for certain non-penal purposes, and typically the Article II definition of genocide is used. Potential immigrants may be denied residency if they have committed genocide. In US immigration law, "Any alien who has engaged in conduct that is defined as genocide for purposes of the International Convention on the Prevention and Punishment of Genocide is inadmissible."[30] An alien once admitted to the United States is deportable if it is discovered that the alien has committed genocide, and again the Convention's definition is used.[31] Certain aliens are granted "temporary protected status," but those otherwise eligible are to be denied this status if they have committed genocide.[32] Under these three statutes, the US Department of Justice makes a judgment based on the definition provided in the Genocide Convention.

Genocide can also be relevant to extradition decisions. Extradition is typically denied for offenses of a political nature, but if genocide is involved, a state may extradite nonetheless. Under the UK Genocide Act, extradition was to be granted, even if it would otherwise fall under the definition of a political offense, if the offense "would be punishable as an offence of genocide" if committed in the UK.[33]

---

29 US Code 18, §1891.

30 US Code 8, §1182(a)(3)(E)(ii).

31 General classes of deportable aliens, US Code 8, §1227(a)(4)(D) ("Any alien described in . . . 8 US Code §1182(a)(3)(E) . . . (ii) is deportable.")

32 US Code 8, §1254a(c)(2)(A)(iii)(III).

33 Genocide Act 1969, §1, *Halsbury's Statutes of England and Wales* (4th ed.), vol. 12, p. 531 (since repealed and replaced).

In US law, genocide is relevant to foreign assistance programs. The US Congress has mandated that the Secretary of State report annually on human rights violations in countries receiving development or military aid from the United States. The Secretary must include certain specific categories of rights violations in these reports. One such category is the commission of genocide. The legislation on military aid states:

> such report shall include consolidated information regarding the commission of war crimes, crimes against humanity, and evidence of acts that may constitute genocide (as defined in article 2 of the Convention on the Prevention and Punishment of the Crime of Genocide and modified by the United States instrument of ratification to that convention and section 2(a) of the Genocide Convention Implementation Act of 1987 [US Code 8, §1091].[34]

The legislation on development assistance includes identical language.[35] The Secretary of State is to decide whether genocide as defined in the Genocide Convention has been committed.

---

34 Human rights and security assistance, US Code 22, §2304(b).
35 Human rights and development assistance, US Code 22, §2151n(d)(8).

PART TWO
CALLING TO ACCOUNT

Chapter 4

Prosecuting Under a Quasi-genocide Statute

The prohibition against genocide would carry little weight without some means of enforcement. The drafters feared that the Genocide Convention might be a dead letter. Governments were not likely to investigate themselves for genocide, and many potential violators would be powerful enough to ensure their own immunity.

Three possibilities presented themselves for enforcement. Genocide could be prosecuted in domestic courts. However, if, as might often be the case, the genocide were supported by the state, prosecution would be unlikely. An international penal tribunal might be the solution to this problem, as it would not be under the authority of local political leaders. But no such tribunal existed in 1948, and there was little prospect that one would soon be set up. Alternatively, lawsuits might be filed by one state against another for genocide. A court had been established under the League of Nations, and then under the United Nations, in which one state could sue another for various violations of international obligations. States were accustomed to suing if the financial interests of a national were violated by another state, but no one knew if states would be willing to sue to protect human rights.

Reasons for Domestic Prosecutions

States have conducted prosecutions for genocide. The prosecutions have fallen into three categories, in terms of their legal basis. Some have been under a statute protecting a particular group. Some have been on the basis of the Genocide Convention, without any local statute. Some have been on the basis of domestically enacted genocide statutes.

Genocide charges have not been brought with great frequency in domestic courts, a fact that is not surprising, given the seriousness of genocide as an offense. In all instances, the charges have involved killings, and convictions carrying significant punishment could have been gained for murder. Given the proof difficulties with genocide, one may inquire why genocide was charged. In order to convict for genocide, a prosecutor must prove both a specific act and genocidal intent. This intent may be difficult to prove against an accused. The specific act will almost certainly be one that is found in the penal code, such as murder or assault, and whose proof would not require showing genocidal intent. Thus, genocide involves proving a common crime plus an intent directed at the group of which the victim or victims were members.

Despite the difficulties of proof, charging genocide is attractive to prosecuting authorities because of the seriousness that the term evokes. Convicting of genocide discredits a person more thoroughly than convicting of murder. Perhaps not surprisingly, genocide has been charged most frequently at the domestic level following a regime change. A new government prosecutes officials of the prior government for genocide. A genocide charge may highlight the evils of the prior government in a way that a murder charge would not. A genocide charge may provide a way of demonstrating to the public that violence used by the prior government was directed not simply against individuals, but against an entire group. A new government may thus seek to enhance its own legitimacy, particularly if it has taken power by non-constitutional means.

Most of the domestic prosecutions for genocide to date have been conducted under genocide articles previously enacted in domestic penal legislation. These cases will be described in Chapter 6. In a few instances, domestic prosecutions have been conducted even though there was no statute on genocide in domestic law. These cases will be examined in Chapter 5.

In one case, a charge was laid under a statute that had been enacted to cover a prior episode of atrocities. This was the case brought in Israel against Adolf Eichmann in 1960, for acts committed as a Nazi official in Europe during World War II.

Israel's Genocide Legislation

The prosecution of Eichmann marked an important event in the history of genocide in two respects. Eichmann was indicted for implementing Hitler's "final solution" against the Jews of Europe. His prosecution thus involved the very situation that prompted the adoption of the Genocide Convention. Additionally, the Eichmann prosecution was the first, on any set of facts, under a statute modeled on Article II of the Genocide Convention.

Israel had written a genocide prohibition tracking Article II into domestic law in 1950, but it was considered to apply only to acts committed from that time forward.[1] Eichmann was prosecuted under another statute, also adopted in Israel in 1950, called the Nazis and Nazi Collaborators (Punishment) Law. Unlike Israel's genocide article, the Nazis and Nazi Collaborators (Punishment) Law provided for retroactive application, specifically for the period of World War II. The Law covered war crimes, crimes against humanity, and crimes against the Jewish people.

Eichmann was charged with all three categories of crime. In the Nazis and Nazi Collaborators (Punishment) Law, "crime against the Jewish people" was defined as

---

1   Crime of Genocide (Prevention and Punishment) Law, *Laws of the State of Israel* 4, p. 101 (1950).

one of seven categories of acts, "committed with intent to destroy the Jewish people in whole or in part." The seven categories of acts were:

1. killing Jews;
2. causing serious bodily or mental harm to Jews;
3. placing Jews in living conditions calculated to bring about their physical destruction;
4. imposing measures intended to prevent births among Jews;
5. forcibly transferring Jewish children to another national or religious group;
6. destroying or desecrating Jewish religious or cultural assets or values;
7. inciting to hatred of Jews.

The categories "crime against humanity" and "war crime" were not defined to limit the circle of victims to Jews.[2]

With respect to all three categories, the Nazis and Nazi Collaborators (Punishment) Law limited its applicability in time and place. Liability for crimes against the Jewish people and for crimes against humanity was limited to acts "done, during the period of the Nazi regime, in an enemy country." Liability for war crimes was limited to acts "done, during the period of the Second World War, in an enemy country." These restrictions reflected the intent to cover only acts committed during World War II and the years immediately preceding. The Law gave precise time definitions for the time period of the Nazi regime and of the Second World War; it defined "enemy country" to mean Germany and its allies, including any territory they controlled.

As for the offense it created, the Nazis and Nazi Collaborators (Punishment) Law was based on Article II but differed in major respects. Five of the acts described (paragraphs 1 through 5) were taken from Article II, as was the "intent to destroy" element. However, only one target group was contemplated, namely, Jews. Two additional categories of acts were inserted. Paragraph 6 added the destruction or desecration of religious or cultural assets, thereby incorporating the "cultural genocide" that had been omitted from Article II. Whereas Article III of the Genocide Convention prohibits "direct and public incitement to commit genocide," paragraph 7 prohibits mere incitement to hatred, and the incitement need not be "direct" or "public."

Jurisdictional Aspects of the Eichmann Prosecution

The Israeli courts, in convicting Eichmann, made significant rulings about the circumstances in which genocide can be prosecuted. Eichmann challenged the court's jurisdiction, on the ground that the acts alleged against him were committed

---

2 Nazi and Nazi Collaborators (Punishment) Law, *Laws of the State of Israel* 4, p. 154 (1950).

outside Israel, and prior in time to the Genocide Convention.[3] The District Court of Jerusalem and, on appeal, the Supreme Court of Israel, rejected these objections.

Eichmann referred to Article VI of the Genocide Convention, which calls on states to prosecute for genocide committed in their territory. Arguing from Article VI, Eichmann said that states have jurisdiction only over genocide committed in their territory. To this argument the two Israeli courts replied that Article VI obliged states to prosecute genocide committed in their territory but was irrelevant to the authority of states to prosecute genocide wherever committed, on the "universal jurisdiction" principle.[4] Both courts found that genocide is prosecutable on the basis of universal jurisdiction, that is, that a court in any state may prosecute for genocide wherever committed.

The two Israeli courts also decided that they could convict Eichmann, even though the Nazis and Nazi Collaborators (Punishment) Law was adopted in 1950, well after the dates of the acts alleged against Eichmann. They did so by ruling that genocide was a crime under customary international law by the time of World War II. By referring to customary international law on this issue, the Israeli courts found that jurisdiction to prosecute for genocide was broader even than the jurisdiction claimed by Israel's parliament.[5]

The question of the propriety of prosecuting for genocide for acts that predate the enactment of a statute defining genocide in the particular jurisdiction would arise again in other domestic courts, and in international courts. We will examine that issue in Chapter 9.

Even though the Nazis and Nazi Collaborators (Punishment) Law was not identical to Article II, the Eichmann prosecution was effectively a genocide prosecution. The Israeli court did not need to rely on paragraphs 6 or 7 to convict Eichmann. And although the Israeli Law did not include all the groups protected under Article II, Jews would fall under Article II. Both the District Court and the Supreme Court in the Eichmann case analyzed substantive and jurisdictional issues on the assumption that Eichmann was being prosecuted for genocide.

As a result, the analysis of the two Israeli courts can be taken as interpretation of the crime of genocide. The two Israeli courts gave important interpretations on the element of an intent to destroy, and in particular, which actions against a people bring about its destruction. These are central issues to the definition of genocide. In Chapter 16, we will revert to the analysis of the Israeli courts in the Eichmann case on these matters.

---

3 Attorney-General of the Government of Israel v. Eichmann, District Court of Jerusalem, 12 December 1961, *International Law Reports* 36, p. 23.

4 Ibid., pp. 34-39.

5 Ibid., p. 26. Supreme Court of Israel, 29 May 1962, ibid., p. 304.

Chapter 5

Prosecuting Without a Genocide Statute

In three instances, genocide has been charged even though domestic statutes contained no genocide article. Genocide was charged in Cambodia in 1979 in a single trial against two former government officials, in Equatorial Guinea in a single trial in 1979 against a group of former government officials, and in Rwanda in multiple trials beginning in 1996. Cambodia and Rwanda had ratified the Genocide Convention, but their parliaments had not legislated on genocide. In Equatorial Guinea, the state of the law in general was muddled. Recently independent from Spain, Equatorial Guinea had not ratified the Genocide Convention and had no penal code.

A basic proposition of penal law is that no one may be prosecuted unless, at the time of the offense, the act was specified in law to be a crime, and unless a punishment was provided by law. The emergence of internationally defined offenses in the mid-twentieth century opened the possibility that an offense might be defined at the international level without having been incorporated into domestic law. It was not clear whether prosecution in such circumstances would violate the requirement that both the act and the penalty must be defined in law.

In Equatorial Guinea, it was left to the prosecutor and the court to determine a legal basis for prosecuting for genocide. In Cambodia and Rwanda, special provisions of law were adopted to establish a legal basis for anticipated prosecutions.

Cambodia: a Special Decree

Genocide was charged in Cambodia against two leaders of the Khmer Rouge, which governed Cambodia from 1975 to 1979. The Khmer Rouge, which had been widely accused abroad of atrocities, was overthrown in 1979 by a dissident Khmer Rouge faction with military backing from Vietnam. Within a few months of taking power, the new Cambodian government set about trying Khmer Rouge officials for genocide.

The reason the Cambodian government charged genocide, rather than murder or assault, was, in all probability, to highlight the seriousness of the conduct of the Khmer Rouge leadership. The overthrown Khmer Rouge continued to be recognized at the United Nations as the legitimate government of Cambodia, while the new Cambodian government was regarded internationally as a usurper, brought to power by a foreign army. Engaged in a struggle for legitimacy, it was anxious to place on the Khmer Rouge leadership a label of great opprobrium.[1]

The Cambodia proceedings did not present the territorial difficulty of the Eichmann trial, since acts in Cambodian territory were alleged. The acts occurred after the Genocide Convention was in force, and at a time when Cambodia was a party. Cambodia, in fact, was one of the earliest ratifiers in 1950.[2] Thus, Cambodia did not need to cope with the problem of acts committed prior to the adoption of the Genocide Convention.

Nonetheless, the absence of a genocide statute presented an obstacle. Article V of the Genocide Convention calls on state parties to adopt genocide legislation, but Cambodia had not done so.[3] To make matters worse, at the time of the contemplated prosecutions, Cambodia, having just undergone a change of government by force of arms, had no functioning parliament. The government decided to handle the problem by issuing a special decree.

By Decree Law No. 1, the government established a special court and instructed it to conduct trials for genocide against Khmer Rouge officials. Article One of Decree Law No. 1 determined:

> To set up a People's Revolutionary Tribunal at Phnom Penh to try the acts of genocide committed by the Pol Pot-Ieng Sary clique, namely, planned massacres of groups of innocent people; expulsion of inhabitants of cities and villages in order to concentrate them and force them to do hard labor in conditions leading to their physical and mental destruction; wiping out of religion; destroying political, cultural and social structures and family and social relations.[4]

Decree Law No. 1 provided for the appointment of a special prosecutor, who was to decide whom to indict.[5] The decree established a penalty of imprisonment or death, in the Tribunal's discretion.[6] Capital punishment was an applicable penalty in the Cambodian penal code of 1956 for premeditated murder (*assassinat*).[7] However, since the Cambodian penal code did not punish genocide, it had no penalty for genocide. The decree did not refer to any penalties in existing Cambodian penal law.

---

1   De Nike, H., J. Quigley and K. Robinson (eds) (2000), *Genocide in Cambodia: Documents from the Trial of Pol Pot and Ieng Sary*, p. 8, University of Pennsylvania Press, Philadelphia.

2   *Multilateral Treaties Deposited with the Secretary-General: Status as at 31 December 2003*, p. 123, UN Doc. ST/LEG/SER.E/22 (2003).

3   Royaume du Cambodge, Ministère de la Justice, *Code pénal et lois pénales* (1956), Phnom Penh.

4   Cambodia, Decree Law No. 1: Establishment of People's Revolutionary Tribunal at Phnom Penh to Try the Pol Pot-Ieng Sary Clique for the Crime of Genocide, 15 July 1979, art. 1, in De Nike, Quigley and Robinson (2000), p. 45.

5   Ibid., art. 4.

6   Ibid., art. 2.

7   *Code pénal et lois pénales*, art. 506.

As to the crime definition, the Decree Law No. 1 referred in a preamble clause to the fact that genocide is defined in international law. Addressing the retroactivity problem, Article 8 of the decree relied on the Genocide Convention. Article 8 provided:

> In accordance with the Convention on the Prevention and Punishment of the Crime of Genocide adopted by the U.N. General Assembly on December 9, 1948, this decree applies to the criminal acts of the Pol Pot-Ieng Sary clique committed prior to its signing.[8]

Thus, the government considered it permissible to try persons for genocide on the basis of a definition to which Cambodia had subscribed by ratifying the Genocide Convention, and on the basis of a penalty specified after the fact by decree.

Article One of Decree Law No. 1 has been construed by some analysts as providing a legislative definition of genocide for incorporation into Cambodian domestic law.[9] Viewing Article One in this light, William Schabas criticized it as an "idiosyncratic definition of genocide closer to crimes against humanity, since it includes wiping out religion and destroying cultural and social structures."[10] Decree Law No. 1, however, introduced no provision of general applicability on genocide into Cambodian law. It was an executive decree and by its terms applied only to a particular set of potential defendants. Rather than defining genocide, it identified practices of the Khmer Rouge on which the special court was being asked to focus as evidence of genocide, as defined by the Genocide Convention. The death penalty envisioned by the decree was not being made a penalty of general applicability for genocide in Cambodian law, but a penalty applicable only in the anticipated trials of Khmer Rouge figures.

Decree Law No. 1 thus took the Genocide Convention as applicable in Cambodian law, even without a legislative enactment. Like the Israeli legislation under which Eichmann was tried, it asserted jurisdiction over acts previously committed. The Israeli statute, as construed in the Eichmann case, was premised on a prohibition against genocide in customary international law. Hence, according to the Israeli courts, punishment was justifiable even for an act committed prior to the date of the legislation. With the Khmer Rouge trials, the Cambodian government viewed capital punishment as justifiable for acts committed prior to any mention of that penalty in Cambodian law as being applicable to genocide.

Israel had not been a party to the Genocide Convention at the time of the acts alleged against Eichmann. Indeed, Eichmann's pre-dated the Genocide Convention. As to the Khmer Rouge proceedings, the Genocide Convention had been in force at the time of the acts alleged, and Cambodia was a party. The Cambodian decree

---

8 Cambodia, Decree Law No. 1, art. 8.

9 Van Schaack, B. (1997), 'The Crime of Political Genocide: Repairing the Genocide Convention's Blind Spot,' *Yale Law Journal* 106, p. 2259, pp. 2271-72 note 78.

10 Schabas, W.A. (2001a), 'Cambodia: Was It Really Genocide?,' *Human Rights Quarterly* 23, p. 470, p. 472.

therefore focused on the Genocide Convention, viewing a charge for genocide as being authorized in domestic law on the basis of the Genocide Convention alone.

Only one trial was held under Decree Law No. 1, a proceeding conducted against Khmer Rouge officials Pol Pot and Ieng Sary. The two were tried *in absentia*. In line with the theory reflected in the decree, the Genocide Convention was used as the applicable law. The indictment against the two men read:

> In light of Article 1 of Decree Law No. 1 of July 15, 1979, of the People's Revolutionary Council of Kampuchea [Cambodia], and with reference to international law punishing the crime of genocide, in particular the Convention on the Prevention and Punishment of the Crime of Genocide of December 9, 1948, we consider that the conscious criminal acts recounted above committed by the Pol Pot-Ieng Sary clique constitute the crime of genocide.[11]

On the basis of this indictment, Pol Pot and Ieng Sary were convicted of genocide and sentenced to death.[12]

In 1999, experts appointed by the United Nations explored the feasibility of trials for genocide of Khmer Rouge figures in the courts of Cambodia. "The 1956 Code does not mention international offences such as genocide," they said. "Whether Cambodian law permits direct prosecution of individuals for international crimes absent codification of those crimes in the penal code remains unresolved."[13] Despite the experts' caution, the jurisdictional basis on which the 1979 trial was conducted was implicitly approved by the UN General Assembly in 2003. The General Assembly provided for jurisdiction on the same basis for anticipated trials of Khmer Rouge figures. By agreement between the UN and Cambodia, trials were, as in 1979, to be held before a specially constituted tribunal of Cambodia, but this time with the participation of international judges and an international prosecutor. The agreement, like Decree Law No. 1 of 1979, specified that trials would be for offenses committed during the period of Khmer Rouge rule.[14] Jurisdiction would include "the crime of genocide as defined in the 1948 Convention on the Prevention and Punishment of the Crime of Genocide."[15] In 2001, Cambodia had adopted a law to create the special tribunal and had, similarly, provided for jurisdiction over genocide on the basis of

---

11 Prosecutor of the Tribunal, Indictment for Genocide Committed by Pol Pot and Ieng Sary, in De Nike, Quigley and Robinson (2000), p. 486.

12 Tribunal, Judgment, 19 August 1979, in De Nike, Quigley and Robinson (2000), p. 549.

13 Identical letters dated 15 March 1999 from the Secretary-General to the President of the General Assembly and the President of the Security Council, UN Doc. A/53/850, S/1999/231, 16 March 1999, Annex: Report of the Group of Experts for Cambodia established pursuant to General Assembly resolution 52/135, p. 26.

14 Draft Agreement between the United Nations and the Royal Government of Cambodia concerning the Prosecution under Cambodian Law of Crimes Committed during the Period of Democratic Kampuchea, arts. 1-2, GA Res. 57/228B, Khmer Rouge trials, UN GAOR, 57th sess., UN Doc. A/57/228B/2003.

15 Ibid., art. 9.

the Genocide Convention.[16] The Cambodian statute recited the content of Articles II and III of the Genocide Convention.[17] The statute referred to the 1956 penal code for penalties but excluded capital punishment.[18]

Equatorial Guinea: a Vacuum of Laws

In September 1979, Francisco Macias Nguema, who had been overthrown one month earlier as president of Equatorial Guinea, was tried by a Special Military Court. Charges were genocide, multiple murders, embezzlement, and other crimes. Ten political associates were similarly charged. All were convicted. Macias and six others were sentenced to death and executed.[19] The others received terms of imprisonment.

Macias, in his capacity as president, was reputed to have been responsible for killing thousands of citizens of Equatorial Guinea and in particular to have targeted intellectuals.[20] Amnesty International had reported frequent torture and extra-judicial executions.[21] According to prosecution evidence, several hundred political opponents had been arrested and then taken from jail cells and executed without trial. Some of these executions occurred shortly after a visit to the jail by Macias, a fact taken as proof that Macias ordered them.[22] Equatorial Guinea was ethnically diverse. Macias belonged to the Fang ethnic group, which constituted 70 per cent of the population. Those killed were political opponents and were not disproportionately of minority ethnic groups.[23]

The legal situation for a genocide prosecution was complex, because Equatorial Guinea had no codes of law at the time, and in particular no penal code and no provision on genocide. Equatorial Guinea gained independence from Spain in October 1968. Under a transition constitution of 1968, the laws in force at the time of independence continued in force. A new constitution adopted in 1973, however, repealed the transition constitution and said nothing about the continuation in force of Spanish law. It was unclear as of 1979 whether Spain's penal code was in force

---

16 Magliveras, K.D. (2002), 'The Unfinished Story of the Cambodia Criminal Tribunal: An Analysis of the Law of August 2001 and its Aftermath,' *International Enforcement Law Reporter* 18, no. 12.

17 Cambodia, Law on the Establishment of Extraordinary Chambers, No. NS/RKM/0801/12, 10 August 2001.

18 Ibid., arts. 3, 39.

19 Artucio, A. (1979), *The Trial of Macias in Equatorial Guinea: The Story of a Dictatorship*, p. 53, International Commission of Jurists & International University Exchange Fund, Geneva.

20 'Death asked for Macias,' *Washington Post*, 28 September 1979, p. A27.

21 *Military Trials and the Use of the Death Penalty in Equatorial Guinea*, pp. 1-2, Amnesty International, New York (1987).

22 Artucio (1979), pp. 32-35.

23 Ibid., pp. 2-3.

in Equatorial Guinea.[24] During Macias' tenure, political opponents were not tried by court. Instead, the security apparatus dispensed summary punishment.[25]

As for the Genocide Convention, as of 1979 Equatorial Guinea had not ratified. It may have been deemed applicable on the basis of Spain's ratification, which occurred one month before Equatorial Guinea's independence. On the basis of the transition constitution, the Genocide Convention might have been considered part of the law that Equatorial Guinea inherited. The Macias indictment referred to the Genocide Convention as providing the applicable law, and the prosecution referred to it during trial.[26] The indictment referred as well to the Spanish penal code and Spanish military justice code as legal norms violated by Macias and the others. Thus, it was apparently considered that Spanish law applied. Spain had ratified the Genocide Convention on 13 September 1968. Spain's parliament inserted a genocide provision in Spain's penal code in 1971, three years after Equatorial Guinea's independence, as Article 137bis.[27]

The Macias indictment did not refer to Article 137bis. Under Spanish law, as we shall see in Chapter 9, the Genocide Convention was not considered to provide a basis for prosecution absent the enactment of a genocide article in the penal code. Thus, if Spanish law were to be followed, Article 137bis could not be used. Moreover, Article 137bis had not been enacted until after Equatorial Guinea's independence, and the transition constitution called for only those laws in force at the time of independence to be carried forward into Equatorial Guinea's law.

During Macias' trial, the court on one occasion referred to Article 137bis but put major emphasis on the Genocide Convention itself.[28] The court did not make it clear on what basis it found the Genocide Convention to be applicable, whether on the basis of Spain's ratification, or perhaps on the basis that it was part of customary international law. In any event, the court appeared to apply the Genocide Convention as the applicable law.

The Macias case stands out as the most confusing of domestic genocide prosecutions from the standpoint of the applicable law. The Macias conviction is also problematic from the standpoint of the identity of the protected group. Spain's Article 137bis did not include political groups as a protected category of group. As we shall see, however, in Chapter 28, the Supreme Court of Spain would, some years later, construe Spain's genocide article to cover situations in which those targeted were political opponents. The court that convicted Macias did not analyze this issue and thus gave no indication of how it determined that genocide might be charged when political opponents were targeted.

---

24 Ibid., pp. 18-19.

25 Sundiata, I.K. (1990), *Equatorial Guinea: Colonialism, State Terror, and the Search for Stability*, p. 69, Westview Press, Boulder.

26 Artucio (1979), p. 26.

27 Spain, Ley 44/1971, 15 November 1971, adding art. 137bis to the Penal Code.

28 Artucio (1979), pp. 29-30.

Rwanda: Genocide as Murder

In 1996, the government of Rwanda undertook prosecutions for genocide for the mass killing of the minority Tutsi population that took place in Rwanda in 1994. The background to this violence was tension between the majority Hutu population and the minority Tutsi population that had in earlier years already led to atrocities. In 1994, a Hutu-led government was trying to suppress a Tutsi insurgency. In that context Hutu killed up to one million Tutsi in the spring of 1994, in what was probably the most concentrated mass killing ever seen.

Unlike most episodes of mass killing, which find soldiers, police, or other officials as the perpetrators, the 1994 episode of killing in Rwanda saw ordinary citizens engaging in killing, along with government personnel. It ended when the Tutsi insurgency prevailed militarily in June 1994, overthrowing the Hutu-led government. Prosecutors working under the new Tutsi-led government initiated genocide prosecutions against Hutu perpetrators.

Like Cambodia, Rwanda was a party to the Genocide Convention, having ratified in 1975.[29] And like Cambodia, Rwanda had failed to write a genocide provision into its penal code.[30] To prosecute for genocide, Rwanda adopted an approach similar to Cambodia's, namely, by creating special judicial institutions to conduct trials relating to the time period of the atrocities. In Rwanda, unlike Cambodia, a parliament was functioning, so the National Assembly of Rwanda adopted a statute for the purpose, which it called an Organic Law.[31]

With many trials anticipated, the National Assembly established special chambers in the civilian and military courts of the country. The jurisdiction of these chambers was limited to genocide, crimes against humanity, and war crimes committed between 1 October 1990 and 31 December 1994.[32] The dates covered more than just the period of mass killing in the spring of 1994. 1 October 1990 was the date of an unsuccessful invasion of Rwanda by the Tutsi-led forces that finally overthrew the government of Rwanda in June 1994. The unsuccessful invasion of 1990 was followed by organized attacks on Tutsi. Acts dating back to 1990 were likely included because violence against Tutsis occurred throughout the period during which the Tutsi insurgency was

---

29 *Multilateral Treaties Deposited with the Secretary-General: Status as at 31 December 2003*, p. 124, UN Doc. ST/LEG/SER.E/22 (2003).

30 Rwanda, *Code pénal: Décret-Loi No. 21/77 du 18 Août 1977 instituant le Code pénal* (1977), Service des Affaires Juridiques de la Présidence de la République, Kigali.

31 Rwanda, Organic Law No. 08/96 of 30 August 1996 on the Organization of the Prosecution of Infractions Constituting the Crime of Genocide or Crimes against Humanity Committed since 1 October 1990, art. 1, Journal officiel, 35th year, no. 17, 1 September 1996.

32 Rwanda, Organic Law No. 08/96, art. 1.

active.[33] The end date of 31 December 1994 roughly reflects the date by which the
new government consolidated power throughout the territory of Rwanda.[34]

The Rwandan prosecutors, while they did charge individual murders, also
charged genocide, doubtless seeking thereby to highlight the seriousness of the
conduct. Since the penal code lacked a provision on genocide, the Organic Law
referred to the Genocide Convention for an offense definition:

> This Organic Law has as its object the trial of persons sought for having committed, after
> October 1, 1990, acts defined and sanctioned by the penal code and which constitute: (a) ...
> crimes of genocide ... as defined in the Convention of December 9, 1948 on the Prevention
> and Punishment of the Crime of Genocide.[35]

The Organic Law created four categories of offenses.[36] The Law provided
penalties for each category, with the death penalty for the first category: "the
planners, organizers, inciters, supervisors, and those who enlist others in the crime
of genocide." The second category included genocide by one who was not a planner,
organizer, inciter, supervisor, or enlister, with a penalty of life imprisonment.[37]
Substantially lower sentences, as terms of imprisonment, were provided by the
Organic Law for a person who agreed not to contest the charges.[38]

The limitation in the Organic Law to "acts defined and sanctioned by the penal
code" was aimed at avoiding a retroactivity problem in the imposition of punishment
for genocide.[39] The reference evidently encompassed acts of violence that could
be a constituent element of genocide, namely, the acts enumerated in the sub-
paragraphs of Article II.[40] According to a Belgian lawyer involved in the Rwanda
genocide proceedings, the offense would have to be "a murder, a premeditated
murder, a serious assault upon physical or mental integrity, or another inhumane act,

---

33 Alvarez, J. (1999), 'Crimes of State/Crimes of Hate: Lessons from Rwanda,' *Yale Journal of International Law* 24, p. 365, p. 395.

34 Drumbl, M.A. (1998), 'Rule of Law Amid Lawlessness: Counseling the Accused in Rwanda's Domestic Genocide Trials,' *Columbia Human Rights Law Review*, p. 545, p. 580. Haile-Mariam, Y. (1999), 'The Quest for Justice and Reconciliation: The International Criminal Tribunal for Rwanda and the Ethiopian High Court,' *Hastings International & Comparative Law Review* 22, p. 667, pp. 682-683.

35 Rwanda, Organic Law No. 08/96, art. 1.

36 Ibid., art. 2.

37 Ibid., art. 14.

38 Ibid., arts. 15-16.

39 Drumbl (1998), p. 576 note 132. Schabas, W.A., and M. Imbleau (1997), *Introduction to Rwandan Law*, p. 35, Editions Yvon Blais, Cowansville, Québec.

40 *The Genocide and the Crimes against Humanity in Rwandan Law* (1997), International Centre for the Study and the Promotion of Human Rights and Information, Editions ASSEPAC.

etc."[41]Under the Rwanda penal code, murder normally carried a life sentence,[42] but the death penalty could be given if the murder were premeditated or committed by lying in wait,[43] if the murder was of one's own parent,[44] or if infanticide,[45] murder by poisoning,[46] murder involving torture or acts of barbarity,[47] or murder accompanied by the commission of a separate crime.[48] Thus, the Rwanda penal code provided for a death penalty for homicide in circumstances that might have been present in genocide prosecuted under the Organic Law.

Of those charged with genocide in the courts of Rwanda, the best known was Froduald Karamira, a vice-president of the Republican Democratic Movement who formed a splinter group called RPD-Power, which actively targeted Tutsis in 1994.[49] According to prosecution evidence, Karamira made radio broadcasts urging the killing of Tutsis. Karamira was convicted of genocide and sentenced to death,[50] and, following an unsuccessful appeal, was executed.[51]

François Twahirwa, a government official, was convicted and sentenced to death as an "organizer, inciter, supervisor, and one who enlisted others," on evidence that he directed others to kill Tutsi in the Sake district of Rwanda.[52] Venuste Niyonzima, a farmer accused of leading a group that killed a dozen Tutsi in his community, was convicted of genocide and sentenced to death.[53]

Agnes Mukantagara was convicted of genocide, but not as an organizer, and was sentenced to life imprisonment, on a finding that she fell within the second, rather

---

41 de Beer, D. (1997), *The Organic Law of 30 August 1996 on the Organization of the Prosecution of Offences Constituting the Crime of Genocide or Crimes Against Humanity: Commentary*, pp. 33-34, Alter Egaux Editions, Brussels.

42 Rwanda, *Code pénal*, art. 311.

43 Ibid., art. 312.

44 Ibid., art. 313.

45 Ibid., art. 314.

46 Ibid., art. 315.

47 Ibid., art. 316.

48 Ibid., art. 317.

49 Haile-Mariam (1999), p. 702 note 171.

50 Public Ministry v. Karamira, Case No. RPO 06/KIG/CS, Tribunal of First Instance, Kigali (special chamber), Judgment, 14 February 1997 (text of this and subsequent Rwanda court decisions available in French text on website of Avocats sans frontières, Brussels). 'Rwandan Tutsi accused of leading '94 genocide is sentenced to death,' *Los Angeles Times*, 15 February 1997, p. A3.

51 McKinley Jr., A.C., 'As crowds vent their rage, Rwanda publicly executes 22,' *New York Times*, 25 April 1998, p. A1.

52 Public Ministry v. Twahirwa, Case No. RP 0042/EX/R1/98/KGO, Tribunal of First Instance, Kibungo, on circuit in Sake (special chamber), Judgment, 16 June 1999.

53 Public Ministry v. Niyonzima, Tribunal of First Instance, Gikongoro (special chamber), 5 February 1997; conviction and sentence confirmed by Court of Appeal, Nyabisindu, 21 May 1997.

than the first, category of offender established by the Organic Law.[54] The court of appeals confirmed that qualification of her offense.[55] An acquittal resulted for Ernest Muhoza, accused of genocide as a category two offender. Muhoza was acquitted for lack of proof of his participation in the acts of killing charged in the indictment.[56] Upon appeal by the Public Ministry, the acquittal was affirmed.[57]

A few prosecutions in Rwanda related to events prior to 1994, but still within the time period covered by the Organic Law. Faustin Ntaganda was convicted of genocide and sentenced to death for a January 1991 killing, the tribunal finding that "he killed and tried to kill Tutsis at Round Point in Kinigi with the intent of exterminating Tutsis of one gender at a time when similar acts were being perpetrated throughout the country." The Tribunal classified Ntaganda in category one and sentenced him to death.[58] Appealing, Ntaganda challenged the evidence of his participation in the January 1991 killings, and of Tutsis of one gender (apparently, male) being killed throughout the country at that time. The court of appeals affirmed the conviction and sentence.[59]

Several thousand Rwandans were tried and convicted in the special chambers of genocide as defined in Article II of the Genocide Convention. The courts found genocidal intent on the rationale that in killing certain Tutsis, the accused acted with intent to destroy Tutsis as a group.

The Rwandan courts complied with the Organic Law by assuring that those convicted had violated the elements not only of genocide, but of some provision of the Rwanda penal code. Thus, those sentenced to death for genocide were sentenced on the basis of having committed a capital offense under the Rwandan code, in most cases premeditated murder under Article 312 of the Rwanda penal code.[60]

Rwanda's technique of convicting of both genocide and murder let the courts punish under penal code provisions that pre-dated the acts charged. In this respect, Rwanda's approach differed from Cambodia's, where the penalty for genocide was prescribed by government decree after the offenses were committed. In Chapter 9,

---

54 Public Ministry v. Mukantagara, Case No. RP Ch. Sp. 003/01/97, Tribunal of First Instance, Kibuye, Decision, 4 April 1997.

55 Public Ministry v. Mukantagara, Case No. RPA 3/Gc/R1/RUH, Court of Appeal of Ruhengeri, Decision, 30 June 1998.

56 Public Ministry v. Muhoza, Case No. RP 023/CS/KIG, Tribunal of First Instance, Kigali, Judgment, 10 March 1998.

57 Public Ministry v. Muhoza, Case No. RPA 40/98/R1/KIG, Court of Appeal, Kigali, Decision, 17 June 1999.

58 Public Ministry v. Ntaganda, Case No. RP 001/R1/97 Tribunal of First Instance, Ruhengeri, Judgment, 20 March 1997.

59 Public Ministry v. Ntaganda, Case No. RPA 01/R1/RUH, Court of Appeal of Ruhengeri, 24 June 1998.

60 Public Ministry v. Ntaganda, Case No. RPA 01/R1/RUH, Court of Appeal of Ruhengeri, 24 June 1998; Rwanda, *Code pénal*, art. 312.

we inquire whether punishing for genocide absent a prior-prescribed penalty violates principles of legality.

Chapter 6

Prosecuting Under a True Genocide Statute

Most domestic prosecutions for genocide have been under genocide provisions in the local penal code. The states are Genocide Convention ratifiers that have written a genocide provision into domestic law prior to the time of the acts alleged as genocide. This chapter reviews these prosecutions. The aim is not to assess these prosecutions for fairness, although a number of them might justifiably be criticized. The aim rather is to examine how the domestic legislation on genocide was applied.

Romania: Destroying a "Collectivity"

Romania had already inserted a genocide provision into its penal code at the overthrow in 1989 of long-time ruler Nicolae Ceausescu. In 1989 and 1990, four genocide trials were held in Romania, on charges stemming from force used by Romanian police. In the first proceeding, Nicolae Ceausescu was charged with genocide and other offenses, along with his wife Elena Ceausescu, who was also accused of instigating the police actions.[1] The charge was laid under the genocide provision of the Romanian penal code.[2]

The genocide charge against the Ceausescus was based on the killing of several hundred civilians by Romanian security police in Timisoara, and then in Bucharest, during street action that, within a few days, led to Ceausescu's fall from power.[3] The Ceausescus refused to respond to any charges or to cooperate with appointed defense counsel.[4] They were both convicted of genocide, sentenced to death, and executed

---

1 'Transcript of the closed trial of Nicolae and Elena Ceausescu, (as aired on Romanian and Austrian television from a military base in Tirgoviste),' 25 December 1989, *Washington Post*, 29 December 1989, p. A26.

2 *Penal Code of the Romanian Socialist Republic* (1976), art. 357, Fred B. Rothman, Hackensack N.J. and Sweet & Maxwell Ltd., London.

3 'Truth and Justice: The Question of Accountability for Stalinist Crimes in Eastern Europe and the Soviet Union,' *New York Law School Journal of Human Rights* 9, p. 603 (1992) (statement of Adrian Nitoiu, General Justice, Military Section, Supreme Court of Justice of Romania).

4 'Transcript of the closed trial of Nicolae and Elena Ceausescu,' *Washington Post*, 29 December 1989, p. A26.

within a few hours.[5] Of all the genocide prosecutions that have been conducted in domestic courts, this was the most summary.

In 1990, three trials were held against Ceausescu associates on charges of genocide. Four former officials were convicted of genocide for being party to the decisions made in December 1989 about the methods of force to suppress the uprising in the streets.[6] Capital punishment was abolished in January 1990 in Romania, and the four men received life sentences.[7] Nicolae Ceausescu's brother, a lieutenant general in the Ministry of Internal Affairs who directed the training school for the security police, was convicted of incitement to genocide for encouraging security police who shot demonstrators.[8] The Ceausescus' son, who had been Communist Party leader in a town in Transylvania, was charged with genocide and other offenses for killings by police of persons demonstrating against the government. He was convicted of the lesser charges only.[9]

The demonstrating civilians shot in Timisoara included ethnic Romanians, but Hungarians, Serbs, and other minorities as well.[10] The ethnic identity of the victims was not stressed by the prosecution in these cases. Romania, as we saw in Chapter 3, had included "collectivity" as a protected category in its genocide article. This category made identification of a protected group less difficult than under genocide statutes that include only the categories of groups specified in Article II of the Genocide Convention.

Bolivia: "Bloody Massacres"

Bolivia signed the Genocide Convention on 11 December 1948, only two days after the adoption of the text by the UN General Assembly. However, Bolivia did not ratify

---

5 'Army executes Ceausescu and wife for "genocide" role, Bucharest says,' *New York Times*, 26 December 1989, p. A1.

6 'Four Ceausescu aides receive life sentence,' *Los Angeles Times*, 2 February 1990, p. 2. Cartner, H. (1990), 'A Rush to Appease...and to Conceal,' *Human Rights Watch/Helsinki* 2, issue no. 6, p. 5.

7 Cartner (1990), p. 5.

8 'Ceausescu's brother draws 15 years for December role,' *New York Times*, 22 June 1990, p. A8.

9 'Ceausescu's son convicted and sentenced to 20 years,' *New York Times*, 22 September 1990, p. A3.

10 Codrescu, A. (1991), *The Hole in the Flag: A Romanian Exile's Story of Return and Revolution*, p. 27, William Morrow, New York.

and thus did not become a party.[11] Nonetheless, the Bolivian parliament enacted a genocide provision.[12]

General Luis García Meza Tejada took power in Bolivia in July 1980. In January 1981, the leadership of the Movement of the Revolutionary Left, which opposed García Meza's assumption of power, assembled to decide on a political strategy. Security police entered the meeting rooms and shot and killed eight of the participants. A complaint was made against the Bolivian government before the Inter-American Commission on Human Rights, which operates under the Organization of American States. The commission inquired into the January 1981 incident, found no justification for it, and said that the government was responsible for arbitrary deprivation of the lives of the victims.[13]

Later in 1981, General García Meza in turn was overthrown. Political groups associated with the Left in Bolivia pressed for accountability for the January 1981 killings, leading to the opening of a criminal investigation. Pre-trial and trial proceedings against General García Meza lasted ten years, even though only a single court was involved. Because of the character of the case, the Supreme Court of Bolivia heard it as a court of first and last instance. Civic organizations that had urged prosecution presented evidence and argument to the court, participating, as provided in Continental criminal procedure, as "civil parties" to the proceedings.[14]

Convicting General García Meza and his associates of genocide, the Supreme Court of Bolivia concluded that "operational plans for the extermination of the leadership of the MIR [Movement of the Revolutionary Left] were worked out in the state security organs, and General García Meza participated in the elaboration of these plans."[15] Bolivia's genocide provision listed "national, ethnic, and religious" as victim groups. Thus, unlike the Romanian code, which included the broader category of "collectivity," the Bolivian code provision did not yield a ready route to a genocide conviction where the victims were political opponents.

The Bolivian genocide article reads: "One who, with the aim of destroying in whole or in part a national, ethnic, or religious group, kills or injures members of the group, or subjects them to inhuman living conditions, or imposes measures designed to impede their reproduction, or by violence removes children or adults to other

---

11 *Multilateral Treaties Deposited with the Secretary-General: Status as at 31 December 2003*, p. 123, UN Doc. ST/LEG/SER.E/22 (2003).

12 Bolivia, *Código Penal: Texto ordenado según Ley No. 1768 de Modificaciones al Código Penal* (1997), art. 138, Editorial Los Amigos del Libro, La Paz.

13 Inter-American Commission on Human Rights, *Report on the Situation of Human Rights in the Republic of Bolivia* (1981), p. 37.

14 Mayorga R.A. (1997), 'Democracy Dignified and an End to Impunity: Bolivia's Military Dictatorship on Trial,' in A.J. McAdams (ed.), *Transitional Justice and the Rule of Law in New Democracies*, p. 61, pp. 70-74, University of Notre Dame Press, Notre Dame and London.

15 Sentencia pronunciada en los juicios de responsabilidad seguidos por el Ministerio Público y coadyuvantes contra Luis García Meza y sus colaboradores, Bolivia, Supreme Court of Justice, 21 April 1993, Sec. VII, Group No. 3 (Genocidio en la Calle "Harrington").

groups shall be imprisoned from ten to twenty years. The same penalty applies to the actor or instigators or others directly or indirectly responsible for bloody massacres in the country."[16]

The Supreme Court of Bolivia did not make it clear on what basis it convicted of genocide. In its verdict the court referred to the incident as "the bloody massacre in Harrington Street," the street where the killings occurred, but spoke of it as involving "the destruction of a group of politicians and intellectuals."[17] The court did not analyze genocidal intent. It did not state that General García Meza intended to destroy a protected group in whole or in part. It is not clear whether the Supreme Court deemed "bloody massacre" to be a characterization of the elements of the offense separate from the basic definition of genocide. It did not identify the victim group as falling into the category of "national," "ethnic," or "religious."

Since the term "bloody massacres" appears only in the second sentence, it seems unlikely that carrying out "bloody massacres" was intended by the Bolivian parliament as an additional means whereby genocide might be committed. "Bloody massacres" appears to be a short-hand reference to some or all of the acts specified in the first sentence.

The International Commission of Jurists, which wrote an analysis of the verdict, said that the Supreme Court understood genocide to include "the destruction of a group of politicians and intellectuals." But the Commission thought that, given the omission of political groups from both the Article II and Bolivian definition of genocide, the Supreme Court had taken "bloody massacre" to be an independent means whereby genocide might be perpetrated and that it convicted General García Meza and the others on that basis.[18]

Since the Bolivian genocide article, like Article II of the Genocide Convention, includes a reference to destroying in whole or in part, the Supreme Court may have deemed the group to be part of one of the three specified categories of groups, perhaps the "national" group. Whether an intent to destroy a leadership, or political, element is genocide will be examined in Chapters 27 and 28.

Ethiopia: Destroying Political Groups

No technical difficulty over acts against political groups confronted the courts of Ethiopia when they heard prosecutions for genocide, beginning in the mid-1990s. The acts alleged, to be sure, involved violence that was politically motivated. Most of the cases related to the period 1977-78, a time known in Ethiopia as the Red Terror.

---

16 Bolivia, *Código Penal*, art. 138.

17 Sentencia pronunciada en los juicios de responsabilidad...

18 'Bolivia: A Historic Ruling Against Impunity,' *Review of the International Commission of Jurists*, No. 51 (1993), p. 1, p. 4.

The prosecutions were against persons associated with the government known as the Dergue that held power in Ethiopia from 1974 to 1991.[19]

Ethiopia was well equipped legally for genocide prosecutions. Ethiopia was the first state to ratify the Genocide Convention.[20] As noted in Chapter 3, Ethiopia wrote a genocide provision into its penal code in 1957. Significantly, that provision, while covering the protected groups listed in Article II of the Genocide Convention, also included political groups.[21]

Because of the scope of the prosecution work contemplated, Ethiopia's Council of Representatives in 1992 established an Office of the Special Public Prosecutor, with "the power to conduct investigation and institute proceedings in respect of any person having committed or responsible for the commission of an offense by abusing his position in the party, the government or mass organizations under the Derg-WPE regime."[22] "Derg," or "Dergue," means "committee" in Amharic, the national language of Ethiopia. "WPE" is the Workers Party of Ethiopia, the sole political party in Ethiopia during the Dergue's tenure. Although a special prosecutor's office was established, trials were to be conducted in the ordinary courts of Ethiopia.

Indictments for genocide charged killing or other physical violence against intellectuals, religious and political figures, and labor union leaders who opposed the Dergue's political program.[23] The Office of the Special Public Prosecutor announced in 1997 that it had indicted 5,198 persons, most of them for genocide. Of those indicted, 146 were said by the Office to be policy-makers, 2,433 to be field commanders, and 2,619 to be perpetrators.[24] Many were outside Ethiopia and were tried *in absentia*.[25] Large numbers were convicted,[26] but many were acquitted for lack of evidence. In one trial, twenty-seven military commanders charged with genocide were acquitted.[27]

---

19 Mayfield, J. (1995), 'The Prosecution of War Crimes and Respect for Human Rights: Ethiopia's Balancing Act,' *Emory International Law Review* 9, p. 553.

20 *Multilateral Treaties Deposited with the Secretary-General: Status as at 31 December 2003*, p. 123, UN Doc. ST/LEG/SER.E/22 (2003) (ratification 1 July 1949).

21 Penal Code of the Empire of Ethiopia, art. 281, Proclamation No. 158 of 1957, Negarit Gazeta, Extraordinary Issue No. 1 of 1957.

22 Haile-Mariam, Y. (1999), 'The Quest for Justice and Reconciliation: The International Criminal Tribunal for Rwanda and the Ethiopian High Court,' *Hastings International & Comparative Law Review* 22, p. 667, pp. 689-690.

23 Ibid., p. 708.

24 'Over 5,000 former government officials charged in Ethiopia,' *Xinhua News Agency*, 13 February 1997.

25 Quintal, A.L. (1998), 'Rule 61: The "Voice of the Victims" Screams Out for Justice,' *Columbia Journal of Transnational Law* 36, p. 688, pp. 739-740.

26 'Federal high court sentences former government officials,' BBC Summary of World Broadcasts (report by Ethiopian radio of 27 October 2000), 30 October 2000.

27 'Mengistu-era officers acquitted of genocide charges,' *Africa News*, 13 June 2001.

The indictments relied heavily on the fact that political groups were included as a protected group in Ethiopia's genocide provision.[28] As a result, prosecutors did not have to characterize the victims as being members of one of the groups protected under Article II of the Genocide Convention.

Lithuania: Acts Pre-dating the Genocide Convention

In the 1990s, prosecutors in Lithuania examined the criminal liability of former officials for killings committed in the 1940s. Kirilas Kurakinas, Petras Bartasevicius, and Jouzas Sakalys, three officials of the Soviet Lithuania's People's Commissariat of Internal Affairs (NKVD), were tried and convicted of genocide in the Regional Court of Vilnius for participating in the murder of a family in hiding from the Soviet (Red) Army in a Lithuanian village in 1945.[29] After a reversal for procedural irregularities,[30] the Regional Court re-convicted the three.[31] Another NKVD officer, Petras Raslanas, was convicted of genocide for organizing the killing of 76 Lithuanians in a village in western Lithuania in 1941.[32]

Lithuanian prosecutors also investigated killings of Jews during Germany's wartime occupation of Lithuania. Kazys Gimzauskas, deputy chief of the security police of Vilnius during the German occupation, was convicted of genocide on a charge of arresting Jews and turning them over to Nazi groups who killed them.[33]

From the statutory standpoint, the prosecutions in Lithuania differed from most other domestic genocide prosecutions in that the genocide statute was adopted only well after the date of the acts alleged. In 1992, Lithuania adopted a genocide provision in its penal law,[34] and in 1996, Lithuania ratified the Genocide Convention. In 2000, Lithuania adopted an amended genocide provision.[35] The Lithuanian courts applied the 1992 or 2000 genocide provisions, whichever was in force at the time of

---

28 Haile-Mariam (1999), p. 710. Mayfield (1995), pp. 572-573.

29 'First trial of genocide concluded in Lithuania,' Baltic News Service, 22 January 1997.

30 'Lithuanian Supreme Court annuls verdict on 3 "people's defenders",' Baltic News Service, 3 June 1998.

31 'Lithuanian court again accuses ex-NKVDs of genocide,' Baltic News Service, 3 December 1998.

32 Siauliai Regional Court, 5 April 2001. 'Lithuanian court gives life sentence to former KGB officer in absentia,' BBC Monitoring, 5 April 2001, from BNS news agency, Tallinn, in English, 1521 gmt, 5 April 2001.

33 Dapkus, L., 'Lithuania court convicts, refuses to sentence Nazi,' *Jerusalem Post*, 15 February 2001, p. 7.

34 Lithuania, Law on Genocide, Law I-2477, Valstybes zinios (1992), no. 13-342, 9 April 1992, codified in Penal Code, art. 71(2).

35 Lithuania, Law VIII-1968, Valstybes zinios, no. 89-2741, 26 September 2000, codified in Penal Code, art. 99.

prosecution and trial, even though those provisions had not been in force at the time of the acts alleged. The courts did not address potential issues of retroactivity.

Lithuania's situation regarding the offense of genocide was complex, as a result of Lithuania having been incorporated into the USSR in 1940, a status that continued until Lithuania once again became independent in 1991. The USSR ratified the Genocide Convention in 1954.[36] Penal codes were at the republic level in the USSR, and none of the fifteen republics put a genocide provision into its penal code. There had thus been no domestic provision on genocide.

A second potential difficulty was the fact that the acts alleged as genocide pre-dated the drafting of the Genocide Convention. With respect to both potential difficulties, Lithuania was in a situation similar to that of Israel in prosecuting Adolf Eichmann. Lithuania handled the problem differently, however. Whereas Israel's parliament had adopted a statute purporting to extend its applicability backward in time, Lithuania adopted a statute silent as to retroactivity. It was left to the prosecutors, and then to the courts, to say that the statute could be applied to acts pre-dating both the adoption of the statute and the emergence of genocide as an internationally defined offense.

As to the characterization of the protected groups, the Lithuanian courts were aided by the inclusion, as noted in Chapter 3, of "social" groups in Lithuania's genocide provision. It was not clear if the courts considered the target group to be national, or social.

Latvia: More Acts Pre-dating the Genocide Convention

In Latvia, as in Lithuania, prosecutors in the 1990s inquired into atrocities by former officials, committed in the 1940s. As to protected groups, the same situation obtained as in Lithuania, since the Latvian code provision included "social" groups as being protected. Regarding sovereignty, Latvia was also in the same situation as Lithuania, having been part of the USSR during the same years as Lithuania. Latvia ratified the Genocide Convention in 1992, earlier than Lithuania, and inserted a genocide provision into its penal code in 1993.[37] A revised Latvia Criminal Code adopted in 1999 also included a genocide provision.[38]

Genocide prosecutions under the 1993 and 1999 Latvian genocide statutes resulted in convictions in three cases. Alfred Noviks, who had been People's Commissar of Internal Affairs of Soviet Latvia, received a life sentence for torturing and executing

---

36 *Multilateral Treaties Deposited with the Secretary-General: Status as at 31 December 2003*, p. 124, UN Doc. ST/LEG/SER.E/22 (2003).

37 Latvia, Penal Code, art. 68-1, as amended 6 April 1993. Ziemele, I. (1999), 'Questions Concerning Genocide: A Note on the Supreme Court Judgements in Cases #PAK-269 of 4 November 1996 and #K-38 of 13 December 1995,' *Latvian Human Rights Quarterly* 7-10, p. 327, p. 340.

38 Latvia, Penal Code, art. 71, Speka Esoss no. 01.04.1999 (Vestnesis, 08.07.1998, no. 199). Ziemele (1999), p. 328.

Latvians, and for deporting Latvians to other parts of the USSR. Acts charged against Noviks occurred between 1940 and 1953.[39] Mikhail Farbtukh, a regional official of the same commissariat in the same era, was sentenced to seven years for deporting thirty-one Latvian families to Siberia.[40] The Supreme Court of Latvia reduced this sentence to five years,[41] and Farbtukh was later released on health grounds.[42]

Jevgenijs Savenko, a criminal investigator for the Committee on State Security (KGB), beginning in 1940, was sentenced to two years in prison on a genocide conviction for instituting allegedly false treason charges that resulted in death sentences.[43] The indictment recited that Savenko took "actions aimed at the physical annihilation of Latvian residents regarded as socially dangerous by the communist regime."[44] Prosecutors alleged that Savenko, dispatched to Latvia immediately after it was incorporated into the USSR, filed the false charges against Latvian officials of the former, independent, government, including border guards, police officers, and army officers. Fifty victims were named in the indictment.[45] Savenko's sentence was reduced by the Supreme Court of Latvia to time served, because of his ill health.[46]

Like the Lithuanian genocide prosecutions, the Latvian prosecutions related to acts committed before the adoption of the applicable genocide statute, and before the drafting of the Genocide Convention. The Supreme Court of Latvia applied the Latvian code provision on genocide to such acts, on the rationale that the Latvian provision was comparable to the definition of genocide in Article II of the Genocide Convention.[47] The Supreme Court presumed, without specific discussion, that genocide was punishable even if committed prior to the adoption of the Genocide Convention.[48]

---

39 Latvia, Riga District Court, Case of Noviks, No. K-38, 13 December 1995, commented in Ziemele (1999), p. 327, and Ziemele, I. (1997), 'The Application of International Law in the Baltic States,' *German Yearbook of International Law* 40, pp. 261-263.

40 Latvia, Riga Regional Court, 27 September 1999.

41 'Latvian court reduces prison sentence passed in genocide case,' Baltic News Service, 12 January 2000.

42 'Latvia releases former Soviet secret policeman,' News Bulletin, Interfax News Agency, 12 March 2002.

43 Latvia, Kurzeme Regional Court, 'Genocide accused sentenced in Latvia,' Baltic News Service, 7 July 2000.

44 'Latvian court examines case of ex KGB officer, accused of genocide,' Interfax News Agency, 26 February 2000.

45 'Latvian court starts reading indictment in genocide case,' Baltic News Service, 28 February 2000.

46 'Latvian court makes ruling allowing former Soviet hit-man to walk free,' Baltic News Service, 7 February 2001.

47 Ziemele (1999), p. 340.

48 Ibid., p. 329.

Rwanda-Bosnia Prosecutions in Europe

The mass killing in Rwanda and Bosnia in the 1990s produced prosecutions of Rwandans or Bosnians in several European states. Those charged were Rwandans who had been in Rwanda in 1994, and Bosnians who had been in Bosnia in 1992-93, but who attracted the attention of prosecutors in European states in which they resided in the late 1990s. They were prosecuted typically after being identified by Rwandans or Bosnians who happened to reside in those states. While the acts occurred abroad and the victims were non-nationals of the forum state, the perpetrators were residents of the forum state.

In Austria, the Salzburg Regional Court tried a Bosnian Serb, Dusko Cvjetkovic, for genocide for acts committed in Bosnia against Bosnian Muslims. A jury that tried the case found the evidence insufficient and acquitted Cvjetkovic.[49] In a Swiss military court, genocide was charged, along with murder and war crimes, against Fulgence Niyonteze, mayor of a Rwandan town, for the killing of Tutsis in Rwanda in 1994. The court convicted Niyonteze of murder and war crimes.[50] It decided, however, that it did not have jurisdiction over genocide.[51]

In Germany, a Bosnian Serb, Dusan Tadic, was arrested and charged with complicity in genocide for acts against Bosnian Muslims in Bosnia. Instead of proceeding to a trial against Tadic, however, Germany extradited him to the UN Yugoslavia tribunal,[52] where he was charged with and convicted of persecution, which is a crime against humanity.[53] Also in Germany, Novislav Djajic, a member of a Bosnian Serb military unit, was tried for complicity in genocide and complicity in murder, in connection with an incident in which fifteen Bosnians Muslims were killed. Djajic was convicted of complicity in murder, but was acquitted of genocide for lack of genocidal intent.[54] The German court decided that the killings were in response to a prior incident in which colleagues of Djajic were killed by a mine, and they therefore were not carried out with intent to destroy the Bosnian Muslims as a group.[55]

---

49   'Bosnian Serb ruled innocent of war crimes,' *Toronto Star*, 1 June 1995, p. A18.

50   'Sentence on former mayor confirmed,' *Africa News*, 5 May 2001.

51   *International Enforcement Law Reporter* 15, no. 5 (May 1999).

52   Cohen, R., 'Bosnian Serb denies all at a war crimes tribunal,' *New York Times*, 27 April 1995, p. A3.

53   Prosecutor v. Tadic, Case No. IT-94-1, Judgment, 7 May 1997.

54   Safferling, C.J.M. (1998), 'Public Prosecutor v. Djajic,' *American Journal of International Law* 92, p. 528.

55   Case of Djajic, Oberlandesgericht, Bavaria, 3 St 20/96, 23 May 1997, *Neue Juristische Wochenschrift* (1998), Book 6, p. 392. 'War Crimes Tribunal Convicts Tadic and German Court Convicts Bosnian Serb of War Crimes,' *International Enforcement Law Reporter* 13, no. 6 (June 1997). 'Bosnian Serb jailed for deaths,' *Independent* (London), 24 May 1997, p. 16. Fischer, H. (1998), 'Some Aspects of German State Practice concerning IHL,' *Yearbook of International*

Germany, however, recorded convictions of Serbs charged with acts against Bosnian Muslims. Nikola Jorgic was tried for killing Bosnian Muslims in Bosnia, including one mass killing of twenty-two persons. A German court convicted Jorgic on eleven counts of genocide and thirty counts of murder and gave him a life sentence.[56] Jorgic's conviction was affirmed by the German Federal High Court. On the question of jurisdiction, the court ruled that all nations have an obligation to prosecute genocide, regardless of where it is committed.[57] Jorgic filed a constitutional challenge, but the German Constitutional Court let the conviction stand.[58] Maxim Sokolovic, head of a Bosnian Serb paramilitary group, was convicted of complicity in genocide and sentenced to nine years in prison, on allegations that he assaulted and unlawfully detained Bosnian Muslims.[59] Sokolovic's conviction was affirmed by the German Federal High Court.[60] Djurdard Kusljic, who ordered the execution of six Bosnian Muslims, was convicted by a Bavarian court of genocide, on a finding that the execution was done to frighten other Muslims into fleeing. The Federal High Court modified the conviction to complicity in genocide, on the theory that while Kusljic did not entertain genocidal intent, he assisted others who did.[61]

In a military court in Bosnia, two Serbian soldiers, Sretko Damjanovic and Borislav Herak, were convicted of genocide on allegations of killing and rape of Bosnian Muslims, on a charge under the Yugoslav penal code's genocide provision, which had been incorporated into Bosnian law after Bosnia separated from Yugoslavia.[62] In Croatia, Milos Horvat, a Serb who headed a Serbian administration that took over a district of Croatia, was convicted of genocide for overseeing the expulsion of the local Croat population. Allegations did not include killing or other acts of violence,

---

Humanitarian Law 1, p. 380, p. 385. Ambos, K. (1998), 'Djajic,' *Neue Zeitschrift für Strafrecht* 3, p. 138.

56 Case of Jorgic, Oberlandesgericht, Dusseldorf, 26 September 1997, 2 StE 8/96. Cowell, A., 'German court sentences Serb to life for genocide in Bosnia,' *New York Times*, 27 September 1997, p. A5. Fischer (1998), p. 385.

57 Case of Jorgic, Bundesgerichtshof, Third Criminal Chamber, 30 April 1999, 3 StR 215/98, *Entscheidungen des Bundesgerichtshofes in Strafsachen* 45, p. 64 (2000).

58 Case of Jorgic, Bundesverfassungsgericht, 12 December 2000, 2 BvR 1290/99. 'German court confirms genocide conviction of Bosnia Serb,' *Agence France Presse*, 16 January 2001.

59 Case of Sokolovic, Oberlandesgericht, Dusseldorf, 29 November 1999, 2 StE 6/97. Ambos, K., and S. Wirth (2001), 'Genocide and War Crimes in the Former Yugoslavia Before German Criminal Courts,' in H. Fischer, C. Kress and S. Luder (eds), *International and National Prosecution of Crimes Under International Law*, p. 769, Berlin Verlag, Berlin.

60 Case of Sokolovic, Bundesgerichtshof, Third Criminal Chamber, 21 February 2001, 3 StR 372/00, *Entscheidungen des Bundesgerichtshofes in Strafsachen* 46, p. 293 (2001).

61 Case of Kusljic, Bundesgerichtshof, Third Criminal Chamber, 21 February 2001, 3 StR 244/00, *Neue Juristische Wochenschrift* 37, p. 2732 (2001).

62 Burns, J. '2 Serbs to be shot for killings and rapes,' *New York Times*, 31 March 1993, p. A6. Death sentence challenged in Human Rights Chamber for Bosnia and Herzegovina, Damjanovic v. Federation of Bosnia and Herzegovina, Case No. CH/96/30, 11 April 1997.

but rather expelling under threat of killing, and property confiscations.[63] Horvat was convicted under a genocide provision of the Croatian penal code.[64]

In Kosovo, where Yugoslav penal law remained applicable, Miroslav Vuckovic was convicted of genocide on an allegation that he forced Albanians out of several villages, at a time when Serbian forces were expelling Albanians.[65] Despite the fact that the Yugoslav penal code includes forcible expulsion as an act constituting genocide, the conviction was reversed by the Supreme Court of Kosovo on the grounds of a lack of genocidal intent.[66] The court said that "the exactions committed by [Serbian President] Milosevic's regime cannot be qualified as criminal acts of genocide, since their purpose was not the destruction of the Albanian ethnic group in whole or in part, but its forceful departure from Kosovo as a result of a systematic campaign of terror including murders, rapes, arsons and severe maltreatments."[67] By refusing to find genocidal intent on these facts, the Supreme Court of Kosovo took a view opposite that of the Croatian court in the Horvat case.

Brazil: Killing for Financial Gain

A group of Brazilian gold prospectors was tried for genocide for killing twelve members of the Yanomami tribe in the Brazilian Amazon jungle in 1993. As Brazil's Superior Tribunal of Justice related, the killings grew out of the efforts of the prospectors to establish themselves in Yanomami territory. According to an anthropologist's report introduced as evidence, the entry of the prospectors adversely affected the Yanomami, who contracted diseases brought in by the prospectors. In addition, mining polluted the rivers on which the Yanomami relied for sustenance.[68] Some prospectors were robbed or assaulted by Yanomami, leading the defendant prospectors to conclude that in order to continue prospecting, they would have to rid themselves of the Yanomami in the area. According to depositions cited by the trial court, the defendants decided to go out to kill local Yanomami.[69]

63　Case of Horvat, Osijek District Court, Croatia, 25 June 1997, Case No. K.64/97-53, accessible at www.icrc.org.

64　Osnovni krivicni zakon Republike Hrvatske [Basic Criminal Law of the Republic of Croatia], art. 119, *Narodne Novine*, no. 31/93, 16 April 1993. Schabas, W.A. (2003), 'National Courts Finally Begin to Prosecute Genocide, the "Crime of Crimes",' *Journal of International Criminal Justice* 1, p. 39, p. 55.

65　'Court sentences Serb to 14 years in jail for committing acts of genocide,' SRNA news agency, Bijeljina, BBC Summary of World Broadcasts, 22 January 2001.

66　'UN court rules no genocide in Kosovo,' United Press International, 7 September 2001.

67　Case of Vuckovic, No. AP.15/2001, Supreme Court of Kosovo, 31 August 2001, quoted in Schabas (2003), p. 56.

68　Recurso Especial No. 222,653 (Roraima) (1999/0061733-9), Brazil, Superior Tribunal of Justice, 22 May 2001, p. 8.

69　Ibid., p. 11.

Brazil had ratified the Genocide Convention in 1952.[70] The genocide charge was laid under a statute that incorporated the Article II definition into Brazilian penal law, stating, in part, "Whoever, with intent to destroy in whole or in part a national, ethnic, racial or religious group as such, kills members of the group, causes serious harm to the physical or mental integrity of members of the group ...".[71] The court viewed it as no obstacle to a genocide conviction that the prospectors, interested in pursuing commercial activity, may have harbored no animus against the Yanomami as a group. The issue of whether genocide requires anti-group animus will be examined in Chapter 18.

70 Brazil, Decree No. 30.822, 6 May 1952, *Lex: Coletanea de Legislaçao* 16, p. 124 (1952).

71 Brazil, Superior Tribunal of Justice, Recurso Especial No. 222,653 (Roraima) (1999/0061733-9), 22 May 2001, p. 14, citing Law No. 2889 (Define e pune o crime de genocidio), art. 1, 1 October 1956, *Lex: Coletanea de Legislaçao* 20, p. 461 (1956).

Chapter 7

Prosecuting in International Courts

The conflicts of the early 1990s in Yugoslavia and Rwanda led to prosecutions for genocide not only at the domestic level, as seen in Chapters 4 to 6, but at the international level. Genocide has been charged before two tribunals specially created by the Security Council of the United Nations to deal with the aftermath of the conflicts in Yugoslavia and Rwanda.

If justice were done to those victimized, it was thought, the population could more readily re-unify and resume a normal existence. Prosecutions for genocide and related offenses might also deter others, whether in the Yugoslav conflict or elsewhere. The International Criminal Tribunal for the Former Yugoslavia opened its offices in The Hague. A year later, when atrocities were committed in Rwanda, again the UN Security Council created a tribunal as a means to restoring the peace. The International Criminal Tribunal for Rwanda began operations in Arusha, Tanzania.

For each tribunal the Security Council wrote a statute, defining offenses and prescribing penalties. Prosecution in the two tribunals was to be handled by a single prosecutor's office, based in The Hague. A single appeals chamber of five judges at The Hague would hear appeals. The jurisdiction of each tribunal was limited in time. The Statute for the Yugoslavia tribunal covered acts committed only "since 1991," the year hostilities broke out in Bosnia.[1] As of 1993, when the Statute of the Yugoslavia tribunal was adopted, the conflict was continuing, and so the Security Council adopted no end date. For the Rwanda tribunal, the atrocities had ended by the time the statute was adopted in November 1994. The Security Council provided in the statute that only acts committed during 1994 would be prosecutable.[2]

International versus Domestic Trials

A lively discussion has centered around the question of whether it is preferable, in situations of widespread atrocities, to try individuals before domestic courts, or before international courts. The argument for domestic courts is that they are closer to the situation, and that their judgments carry greater moral authority with the

---

1   Statute of the International Criminal Tribunal for the Former Yugoslavia, art. 7, appended to SC Res. 827, UN SCOR, 48th sess., 3217th meeting, UN Doc. S/RES/827 (1993).

2   SC Res. 955, art. 1, UN SCOR, 49th sess., 3453rd meeting, UN Doc. S/RES/955 (1994).

public.[3] International courts may be viewed as an outside imposition and generate a backlash.

An argument in support of the use of international courts is that they are more likely to observe due process and to apply more accurately the offense definitions for internationally defined crimes. Practical considerations may also play a role. Germany, as noted in Chapter 6, tried three Bosnian Serbs for genocide. It did so only after conferring with the Yugoslavia tribunal, and in order to ease the latter's caseload.[4] Germany turned over one other genocide suspect, Dusan Tadic, to the Yugoslavia tribunal.

The concept for the Yugoslavia and Rwanda tribunals was that they would try major offenders. For Yugoslavia, domestic trials were not expected, and only a few trials were held, in Bosnia and in Serbia, for atrocities. With the Rwanda tribunal, to the contrary, mention was made in the Security Council resolution of the need "to strengthen the courts and judicial system of Rwanda, having regard in particular to the necessity for those courts to deal with large numbers of suspects."[5] The Rwandan courts actively prosecuted. For Ethiopia, the creation of an international tribunal was contemplated, but in the end all cases were tried domestically.

In Cambodia, as described in Chapter 5, a domestic trial was held of two major Khmer Rouge figures, but years later, an international effort was mounted to conduct international proceedings against others. The United Nations considered establishing an *ad hoc* tribunal, but Cambodia insisted on domestic proceedings. The United Nations and Cambodia negotiated to arrange trials to be conducted in Cambodia under Cambodian law, but with participation by internationally appointed jurists in the prosecution team and the tribunal panels.[6]

Genocide Prosecutions in the Rwanda Tribunal

Indictments for genocide were laid before the Yugoslavia and Rwanda tribunals. In the Rwanda tribunal, nearly all acts charged were committed prior to 8 November 1994, the date of the Statute. In the Yugoslavia tribunal, some indictments for genocide related to acts committed prior to 25 May 1993, the date of the Statute. Thus, prosecutions were instituted for acts committed before the tribunal came into existence, and before a penalty had been legislated that the tribunal could use.

---

3   Alvarez, J. (1999), 'Crimes of State/Crimes of Hate: Lessons from Rwanda,' *Yale Journal of International Law* 24, p. 365, pp. 403-404.

4   'War criminal sentenced to 40 years,' *Facts on File World News Digest*, 31 December 1999, p. 975 G2.

5   SC Res. 955, preambular para. 9, UN SCOR, 49th sess., 3453d meeting, UN Doc. S/RES/955 (1994).

6   GA Res. 57/228B, UN GAOR, 57th sess., UN Doc. A/57/228B/2003. 'Deal is reached on Khmer Rouge trials,' *New York Times*, 7 June 2003, p. A5.

Whether this practice constitutes a violation of principles of legality is considered in Chapter 9.

Of the two *ad hoc* tribunals, the Rwanda tribunal produced more genocide indictments and convictions. In all cases the victims were Tutsis. The Rwanda tribunal was the first of the two tribunals to enter a genocide conviction. Jean-Paul Akayesu, a town mayor, was found guilty of organizing the killing of Tutsis in his town.[7] A guilty plea was accepted from the Rwanda tribunal's most prominent defendant, Jean Kambanda, who was prime minister of Rwanda in 1994 and was charged for directing the killing of Tutsis throughout the country.[8]

Other members of the 1994 government cabinet were convicted for participating in or organizing attacks on Tutsi: Eliézer Niyitegeka, minister of information,[9] Jean Kamuhanda, minister of higher education,[10] and Emmanuel Ndindabahizi, finance minister.[11]

Andre Ntagerura, transportation minister of Rwanda in 1994, Emmanuel Bagambiki, a town mayor, and Samuel Imanishimwe, commander of a military barracks, were jointly indicted for promoting killings of Tutsis in Cyangugu province. Imanishimwe was convicted, but Ntagerura and Bagambiki were acquitted for lack of evidence.[12]

Numerous officials and private persons, some associated with militia organizations, were convicted of genocide or inciting to genocide. Omar Serushago, leader of a Hutu militia, pleaded guilty of the killing of Tutsis.[13] Clément Kayishema, a provincial governor, and Obed Ruzindana, a businessman, were jointly convicted, Kayishema for mass killings at four locations, Ruzindana for attacking Tutsis who had taken refuge in a building complex.[14] Laurent Semanza, a town mayor, was convicted for organizing and participating in the killing of Tutsis, and for encouraging the rape

---

7 Prosecutor v. Akayesu, Case No. ICTR-96-4-T, Judgment, 2 September 1998; confirmed on appeal as Case No. ICTR-96-4-A, 1 June 2001.

8 Prosecutor v. Kambanda, Case No. ICTR 97-23-S, Judgment and Sentencing, 4 September 1998.

9 Prosecutor v. Niyitegeka, Case No. ICTR 96-14-T, Judgment and Sentencing, 16 May 2003, confirmed on appeal as Case No. ICTR 96-14-A, 9 July 2004.

10 Prosecutor v. Kamuhanda, Case No. ICTR-99-54A-T, Judgment and Sentencing, 22 January 2004.

11 Prosecutor v. Ndindabahizi, Case No. ICTR-01-71-T, Judgment and Sentencing, 15 July 2004.

12 Prosecutor v. Ntagerura, Bagambiki & Imanishimwe, Case No. ICTR-99-46-T, 25 February 2004. Confirmed on appeal as Case No. ICTR-99-46-A, 8 February 2006.

13 Prosecutor v. Serushago, Case No. ICTR 98-39-S, Judgment and Sentencing, 5 February 1999, confirmed on appeal as Case No. ICTR 98-39-A, 14 February 2000.

14 Prosecutor v. Kayishema & Ruzindana, Case No. ICTR-95-1-T, Judgment, 21 May 1999, confirmed on appeal as Case No. ICTR-95-1-A, 1 June 2001.

of Tutsi women.[15] Juvenal Kajelijeli, a town mayor, was convicted for organizing killings.[16]

Elizaphan Ntakirutimana, pastor of a Seventh Day Adventist church, and his son Gerald Ntakirutimana, a medical doctor, were convicted for attacks on Tutsis at a church complex.[17] George Rutaganda, vice-president of the national committee of the Interahamwe, a paramilitary group that carried out much of the killing, was convicted for an attack on Tutsis who had taken refuge in a school.[18] Alfred Musema, director of a state-owned tea factory, was convicted for participating in deadly attacks on Tutsis.[19] Aloys Simba, a retired army officer, was convicted for organizing several mass killings of Tutsis.[20]

Convictions for promoting the killing of Tutsis through the media were entered against Ferdinand Nahimana, a radio and television station director; Hassan Ngeze, a newspaper editor; and Jean Bosco Barayagwiza, director of political affairs of the foreign affairs ministry.[21] Georges Ruggiu, a Belgian working in Rwanda as a radio announcer, pleaded guilty of broadcasting encouragement to kill Tutsis.[22] Samuel Musabyimana was charged for identifying Tutsis to be killed by others.[23] Musabyimana died before being tried.

Acquittal on genocide charges came at trial for Ignace Bagilishema, a town mayor indicted for promoting the killings of large numbers of Tutsis. He was acquitted when two of the trial chamber's three judges concluded that it was not proven that he had promoted these killings.[24] One judge who dissented considered the evidence

---

15 Prosecutor v. Semanza, Case No. ICTR-97-20-T, Judgment and Sentencing, 15 May 2003, confirmed with modification on appeal as Case No. ICTR-97-20-A, 20 May 2005.

16 Prosecutor v. Kajelijeli, Case No. ICTR-99-44A-T, Judgment and Sentencing, 1 December 2003, confirmed with modification on appeal as Case No. ICTR-99-44A-A, 23 May 2005.

17 Prosecutor v. Ntakirutimana, Ntakirutimana & Sikubwabo, Case No. ICTR-96-10-T, Judgment and Sentencing, 19 February 2003, confirmed with modification on appeal as Case No. ICTR-96-10A, 13 December 2004.

18 Prosecutor v. Rutaganda, Case No. ICTR-96-3-T, Judgment, 6 December 1999, confirmed on appeal as Case No. ICTR-96-3-A, 26 May 2003.

19 Prosecutor v. Musema, Case No. ICTR-96-13-T, Judgment, 27 January 2000, confirmed on appeal as Case No. ICTR-96-13-A, 16 November 2001.

20 Prosecutor v. Simba, Case No. ICTR-01-76, Judgment, 13 December 2005.

21 Prosecutor v. Nahimana, Ngeze & Barayagwiza, Case No. ICTR-99-52-T, 3 December 2003.

22 Prosecutor v. Ruggiu, Case No. ICTR 97-32-S, Judgment and Sentencing, 1 June 2000.

23 Prosecutor v. Musabyimana, Case No. ICTR-01-62, Indictment, 15 March 2001, para. 15.

24 Prosecutor v. Bagilishema, Case No. ICTR-95-1A-T, Judgment, 7 June 2001.

sufficient to prove Bagilishema's complicity in genocide.[25] The prosecutor appealed the acquittal, but the appeals chamber upheld it.[26]

Genocide Prosecutions in the Yugoslavia Tribunal

In the Yugoslavia tribunal, genocide was charged more sparingly than in the Rwanda tribunal. Dusko Sikirica, a prison camp security officer, was indicted for genocide in connection with the killings of Bosnian Muslim detainees. At trial, Sikirica challenged the genocide charge, and the court dismissed it for lack of genocidal intent.[27] A genocide indictment against Goran Jelisic, for killing Muslims under detention, resulted in an acquittal on that charge, after the trial chamber decided that the prosecution had presented insufficient evidence of genocidal intent. The trial chamber convicted Jelisic of other charges and sentenced him to forty years in prison.[28] The appeals chamber thought that the trial chamber had improperly decided that the evidence of genocidal intent had been insufficient, but it let the forty-year sentence stand rather than order a re-trial.[29]

Radislav Krstic was a Bosnian Serb military commander in charge of the troops that executed several thousand Bosnian Muslim military-age males in the town of Srebrenica in 1995. As indicated in Chapter 2, Krstic was convicted of genocide.[30] The appeals chamber changed the genocide conviction to one of complicity in genocide.[31] Genocide indictments were also issued for the Srebrenica killings against General Ratko Mladic, commander of the army of the Bosnian Serb administration, and Radovan Karadzic, president of the Bosnian Serb administration.[32] Several other commanders were indicted for genocide. One was Vinko Pandurevic, a brigade commander.[33] Dragan Obrenovic, a brigade chief of staff, was indicted for complicity in genocide, but the charge was dismissed when Obrenovic pleaded guilty to crimes against humanity involving the same acts.[34] Vidoje Blagojevic, a colonel in the Army

---

25 Prosecutor v. Bagilishema, Case No. ICTR-95-1A-T, Judgment, 7 June 2001 (dissenting opinion, Güney).

26 Prosecutor v. Bagilishema, Case No. ICTR-95-1A-A, 3 July 2002.

27 Prosecutor v. Sikirica, Case No. IT-95-8, Judgment on Defence Motions to Acquit, 3 September 2001.

28 Prosecutor v. Jelisic, Case No. IT-95-10-T, Judgment, 14 December 1999, confirmed on appeal as Case No. IT-95-10-A, 5 July 2001.

29 Prosecutor v. Jelisic, Case No. IT-95-10-A, Decision, 5 July 2001.

30 Prosecutor v. Krstic, Case No. IT-98-33-T, Judgment, 2 August 2001.

31 Prosecutor v. Krstic, Case No. IT-98-33-A, Judgment, para. 218, 19 April 2004.

32 Prosecutor v. Karadzic & Mladic, Cases No. IT-95-5-R61, IT-95-18-R61, Review of Indictment Pursuant to Rule 61, 11 July 1996.

33 Prosecutor v. Pandurevic, Case No. IT-05-86-I, 10 February 2005.

34 Prosecutor v. Obrenovic, Case No. IT-02-60/2-S, 10 December 2003.

of Republika Srpska and in command of an area near Srebrenica, was convicted of complicity in genocide in the Srebrenica killings.[35]

Slobodan Milosevic, president of Yugoslavia, was indicted for genocide for killings and other injuries to Bosnian Muslims and Bosnian Croats throughout the territory of Bosnia.[36] Milosevic died before his trial was completed. Biljana Plavsic and Momcilo Krajisnik, co-presidents, along with Radovan Karadzic, of the Bosnian Serb Assembly, were indicted for killings of detainees and for killings in an ethnic cleansing context in many localities of Bosnia.[37] Genocide charges against Plavsic were dropped when she pleaded guilty to other charges.[38]

Three members of the Prijedor Crisis Committee, Milomir Stakic, Milan Kovacevic, and Simo Drljaca, were charged for organizing assaults on Croats and Muslims.[39] Stakic was acquitted for lack of genocidal intent.[40] The case against Kovacevic was dropped following his death.[41] Zeliko Meakic, in charge of the Omarska prison camp in Prijedor, was indicted for atrocities in that camp,[42] but the genocide charge was later dropped.[43] Radoslav Brdjanin, Momir Talic, and Stojan Zupljanin, regional officials of the Serbian administration, were charged for organizing ethnic cleansing.[44] Brdjanin was acquitted of genocide but convicted of other charges.[45] The genocide charge against Zupljanin was later dropped.[46]

---

35 Prosecutor v. Blagojevic, Case No. IT-02-60-T, 17 January 2005.

36 Prosecutor v. Milosevic, Case No. IT-02-54, Indictment, 21 April 2004.

37 Prosecutor v. Plavsic, Case No. IT-00-40-I, 3 April 2000; Prosecutor v. Krajisnik, Case No. IT-00-39-I, 21 March 2000, consolidated indictment of Plavsic and Krajisnik replacing the earlier individual indictments, 23 February 2001.

38 Prosecutor v. Plavsic, Case No. IT-00-40, Sentencing Judgment, 27 February 2003.

39 Prosecutor v. Stakic, Case No. IT-97-24-PT, 10 April 2002. Prosecutor v. Kovacevic, Case No. IT-97-24-I, 28 January 1998. Prosecutor v. Drljaca, Case No. IT-97-24-I, 13 March 1997.

40 Prosecutor v. Stakic, Case No. IT-97-24-T, Judgment, 31 July 2003, para. 519.

41 Prosecutor v. Kovacevic, Case No. IT-97-24-T, 24 August 1998.

42 Prosecutor v. Meakic, Case No. IT-95-4-I, 13 February 1995.

43 Prosecutor v. Meakic, IT-02-65-I, 5 July 2002.

44 Prosecutor v. Brdjanin, Talic & Zupljanin, Case No. IT-99-36, 17 December 1999.

45 Prosecutor v. Brdjanin, Case No. IT-99-36, Sentencing, 1 September 2004.

46 Prosecutor v. Zupljanin, Case No. IT-99-36-I, Indictment, 6 October 2004.

Chapter 8

Suing in the World Court

In addition to the prosecution of individuals for genocide, lawsuits for state-perpetrated genocide have been filed by states against other states. In one respect, genocide is a crime for which individuals are held responsible, but genocide is also a wrong for which states are accountable. In customary international law, the unwritten body of law based on state practice, states are prohibited from perpetrating genocide: "A state violates international law if, as a matter of state policy, it practices, encourages, or condones ... genocide."[1] In 1951, the International Court of Justice said that the prohibition against genocide was "recognized by civilized nations as binding on States, even without any conventional obligation."[2] The court was using the term "convention" in the sense of treaty. Its point was that states are prohibited from committing genocide, even apart from the Genocide Convention.

The UN General Assembly has also referred to genocide as a wrong for which states may be legally responsible. In the resolution mentioned in Chapter 1, in which it asked the UN Economic and Social Council to draft a genocide treaty, the General Assembly declared that genocide was "an international crime entailing national and international responsibility on the part of individuals and States."[3]

The impetus behind the drafting of the Genocide Convention was for a treaty that would ensure the liability of individuals. The Genocide Convention uses penal law terminology, and in defining punishable acts, it uses criminal law categories that apply in domestic law to individuals: conspiracy, incitement, attempt, complicity. Nonetheless, the prohibition against genocide also applies to states.

Lawsuits for Genocide

State-to-state suits add a weapon to the international arsenal against genocide, because they can accomplish two goals that are not easily attained through the prosecution of individuals, even high-ranking individuals. First, a suit against a state can lead to an injunction against ongoing genocide, thereby helping to stop genocide

---

1 *Restatement (Third): Foreign Relations Law of the United States* (1987), §702, American Law Institute, St. Paul.

2 Reservations to the Convention on the Prevention and Punishment of the Crime of Genocide (adv. op.), 1951 ICJ Rep., p. 15, p. 23.

3 Draft convention on genocide, GA Res. 180, preamble, UN GAOR, 2nd sess., *Resolutions*, p. 129, UN Doc. A/519 (1948).

while it is actually occurring. Second, states, more than individuals, are likely to be sufficiently solvent to pay money damages to victims.

The United Nations created a court for suits between states, often called the world court, but whose formal title is the International Court of Justice. It is located in The Hague, Netherlands, a fact that leads to confusion with the *ad hoc* Yugoslavia tribunal, which is also located in The Hague.

Nor should the ICJ be confused with the International Criminal Court, which may hear prosecutions of individuals for genocide but which has no jurisdiction over suits against states.

Lawsuits by states against states for genocide differ markedly from the prosecution of individuals for genocide. In the prosecution of individuals, a prosecutor surveys evidence and determines whom to prosecute. The outcome is either an acquittal or a conviction, and if a conviction, then a penalty against the individual person.

Jurisdiction over Genocide Suits

With suits against a state for genocide, the decision to file is made by some other state. Whether that other state must have some connection to the alleged genocide is a matter of controversy that will be examined in Part Eight. A state seeking to sue another state for genocide faces procedural hurdles. In the ICJ a state can be sued against its will only if it has so agreed in advance. The fact of its being a UN member is not enough. Some states have opened themselves to being sued in the court for any breach of international law by filing a consent statement with the court. By that route, which is regulated by the court's Statute, a state agrees that any other state that similarly subjects itself to suit may sue it. Since the perpetration of genocide is a violation of international law, the court would have jurisdiction.

Other states have opened themselves to ICJ suit for genocide by becoming parties to the Genocide Convention. In Article IX, the Genocide Convention allows a state party to sue another state party for violating obligations found in the Convention. Article IX has, to date, been the only jurisdictional mechanism under which a case has been filed against a state alleging genocide.

The scope of suits permitted under Article IX has been the subject of debate. As we shall see in Part Eight, by one view only if a state failed to stop genocide being committed by individuals could it be sued. By another view, a state could also be sued if it committed genocide itself. The ICJ, as we shall see, adopted the latter view, which means that a state can be sued by another state for committing genocide. However, some states that are party to the Genocide Convention have tried to insulate themselves from suit by filing a reservation to Article IX. A reservation exempts a state from a particular clause of a treaty. How the ICJ has dealt with states that have filed a reservation to Article IX will be analyzed in Part Eight.

A complaint filed by a state alleging genocide by another is like a civil lawsuit that one private party might file against another. A "plaintiff" state sues a "defendant" state, asserting that it is committing or has committed genocide, and asking for a remedy. If the genocide is ongoing, the "plaintiff" state may seek an injunction from the court, to order the "defendant" to stop committing genocide. Whether the genocide is ongoing or has ended, the "plaintiff" state may ask for redress, which might include financial compensation. If victims have been displaced from their home areas, the "plaintiff" state might ask for a court order to the "defendant" state to repatriate the displaced.

If a state successfully sues another for genocide, the outcome may be an order to stop ongoing genocidal activity. Or it might be an order to compensate, and otherwise assist, victims. A state that gains an order from the court against another state may not necessarily get the action it seeks. Enforcement of the court's orders is far from automatic. If the "defendant" state refuses to comply, the "plaintiff" state may approach the UN Security Council, and ask it to take coercive measures against the "defendant" state. The UN Security Council, however, is a highly political body, and the measures at its command are not ideally suited to enforcement of a court judgment. The Security Council has been of little use to states seeking to enforce a court order against an unwilling state.

A 1973 case in the ICJ related to genocide but did not involve an allegation of genocide against a state. After India captured Pakistani soldiers in the 1971 fighting between the two countries, it turned some of them over to the new state of Bangladesh for trial on genocide charges. Pakistan objected that it alone had jurisdiction under the Genocide Convention, since the alleged genocide occurred in Pakistani territory. Pakistan sued India in the ICJ to stop any trials but settled the matter with India and dismissed the case.[4] Bangladesh repatriated the POWs to Pakistan without trying them.[5]

Three Suits Alleging Genocide

Despite the obstacles, three states have sued another state for genocide. All three cases came out of conflict in the Balkans. The first was filed in 1993 by Bosnia against Yugoslavia, alleging "ethnic cleansing," as atrocities were being perpetrated in Bosnia during the hostilities that accompanied the breakup of Yugoslavia. Thus, the situation that led to prosecution of individuals for genocide also yielded allegations against a state.

Bosnia sought an injunctive order on an emergency basis, and the court issued an order asking Yugoslavia not to commit genocide in Bosnia. While the case was still pending, Yugoslavia filed a counter-claim against Bosnia, alleging genocide by

---

4   Case Concerning Trial of Pakistani Prisoners of War (Pakistan v. India), Order, 1973 ICJ Rep., p. 328, p. 347.

5   Salunke, S.P. (1977), *Pakistani POWs in India*, p. 104, Vikas Publishing, New Delhi. Bangladesh, India, Pakistan Agreement Signed in New Delhi on April 9, 1974, para. 15, *International Legal Materials* 13, p. 501 (1974).

Bosnia during the same hostilities. Thus, this case involved two cross-allegations of state-perpetrated genocide.

The second genocide suit was filed by Yugoslavia, the state against whom the 1993 suit had been brought. In 1999, NATO began aerial bombardment of Yugoslavia, in response to Yugoslavia's actions in Yugoslavia's Kosovo province. Yugoslavia sued ten NATO states for genocide and sought an injunctive order against the bombing campaign. As will be explained in Chapter 32, the court did not oblige, but the case continued nonetheless.

In 1999, a third genocide suit was filed by Croatia against Yugoslavia. This suit alleged genocide by Yugoslavia during Yugoslavia's invasion of sectors of Croatia in 1991.[6] That invasion led to a large sector of Croatia's territory being controlled by Yugoslavia until Croatia re-took it in 1995.

Key aspects of these suits will be examined in Part Eight. These suits have opened the possibility of stopping genocide by court order. Even if the court as presently structured is not always able to get its orders enforced, this development is potentially path-breaking in the quest to prevent atrocities. By entertaining such suits, the ICJ potentially pressures states committing atrocities.

Absence of Penal Prosecutions in the World Court

One may wonder why, with all the international interest in prosecuting for genocide, the ICJ has no role in such prosecutions. It is, after all, the court of the United Nations, established as an adjunct of the international organization. It is the successor to a court that functioned under the auspices of the League of Nations, called the Permanent Court of International Justice.

In discussions over the establishment of the Permanent Court of International Justice, a role was proposed for the court in prosecutions of individuals for internationally defined offenses.[7] When a statute for the Permanent Court of International Justice was finalized, however, the court was given jurisdiction only over states.

When the League of Nations was replaced by the United Nations, the Permanent Court of International Justice was re-named the International Court of Justice. No changes in jurisdiction were made. No role was created to try individuals. As a result, when the Genocide Convention was drafted in 1948, there was no possibility of referring prosecutions to the ICJ. The Genocide Convention required states parties to conduct trials in their own courts, or to extradite to another state for trial there. It provided for a state to be sued in the ICJ if it failed in these obligations.

---

6   Application of the Convention on the Prevention and Punishment of the Crime of Genocide (Croatia v. Yugoslavia), Application, 2 July 1999.

7   Saldaña, Q. (1925), 'La Justice pénale internationale,' *Recueil des cours* (Hague Academy of International Law) 10, p. 227, p. 368.

Additionally, the Genocide Convention said, in Article VI, that jurisdiction would lie for prosecutions in "such international penal tribunal as may have jurisdiction with respect to those Contracting Parties which shall have accepted its jurisdiction." No such "international penal tribunal" existed at the time, although the UN General Assembly did have the establishment of such a tribunal on its agenda for study.

That effort languished until the experience of the *ad hoc* tribunals for Rwanda and Yugoslavia in the 1990s gave new impetus. In 1998 the text was finalized for the Statute of the International Criminal Court. The Statute, a treaty, entered into force in 2002. Despite the label "international," the International Criminal Court does not have universal jurisdiction. It may prosecute only if a suspect's state of nationality has ratified the statute, or if the suspect's act occurred in the territory of a state that has ratified.[8] The statute made provision for prosecutions for genocide, using the definition in Article II of the Genocide Convention. The court thus has jurisdiction to prosecute for genocide, but only under the circumstances indicated.

The availability of criminal prosecution and of state-to-state suits raises two serious questions. First, one can contrast the two mechanisms and ask whether criminal prosecution is more effective than lawsuits, and vice versa. One can also ask whether it is necessary to have both mechanisms, or whether one or the other would suffice. More broadly, one can ask whether there is utility in either mechanism. Genocide has been committed not infrequently during the time the Genocide Convention has been in force. The question of criminal prosecution versus lawsuit, and the question of the efficacy of a genocide prohibition will be examined in Part Nine.

---

8 Statute of the International Criminal Court, art. 12, 17 July 1998, UNTS 2187, p. 3.

PART THREE
GENOCIDE'S LEGAL
ENVIRONMENT

Chapter 9

Ex Post Facto Genocide

Technical problems followed the adoption of the Genocide Convention. The states were supposed to pass statutes on genocide in their penal codes. Some did, but others did not. As we saw in Chapter 5, some of the states that did not pass statutes prosecuted for genocide nonetheless. The Genocide Convention did not give an express answer to whether this practice was lawful.

Another difficulty in the legal environment in which the Genocide Convention operated was ambiguity as to the proper rules by which the text should be construed. History had never seen a treaty that attempted to define a penal offense in the style of domestic penal legislation. Specific rules apply to the interpretation of penal legislation, while quite different rules apply to the interpretation of treaties. The Genocide Convention was neither fish nor fowl.

Another problem was whether the Genocide Convention was the last word on genocide. Genocide already existed in customary international law both as a penal offense and as a wrong that could be committed by states. The Genocide Convention did not totally displace genocide as a customary norm. Hence genocide in customary law might, in principle, mean something different from genocide as defined by the Genocide Convention.

Beyond the problem of customary law lay another potential challenge to the Genocide Convention as the ultimate determinant of the definition of genocide. The UN Security Council deals with war and peace and, under the UN Charter, the Council's decisions on such matters are legally binding on states. Genocide may be committed during armed hostilities. The Security Council has the power to order specific action by combatting parties and to take measures it views as appropriate to restore order. The Security Council potentially could direct a resolution to a conflict that has the effect of protecting those who commit genocide. It might, in effect, give amnesty to persons whom states are required under the Genocide Convention to prosecute.

The Security Council also has the power to organize economic sanctions or armed action to deal with a breach of the international peace. Such sanctions or armed action might potentially result in death or other severe harm to members of the population of the state against which they are directed. Thus, the Security Council may act in a role in which it itself might commit genocide. Since its actions are legally binding, one would be confronted with the anomalous situation of genocide backed by the power of the law.

These issues—domestic implementation of the Genocide Convention, the rules for its interpretation, genocide as a customary norm, and the role of the UN Security

Council—serve to define the legal environment in which the Genocide Convention operates. They are examined in Part Three.

The first of these issues is implementation by the state parties. The principal forum for enforcement of the crime defined by the Genocide Convention was to be the courts of the state parties. Ratification of the Convention by a state would not, however, automatically put genocide into that state's domestic law. Moreover, the Genocide Convention did not specify a penalty for genocide. Each state would have to determine a penalty, which might differ from one state to another. Precisely what legislation action was required before states could prosecute was not made clear by the Genocide Convention.

Lawyers still use Latin for principles that limit criminal prosecutions, and two in particular have been invoked in regard to genocide. One is *ex post facto*, the principle that a legislature may not reach back in time to penalize conduct that was not a crime when done. A related principle is *nullum crimen, nulla poena sine lege*—no crime, no penalty, without a statute. At the time of the act, there must have been in force an offense covering the act. The rationale is that it is unfair to punish for crime unless the public knows in advance that certain acts are forbidden. The two principles are sometimes called the principle of legality.

These principles have come under strain in genocide prosecutions. Could states prosecute for genocide only after first enacting their own penal provisions on genocide? Could an international tribunal convict of genocide if no legislation at the international level first prescribed a penalty?

Genocide Legislation

Article V of the Genocide Convention requires states to enact the necessary legislation and to provide for penalties. Article V thus recognizes that the Genocide Convention does not provide penalties, but that this task falls to the states. Finding this aspect of the Genocide Convention curious, Adolfo Molina commented that Articles II and III were "no more than the necessary antecedent to the imposition of a penalty."[1]

The expectation was that states would insert provisions on genocide into their penal codes, legislate a penalty, and use that provision to prosecute. Not all ratifying states have done so. Australia, after ratifying, did not enact a penal provision, and the courts there have said that as a result there can be no prosecution in Australia for genocide.[2] New Zealand took the view that it need not enact a genocide crime,

---

1   Molina, A. (1950), 'El delito de genocidio en la legislación Guatemalteca,' *Revista de la Facultad de Ciencias Jurídicas y Sociales de Guatemala*, p. 25, p. 33.

2   Re Thompson; ex parte Nulyarimma and Others, Supreme Court of the Australian Capital Territory, Australian Capital Territory Reports 136, p. 9 (1998).

because prosecution could be brought under existing statutes on crimes against the person.[3]

The Philippines, when it ratified the Genocide Convention, filed an "understanding" on the obligation in Article VII to extradite genocide suspects. It explained that it could not extradite until it enacted a penal provision on genocide, a provision that, it said, would have no retroactive effect:

> With reference to article VII of the Convention, the Philippine Government does not undertake to give effect to said article until the Congress of the Philippines has enacted the necessary legislation defining and punishing the crime of genocide, which legislation, under the Constitution of the Philippines, cannot have any retroactive effect.[4]

Thus, the Philippines indicated that it did not intend for its future penal provision on genocide to apply to acts committed prior to the enactment.

Prosecutions Absent a Prior-enacted Offense

The states that have conducted genocide prosecutions without an applicable genocide provision in their domestic penal law have all recognized the problem. As indicated in Chapters 4 and 5, they dealt with it in various ways. Israel adopted a statute with retroactive effect. Cambodia decreed a penalty to be applied to previously committed genocide and relied on the Genocide Convention for the existence of an offense in domestic law. Rwanda allowed for conviction and punishment only for a constituent offense of genocide, such as murder, even though prosecutors were required to prove the elements of genocide.

The Genocide Convention does not leave it clear how a state might deal with this problem. Article V might mean that a state may punish for genocide only after it has enacted a domestic definition of genocide including a penalty, and that prosecution may relate only to acts committed after the enactment. If a state can punish for genocide without a domestic provision, it would be punishing for an act for which no penalty were prescribed at the time the act was committed.

A trial chamber of the Rwanda tribunal, in the Akayesu case, asked itself whether genocide had been a punishable offense in Rwanda in 1994. By referring to the legal situation in Rwanda in 1994, the trial chamber showed concern that the statute creating the Rwanda tribunal might not suffice, even with the Genocide Convention, to give it jurisdiction. The trial chamber said:

---

3   Clark, R. (2000), 'The Development of International Criminal Law,' pp. 9-10, unpublished paper presented at Conference: "Just Peace? Peace Making and Peace Building for the New Millennium," Massey University, Auckland, New Zealand, 24-28 April 2000.

4   *Multilateral Treaties Deposited with the Secretary-General: Status as at 31 December 2003*, p. 125, UN Doc. ST/LEG/SER.E/22 (2003).

The Chamber notes that Rwanda acceded, by legislative decree, to the Convention on Genocide on 12 February 1975. Thus, punishment of the crime of genocide did exist in Rwanda in 1994, at the time of the acts alleged in the Indictment, and the perpetrator was liable to be brought before the competent courts of Rwanda to answer for this crime.[5]

But the Rwandan National Assembly evidently did not think that Rwandan courts could punish for genocide, since it provided in the Organic Law of 1996 that the penalties to be applied were those for other crimes against the person as found in Rwanda's penal code. The trial chamber's analysis did not address the issue that when Akayesu acted, no penalty existed in Rwandan law for genocide.

The statutes creating the Yugoslavia and Rwanda tribunals did not set any penalties. Apparently out of a desire to avoid impinging on local prerogatives, the two statutes referred the international judges to penalties found in local law in the two countries. The Statute for the Yugoslavia tribunal said that terms of imprisonment would be the applicable penalty and directed the tribunal to "have recourse to the general practice regarding prison sentences in the courts of the former Yugoslavia."[6] This formulation did not direct the judges to convict for specific offenses, such as murder, found in local law, but rather to be guided by the general level of penalties. Yugoslavia, as noted in Chapter 3, did have a penal prohibition against genocide, so that its parliament had expressed itself on a penalty.

The Statute for the Rwanda tribunal similarly provided for imprisonment for genocide and directed the tribunal to "have recourse to the general practice regarding prison sentences in the courts of Rwanda."[7] Here too, the international judges were not to convict for offenses against the person found in the law of Rwanda, but were to be guided by the general level of penalties found there. For Rwanda, they would be convicting for genocide despite the fact that, at the time of the acts alleged, no penalty existed either in international or domestic law for genocide. Unlike Yugoslavia, Rwanda had no genocide provision in its penal code.

Arguably there was a deficit of legality in the statutes of the Yugoslavia and Rwanda tribunals. If the idea of a prior enacted offense is to give notice to potential violators that the conduct is penalized, then perhaps the precise penalties too would be required. A reference to the "general practice regarding prison sentences" in a particular country might not suffice.

---

5   Prosecutor v. Akayesu, Case No. ICTR-96-4-T, Judgment, 2 September 1998, para. 496 (footnote omitted).

6   Statute of the International Criminal Tribunal for the Former Yugoslavia, art. 24, appended to SC Res. 827, UN SCOR, 48th sess., 3217th meeting, UN Doc. S/RES/827 (1993).

7   SC Res. 955, art. 23, UN SCOR, 49th sess., 3453d meeting, UN Doc. S/RES/955 (1994).

Retroactivity under Article VI of the Genocide Convention

The tension here is between a desire, on the one hand, to punish for such a serious act as genocide, and, on the other, to conform to generally recognized standards of legality as regards criminal convictions and sentences. Nonetheless, the principle of legality may not preclude convicting and punishing for genocide even absent a prior-enacted domestic provision and penalty. There is international precedent for convictions and sentences for internationally defined offenses even absent a prior-enacted penalty. The Genocide Convention itself may contemplate trial under such circumstances. Finally, the principle of legality may not be as strict for crimes like genocide as it is for other offenses.

Article VI of the Genocide Convention contemplates international prosecutions to take place in the future, even though the Genocide Convention established no penalties. It said that trials might be held before an international penal tribunal yet to be established. While Article VI did not specifically address the question of whether such future tribunal might try for acts committed prior to the time the tribunal would fix a penalty, it did not, by the same token, forbid such. The expectation was apparently that genocide could be charged before an international court yet to be constituted.

If international proceedings could be conducted for genocide in the absence of an already enacted penalty, presumably it would not be unlawful for states to do the same. One other option, of course, was possible, namely that an international tribunal would establish a penalty and assert jurisdiction only for acts committed after that enactment. This is precisely what was done when the International Criminal Court was established. According to the Statute of the International Criminal Court, adopted in 1998, the court would have jurisdiction for the offenses within its jurisdiction, including genocide, "only with respect to crimes committed after the entry into force of this Statute."[8] The Statute entered into force on 1 July 2002. The Statute thus avoided any possible argument that it created crimes after the fact.

Article VI, however, does not seem to require the time limitation written into the Statute of the International Criminal Court. By defining genocide and stating that it can be prosecuted before "such international penal tribunal as may have jurisdiction with respect to those Contracting Parties which shall have accepted its jurisdiction," Article VI appears to contemplate that prosecutions could relate to acts committed prior to the constitution of "such" tribunal. The *ad hoc* tribunals for Rwanda and Yugoslavia, as noted in Chapter 7, have convicted for genocide for acts pre-dating the statutes of those tribunals.

Precedents for Punishing Absent a Prior-enacted Penalty

Article VI was drafted only shortly after the prosecutions of Third Reich officials for crimes against humanity committed during World War II. At the Nuremberg trials,

---

8   Statute of the International Criminal Court, art. 11.

internationally defined offenses were charged even though no penal enactment had been promulgated by any authority, domestic or international, prior to the date of the acts charged. Adolfo Miaja de la Muela, writing in 1950, foresaw that trials might be held under the Genocide Convention before a penalty was provided in the particular jurisdiction. He found the problem solved by international precedent dating not only from World War II, but also from World War I. Miaja de la Muela concluded that genocide can be charged in the courts of a state party on the basis of Article II alone:

> The Convention does not specify penalties. The principle of legality thus is fulfilled only in part, since the offenses are defined prior in time to being committed, but the sanctions will be imposed *without a prior penal statute*. The only solution is judicial discretion, for which one has the precedents of Article 227 of the Treaty of Versailles and that found in the London Agreement, unlike the laws pronounced by the victorious states to try crimes of war. And the application of this discretion presents no practical difficulty, since national tribunals must apply to genocide the penalties provided in their national laws ...[9]

Article 227 of the Treaty of Versailles called for trial of the German Kaiser by a tribunal to be specially constituted, "for a supreme offense against international morality and the sanctity of treaties." As to penalty, Article 227 provided that the tribunal should "fix the punishment which it considers should be imposed."[10] This World War I precedent thus stood for the proposition that with certain offenses of substantial seriousness, it does not violate legality to determine the penalty after the fact.

The London Agreement, to which Miaja de la Muela referred, was the treaty in which the World War II allies decided to prosecute Nazis. In the Charter of the International Military Tribunal, which was annexed to the London Agreement, that tribunal was empowered to impose "death, or such other punishment as shall be determined by it to be just."[11] Here too, no penalty would have existed in any legislative form at the time of the acts to be alleged.

The retroactivity issue surfaced in the post-World War II prosecutions, as Nazi defendants argued that they were being tried for crimes that had not been defined at the time of their alleged acts, and for which no penalty had been prescribed. The International Military Tribunal at Nuremberg, which tried the major war criminals, and the courts of the Allied powers that tried other Nazis gave short shrift to this argument. "Under written constitutions," ruled a US military court in Germany, "the

---

9   Miaja de la Muela, A. (1951-52), 'El genocidio, delito internacional,' *Revista española de derecho internacional* 4, p. 363, p. 401.

10 Treaty of Peace with Germany (Versailles), art. 227, 28 June 1919, in Bevans, C., *Treaties and Other International Agreements of the United States of America, 1776-1949*, vol. 2, p. 43, US Department of State, Washington.

11 Charter of the International Military Tribunal, art. 27, appended to Agreement for the Prosecution and Punishment of the Major War Criminals of the European Axis, 8 August 1945, UNTS 82, p. 279.

ex post facto rule condemns statutes which define as criminal, acts committed before the law was passed, but the *ex post facto* rule cannot apply in the international field as it does under constitutional mandate in the domestic field." The court referred to the fact that in English common law the judges decided what was criminal from case to case, even if there were no statute on the subject: "Even in the domestic field the prohibition of the rule does not apply to the decisions of common law courts, though the question at issue be novel."

Then the court said that the rule did not in any event apply to international prosecutions: "International law is not the product of statute for the simple reason that there is as yet no world authority empowered to enact statutes of universal application. International law is the product of multipartite treaties, conventions, judicial decisions and customs which have received international acceptance or acquiescence. It would be sheer absurdity to suggest that the *ex post facto* rule, as known to constitutional states, could be applied to a treaty, a custom, or a common law decision of an international tribunal."[12]

Jordan Paust, reviewing international practice, concluded that international criminal laws that do not set forth a penalty do not violate the principle of legality.[13] The rationale is that the potential defendants have notice of the prohibition and that the offense is of such gravity that they must know that the offense would bring a substantial penalty.

Like Israel, a number of states enacted statutes after World War II to give themselves jurisdiction over World War II-era crimes. Penalties were set only after the war, to apply to acts committed during the war. Under the United Kingdom's War Crimes Act, UK courts assumed jurisdiction over culpable homicide in violation of the laws and customs of war, if the crime was committed between 1 September 1939 and 5 June 1945, in Germany or in territory under German occupation.[14] Australia's War Crimes Act, adopted in 1945, gave Australian military courts jurisdiction over acts in violation of the laws of war, committed since 2 September 1939, and gave these courts the power to impose capital punishment or imprisonment.[15]

Principle of Legality in Human Rights Law

In the Eichmann case, the Supreme Court of Israel rejected the *ex post facto* contention of defense counsel by saying that no principle of international law forbids

---

12 USA v. Altstoetter et al. (Justice Case: Case 3), Opinion and Judgment, in *Trials of War Criminals Before the Nuernberg Military Tribunals under Control Council Law No. 10, 1946-1949*, vol. 3, pp. 974-975, US Government Printing Office, Washington (1951).

13 Paust, J. (1997), 'It's No Defense: *Nullum Crimen*, International Crime and the Gingerbread Man,' *Albany Law Review* 60, p. 657, p. 664.

14 War Crimes Act, 1991, ch. 13, §1(1), *Halsbury's Statutes of England and Wales*, vol. 12 (4th ed. 2002 reissue), p. 1116.

15 War Crimes Act 1945, *Acts of the Australian Parliament 1901-1973*, vol. 12, p. 427.

a state from applying penal laws *ex post facto*. "[T]he principle *nullum crimen sine lege, nulla poena sine lege*," it said, "in so far as it negates penal legislation with retroactive effect, has not yet become a rule of customary international law."[16] In this statement, the court did not limit itself to prosecution for internationally defined offenses but spoke about penal offenses generally.

In 1962 it may have been true that no customary norm required the principle of legality in criminal proceedings. By the late twentieth century, such a norm had developed. According to Article 15 of the International Covenant on Civil and Political Rights, which was widely ratified in the second half of the twentieth century:

> No one shall be held guilty of any criminal offense on account of any act or omission which did not constitute a criminal offense, under national or international law, at the time when it was committed. Nor shall a heavier penalty be imposed than the one that was applicable at the time when the criminal offense was committed.

If genocide were charged in a state that, at the time of the act, had not enacted a penalty for genocide, the offense would still have been in existence, under international law, at least if the act occurred after genocide came to be considered an international offense. While Article 15 prohibits sentencing a person to a penalty higher than that in effect at the time of the act, it does not require that there be a penalty in effect at the time of the act. The prohibition against imposing a penalty higher than one that was in effect at the time of the act does not, writes Alicia Gil Gil, require that a particular penalty be previously set. All that is required, she writes, is "the recognition of the criminality of the conduct, even if the penalty to be imposed has not been set."[17]

Even if a particular previously set penalty were required in human rights law, that requirement would not apply to genocide. Article 15 of the International Covenant on Civil and Political Rights contains a second paragraph that provides:

> Nothing in this article shall prejudice the trial and punishment of any person for any act or omission which, at the time when it was committed, was criminal according to the general principles of law recognized by the community of nations.[18]

This paragraph was copied, practically *verbatim*, from Article 7 of the 1950 European Convention for the Protection of Human Rights and Fundamental Freedoms, where it had been included primarily to accommodate statutes adopted in European states, like the UK statute mentioned above, in the aftermath of World War II, penalizing

---

16 Attorney-General of the Government of Israel v. Eichmann, Supreme Court of Israel, 29 May 1962, *International Law Reports* 36, p. 281.

17 Gil Gil, A. (1999), *Derecho Penal Internacional: Especial Consideración del Delito de Genocidio*, p. 92, Editorial Tecnos, Madrid.

18 International Covenant on Civil and Political Rights, art. 15, para. 2, UNTS 999, p. 171.

war crimes and other offenses committed during the war.[19] The reference to "general principles" was apparently intended to include acts that are crimes under international law.[20] Thus, the reference includes the prohibition against genocide, as a crime found in international law.[21] For genocide, therefore, it suffices that the offense was internationally defined at the time committed, but not that a penalty was prescribed.

This exception is made so that such major offenses will be prosecutable. The International Law Commission followed that rationale when it considered internationally defined offenses. In its Draft Code of Crimes against Peace and Security of Mankind, the Commission said that, with regard to internationally defined crimes including genocide, it is "not necessary for an individual to know in advance the precise punishment so long as the actions constitute a crime of extreme gravity for which there will be severe punishment." As authority, the Commission cited the Nuremberg judgment and Article 15 of the International Covenant on Civil and Political Rights.[22]

Some states in their domestic law take the principle of legality further, to require that a specific penalty have been in effect at the time of the act, even for an internationally defined crime. Gil Gil notes that this is the case in Spain. Even though under Spanish law a treaty, like the Genocide Convention, is automatically incorporated into domestic law when it enters into force for Spain, it would not have the effect of creating a penal prohibition that the Spanish courts could apply. A conviction would be proper under Spanish law only after the parliament enacts a penalty for genocide, and only for acts after that date.[23]

That approach, however, is not required by international norms. States like Cambodia and Rwanda violated no internationally protected right when they initiated genocide prosecutions based on their adherence to the Genocide Convention, but without a domestic genocide statute specifying a penalty. Israel, Lithuania, and Latvia did not violate the principle of legality by prosecuting for acts committed in the early 1940s. Genocide was recognized by the UN General Assembly in 1946 as an offense that already existed in international law and thus pre-dated 1946. The General Assembly said that genocide was a crime under international law for which individuals are punishable and characterized genocide as "a denial of the right of existence of entire human groups, as homicide is the denial of the right to live of

---

19 X v. Belgium, European Commission of Human Rights, Case No. 268/57, Decision, 20 July 1957, *Documents and/et Décisions 1955-1956-1957*, p. 239. Huet, A. and R. Koering-Joulin (1994), *Droit pénal international*, p. 135, Presses Universitaires de France, Paris.

20 Nowak, M. (1993), *U.N. Covenant on Civil and Political Rights: CCPR Commentary*, p. 281, N.P. Engel, Kehl, Strasbourg and Arlington.

21 Schabas, W.A. (1996), 'Justice, Democracy, and Impunity in Post-genocide Rwanda: Searching for Solutions to Impossible Problems,' *Criminal Law Forum* 7, p. 523, pp. 536-537.

22 Draft Code of Crimes against the Peace and Security of Mankind (commentary), *Report of the International Law Commission on the work of its forty-eighth session 6 May - 26 July 1996*, UN GAOR, 51st sess., Supp. (No. 10), pp. 29-30, UN Doc. A/51/10 (1996).

23 Gil Gil (1999), p. 92.

individual human beings."[24] In 2001, a trial chamber of the Yugoslavia tribunal said that "the Convention has been viewed as codifying a norm of international law long recognised."[25]

24 GA Res. 96, UN GAOR, 1st sess., Part 2, *Resolutions*, p. 188, UN Doc. A/64/Add.1 (1946).

25 Prosecutor v. Krstic, Case No. IT-98-33-T, Judgment, 2 August 2001, para. 541.

Chapter 10

Treaty Violation or Crime

Retroactivity is an issue peculiar to penal law. But the Genocide Convention is a treaty. Treaties are normally interpreted by rules specific to treaties. If the Genocide Convention is to be interpreted only by the rules applicable to treaty interpretation, the issue of retroactivity might not arise. Yet most commentators assume that it is an issue, however they may resolve it.

The question of whether the Genocide Convention is to be construed as a treaty, or as a penal statute is also key to interpreting the definition of genocide itself. The definition as written into the Genocide Convention left many questions unanswered. The sparse language of Article II hid a multitude of problems. Later chapters explore some of them. Before specific issues can be approached, however, it is necessary to understand the legal character of the Genocide Convention.

Interpretation of the Genocide Convention is particularly complex because of its dual character as a source of obligations between states, on the one hand, and as a penal prohibition applicable to individuals. One set of rules of construction applies to treaties. Another applies to penal statutes. Genocide is both.

It is also useful to understand the character of the institutions that perform the interpretation. International law does not have a single hierarchy of institutions that refine the rules that have been agreed upon by the international community. Genocide falls within the jurisdiction of more than one judicial institution. They may differ on particular points, and no one of them has the authority to reconcile. In this respect the international legal order differs from a domestic legal order, where typically a single court has the final word on points of law.

A Community of Interpreters

In the early decades of the Genocide Convention, interpretation was the province of scholars. A spate of articles and monographs in the 1950s and 1960s by international lawyers examined issues of potential controversy. As various states incorporated genocide into penal codes, genocide entered the domain of criminal law specialists. Penal code commentaries, the major form of analysis in Continental law, included glosses on the genocide provisions.

As these scholars examined the Genocide Convention, they were aided by the drafting work of 1948 that led to the final text. The detailed attention devoted to each provision of the draft convention by the Sixth Committee of the UN General

Assembly left a wealth of documentation. Scholars parsed the published proceedings of the Sixth Committee for clues as to the meaning of particular provisions.[1]

In the 1990s, judges took center stage in construing genocide. The case law that emerged in both domestic courts and international tribunals applied the genocide definition to real-life facts. An informal consortium of interpreters came into being. The Rwanda and Yugoslavia tribunals each had several trial chambers, and the two had a common appellate chamber. Within each tribunal, the chambers began their task of interpretation, not always agreeing with each other. Chambers of the Rwanda tribunal did not necessarily agree with chambers of the Yugoslavia tribunal. The common appellate chamber was, in theory, to provide a uniform interpretation.

Domestic courts were part of the informal consortium. Domestic prosecution of genocide gained speed in the 1990s. Domestic courts gave their own reading to the Genocide Convention, as incorporated into their domestic law. On occasion they referred to the interpretations given by international tribunals. The German Supreme Court, for example, referred to the Rwanda tribunal's Akayesu decision in parsing Article II as incorporated into the German penal code.[2]

The international tribunals in turn read the genocide decisions of domestic courts. The first trial chamber of the Yugoslavia tribunal to convict of genocide stated that, in determining the meaning of genocide, it "looked for guidance in the legislation and practice of States, especially their judicial interpretations and decisions."[3]

Scholars continued to play a role, as they analyzed the rulings of both domestic courts and international tribunals. Scholars influenced the decisions of both the domestic courts and international tribunals. In Continental law, scholars are regarded as authoritative interpreters of statutes. The German courts in particular relied, in their first genocide prosecutions, on the commentaries written by German criminal law specialists.[4]

The international tribunals as well looked to scholars for guidance. International tribunals, drawing on Continental practice, accord great weight to scholars as they construe treaties. When the International Criminal Court was being created, with genocide as one offense within its jurisdiction, a genocide definition was elaborated, again based on Article II. A panel of experts wrote a gloss on Article II, to direct the International Criminal Court in applying genocide. This exercise introduced yet another party into the increasingly complex fabric of genocide interpretation.[5] Controversial issues of interpretation abounded. Commentators, some fresh from

---

1   UN GAOR, 3rd sess., Part 1, *Summary Records of Meetings 21 September - 10 December 1948*, UN Doc. A/C.6/SR.61-140 (1948).

2   Case of Jorgic, Bundesgerichtshof (Third Criminal Chamber), 30 April 1999, 3 StR 215/98, *Entscheidungen des Bundesgerichtshofes in Strafsachen*, vol. 45, p. 65, p. 80 (2000).

3   Prosecutor v. Krstic, Case No. IT-98-33-T, Judgment, 2 August 2001, para. 541.

4   Case of Jorgic, Bundesgerichtshof (Third Criminal Chamber), 30 April 1999, p. 80.

5   Clark, R. (2001), 'The Mental Element in International Criminal Law: The Rome Statute of the International Criminal Court and the Elements of Offenses,' *Criminal Law Forum* 12, p. 291.

experience with the domestic cases or the international tribunals, wrote articles and treatises praising or criticizing the case law.

Construction as a Penal Statute

The issue of whether the Genocide Convention is to be interpreted like a treaty or like a penal statute got little attention from the drafters of the Genocide Convention. One rare mention came from the Dominican Republic, which argued that the definition of genocide should be "as complete as possible," because of "the fact that the penal provisions gave rise to limited interpretation."[6]

Hints at a conflict between the two approaches can be discerned in cases before the Yugoslavia and Rwanda tribunals, although the tribunals have not directly confronted the issue. Treaties are construed to ascertain the plain meaning of a term or phrase, and in case of an ambiguity no preference works in the direction of a more expansive or a less expansive reading.[7] Penal statutes are construed, in case of an ambiguity, according to the principle *in dubio pro reo*, or presumption of innocence, which results in a preference for the accused. The Genocide Convention is the first treaty that is simultaneously a penal statute. Nothing in the Convention's text indicates how it is to be construed.

The matter is addressed in the Statute of the International Criminal Court, which has jurisdiction over genocide, along with other internationally defined offenses. For genocide, the Statute gives a definition that comes *verbatim* from Article II of the Genocide Convention.[8] The Statute also contains a provision on construction applicable to all offenses within the court's jurisdiction. This provision requires that all offense definitions, including that for genocide, be read like penal statutes: "The definition of a crime shall be strictly construed and shall not be extended by analogy. In case of ambiguity, the definition shall be interpreted in favour of the person being investigated, prosecuted or convicted."[9]

Thus, the approach of the Statute is that even though the Statute is a treaty, principles of construction of penal law shall be employed. Analogy is a concept found in Continental law in statutory construction. Analogy allows a court to read a statute to apply to matters similar to those specifically mentioned, on the theory that they fall within the legislator's intent, even though not mentioned. In Continental law, construction by analogy is generally not used in penal law, however, in order to ensure that persons be punished only for conduct the legislature specifically contemplated, and not for other conduct similar, in a court's estimation, to that

---

6   UN GAOR, 3rd sess., Part 1, *Summary Records of Meetings 21 September - 10 December 1948*, p. 81, UN Doc. A/C.6/SR.71 (Mr. Messina, Dominican Republic).

7   Vienna Convention on the Law of Treaties, art. 31, UNTS 1155, p. 331.

8   Statute of the International Criminal Court, art. 6, 17 July 1998, UNTS 2187, p. 3.

9   Ibid., art. 22, para. 2.

specified. The Continental prohibition against analogy in reading penal statutes is deemed a fundamental guarantee of legality.

Strict construction is the other technical term used in the International Criminal Court's statute. Strict construction is a term found in Anglo-American law in the analysis of penal statutes. A penal statute is to be confined to conduct clearly within its terms. If there are two logical readings of a statute, one broader that would cover the accused's conduct, and one narrower that would not, the latter is to be used. The statute, in this instance, is said to be construed strictly against the state. This approach is similar to the *in dubio pro reo* analytical technique of Continental law, and to the prohibition against analogy. These canons of construction are aimed at ensuring that only those individuals are punished who engaged in conduct the legislature obviously deemed to merit sanction.

Construction in State-to-state Cases

If the Genocide Convention is to be regarded as a penal statute when an individual is being prosecuted, should the same be true when one state sues another? If, in a prosecution against an individual, an international tribunal or domestic court gives a construction in keeping with penal principles, limiting the scope of liability, should the ICJ ignore that interpretation in a state-to-state genocide case? The consideration of protecting individuals from being convicted for conduct not clearly covered by a provision would not seem to be relevant to interpretation of genocide if one state is suing another.

The ICJ, according to Article 34 of its Statute, hears only cases involving states. The ICC, like the Rwanda and Yugoslavia tribunals, enjoys jurisdiction only over natural persons.[10] With the ICJ policing states, and other tribunals policing individuals, a potential arises for varying approaches to construction of the Genocide Convention. A question of judicial training and background may enter the picture. ICJ judges are typically international law specialists, whereas among judges on the tribunals trying individuals, one finds both international law specialists and persons whose background is in criminal law, or as judges in courts of general jurisdiction. A judge with a criminal law background is more likely to assume that the genocide definition must be read like a penal statute.

Still another canon of construction may play a role when genocide is being interpreted in domestic courts. When treaties are written into domestic law, the domestic statute is typically construed consistently with the treaty, on the rationale that the intent behind incorporation of the treaty was to make the treaty into domestic law.[11] Thus, a domestic court construing a domestic genocide provision copied from

---

10 Statute of the International Criminal Court, art. 25, para. 1.

11 Immigration and Naturalization Service v. Cardoza-Fonseca, USA, Supreme Court, 480 U.S. 421, 436-437 (1987).

Article II of the Genocide Convention might attempt to find a construction consistent with Article II as understood by relevant international institutions.

From the other side, the ICJ might attempt to render its reading of the Genocide Convention consistent with principles of construction of penal law. The Genocide Convention was drafted as a penal prohibition applicable to individuals, and this aspect might well be found by the court to be central, even though states too are potentially liable.

On the other hand, when the ICJ entertains a complaint of genocide against a state, the policy considerations calling for strict construction do not apply. If State A sues State B for committing genocide, there is no reason to favor the defendant state, in case of ambiguity in the definition of genocide. State-to-state cases are more analogous to civil cases than to criminal cases.

To date, in its consideration of state-to-state genocide complaints, the ICJ has not referred to strict construction, although, to be sure, the court has not yet issued a final judgment on the merits in a genocide case. If the court takes this position, and if in the prosecution of individuals by other tribunals the strict construction approach is taken, differences in construction could emerge.

While any such differences may seem to be an unacceptable inconsistency, one often finds differences in law between penal and civil proceedings, leading to differing results. Another possible difference is in quantum of proof. The Statute of the International Criminal Court calls for a presumption of innocence and permits conviction only if the prosecutor proves guilt beyond a reasonable doubt.[12] In a state-to-state proceeding for genocide, the ordinary standard of proof would apply. As a result, it is possible that on the same set of facts, the prosecution of an individual would result in an acquittal, whereas a suit against a state on whose behalf the same individual acted would result in a finding of liability.

Evolutive Interpretation of Human Rights Treaties

Another potential conflict in rules for interpretation stems from the fact that the Genocide Convention is a treaty aimed at protecting the rights of individuals. With most treaties, the obligations of a state are static. If anyone tries to argue that the treaty's obligations today encompass more than they did originally, a state may legitimately object that it is being held to an obligation it did not undertake.

The ICJ has characterized the Genocide Convention as a treaty of a special type, however, because of its humanitarian character. The Genocide Convention was intended, the court explained, to protect individuals.[13] That aspect of the Genocide Convention might lead to expansive interpretation, in order to ensure that victims are protected.

---

12 Statute of the International Criminal Court, art. 66.

13 Reservations to the Convention on the Prevention and Punishment of the Crime of Genocide (adv. op.)., 1951 ICJ Rep., p. 15, p. 23.

Two international courts have said that the content of at least certain norms in human rights treaties may expand over time. The Inter-American Court of Human Rights examined the question of due process of law for a criminal accused, as found in the International Covenant on Civil and Political Rights, when the accused is a foreigner. The court said that, for a foreign national, due process includes the right to be informed of the right to contact one's home-country consulate for assistance and advice. The court arrived at this conclusion even though it could not say that such a right was intended to be included in the concept of due process at the time the International Covenant was adopted. "Human rights treaties," said the court, "are living instruments whose interpretation must consider the changes over time and present-day conditions."[14]

The Inter-American Court of Human Rights drew on an earlier decision by the European Court of Human Rights. The European Court had been asked to decide whether the use of caning as a judicially imposed criminal punishment constituted a "degrading punishment," which would be prohibited by the European Convention for the Protection of Human Rights and Fundamental Freedoms. Concluding that caning was a degrading punishment, the court referred to the fact that corporal punishment had been abandoned in most European jurisdictions. "The Court must also recall," it said, "that the convention is a living instrument which ... must be interpreted in the light of present-day conditions. [T]he Court cannot but be influenced by the developments and commonly accepted standards in the penal policy of the member States of the Council of Europe in this field."[15]

In a later case, the European Court of Human Rights faced the issue of whether the right to family life, as guaranteed by the European Convention, was violated by a Belgian law that failed to recognize the maternal rights of a woman to whom a child was born out of marriage. The court decided that the right to family life did cover a mother-child relationship absent a marriage, even though it said, "It is true that, at the time when the Convention ... was drafted, it was regarded as permissible and normal in many European countries to draw a distinction in this area between the 'illegitimate' and the 'legitimate' family. However," said the court, referring to its caning case, "this Convention must be interpreted in light of present-day conditions."[16]

---

14 The Right to Information on Consular Assistance in the Framework of the Guarantees of the Due Process of Law, Inter-American Court of Human Rights, Advisory Opinion No. 16 (1999).

15 Case of Tyrer, European Court of Human Rights, Judgment of 25 April 1978, vol. 26 (Ser. A), pp. 15-16.

16 Case of Marckx, European Court of Human Rights, Judgment of 13 June 1979, vol. 31 (Ser. A), p. 19.

Characterization of the Genocide Convention

The characterization of the Genocide Convention as a "humanitarian" or human rights treaty has not gone unchallenged. Arthur Kuhn viewed it as a war-prevention treaty, on the rationale that genocide may spark warfare with neighboring states. "Mass exterminations," he wrote, may engender "a spirit of vengeance continuing for generations and even for centuries both within the state and in other states where related groups seek action to revenge the crime."[17]

Kuhn, to be sure, was making an argument to the Senate of the United States that it consent to the ratification of the Genocide Convention by the United States. Kuhn was aware that many Senators were reluctant to consent to human rights treaties, fearing international attention to racial practices in the United States. Kuhn wanted the Senators to view the Genocide Convention through the lens of World War II, rather than through the lens of law-enforced segregation, as then practiced in the American South.

The ICJ viewed the Genocide Convention as being aimed at protecting groups of people. Nonetheless, the Genocide Convention is distinguishable from the run of human rights treaties in that it defines a crime. A typical human rights treaty prohibits certain conduct by states but does not provide for the punishment of individuals.

Since human rights treaties typically do not define crimes, one cannot necessarily use the logic of decisions about an evolutive interpretation to expand the Genocide Convention's definition in any particular direction. To date no judicial tribunal has explicitly stated that it was construing the Genocide Convention to reflect any evolution of its meaning since the time of adoption. However, the Convention's requirement of criminal intent has been read in ways that were not anticipated by early commentators on the Convention. Moreover, apart from whether the Genocide Convention can change in meaning as a human rights treaty, another interpretive factor applies to treaties of any type, namely, international customary law, a topic to which we now turn.

---

17 Kuhn, A.K. (1949), 'The Genocide Convention and State Rights,' *American Journal of International Law* 43, p. 498, p. 501.

Chapter 11

Genocide in Customary Law

Even if issues of construction of the Genocide Convention can be resolved, there exists a separate, and potentially competing, body of genocide law, namely, genocide under customary international law. Genocide is prohibited under customary international law, which provides a distinct source of obligation for both individuals and states. Although the issue has not been definitively resolved, there may, on certain points, be a difference between genocide as defined in customary law and in the Genocide Convention. Customary law, moreover, evolves more readily than treaty norms. Customary law potentially introduces another dynamic factor in the definition of genocide.

Customary Norms Affecting the Genocide Convention

A trial chamber of the Yugoslavia tribunal posed the issue of the relevance of customary law, when it provided a guide on how it would construe the definition of genocide under its own Statute, which tracks Article II of the Genocide Convention *verbatim*. Dealing with an accused charged with genocide involving mass killing in 1995 at the Bosnian town of Srebrenica, the trial chamber, perhaps surprisingly, said that it would construe Article 4 in line with customary law at the time of the acts alleged against the accused, namely, 1995, rather than strictly in line with Article II as written in 1948. The trial chamber indicated that it used multiple sources to arrive at the definition of genocide that it applied. Its statement of interpretive sources merits quotation in full:

> The Trial Chamber must interpret Article 4 of the Statute taking into account the state of customary international law at the time the events in Srebrenica took place. Several sources have been considered in this respect. The Trial Chamber first referred to the codification work undertaken by international bodies. The Convention on the Prevention and Punishment of the Crime of Genocide ... whose provisions Article 4 adopts *verbatim*, constitutes the main reference source in this respect. Although the Convention was adopted during the same period that the term "genocide" itself was coined, the Convention has been viewed as codifying a norm of international law long recognised and which case-law would soon elevate to the level of a peremptory norm of general international law (*jus cogens*). The Trial Chamber has interpreted the Convention pursuant to the general rules of interpretation of treaties laid down in Articles 31 and 32 of the Vienna Convention on the Law of Treaties. As a result, the Chamber took into account the object and purpose of the convention in addition to the ordinary meaning of the terms in its provisions. As a supplementary means of interpretation, the Trial Chamber also consulted the preparatory work and the circumstances which gave

rise to the Convention. Furthermore, the Trial Chamber considered the international case-law on the crime of genocide, in particular, that developed by the ICTR. The Report of the International Law Commission (ILC) on the Draft Code of Crimes against Peace and Security of Mankind received particular attention. Although the report was completed in 1996, it is the product of several years of reflection by the Commission whose purpose was to codify international law, notably on genocide: it therefore constitutes a particularly relevant source for interpretation of Article 4. The work of other international committees, especially the reports of the Sub-Commission on Prevention of Discrimination and Protection of Minorities of the UN Commission on Human Rights, was also reviewed. Furthermore, the Chamber gave consideration to the work done in producing the Rome Statute on the establishment of an international criminal court, specifically, the finalised draft text of the elements of crimes completed by the Preparatory Commission for the International Criminal Court in July 2000. Although that document post-dates the acts involved here, it has proved helpful in assessing the state of customary international law which the Chamber itself derived from other sources. In this regard, it should be noted that all the States attending the conference, whether signatories of the Rome Statute or not, were eligible to be represented on the Preparatory Commission. From this perspective, the document is a useful key to the *opinio juris* of the States. Finally, the Trial Chamber also looked for guidance in the legislation and practice of States, especially their judicial interpretations and decisions.[1]

The Krstic trial chamber thus referred to a variety of sources to arrive at its definition of genocide, starting from Article II of the Genocide Convention, but also using construction of Article II by domestic and international courts and other bodies. The most important point the trial chamber makes here is that it was using customary law to determine the meaning of Article 4.

Customary Norm versus Treaty Norm

One might question the correctness of the Krstic trial chamber's approach of using customary law. Since Article 4 of the Statute of the Yugoslavia tribunal is taken *verbatim* from Article II, the trial chamber should arguably confine itself to construing Article II and ignore customary law.

The issue of treaty norm versus customary norm was considered by the ICJ, in a case involving a different international norm, the prohibition against use of force by one state against another. Nicaragua charged the USA with violating this norm as it is found in a treaty, the UN Charter. The case was before the court on the basis of a submission to jurisdiction filed by the USA in 1946, which excluded disputes over treaties unless other parties to the treaty were also parties to the case, and on this basis the court said that it could not resolve the matter under the UN Charter. Instead, it considered Nicaragua's allegations under the customary international law on use of force. This approach presented difficulty, however, since most instances of state

---

1   Prosecutor v. Krstic, Case No. IT-98-33-T, Judgment, 2 August 2001, para. 541 (notes omitted).

practice on use of force have involved allegations of violation of the UN Charter provisions on use of force.

The court said that the two norms on use of force are separate sources of obligation for states, the customary norm maintaining "a separate existence."[2] "[T]he fact," it said, "that ... principles ... have been codified or embodied in multilateral conventions does not mean that they cease to exist and to apply as principles of customary law, even as regards countries that are parties to such conventions."[3] Thus, a state member of the United Nations is prohibited from committing aggression both by the UN Charter and by customary international law.

The court did not find differences between the UN Charter and customary international law in prohibiting the use of force by states. However, the court's opinion is open to the interpretation that if a customary rule imposes greater obligations than a treaty on the same subject matter, states that are party to the treaty may nonetheless be required to fulfill the greater obligations imposed by customary law.[4] If genocide as defined in customary law were in some fashion broader than genocide as defined in Article II, then states, even those party to the Genocide Convention, would be bound by the norm as more broadly defined in customary law.[5]

The Krstic trial chamber was probably correct in endeavoring to arrive at a definition of genocide that is based on Article II but that reflects customary law. The potentiality of a difference between the two may be more theoretical than real, however, because in construing a treaty the practice of states in implementing it is relevant. According to the Vienna Convention on the Law of Treaties, one takes account of "any subsequent practice in the application of the treaty which establishes the agreement of the parties regarding its interpretation."[6] As seen in Chapter 10, an evolutive approach may be taken to construing human rights treaties, and state practice would be relevant in determining whether a human rights norm had evolved.

The sources the Krstic trial chamber referenced all involved efforts to construe Article II, so that even if one were to conceive the project as simply to interpret Article II, one would probably take the same sources into account, either as instances of implementation of the relevant article of the Genocide Convention, or as instances of customary norms covering the same subject matter. All the sources to which the Krstic trial chamber refers might legitimately be used to construe Article II of the

---

2   Military and Paramilitary Activities In and Against Nicaragua (Nica. v. USA), Merits, Judgment, 1986 ICJ Rep., p. 14, p. 95.

3   Military and Paramilitary Activities In and Against Nicaragua (Nica. v. USA), Jurisdiction of the Court and Admissibility of the Application, 1984 ICJ Rep., p. 392, p. 424.

4   Schachter, O. (1989), 'Entangled Treaty and Custom,' in Y. Dinstein (ed.), *International Law at a Time of Perplexity*, p. 717, p. 720, Martinus Nijhoff Publishers, Dordrecht.

5   Van Schaack, B. (1997), 'The Crime of Political Genocide: Repairing the Genocide Convention's Blind Spot,' *Yale Law Journal* 106, p. 2259, pp. 2274-2277.

6   Vienna Convention on the Law of Treaties, art. 31, para. 3(b), UNTS 1155, p. 331.

Genocide Convention, without referring to any different or broader concept of genocide that may exist in customary international law.

Reference to customary law might pose a difficulty if suggested in a state-to-state genocide case in the ICJ. If the court's jurisdiction were based on the Article IX submissions clause, the court would be limited to construing the Genocide Convention. In the case of Nicaragua v. USA, the court's jurisdiction was based on a broader ground, so that the court had jurisdiction over any relevant rules of international law. The court's jurisdiction under Article IX will be considered more fully in Part Eight.

Amending the Genocide Convention

At various times, proposals have been made by analysts to amend the Genocide Convention to remedy perceived defects by broadening its coverage. Analysts concerned that political groups are not among the protected groups suggest amendment to add political groups. Analysts concerned that the mental element regarding the destruction of groups is too narrowly framed suggest amendment to provide that mental elements short of purpose, such as recklessness, or even negligence, should suffice.

The possibility of amendment is slim, however. The historical record with human rights treaties shows no instance of subsequent revision. Treaties once adopted remain as they are. The reasons are more practical than conceptual. Treaties cannot be revised by majority vote of the states parties. Once a treaty is distributed for ratification, states begin to subscribe to it. Any revision runs the risk that those states that have ratified will decline to accept the changes.

An approach that has enjoyed success in Europe is the practice of adopting subsequent protocols. Thus, a treaty on human rights was adopted as a regional instrument in 1950, the Convention for the Protection of Human Rights and Fundamental Freedoms. Since 1950, numerous proposals have been made to add new rights. These proposals have been handled not as amendments to the 1950 treaty, but as protocols to it. A right to property, a right to return to one's country, and a prohibition against capital punishment have all been adopted by the states of Europe by protocols to the 1950 treaty. The text of the 1950 treaty has not been touched. Those states that agree with the new rights provisions are free to subscribe to the appropriate protocol, but the circle of states that adhered to the 1950 treaty is not affected.

While the protocol approach is helpful in adding new rights, it is less useful in altering or explaining the meaning of existing language. It would be more feasible in regard to adding political groups, than to altering or explaining the intent element. Nonetheless, neither the amendment process or the protocol approach holds great prospect in regard to the Genocide Convention. Either process is arduous, as at least some states must initially agree on new language in the hope that it will appeal to other states. There has been no movement towards either amendment of or protocols to the Genocide Convention. The more likely avenue to coping with controversial issues is a process of construction of the terms adopted in 1948.

Chapter 12

The UN Security Council and Genocide

Article VIII of the Genocide Convention acknowledges a UN role in enforcing the prohibition against genocide. "Any Contracting Party," it states, "may call upon the competent organs of the United Nations to take such action under the Charter of the United Nations as they consider appropriate for the prevention and suppression of acts of genocide or of any of the other acts enumerated in article III."

The "competent organ" most directly in a position to stop genocide is the Security Council, which is the only UN organ that has the power to compel states to act, or to refrain from acting, in a certain way. Under Article 25 of the UN Charter, states are required to carry out decisions of the Security Council. No other UN organ has that power.

The coercive power of the Security Council relates to dealing with threats to, or breaches of, the international peace. No mention is made in regard to the powers of the Security Council about genocide, or human rights, or protection of individual persons. Clearly the Security Council could become involved if a war of an international character were ongoing, in which genocide was being committed.

Moreover, the Security Council has construed "international peace" broadly to allow itself to deal with situations that are primarily internal. The foremost example is its determination in 1994 of a threat to the peace in Haiti because of the refusal of a military junta that had taken power from an elected president to reinstate the elected president. The Council

> authorize[d] Member States to form a multinational force under unified command and control and, in this framework, to use all necessary means to facilitate the departure from Haiti of the military leadership, ... the prompt return of the legitimately elected President and the restoration of the legitimate authorities of the Government of Haiti ...[1]

At the time, Haiti was involved in no hostilities. It was not threatening, nor was it being threatened by, any foreign state.

To date, the Security Council has not taken military action to stop genocide. In Rwanda in 1994, it was called upon to do so but declined. It did authorize a military force to go to Rwanda, but not in time to stop the mass killing.[2] Moreover, the force

---

1 SC Res. 940, UN SCOR, 49th sess., *Resolutions & Decisions*, p. 51, UN Doc. S/INF/50 (1994).

2 SC Res. 929, UN SCOR, 49th sess., *Resolutions & Decisions*, p. 10, UN Doc. S/INF/50 (1994).

that it authorized was, in the event, headed by France, which had sided with the government of Rwanda, the party responsible for the genocide.

When genocide was ongoing in Bosnia in 1993, the Security Council was asked to remove an arms embargo it had imposed on Yugoslavia before its breakup, an embargo that as of 1993 was still in force in Bosnia and was preventing the government of Bosnia from acquiring arms from outside the country. Bosnia argued that it needed arms to stop the genocide. The Security Council kept the embargo in place, leading to criticism that it allowed the genocide to continue.

Since the Security Council has coercive power, it can mandate action, or inaction, by states in situations involving a threat to, or breach of, the peace, in which genocide may be involved. Ideally, the Security Council will employ that power to stop genocide, but if it employs it in a fashion that facilitates ongoing genocide, states are obligated to do what the Security Council tells them.

If genocide is taking place in a particular state, at least that state, and perhaps others, would be obliged, under Article I of the Genocide Convention, to try to stop it. But if the Security Council, having determined the existence of a threat to, or breach of, the peace, told it not to do so, the latter obligation would take precedence. According to Article 103 of the UN Charter, "In the event of a conflict between the obligations of the Members of the United Nations under the present Charter and their obligations under any other international agreement, their obligations under the present Charter shall prevail."

An obligation under the UN Charter prevails over a conflicting obligation based on any other treaty, at least as regards states that are members of the United Nations. To be sure, in regard to both Rwanda and Yugoslavia, the Security Council did, as we saw in Chapter 7, establish special tribunals to conduct trials for genocide. In those statutes, the Security Council followed the definition of genocide found in Article II of the Genocide Convention.

The Security Council, in its role of protecting the international peace, may, as indicated, undertake its own military actions. This role puts it in the position of being responsible for troops in the field and thus makes it, potentially, a perpetrator of a variety of war crimes, and even of genocide. Moreover, the Security Council has a power to take coercive action short of use of force, involving economic or diplomatic sanctions. That power also puts the Security Council in a position to affect the livelihood of civilian populations.

It may seem absurd to contemplate that the Security Council might undertake action that might constitute genocide, since the Security Council was established to preserve the international peace and to protect against such atrocities as genocide. Nonetheless, one can, without departing from the realities of international practice, imagine situations in which the Security Council might itself commit genocide. Iraq accused the Security Council of genocide against its population for the economic sanctions the Council imposed on Iraq after the Persian Gulf war. As viewed by Iraq, these sanctions caused thousands of foreseeable civilian deaths.[3]

Whatever the validity of the criticisms of the UN Security Council over Rwanda, Bosnia, and Iraq, it is clear that the Security Council can play a role in situations involving genocide. From the enforcement aspect, its role must be viewed as one that complements the role of courts in prosecuting genocide perpetrators, and the role of the ICJ in hearing lawsuits against states that are allegedly perpetrating genocide.

In 2005, the Security Council referred the situation in the Darfur region of Sudan to the International Criminal Court, asking it to investigate individuals who might have committed crimes within the jurisdiction of the ICC. Although the Security Council did not specify particular crimes, genocide is within the jurisdiction of the ICC, and a report the Security Council mentioned (described in Chapter 24 below) spoke of genocide as a crime that may have been committed in Darfur.[4]

The Security Council's strength in carrying out its role is that the Council is dominated by the major powers, who, as a result of their position, are able to affect events. That strength is, at the same time, the Council's weakness. The major powers may have their own agendas in regard to crisis situations. They may view their national interests as being contrary to protection against genocide, depending on which parties are accused of the perpetration of genocide. Each of the five major powers that sits permanently on the Security Council enjoys veto power. Hence if any one of them fails to agree, the Council is unable to act.

The role of the Security Council is, in any event, part of the legal environment in which the Genocide Convention functions. In analyzing the Convention, that environment is important to keep in mind. The Genocide Convention does not operate in a vacuum, but as part of an international legal order that remains a work in progress. From that context, the next set of chapters addresses the most puzzling aspect of the definition of genocide, the question of genocidal intent.

---

3   Bisharat, G.E. (2001), 'Sanctions as Genocide,' Transnational Law & Contemporary Problems 11, p. 379.

4   SC Res. 1593, UN SCOR, 60th sess., UN Doc. S/RES/1593 (2005).

PART FOUR
GENOCIDAL INTENT

Chapter 13

The Acts of Genocide

Intent is key to the definition of genocide. Intent is relevant whether an individual is being prosecuted, or a state is suing another. Since the intent must be directed towards a group of a certain kind, Part Five deals with the question of which groups are protected, and how the existence of such groups is determined. Part Six examines another aspect of intent, the quantitative requirements of genocide. Part Seven examines genocide committed by particular techniques, each of which raises a question of genocidal intent.

Part Four considers a number of basic issues involved in the intent element of genocide. This chapter and the next examine the intent required for the acts directed against particular members of the group. Chapter 15 focuses on "destroy," inquiring what it means to intend to destroy a group. Whether the destruction of the group occurs by virtue of the acts against particular members, without more, is the topic of Chapter 16. Whether "intent" is present only when the destruction of a group is actively sought is considered in Chapter 17. The motives for genocide are examined in Chapter 18. Where the actor is involved with others in perpetrating atrocities, the intent may relate to more than one person, an issue examined in Chapter 19.

The drafters of the Genocide Convention settled upon a definition of the offense that focused on intent. A perpetrator would commit an act involving actual or potential harm to particular victims, while harboring an intent to destroy the group of which the victims were members. In most prosecutions to date, it has been clear that the accused caused harm to specific victims in ways falling within the sub-paragraphs of Article II of the Genocide Convention. What the accused has typically denied is having acted with intent to destroy the group of which the victims were members. The several acquittals that have been entered on genocide charges have resulted from the court's conclusion that the prosecution had not proved intent to destroy.

Nonetheless, intent is required regarding the act against the immediate victims. Article II defines genocide as one of the acts enumerated in sub-paragraphs (a) through (e), committed with intent to destroy a group. These enumerated acts carry an element of intent, some expressly, some impliedly.

Implied Intent

Subparagraph (b) says, "Causing serious bodily or mental harm to members of the group" and thus does not specify any requirement of criminal intent. Taken alone, this phrase could encompass causing harm through an innocent act, for example, doing so accidentally, or in self-defense. However, a criminal intent requirement is implicit. William Schabas has argued, in regard to sub-paragraph (b), that the actor must have "the specific intent to cause serious bodily or mental harm to a member of the group."[1]

The International Law Commission, which drafts treaties for the UN General Assembly, drew up a Draft Code of Crimes against the Peace and Security of Mankind. The commission decided to include a genocide provision and took the Article II definition without change. In a commentary, the commission analyzed the intent level for the sub-paragraph acts. It said, "The prohibited acts enumerated in subparagraphs (a) to (e) are by their very nature conscious, intentional or volitional acts which an individual could not usually commit without knowing that certain consequences were likely to result."[2]

Some culpability is clearly implied, though not stated. Sub-paragraph (c) includes a culpability term, prohibiting the act of "deliberately inflicting on the group conditions of life calculated to bring about its physical destruction in whole or in part." The actor must inflict the conditions "deliberately." When the Genocide Convention was being drafted, the UN Secretary-General commented on what the actor must understand regarding the destruction that flows from the conditions. He said:

> Obviously, if members of a group of human beings are placed in concentration camps where the annual death rate is thirty per cent to forty per cent, the intention to commit genocide is unquestionable. There may be borderline cases where a relatively high death rate might be ascribed to lack of attention, negligence or inhumanity, which, though highly reprehensible, would not constitute evidence of intention to commit genocide.[3]

By this view, while the infliction of conditions must be deliberate, the actor need not necessarily desire that the resulting harm should follow. The term "deliberately" is used with regard to creating the conditions, but deliberately harming is not required. It suffices that the conditions, deliberately created, are "calculated" to bring about physical destruction.

By the same reasoning, sub-paragraph (b) on causing harm, which omits any culpability term, must encompass one nonetheless, but probably at a level less than that of desiring to bring about the harm. If an actor creates a situation of danger for a victim, such that harm can be anticipated, and if such harm results, the actor has probably "caused" harm within the meaning of sub-paragraph (b).

---

1   Schabas, W.A. (2000), *Genocide in International Law: The Crime of Crimes*, p. 242, Cambridge University Press, Cambridge.

2   Draft Code of Crimes against the Peace and Security of Mankind (commentary), *Report of the International Law Commission on the work of its forty-eighth session 6 May - 26 July 1996*, UN GAOR, 51st sess., Supp. (No. 10), p. 88, UN Doc. A/51/10 (1996).

3   UN ECOSOCOR, 2nd sess., *Draft Convention on the Crime of Genocide*, p. 25 (Report of Secretary-General, 26 June 1947), UN Doc. E/447 (1947).

Domestic Law Analogies

The concept that penal statutes require some proof of culpability, even if they omit any words to that effect, derives from domestic penal law. When the ILC or Secretary-General opine about the culpability requirements in the Genocide Convention, they speak against a background of culpability concepts as found in domestic penal law. International law has not independently developed such concepts but draws on domestic law, where such matters have been analyzed by courts in great detail. The presumption is that when treaty drafters formulate a penal offense, they operate from concepts found in domestic penal law.

Drawing on domestic law is a process not without its hazards, however. Domestic penal law is not uniform throughout the world, and thus one can find more than one solution for a given culpability situation. One could look to the domestic law of the country of the particular drafters, on the assumption that they understood particular terms as they are used in their own law. That approach faces difficulties on several counts. First, it gives primacy to the legal systems of some states over others.

Second, the premise that drafters are thinking of their own legal system may be unwarranted. When treaty drafters use a particular term, they may be thinking of its use in domestic law generally. Additionally, since a treaty is drafted as a collective effort, drafters from various countries may be involved. There is no assurance that all the drafters had a like understanding of a given term. Some may have understood "intent" quite differently from others. The normal approach is to attempt to identify domestic law concepts that seem to be accepted widely.

Statute of the International Criminal Court

The Rome Statute of the International Criminal Court contains some learning on culpability in the definition of genocide. Genocide is one of the offenses subject to the court's jurisdiction. Whereas the Genocide Convention gives no explanation of the culpability terms it uses, the Rome Statute contains a detailed provision headed "Mental Element," applicable to genocide and the other offenses subject to the court's jurisdiction. It reads:

> 1. Unless otherwise provided, a person shall be criminally responsible and liable for punishment for a crime within the jurisdiction of the Court only if the material elements are committed with intent and knowledge.
> 2. For the purposes of this article, a person has intent where:
> (a) In relation to conduct, that person means to engage in the conduct;
> (b) In relation to a consequence, that person means to cause that consequence or is aware that it will occur in the ordinary course of events.

3. For the purposes of this article, "knowledge" means awareness that a circumstance exists or a consequence will occur in the ordinary course of events. "Know" and "knowingly" shall be construed accordingly.[4]

This provision gives a default mental element. It applies, as indicated in paragraph 1, "unless otherwise provided." As for sub-paragraph (c), which uses the terms "deliberately" and "calculated," presumably those terms would govern. The other four sub-paragraphs contain no culpability term, so that this default mental element would govern.

The Rome Statute's default culpability provision employs a solution consistent with that found in domestic penal law. It applies to conduct and its consequences, that is, in an assault on a person, to the conduct involved in the assault (for example, striking the person), and to the consequences (for example, the death of, or harm to, the person). As to the conduct, the provision evidently means that it must be volitional. As to consequences, the actor must at least be aware that a harmful consequence will occur in the ordinary course of events.

That formulation may not resolve all cases. Attributing knowledge to an actor is not always easy in domestic penal law. Even if actual awareness on the part of the actor cannot be ascertained, circumstances may suggest that the actor must have been aware. In such a situation, domestic courts may determine that the actor was aware. To date, genocide prosecutions have not yielded great refinement in the analysis of awareness.

---

4   Statute of the International Criminal Court, art. 30, UN Doc. A/CONF.183/9, 17 July 1998, *International Legal Materials* 37, p. 999 (1998).

Chapter 14

Genocide by Killing

The sub-paragraph that has figured most prominently in genocide cases is sub-paragraph (a), which prohibits killing. The term "killing" reads oddly in this context. "Killing" is not a term ordinarily used to define crime in English-speaking countries, since it implies no culpability. A killing can be accidental, or in self-defense. John van der Vyver suggests that "killing" as used in Article II should be taken to mean "homicide committed with the intent to cause death."[1]

"Kill" vs. "Murder"

Determining which culpability level should apply to "killing" in sub-paragraph (a) is complicated by the fact that the Genocide Convention was concluded in Chinese, English, French, Russian, and Spanish. In some of the five texts, terms are used for "killing" that imply mental culpability, whereas in others, like English, the term implies no mental culpability. The Genocide Convention recites, in Article X, that the texts in all five languages are equally authentic. Under accepted rules of interpretation, treaty terms "are presumed to have the same meaning in each authentic text." In case of a difference, "the meaning which best reconciles the texts" is to be sought.[2]

The Spanish text uses "*matanza*," which, like "killing" in English, covers any killing, regardless of culpability. It is not a term used in penal legislation in Spanish-speaking countries for culpable forms of homicide. The Chinese term also corresponds to "killing," with no implication of culpability. The Russian text uses "*ubiistvo*," a term found in Russian penal legislation for culpable forms of homicide, but which, in addition, can include non-culpable forms. Thus, the Russian term could mean either a culpable or a non-culpable homicide.

The French text uses "*meurtre*," a term found in French penal legislation for culpable forms of homicide. French has a verb "*tuer*" that means "kill," and a corresponding noun "*tuerie*" for "killing," but "*meurtre*" was selected to be used in Article II.

The French term requires culpability. The Russian term may, but may not. The Spanish, English, and Chinese terms do not require culpability but could be construed

---

1   van der Vyver, J.D. (1999), 'Prosecution and Punishment of the Crime of Genocide,' *Fordham International Law Journal* 23, p. 286, p. 299.

2   Vienna Convention on the Law of Treaties, art. 33, UNTS 1155, p. 331.

to be limited to culpable killings without departing from the meaning. Therefore, a reading that accommodates all five texts conforms to the French term, since "*meurtre*" cannot be read to cover a non-culpable homicide. The proper construction of the term is that it designates a culpable homicide only.

This conclusion was reached by a trial chamber of the Rwanda tribunal, in Akayesu, its first genocide case. The chamber noted the discrepancy between "killing" in the English text and "*meurtre*" in the French text:

> the term "killing" used in the English version is too general, since it could very well include both intentional and unintentional homicides, whereas the term "*meurtre*", used in the French version, is more precise. It is accepted that there is murder when death has been caused with the intention to do so ...[3]

The chamber said that it would apply the French "*meurtre*" in preference to the English "killing." The chamber did not refer to principles for construing plurilingual treaties. Instead it reached this result by referring to the presumption of innocence as requiring the construction more favorable to the accused, and also to the Penal Code of Rwanda, which uses "*meurtre*."[4]

In the Rwanda tribunal's next genocide trial, that against Kayishema and Ruzindana, a different trial chamber reached the same result, albeit by different reasoning. It agreed with the Akayesu trial chamber that a doubt in construction must benefit the accused. Instead, however, of resolving the difference between "killing" and "*meurtre*," it referred to the fact that any of the sub-paragraph acts must be committed with the intent to destroy a group. It said that a killing must be of a culpable type before it can be committed with the intent to destroy a group.[5]

The Kayishema-Ruzindana trial chamber's approach was similar to a view expressed by the United States during the drafting of Article II. The United States recognized that "killing" did not necessarily imply culpability but thought that the text implied a culpability requirement, because "the idea of intent had been made sufficiently clear in the first part of article II."[6] The first part of Article II is the phrase about intent to destroy a group.

This is the approach taken by the Assembly of States Parties to the Rome Statute of the International Criminal Court, in the Elements of Offenses it adopted for genocide prosecutions in the ICC. The Elements of Offenses were drafted by the Preparatory Commission for the court.[7] The ICC Statute follows Article II *verbatim*

3   Prosecutor v. Akayesu, Case No. ICTR-96-4-T, Judgment, 2 September 1998, para. 500.

4   Ibid., para. 501.

5   Prosecutor v. Kayishema & Ruzindana, Case No. ICTR-95-1-T, Judgment, 21 May 1999, paras. 103-104.

6   UN GAOR, 3rd sess., Part 1, *Summary Records of Meetings 21 September - 10 December 1948*, p. 177, UN Doc. A/C.6/SR.81 (Mr. Maktos, USA).

7   Oosterveld, V. (2001), 'The Elements of Genocide,' in R. Lee (ed.), *The International Criminal Court: Elements of Crimes and Rules of Procedure and Evidence*, pp. 41-49,

in defining genocide. In the French text of the Elements of Offenses, however, "*tuer*" is used in place of the "*meurtre*" that is used in the Statute. In both the English and French texts of the Elements of Offenses, an explanatory footnote was added to "kill" stating, "The term 'killed' is interchangeable with the term 'caused death'."[8]

The Preparatory Commission and the Assembly apparently thought that the culpability element relating to the group necessarily required culpability with respect to killing a particular victim. Whether one focuses on the meaning of "*meurtre*," or on the intent to destroy a group, it seems clear that culpability is required for the acts listed in the sub-paragraphs of Article II. Innocent acts that result in harm to persons cannot be the basis for a charge of genocide.

Level of Culpability Required in Sub-paragraph (a)

British-derived and Continental legal systems distinguish two grades of homicide. In British law they are called murder and manslaughter. In American law, a killing qualifies as murder if caused, even unintentionally, while committing another crime, such as robbery. A typical example is a killing with a firearm by a person who is committing robbery in a retail establishment. The crime is murder even if the weapon discharges accidentally, on the rationale that the person created a situation of extreme danger by robbing with a weapon.[9]

A killing also qualifies as murder if the actor commits a serious crime against the person, and the victim, in order to escape, brings about his or her own death, for example, by leaping from a window. Here too, even though the death was not intended, or even caused, in a direct sense, by the actor, the crime is murder, again on the rationale that the actor created a situation of danger.[10]

The American Law Institute drafted a Model Penal Code that has been used by many states in the United States in drafting their penal codes. The Model Penal Code defines murder as killing either purposely or knowingly.[11] The Code defines "knowingly" in regard to results of conduct as follows: "if the element involves a result of his conduct, he [the actor] is aware that it is practically certain that his conduct will cause such a result."[12] On this definition, one who understands that his action will result in death is guilty of murder, even absent a desire to cause death.

In Continental law, murder can be committed with "direct intent," which means a conscious design to achieve a result, or by "indirect intent," which means

---

Transnational, Ardsley NY.

8   Assembly of States Parties to the Rome Statute of the International Criminal Court, *Official Records*, 1st sess., 3-10 September 2002, p. 113 (English text), p. 116 (French text), UN Doc. ICC-ASP/1/3 (2002).

9   Ibid., pp. 515-516.

10   Ibid., p. 190.

11   *Model Penal Code*, §210.2, American Law Institute, Philadelphia (1962).

12   Ibid., §2.02(2)(b).

understanding the dangerous character of an act and foreseeing the result, but allowing the result to occur. Thus, the Russian penal code defines "intentional commission" of crime: "A crime is deemed to be committed intentionally if the person committing it realized the socially dangerous character of his act or omission, foresaw its socially dangerous consequences, and desired them or consciously allowed these consequences to follow."[13] If the actor "desires" the result, the crime is said to be committed with direct intent. If the actor "consciously allows" the result, the crime is said to be committed with indirect intent.[14] German law takes the same approach.[15] One finds comparable culpability distinctions in other legal systems. In Islamic law, culpable homicide is graded on the basis of factors reflecting the concepts that in British-derived or Continental law are termed purpose or knowledge.[16]

If, as suggested above, the "killing" specified in sub-paragraph (a) must constitute murder, there remains flexibility in the characterization of the mental element. Murder is a term defined in domestic law, and one must assume that when it is incorporated into a treaty, the meaning as found in domestic law is what is intended. While domestic law definitions vary somewhat, murder is not limited to instances in which the actor consciously desires to cause death.

Numbers Killed or Injured

Although it was the mass killings by Germany in World War II that inspired the Genocide Convention, Article II does not require the killing of large numbers. If genocide is alleged on the basis of killings, rather than one of the other sub-paragraph acts, Article II requires the killing of "members," without specifying a minimum number.

The Genocide Convention was intended to allow action before mass killing occurs. "Society must not wait," writes Daniel Nsereko, "until such a person has injured a large number of people before it can find him liable [for genocide]."[17] The

13 Russia, *Ugolovnyi kodeks RSFSR* [Criminal Code of the Russian Soviet Federated Socialist Republic], art. 8 (1960).

14 Nikiforov, B.S. (1963), *Nauchno-prakticheskii kommentarii ugolovnogo kodeksa RSFSR* [Scholarly and Practical Commentary to the Criminal Code of the RSFSR], p. 17, Juridical Literature, Moscow.

15 Fletcher, G.P. (1978), *Rethinking Criminal Law*, pp. 325-326, Little, Brown & Co., Boston.

16 Forte, D.F. (1999), *Studies in Islamic Law: Classical and Contemporary Application*, pp. 91-93, Austin & Winfield, Lanham MD. Schacht, J. (1964), *An Introduction to Islamic Law*, pp. 181-82, Clarendon Press, Oxford.

17 Nsereko, D.D.N. (2000), 'Genocide: A Crime Against Mankind,' in G.K. McDonald and O. Swaak-Goldman (eds), *Substantive and Procedural Aspects of International Criminal Law: The Experience of International and National Courts*, vol. 1, p. 113, pp. 125-126, Kluwer, The Hague.

trial chamber that reviewed the Mladic-Karadzic indictment said that the destruction of the group relates to the actor's intent but need not necessarily be brought about by the act, so long as the requisite intent accompanies the act. The trial chamber said, "The degree to which the group was destroyed in whole or in part is not necessary to conclude that genocide has occurred. That one of the acts enumerated in the definition was perpetrated with a specific intent suffices."[18] It is thus not accurate to refer to genocide as a "mass crime" or a "massive crime" as one sometimes reads. The actor need not harm substantial numbers of people to commit genocide.

The Krstic trial chamber of the Yugoslavia tribunal said that genocide may be committed "by a single or a few murders."[19] The Croatian court that, as seen in Chapter 6, convicted Milos Horvat, similarly said, "For bringing charges against the defendant for genocide [it] would be enough to mention only one action against only one person in case his intention was to partly or entirely annihilate some of the groups as mentioned in the Article 119 Basic Criminal Law of the Republic of Croatia."

That view accurately reflects Article II.[20] In 1948, France told the Sixth Committee that the killing of one person would suffice, if the requisite anti-group intent were present.[21] Stefan Glaser writes that genocide under Article II is present "even where the act (murder, etc.) was committed against a single member of one of the specified groups, with intent to destroy it 'in whole or in part'."[22] A commentary to the Austrian penal code, addressing genocide as it appears in the Austrian penal code, states: "The killing of a single member of the group can in general be regarded as genocide, if it is part of a plan to destroy the group, for example, if thereby to work towards the killing of other members of the group."[23]

The Preparatory Commission for the International Criminal Court affirmed this understanding of genocide in its Elements of Offenses. The Commission provided that genocide by killing is committed if an actor kills "one or more persons."[24] The German parliament made this result explicit in its 2002 genocide provision by

---

18 Prosecutor v. Karadzic & Mladic, Cases No. IT-95-5-R61, IT-95-18-R61, Review of Indictment Pursuant to Rule 61, 11 July 1996, para. 92.

19 Prosecutor v. Krstic, Case No. IT-98-33-T, Judgment, 2 August 2001, para. 685.

20 Gil Gil, A. (1999), *Derecho Penal Internacional: Especial Consideración del Delito de Genocidio*, p. 194, Editorial Tecnos, Madrid.

21 UN GAOR, 3rd sess., Part 1, *Summary Records of Meetings 21 September - 10 December 1948*, p. 90-91, UN Doc. A/C.6/SR.73 (1948) (Mr. Chaumont, France).

22 Glaser, S. (1970), *Droit international pénal conventionnel*, p. 112, Bruylant, Brussels.

23 Foregger, E. and E. Serini (eds) (1978), *Strafgesetzbuch samt den wichtigsten Nebengesetzen*, p. 516, Manz Verlag, Vienna.

24 Assembly of States Parties to the Rome Statute of the International Criminal Court, *Official Records*, 1st sess., 3-10 September 2002, p. 113 (English text), p. 116 (French text), UN Doc. ICC-ASP/1/3 (2002).

changing the phrase "kills members of the group" to read "kills a member of the group."[25]

This approach follows from the concept behind the Article II definition of genocide. An actor is responsible for entertaining the intent to destroy a group, when an act is carried out in pursuance of that intent, directed against individual members of the group. In principle, the act could be directed against a single member.

Whether Deaths Must Ensue

Even a single death may not be essential for genocide liability. Since the Genocide Convention, in Article III, includes "attempt," presumably even an unsuccessful effort to kill one person would suffice, if committed with the requisite intent. Thus, Alicia Gil Gil writes that "there would be an attempt where an actor tries to kill a member of a specific group, with intent to destroy the group, but without achieving the result of death for reasons not dependent on the will of the actor."[26]

Italy's genocide provision indicates that no death need result for genocide liability. The Italian code provision includes a paragraph titled "Aggravating circumstance" that calls for a higher penalty "if the death of one or more persons results from any of the acts provided in the preceding articles." A lower penalty applies if genocide is committed without killing anyone.[27]

Whether Multiple Acts are Required

The issue of whether a single act against members of a group might constitute genocide was raised by one judge in Bosnia's ICJ case against Yugoslavia. When Yugoslavia asserted a counter-claim for genocide against Bosnia, the court struggled with the question of whether Yugoslavia's genocide allegations could properly be heard in the same case as the genocide allegations asserted by Bosnia. Bosnia said that a counter-claim was proper only if there were a direct connection between the facts it alleged against Yugoslavia, and the facts Yugoslavia alleged against it. But Yugoslavia was alleging, as proof of Bosnia's genocide, incidents different from those alleged by Bosnia. Yugoslavia said that even if different incidents were involved, a counter-claim was proper so long as the facts came out of the same hostilities, as they did.

---

25 Germany, Strafgesetzbuch §220a, superseded by Code of Crimes Against International Law, §6, Federal Gazette I, p. 2254 (2002), translated in *Criminal Law Forum* 13, p. 214 (2002). Zimmerman, A. (2003), 'Main Features of the New German Code of Crimes against International Law (*Völkerstrafgesetzbuch*),' in M. Neuner (ed.), *National Legislation Incorporating International Crimes: Approaches of Civil and Common Law Countries*, p. 137, p. 140, Berliner Wissengeschafts Verlag, Berlin.

26 Gil Gil (1999), p. 328.

27 Italy, Law of 9 October 1967, no. 962.

Judge *ad hoc* Lauterpacht, appointed by Bosnia for the case, said that the definition of genocide was relevant to which approach to counter-claims was correct. He stated:

> the choice between these two approaches must depend to a large extent on the nature of the concept "genocide." Can what we conceive of as amounting to genocide be constituted by a single act of a horrific nature? Or can it only be constituted by a series of acts which, while individually being no more than murder or causing serious bodily harm to individuals or such like, are, when viewed cumulatively, evidence of a pattern of activity amounting to genocide? ... The second alternative seems logically to be the more cogent. A single murder or other horrific act cannot be genocide. Only a series or accumulation of such acts, if they reveal collectively the necessary intent and are directed against a group identifiable in the manner foreseen in Article II of the Convention, will serve to constitute genocide—whereupon liability for the individual component crimes, as well as for the special crime of genocide, will fall not only upon the individuals directly responsible but also upon the State to which their acts are attributable.[28]

In his analysis of Yugoslavia's allegations as they related to Bosnia's allegations, Lauterpacht was working against the background of events in Bosnia, which involved killings by opposing forces over a period of time. In that context, it may have seemed logical to consider as genocide only a series of acts. However, Article II requires only a single act accompanied by the intent to destroy. The analysis of the commentators to the German and Austrian codes, as seen above, that a single act can constitute genocide accurately reflects Article II. While a series of acts of violence against members of a group may evidence an intent to destroy the group, other evidence may suffice, even if the actor commits only a single act.

---

28 Application of the Convention on the Prevention and Punishment of the Crime of Genocide (Bosnia and Herzegovina v. Yugoslavia), Counter-claims, Order, 1997 ICJ Rep., p. 243, p. 282 (separate opinion, Lauterpacht).

Chapter 15

Destroying a Group

While the number of persons killed may not need to be high to satisfy the requirements of sub-paragraph (a), the number may facilitate the proof of an "intent to destroy." Over and above the mental element required in relation to immediate victims, Article II of the Genocide Convention requires proof of a mental element in relation to the group of which the victims are members. The phrase "intent to destroy, in whole or in part, a national, ethnical, racial or religious group, as such" is the Genocide Convention's formulation of the mental element applicable to the group.

A trial chamber of the Rwanda tribunal quoted Brazil's statement in the Sixth Committee about the importance of this secondary intent element: "genocide [is] characterised by the factor of particular intent to destroy a group. In the absence of that factor, whatever the degree of atrocity of an act and however similar it might be to the acts described in the convention, that act could still not be called genocide."[1] The acts specified in the Article II sub-paragraphs, even if accompanied by the intent required for those acts, result in genocide liability only if an intent to destroy the group was also present.

Article II uses "destroy" without defining it. Forcing a group out of its home area arguably destroys it. Forced removal will be considered in Chapters 29 and 30. Forced assimilation arguably destroys a group. As a result of threats or legal prohibitions, a group's members may refrain from speaking its language, or from practicing its religion or customs. The group may cease to be identifiable as such. In this chapter, two possible ways of intending to destroy a group are considered: an intent to injure, but short of killing; and an intent to destroy the group's social identification.

Intent to Injure

Alicia Gil Gil views an intent to harm falling short of an intent to kill as insufficient to satisfy the "intent to destroy" element of Article II. Intent to destroy, she reasons, requires an intent to kill, and therefore intending merely to cause injury, even

---

1 Prosecutor v. Akayesu, Case No. ICTR-96-4-T, Judgment, 2 September 1998, para. 519, from UN GAOR, 3rd sess., Part 1, *Summary Records of Meetings 21 September - 10 December 1948*, p. 87, UN Doc. A/C.6/SR.72 (1949) (Mr. Amado, Brazil) (incorrectly cited by ICTR as being at p. 109).

serious injury, does not suffice.[2] The drafting history reveals discussion, however, of destruction by means short of killing.[3] The UN Secretary-General thought that the intent to destroy, as found in an early draft of the Genocide Convention, involved acts intended to "cause the death of members of a group, or injuring their health or physical integrity."[4]

Under this reading, one may be guilty of genocide for intending harm short of death. During the drafting, the issue was discussed principally in relation to actions by Japan in China. China said that Japan, occupying China in the 1930s, had encouraged opium use among the Chinese people. Such activity, it thought, should be included as genocide. "If those acts were not as spectacular," it suggested, "as Hitlerite killings in gas-chambers, their effect had been no less destructive. In drawing up a convention of universal scope it was appropriate to keep in mind not only the atrocities committed by Nazis and fascists, but also the horrible crimes of which the Japanese had been guilty in China."[5] Addicting a population to opium, in China's view, would destroy it.

"The record of the deliberations of the Ad Hoc Committee," wrote Stephen Gorove, "makes it clear that the case that was specifically in mind was the claim of the Chinese with reference to the dissemination by the Japanese of opium drugs to the Chinese population."[6] The term "mental" was added in sub-paragraph (b) of Article II, to include at least the spreading of opium as genocide. In ratifying the Genocide Convention, the United States filed an "understanding" regarding the term "mental harm," stating that it "means permanent impairment of mental faculties through drugs, torture or similar techniques."[7] The US understanding presupposes that one may destroy a group by weakening its members, physically or mentally, short of killing them.

A trial chamber of the Yugoslavia tribunal said that acts of physical abuse may reflect an intent to destroy the group through the physical or mental harm inflicted on members of the group.[8] The trial chamber was reviewing the first indictment of Karadzic and Mladic, which charged genocide for killing and other atrocities

2   Gil Gil, A. (1999), *Derecho Penal Internacional: Especial Consideración del Delito de Genocidio*, pp. 210-211, Editorial Tecnos, Madrid.

3   UN GAOR, 3rd sess., Part 1, *Summary Records of Meetings 21 September - 10 December 1948*, pp. 59-60, UN Doc. A/C.6/SR.69 (1948) (Mr. Li, China).

4   UN ECOSOCOR, 2nd sess., *Draft Convention on the Crime of Genocide*, p. 25 (Report of Secretary-General, 26 June 1947), UN Doc. E/447 (1947).

5   UN GAOR, 3rd sess., Part 1, *Summary Records of Meetings 21 September - 10 December 1948*, p. 175, UN Doc. A/C.6/SR.81 (Mr. Li, China).

6   Gorove, S. (1951), 'The Problem of "Mental Harm" in the Genocide Convention,' *Washington University Law Quarterly*, p. 174, p. 185.

7   *Multilateral Treaties Deposited with the Secretary-General: Status as at 31 December 2003*, p. 126, UN Doc. ST/LEG/SER.E/22 (2003).

8   Prosecutor v. Karadzic & Mladic, Cases No. IT-95-5-R61, IT-95-18-R61, Review of Indictment Pursuant to Rule 61, 11 July 1996, para. 94.

committed in detention camps under their control. The indictment charged as follows:

> 17. Radovan Karadzic and Ratko Mladic, from April 1992, in the territory of the Republic of Bosnia and Herzegovina, by their acts and omissions, committed genocide.
> 18. Bosnian Muslim and Bosnian Croat civilians were persecuted on national, political and religious grounds through the Republic of Bosnia and Herzegovina. Thousands of them were interned in detention facilities where they were subjected to widespread acts of physical and psychological abuse and to inhumane conditions. Detention facility personnel who ran and operated the Omarska, Keraterm and Luka detention facilities, among others, ... intended to destroy Bosnian Muslim and Bosnian Croat people as national, ethnic, or religious groups and killed, seriously injured and deliberately inflicted upon them conditions intended to bring about their physical destruction.[9]

This indictment thus alleges, along with killings, the infliction of injuries. It states that by inflicting injuries, the accused manifested an intent to destroy the two groups. The physical destruction of a group does not necessarily require the deaths of its members. As was understood by the drafters, the infliction of harm that renders group members unable to function effectively also destroys the group.

Social Identification of a Group

Another potential means of destroying a group short of killing its members is the elimination of the group's ability to function on the basis of its customs and traditions. As we saw in Chapter 4, the Israeli statute under which Adolf Eichmann was prosecuted included as an act of genocide "destroying or desecrating Jewish religious or cultural assets or values."[10] The inclusion of that category as acts that might be committed with intent to destroy suggests that for the Israeli legislator a group could be destroyed by the eradication of its religious or cultural life.

Unlike the Israeli Statute, the Genocide Convention omits desecration of religious or cultural assets in the listing of acts that constitute genocide. As related in Chapter 2, early drafts included a clause on destruction of culturally important objects. The final text of Article II did not.

The destruction of religious or cultural objectives has, however, figured in genocide prosecutions. The trial chamber of the Yugoslavia tribunal reviewing the Karadzic-Mladic indictment suggested that the prosecution broaden the genocide indictment to include other acts aimed at forcing departure. It said:

> the specific nature of some of the means used to achieve the objective of "ethnic cleansing" tends to underscore that the perpetration of the acts is designed to reach the very foundations

---

9   Prosecutor v. Karadzic & Mladic, Cases No. IT-95-5, IT-95-18, Indictment, 24 July 1995, paras. 17-18.

10 Nazi and Nazi Collaborators (Punishment) Law, *Laws of the State of Israel* 4, p. 154 (1950).

of the group or what is considered as such. The systematic rape of women, to which material submitted to the Trial Chamber attests, is in some cases intended to transmit a new ethnic identity to the child. In other cases, humiliation and terror serve to dismember the group. The destruction of mosques or Catholic churches is designed to annihilate the centuries-long presence of the group or groups; the destruction of the libraries is intended to annihilate a culture which was enriched through the participation of the various national components of the population.[11]

Here, in addition to considering acts causing physical or mental harm, the trial chamber included efforts to eradicate a group's culture as indicative of an intent to destroy the group.

The trial chamber that convicted Krstic also alluded to the destruction of cultural objects:

where there is physical or biological destruction there are often simultaneous attacks on the cultural and religious property and symbols of the targeted group as well, attacks which may legitimately be considered as evidence of an intent to physically destroy the group. In this case, the Trial Chamber will thus take into account as evidence of intent to destroy the group the deliberate destruction of mosques and houses belonging to members of the group.[12]

UN-appointed experts made a similar analysis in regard to religious and ethnic groups in Cambodia, using acts against a group's way of interacting as evidence of an intent to destroy. Thus, regarding a possible genocide charge against Khmer Rouge figures for acts against the Buddhist monkhood of Cambodia, the experts wrote:

[I]n the case of the Buddhist monkhood, their intent [that of Khmer Rouge leaders] is evidenced by the Khmer Rouge's intensely hostile statements towards religion, and the monkhood in particular; the Khmer Rouge's politics to eradicate the physical and ritualistic aspects of the Buddhist religion; the disrobing of monks and abolition of the monkhood; the number of victims; and the executions of Buddhist leaders and recalcitrant monks.

As for ethnic minorities of Cambodia, the experts similarly found acts against maintenance of cultural traditions to evidence genocide:

[I]n addition to the number of victims, the intent to destroy the Cham and other ethnic minorities appears evidenced by such Khmer Rouge actions as their announced policy of homogenization, the total prohibition of these groups' distinctive cultural traits, their dispersal among the general population and the execution of their leadership.[13]

---

11 Prosecutor v. Karadzic & Mladic, Cases No. IT-95-5-R61, IT-95-18-R61, Review of Indictment Pursuant to Rule 61, 11 July 1996, para. 94.

12 Prosecutor v. Krstic, Case No. IT-98-33-T, Judgment, 2 August 2001, para. 580.

13 Identical letters dated 15 March 1999 from the Secretary-General to the President of the General Assembly and the President of the Security Council, UN Doc. A/53/850, S/1999/231, 16 March 1999, Annex: Report of the Group of Experts for Cambodia established pursuant to General Assembly resolution 52/135, p. 20.

Under Article II, destruction of culture is not an act of genocide. However, if acts listed in the sub-paragraphs of Article II are committed, the destruction of cultural objectives may provide evidence that such acts were done with intent to destroy the group.

Chapter 16

Instant Destruction

It is often said that, for genocide, additional acts must be envisioned against group members, beyond the act committed in violation of one of the sub-paragraphs of Article II. Or that the actor must know that others are similarly acting against group members in ways that violate one of the sub-paragraphs. On the other hand, one finds reference to destruction of a group by virtue of an act committed against group members on account of their membership in the group. A group is said to be destroyed by virtue of an act against one or more members.

If an actor selects a victim and carries out an act of violence against that victim because of the victim's membership in a group, one might say that the actor intends to destroy the group. Harming victims based on their group membership, however, constitutes persecution, a crime against humanity, so perhaps some additional element is needed for genocide liability.

Distinguishing the two states of mind has, however, proved problematic. The actor need only intend to destroy the group "in part," a phrase that does not expressly require that the part be a substantial part. Moreover, it may not be possible meaningfully to draw a line between killing because of a victim's group membership and killing with intent to destroy the group. Several courts have found an intent to destroy based on acts against immediate victims and have not seemed to require proof of further planned acts.

Intent to Destroy via Acts against Group Members

The Akayesu trial chamber used acts constituting "serious bodily or mental harm" as a base for a genocide conviction. It found genocidal intent from these same acts. The acts involved rape of Tutsi women, carried out in public places by Hutu militia as a humiliation technique. Rape of this type was carried out, the chamber found, against large numbers of Tutsi women. The chamber said that such rapes were part of a plan of physical destruction of Tutsis as a group and thus manifested an "intent to destroy." The chamber said:

> These rapes resulted in physical and psychological destruction of Tutsi women, their families and their communities. Sexual violence was an integral part of the process of destruction, specifically targeting Tutsi women and specifically contributing to their destruction and to the destruction of the Tutsi group as a whole.[1]

---

1   Prosecutor v. Akayesu, Case No. IT-96-4-T, Judgment, 2 September 1998, para. 731.

The trial chamber thought that an act directed against immediate victims could by itself "destroy" the group. Thus, the group, or part of it, is "destroyed" by the act of the killing of one member. The Akayesu trial chamber stated this view explicitly:

> Thus, the victim is chosen not because of his individual identity, but rather on account of his membership of a national, ethnical, racial or religious group. The victim of the act is therefore a member of a group, chosen as such, which, hence, means that the victim of the crime of genocide is the group itself and not only the individual.[2]

Hence, if a victim is selected because of group membership, and one of the sub-paragraph acts is committed against that victim, the group is thereby destroyed. In the context of rape as committed in Rwanda, it has been suggested that those who promoted the widespread rape of Tutsi women did so with the understanding that it would tear Tutsi society apart. As known to the Hutus, Tutsi men were likely to reject Tutsi women who had been raped. Tutsi girls would be ineligible for marriage. Tutsi married women might be divorced. Many of the rape victims would contract AIDS. Raping Tutsi women in large numbers would make it difficult for Tutsis to continue their social existence.[3]

In the Eichmann case, the District Court of Jerusalem explained its view that acts directed against group members destroy the group:

> But it is not only in respect of *intention* that a distinction lies between the crime of genocide and the individual crimes of homicide perpetrated during the commission of that crime. The criminal act itself (*actus reus*) of genocide also differs *in its nature* from the combination of all the individual acts of murder and the other crimes committed during its execution. The people, in whole or in part, is the victim of the extermination which befalls it in consequence of the extermination of its sons and daughters.[4]

Whereas in homicide the victim is the person killed, in genocide the victim is dual: both the person killed and the group. The "consequence" of the killing of individuals is the destruction of the group. The destruction of the group is not a possible future event, but a present reality.

Both the Akayesu trial chamber and the District Court of Jerusalem read "destroy" in the context of an intent to destroy the group to mean that harming the immediate victims constitutes destruction of the group, and therefore that the act directed against the immediate victims itself constitutes destruction of the group.

In the Rwanda tribunal, the trial chamber that had heard the Akayesu case later heard the Rutaganda case and took the same approach by saying that victimization

---

2   Ibid., paras. 520-521.

3   Peter Landesman, 'A woman's work,' *New York Times Sunday Magazine*, 15 September 2002, p. 82.

4   Attorney-General of the Government of Israel v. Eichmann, District Court of Jerusalem, Judgment, 12 December 1961, *International Law Reports* 36, p. 233 (1962).

of Tutsi because they were Tutsi manifested an intent to destroy the Tutsi as a group.
The trial chamber said:

> The victims were systematically selected because they belonged to the Tutsi group and for the
> very fact that they belonged to the said group. As a result, the Chamber is satisfied beyond any
> reasonable doubt that, at the time of commission of all the above-mentioned acts which in its
> opinion are proven, the Accused had indeed the intent to destroy the Tutsi group as such.[5]

The Rutaganda trial chamber did note, to be sure, that others all over Rwanda were
similarly attacking Tutsi because they were Tutsi. Rutaganda was not acting alone. It
referred to this as "a general context within which acts aimed at destroying the Tutsi
group were perpetrated."[6] It did not say that this context was essential to establishing
the intent of Rutaganda, which, as indicated, the chamber appeared to base on his
own attacks on Tutsi for the fact of their being Tutsi.

Support for that view of "destruction" was expressed during the drafting of
the Genocide Convention. France proposed an amendment, which it subsequently
withdrew, to define genocide as an attack against an individual as a member of a
group. France considered: "The group was an abstract concept; it was an aggregate of
individuals; it had no independent life of its own; it was harmed when the individuals
composing it were harmed."[7] France was expressing the same view as the District
Court of Jerusalem and the Akayesu trial chamber, namely that the destruction, or
harm, to the group occurs by virtue of the harm to the individual victims, as a result
of the harm to the individual victims.

The "destruction" of the group, under this view, is brought about by the harm
inflicted on certain of its members. The "destruction" of the group is not something
that necessarily is contemplated as occurring at a later time as a result of further acts
of violence against group members.

Distinction Between Persecution and Genocide

A potential difficulty with the approach of the Rwanda tribunal and the District Court
of Jerusalem is that the distinction between genocide and persecution may be blurred.
The crime of persecution, which, as indicated in Chapter 2, is a species of crime
against humanity, involves acts against individuals because of their membership in a
group, though not necessarily the same limited types of group enumerated in Article
II.

---

5   Prosecutor v. Rutaganda, Case No. ICTR 96-3-T, Judgment, 6 December 1999, para.
399.

6   Ibid., para. 400.

7   UN GAOR, 3rd sess., Part 1, *Summary Records of Meetings 21 September - 10 December
1948*, p. 91, UN Doc. A/C.6/SR.73 (Mr. Chaumont, France).

Stefan Glaser and William Schabas have written that a racially motivated murder does not necessarily reflect an intent to destroy the group.[8] The Krstic trial chamber distinguished the mental element in genocide from the mental element in persecution, saying that targeting an individual because of group membership constitutes the mental state for persecution, but not for genocide:

> The Convention thus seeks to protect the right to life of human groups, as such. This characteristic makes genocide an exceptionally grave crime and distinguishes it from other serious crimes, in particular persecution, where the perpetrator selects his victims because of their membership in a specific community but does not necessarily seek to destroy the community as such.[9]

The Krstic trial chamber apparently did not view acts against a victim because of the victim's group membership as constituting, in and of itself, destruction of the group.

Whether the Eichmann court's concept of intent to destroy the group is too metaphysical to apply in court cases is a question that can fairly be raised. On the other hand, it is difficult to pinpoint what, additionally, must be in the mind of an actor who victimizes a group member because of his group membership, to constitute an intent to destroy the group. Rape was used, not only in Rwanda, but in Bosnia, with an anti-group intent. Raping was arguably aimed at destroying the social fabric of the group.

In Rwanda, as the trial chamber pointed out, rape of Tutsi women in the manner described was not an isolated incident but was being carried out on a significant scale at many locations. Thus, the trial chamber was not presented with an isolated case of rape carried out in public as a humiliation technique. Nonetheless, even in such a situation, one might equally argue that such rape manifests an intent to destroy the group. It might be harder to say that the group was actually destroyed, but actual destruction is not required for genocide. A mere intent to destroy suffices.

If an actor rapes or kills members of a group on account of their group membership, it is plausible to conclude that the actor intends to destroy the group. The actor's animus is not directed against the immediate victim as such, but against the immediate victim because of the latter's membership in the group. Thus, the animus is directed against the group. In some cases, a court may have evidence of the actor's attitude to the group, such as the actor's own explanation that the killing was prompted by a desire to harm the group, or the actor's association with and acceptance of the views of an organization that seeks to eliminate the group. In other cases, as in the Rutaganda case, the court may not find such additional evidence. It is confronted only with the fact of killing group members on account of their membership. While

---

8   Glaser, S. (1970), *Droit international pénal conventionnel*, p. 109, Bruylant, Brussels. Schabas, W.A. (2000), *Genocide in International Law: The Crime of Crimes*, p. 234, Cambridge University Press, Cambridge.

9   Prosecutor v. Krstic, Case No. IT-98-33-T, Judgment, 2 August 2001, para. 553.

a distinction between the mental intent involved in persecution and that involved in genocide has often been stated, it is difficult to apply in practice.

Chapter 17

Intent Without Intent

Equally as problematic as the term "destroy" in Article II is the term "intent." A common meaning of "intend" is to try to bring about a particular end. In the criminal law, the term "intent" is encumbered by considerable baggage. It is used in more than one meaning. It characterizes more than one state of mind in the law of homicide. As used in Article II of the Genocide Convention, "intent" is open to a number of possible readings.

Otto Triffterer finds the default provision on culpability in the Statute of the International Criminal Court, quoted in Chapter 13, to apply to the Article II intent to destroy.[1] That provision, it will be recalled, defines intent as encompassing both an aim to achieve a result, and knowledge that a result will follow. However, the provision is limited to specific types of elements. It applies to conduct, in which case intent means an aim to achieve a particular result, and it applies to consequences, in which case intent means knowledge of the result. The element of a further intent to destroy a group is neither "conduct" nor a "consequence." Hence, the default provision gives no guidance as to the meaning of "intent to destroy."[2]

An intent to destroy would clearly be present if an actor actively desires the destruction of a group. But an accused may well deny harboring such an intent. The prosecutor may need to prove the intent on the basis of actions and prior words of the accused that leave it unclear whether the actor actively desired the destruction of the group.

A prosecutor might be able to demonstrate that an actor engaged in conduct calculated to bring harm to substantial numbers of members of a group. One scenario would be that of an actor who engages in conduct that may bring about the destruction of the group, and who realized that destruction may follow but is indifferent to that result. Another would be that of an actor who engages in conduct that may bring about the destruction of the group and who does not realize that destruction may follow but, under the circumstances, should so realize.

One can imagine situations of potential environmental harm that could constitute genocide if the culpability standard requires less than a purpose to bring about a result. Allowing a nuclear generator to operate in the face of knowledge that it is

---

1   Triffterer, O. (2001), 'Genocide, Its Particular Intent to Destroy in Whole or in Part the Group as Such,' *Leiden Journal of International Law* 14, p. 399, p. 406.

2   Garraway, C. (2001), 'Elements of the Specific Forms of Genocide,' in R. Lee (ed.), *The International Criminal Court: Elements of Crimes and Rules of Procedure and Evidence*, p. 50, Transnational, Ardsley NY.

emitting radioactive material to the surrounding area might be taken as evidence of an intent to destroy a group.

Analysts have struggled with the proper construction of "intent to destroy." Some have found it to encompass purpose only. Roger Clark, writing before Article II had been subjected to interpretation in many cases, said that the prosecution "would have to prove purpose/intent. Nothing else will do. All cases short of intent may be genocide in ordinary usage but fall short of criminal genocide as understood in the Convention." However, Clark considered "purpose" as too confining a requirement and suggested that "the Genocide Convention should be expanded to include negligent as well as reckless everyday genocide within its ambit."[3]

Alexander Greenawalt, writing more recently, said that Article II has generally been read to require a purpose to destroy but, like Clark, disputes the propriety of such a limitation. Agreeing with Clark that purpose is too confining a standard, Greenawalt suggested that the term "intent" in Article II can fairly be construed to include knowledge of the consequences of one's acts.[4]

Some analysts have suggested that "intent to destroy" is present in still broader situations. Leo Kuper wrote that it is present "if the foreseeable consequences of an act are, or seem likely to be, the destruction of a group."[5] Ben Whitaker, studying genocide for the UN Commission on Human Rights, reported a view that an intent to destroy a group may be inferred from "actions or omissions of such a degree of criminal negligence or recklessness that the defendant must reasonably be assumed to have been aware of the consequences of his conduct."[6]

Ad Hoc Tribunals

In court practice, Article II has been read to encompass an intent broader than only a purpose to bring about a result. The Akayesu trial chamber referred to Continental law, where it found a concept of "special intent": "Special intent is a well-known criminal law concept in the Roman-continental legal systems. It is required as a

3   Clark, R. (1981), 'Does the Genocide Convention Go Far Enough? Some Thoughts on the Nature of Criminal Genocide in the Context of Indonesia's Invasion of East Timor,' *Ohio Northern University Law Review* 8, p. 321, pp. 327-328.

4   Greenawalt, A.K.A. (1999), 'Rethinking Genocidal Intent: The Case for a Knowledge-Based Interpretation,' *Columbia Law Review* 99, p. 2259, p. 2288.

5   Kuper, L. (1985), *The Prevention of Genocide*, p. 12, Yale University Press, New Haven.

6   *Revised and updated report on the question of the prevention and punishment of the crime of genocide prepared by Mr. B. Whitaker*, 2 July 1985, Commission on Human Rights, UN Doc. E/CN.4/Sub.2/1985/6, p. 19.

constituent element of certain offences and demands that the perpetrator have the clear intent to cause the offence charged."[7]

Explaining the "special intent" required by Article II, however, the Akayesu trial chamber gave the phrase a wider meaning:

> With regard to the crime of genocide, the offender is culpable only when he has committed one of the offences charged under Article 2(2) of the Statute [of that tribunal] with the clear intent to destroy, in whole or in part, a particular group. The offender is culpable because he knew or should have known that the act committed would destroy, in whole or in part, a group. In concrete terms, for any of the acts charged under Article 2(2) of the Statute to be a constitutive element of genocide, the act must have been committed against one or several individuals, because such individual or individuals were members of a specific group, and specifically because they belonged to this group. Thus, the victim is chosen not because of his individual identity, but rather on account of his membership of a national, ethnical, racial or religious group. The victim of the act is therefore a member of a group, chosen as such, which, hence, means that the victim of the crime of genocide is the group itself and not only the individual.[8]

With respect to intent to destroy the group, the Akayesu trial chamber said that this "special intent" is satisfied if the actor knew or should have known that the act would destroy the group. Thus, the trial chamber read "intent" to include situations in which the actor knew what result would ensue, even absent a desire that it ensue. The trial chamber also includes situations in which the actor should have known, even though the actor did not know.

The Akayesu trial chamber's reasoning was misinterpreted by Greenawalt, who took the relevant paragraphs of the Akayesu judgment to mean that the actor "must desire the destruction of the group as a group." Greenawalt characterized the position he erroneously drew from the Akayesu judgment as reflecting "the prevalent understanding of genocide."[9] He then proposed a standard quite close to the one Akayesu actually reflects as the proper reading of Article II, namely that "intent to destroy" is satisfied by knowledge that the effect of the actor's conduct is the destruction of the group in whole or in part.[10]

In Jelisic, a genocide case before a trial chamber of the Yugoslavia tribunal, the prosecutor argued that the "intent to destroy" is satisfied if the accused "knows that his acts will inevitably, or even only probably, result in the destruction of the group," even if the accused did not "seek the destruction."[11] The trial chamber acquitted

---

7   Prosecutor v. Akayesu, Case No. ICTR-96-4-T, Judgment, 2 September 1998, para. 518.

8   Ibid., paras. 520-521.

9   Greenawalt (1999), p. 2265.

10   Ibid., p. 2288.

11   Prosecutor v. Jelisic, Case No. IT-95-10-T, Judgment, 14 December 1999, para. 85. Quotations here and subsequently from the Jelisic Judgment are from the tribunal's English version, rather than its French version, which is authoritative, but unavailable.

Jelisic of genocide, finding a lack of intent to destroy the group in his acts against individual victims. Jelisic had been in charge of a Bosnian Serb prison in which Bosnian Muslims were incarcerated. The trial chamber found that Jelisic killed a number of the Bosnian Muslim inmates. Analyzing why he killed them, however, the trial chamber found that he killed victims "randomly,"[12] and as a result of his "disturbed personality."[13] On the basis of that evidence, the trial chamber found that Jelisic killed out of personal motivations, rather than out of an intent to destroy Bosnian Muslims as a group. The trial chamber stated, "the acts of Goran Jelisic are not the physical expression of an affirmed resolve to destroy in whole or in part a group as such."[14] It said, "although he obviously singled out Muslims, he killed arbitrarily rather than with the clear intention to destroy a group."[15]

Upon the prosecutor's appeal, the appeals chamber ruled that the trial chamber had inappropriately acquitted Jelisic. Citing evidence that he desired to kill Bosnian Muslims on the basis of their identity as such, the appeals chamber found that when Jelisic killed, he intended to destroy the Bosnian Muslims, notwithstanding his personality or the random character of the killings.[16]

In analyzing the term "intent," the Jelisic trial chamber mis-characterized the reasoning of the Akayesu trial chamber:

> The *Akayesu* Trial Chamber found that an accused could not be found guilty of genocide if he himself did not share the goal of destroying in part or in whole a group even if he knew that he was contributing to or through his acts might be contributing to the partial or total destruction of a group. It declared that such an individual must be convicted of complicity in genocide.[17]

However, as indicated, the Akayesu trial chamber said that the intent required for liability, even as a principal, can be satisfied by less than purpose. The Akayesu trial chamber specifically found that "intent" is satisfied if the accused knew or should have known that the acts against specific victims would destroy the group.[18] The Jelisic trial chamber, in acquitting Jelisic, did not make clear what level of intent is required. Presumably, it had in mind situations in which the facts make it plain that a given harm will result, and the actor should have so understood, even if the actor did not actually so understand. This would involve a culpability level lower than "knowledge," akin to "recklessness."

The Krstic trial chamber considered what Krstic must have known, when it inquired whether he had an intent to destroy the Bosnian Muslim group at Srebrenica:

---

12 Ibid., para. 106.

13 Ibid., para. 105.

14 Ibid., para. 107.

15 Ibid., para. 108.

16 Prosecutor v. Jelisic, Case No. IT-95-10-A, Judgment, 5 July 2001, para. 72.

17 Prosecutor v. Jelisic, Case No. IT-95-10-T, Judgment, 14 December 1999, para. 86, *citing* Prosecutor v. Akayesu, Case No. ICTR-96-4-T, Judgment, 2 September 1998, para. 485.

18 Prosecutor v. Akayesu, Case No. ICTR-96-4-T, Judgment, 2 September 1998, para. 520.

The Bosnian Serb forces could not have failed to know, by the time they decided to kill all the men, that this selective destruction of the group would have a lasting impact upon the entire group. ... Furthermore, the Bosnian Serb forces had to be aware of the catastrophic impact that the disappearance of two or three generations of men would have on the survival of a traditionally patriarchal society.[19]

Thus, it sufficed that the Bosnian Serb forces, and, by implication, Krstic, must have known that the killing would destroy the group. The trial chamber did not require the prosecution to prove that Krstic desired to destroy. The appeals chamber in Krstic's case would have more to say, as will be seen in chapter 19.

Domestic Law Analogies

Domestic law provides examples of offenses defined in a format similar to that of the Genocide Convention, namely by the commission of an act with the intent to commit some other act. But such statutes do not provide a ready answer to the appropriate mental element applicable to the "further intent." In German and Austrian law, one finds an offense of fraud, defined to include an intent to deceive another, but with the additional element of a further intent of securing illegal profit. As Otto Triffterer points out, the content of this further intent, sometimes called *dolus specialis*, may vary, depending on what the particular legislature deems appropriate.[20]

In US law, one finds statutes on assault accompanied by an intent to commit some additional offense—assault with intent to rape, assault with intent to kill, assault with intent to rob. The use of the term intent in this context requires a conscious design: a person assaults, seeking to rape, to kill, or to rob.[21] These statutes, say the courts, require, in addition to the intent that applies to the assault, an "additional deliberate and conscious purpose or design of accomplishing a very specific and more remote result."[22] The further intent is said to be a "special intent."

These assault statutes do not present a perfect analogy to Article II. In the assault statutes, the further intent relates to an additional act to be performed by the actor, in addition to the basic act. In Article II, the further intent relates to a result that might flow from the basic act. As a result, one cannot necessarily apply the intent level for the further act found in the assault statutes to the intent level for the intent to destroy in Article II.

As both Triffterer and William Schabas have argued, the vagaries of potential analogies to domestic law caution against over-reliance on them in determining the

---

19 Prosecutor v. Krstic, Case No. IT-98-33-T, Judgment, 2 August 2001, para. 595.

20 Triffterer (2001), pp. 403-404.

21 U.S. v. Short, USA, 4 U.S. Court of Military Appeals 437 (1954). Dressler, J. (2001), *Understanding Criminal Law*, pp. 136-137, Matthew Bender, New York.

22 'Developments in Maryland Law, 1986-87: III. Criminal Law,' *Maryland Law Review* 47, p. 793 (1988).

content of "intent to destroy" in Article II.[23] Moreover, where both the "act" element and the "intent" element are directed to the same individual, as with assault with intent to kill, there is greater reason for reading "intent" to mean "purpose" than when the "intent" element is directed to a different party. Genocide is an offense against the group in its primary aspect. The act against a specific victim is only, as the District Court of Jerusalem said, "part performance." The technique of requiring an act against immediate victims, with intent to destroy the group, was a device for correlating the two aspects and for providing evidence that the actor was willing to destroy the group.

The animus required for an "intent to destroy" is not further defined by the Genocide Convention. The term "intent" in most legal systems is used in penal law to encompass two distinct states of mind. The first is that in which the actor acts with a purpose to effect a given consequence. In some legal systems, this is called "direct intent," or "purpose." The second is that in which the actor understands that a particular consequence will follow and consciously allows that result to occur, albeit without desiring that result. In domestic legal systems, this is called a killing with "indirect intent," or a killing carried out with knowledge that death is likely to result. In these situations, the accused is guilty of murder.

The appeals chamber hearing Jelisic's case struggled with the question of whether to refer to the intent required by Article II as "specific intent." It said that it would use the term in its analysis of Article II, but that it did "not attribute to this term any meaning it might carry in a national jurisdiction."[24] Appropriately, the appeals chamber was unwilling to apply to Article II the restrictive notion of specific intent as found, in particular, in the US assault statutes.

Factual Circumstances Tending to Prove Intent

The issue can also be addressed from the standpoint of what proof may be required to show intent. If an actor uses racially pejorative language towards the victim, this may evidence state of mind with regard to the group. Or the actor might use pejorative language with regard to the group as a whole. Taken with other evidence of an intent to destroy a group, the use of such language might be probative on the issue of intent to destroy. The Preparatory Commission for the International Criminal Court, in its Elements of Offenses, repeated a proposition commonly found in domestic penal law, namely that "intent and knowledge can be inferred from relevant facts and circumstances."[25]

---

23 Triffterer (2001), p. 404. Schabas, W.A. (2001c), 'The *Jelisic* Case and the *Mens Rea* of the Crime of Genocide,' *Leiden Journal of International Law* 14, p. 125, p. 129.

24 Prosecutor v. Jelisic, Case No. IT-95-10-A, Decision, 5 July 2001, para. 45 note 81.

25 Preparatory Commission for the International Criminal Court, *Finalized draft text of the Elements of Crimes*, 2 November 2000, General Introduction, para. 3, UN Doc. PCNICC/2000/1/Add.2 (2000), confirmed by Assembly of States Parties to the Rome Statute of the International

Tribunals determining the anti-group intent required by Article II have followed this approach, employing both direct and indirect evidence. In some cases, they have found that the actor expressed the anti-group intent, as, for example, by exhorting others to kill members of the group. Such statements have been considered by the tribunal in the context in which they were made. Thus, the Akayesu trial chamber found genocidal intent on the basis, in part, of statements by Akayesu. The chamber said:

> it is possible to infer the genocidal intention that presided over the commission of a particular act, *inter alia*, from all acts or utterances of the accused, or from the general context in which other culpable acts were perpetrated systematically against the same group, regardless of whether such other acts were committed by the same perpetrator or even by other perpetrators.[26]

The "utterances" involved calls by Akayesu to others to kill Tutsi.

As regards "other culpable acts" that were "perpetrated systematically against the same group," the trial chamber's rationale was that if Akayesu was killing Tutsi at the same time as others were killing Tutsi, he must have been killing them with the intent to destroy them as a group. The chamber explained:

> the Chamber has already established that genocide was committed against the Tutsi group in Rwanda in 1994, throughout the period covering the events alleged in the Indictment. Owing to the very high number of atrocities committed against the Tutsi, their widespread nature not only in the commune of Taba, but also throughout Rwanda, and to the fact that the victims were systematically and deliberately selected because they belonged to the Tutsi group, with persons belonging to other groups being excluded, the Chamber is also able to infer, beyond reasonable doubt, the genocidal intent of the accused in the commission of the above-mentioned crimes.[27]

A trial chamber of the Yugoslavia tribunal referred to still another circumstance as an indication of genocidal intent, namely the political doctrine that gave rise to specific acts of violence. In confirming a genocide indictment against Radovan Karadzic and Ratko Mladic, the political and military leaders, respectively, of the Bosnian Serbs, the chamber said that such political doctrine may indicate genocidal intent even if the accused did not expressly state a genocidal intent:

> The intent which is peculiar to crime of genocide need not be clearly expressed...[T]he intent may be inferred from a certain number of facts such as the general political doctrine

---

Criminal Court, *Official Records*, 1st sess., 3-10 September 2002, p. 112, UN Doc. ICC-ASP/1/3 (2002).

26 Prosecutor v. Akayesu, Case No. ICTR-96-4-T, Judgment, 2 September 1998, para. 728.

27 Ibid., para. 730.

which gave rise to the acts possibly covered by the definition in Article 4, or the repetition of destructive and discriminatory acts.[28]

The trial chamber found that the "political doctrine" underlying the acts alleged against Karadzic and Mladic involved the use of violence to force non-Serbs out of a given territory in Bosnia.[29]

The appeals chamber in Jelisic's case also said that circumstances might prove the Article II intent, namely "the general context, the perpetration of other culpable acts systematically directed against the same group, the scale of atrocities committed, the systematic targeting of victims on account of their membership of a particular group, or the repetition of destructive and discriminatory acts."[30]

This approach of using factual circumstances to establish culpability is routinely used in domestic penal law. Criminal intent is frequently found on the basis of the circumstances in which the accused acted.[31] There are, to be sure, hazards in this approach. Even though others may have been acting to destroy a given group, the specific accused person may have been acting outside that context, pursuing wholly different objectives. The Jelisic trial chamber, as indicated, refused to find genocidal intent, even though Jelisic was acting in circumstances in which many were carrying out acts of violence against Bosnian Muslims in furtherance of the "political doctrine" to which the Karadzic-Mladic trial chamber referred.

Despite that fact, the trial chamber said that Jelisic's acts of violence against Bosnian Muslims were committed for reasons relating to Jelisic's psychological make-up, rather than in furtherance of the "political doctrine." The Jelisic trial chamber's approach shows that it was sensitive to the fact that because the accused is acting at a time when others are acting does not necessarily mean that a particular accused was acting out of a genocidal intent.

The Bagilishema trial chamber sounded a similar note of caution in using context to determine the intent of a particular person. It said that "the use of context to determine the intent of an accused must be counterbalanced with the actual conduct of the accused ... the Accused's intent should be determined, above all, from his words and deeds, and should be evident from patterns of purposeful action."[32] Nonetheless, when tribunals use factual circumstances to infer intent, the difference narrows between a desire to achieve a result, and knowledge that given consequences will ensue.

---

28 Prosecutor v. Karadzic & Mladic, Cases No. IT-95-5-R61, IT-95-18-R61, Review of Indictment Pursuant to Rule 61, 11 July 1996, para. 94.

29 Ibid., para. 94.

30 Prosecutor v. Jelisic, Case No. IT-95-10-A, Decision, 5 July 2001, para. 47.

31 LaFave, W.R. (2000), *Criminal Law*, p. 241, West Group, St. Paul.

32 Prosecutor v. Bagilishema, Case No. ICTR-95-1A-T, Judgment, 7 June 2001, para. 63.

The Proper Standard for "Intent"

The analogy to specific intent in British-derived legal systems, and to *dolus specialis* in Continental legal systems, is inviting. However, the Akayesu trial chamber is on strong ground in deviating from strict adherence to that standard. If an actor does violence to immediate victims, understanding that thereby harm is brought to the group, or even having reason to know that harm is thereby brought to the group, the elements of genocide would seem to be satisfied. The humanitarian purpose of the Genocide Convention, referenced by the ICJ in the *Reservations* case, supports such a reading.

The state of mind termed "wilful blindness" may also be included in the Article II formulation.[33] "Wilful blindness" refers to a situation in which an actor lacks actual knowledge but is aware of a high probability of the existence of a fact and fails to inquire into circumstances that would have made him aware of the existence of the fact.[34] Although the issue has not been directly addressed in the genocide cases, the frequent references to situations in which an actor should have known of consequences suggest that the tribunals find it a fair reading of Article II to include persons who do not have actual knowledge of the consequences, but who should, on the basis of facts they knew, have understood the consequences.

---

33 Schabas, W.A. (2000), *Genocide in International Law: The Crime of Crimes*, pp. 212-213, Cambridge University Press, Cambridge.

34 Dressler (2001), p. 126.

Chapter 18

The Motives for Genocide

Article II uses the phrase "as such" in identifying the target group. The meaning of this phrase in this context is not immediately apparent. The phrase was included as a result of a drafting process that began with other language. The draft by the Economic and Social Council's *ad hoc* committee, as we saw in Chapter 2, would have required an intent to destroy one of the protected groups "on grounds of the national or racial origin, religious belief" of its members.[1]

That formulation was open to the reading that the act must be motivated by animosity towards the group, based on the group's national identity, its race, or its religion. In penal law, however, motive is typically not required. Motive may be useful for a prosecutor to demonstrate, in order to convince the trier of fact that the accused committed the act charged. However, as a matter of the definition of crime, motive is not an element separate from intent that must be proved.

Genesis of the "As Such" Formula

The phrase "as such" was inserted in Article II by the Sixth Committee.[2] The Sixth Committee adopted the phrase on a proposal by Venezuela.[3] Venezuela suggested this formulation as an alternative to either the inclusion, or non-inclusion, of a list of motives. It explained that this language:

> omitted the enumeration appearing in article II of the *Ad Hoc* Committee's draft, but re-introduced the motives for the crime without, however, doing so in a limitative form which admitted no motives other than those which were listed. The aim of the amendment was to give wider powers of discretion to the judges who would be called upon to deal with cases of genocide. The General Assembly had manifested its intention to suppress genocide as fully as possible. The adoption of the Venezuelan amendment would enable the judges to take into account other motives than those listed in the *Ad Hoc* Committee's draft.[4]

---

1 UN ECOSOCOR, 3rd sess., *Report of the Ad Hoc Committee on Genocide 5 April to 10 May 1948*, Supp. (No. 6), p. 5, UN Doc. E/794 (1948).

2 Schabas, W.A. (2000), *Genocide in International Law: The Crime of Crimes*, pp. 245-246, Cambridge University Press, Cambridge.

3 UN GAOR, 3rd sess., Part 1, *Summary Records of Meetings 21 September - 10 December 1948*, p. 133, UN Doc. A/C.6/SR.77 (1948).

4 Ibid., p. 131 (Mr. Pérez Perozo, Venezuela).

Venezuela argued that a listing of motives would be "dangerous, as such a restrictive enumeration would be a powerful weapon in the hands of the guilty parties and would help them to avoid being charged with genocide."[5] The United Kingdom supported Venezuela's approach, making the same argument that a list of motives would allow the guilty to exonerate themselves by denying that they had been impelled by motives contained in the proposed list.[6]

Venezuela said, at the same time, that the "as such" formula "should meet the views of those who wished to retain a statement of motives; indeed, the motives were implicitly included in the words 'as such'."[7] That statement has led William Schabas to argue that a motive requirement in fact is present in Article II.[8] But delegates seemed satisfied that the "as such" formula did not require the prosecution to prove a motive. Brazil supported the Venezuelan amendment, "because it did not include the motives for the crime, but stressed the element of intention."[9] Haiti said that the amendment embodied all possible motives, which meant there was no need to prove any particular motive.[10]

In prosecutions for genocide, tribunals have not required proof of a motive as an element. The ILC, in its work on a Draft Code of Crimes against the Peace and Security of Mankind, sought to define genocide using the Convention's definition. In a commentary on its genocide provision, the Commission stated:

> The prohibited act must be committed against an individual because of his membership in a particular group and as an incremental step in the overall objective of destroying the group. It is the membership of the individual in a particular group rather than the identity of the individual that is the decisive criterion in determining the immediate victims of the crime of genocide. The group itself is the ultimate target or intended victim of this type of massive criminal conduct.[11]

---

5   UN GAOR, 3rd sess., Part 1, *Summary Records of Meetings 21 September - 10 December 1948*, at 124, UN Doc. A/C.6/SR.76 (Mr. Pérez Perozo, Venezuela).

6   UN GAOR, 3rd sess., Part 1, *Summary Records of Meetings 21 September - 10 December 1948*, p. 118, UN Doc. A/C.6/SR.75 (Mr. Fitzmaurice, UK).

7   UN GAOR, 3rd sess., Part 1, *Summary Records of Meetings 21 September - 10 December 1948*, at 124-125, UN Doc. A/C.6/SR.76 (Mr. Pérez Perozo, Venezuela).

8   Schabas, W.A. (2001b), 'The Crime of Genocide in the Jurisprudence of the International Criminal Tribunals for the Former Yugoslavia and Rwanda,' in H. Fischer, C. Kress and S. Luder (eds), *International and National Prosecution of Crimes Under International Law*, p. 447, pp. 457-458, Berlin Verlag, Berlin.

9   UN GAOR, 3rd sess., Part 1, *Summary Records of Meetings 21 September - 10 December 1948*, p. 132, UN Doc. A/C.6/SR.77 (Mr. Amado, Brazil).

10 Ibid., p. 137 (Mr. Demesmin, Haiti).

11 Draft Code of Crimes against the Peace and Security of Mankind (commentary), *Report of the International Law Commission on the work of its forty-eighth session 6 May - 26 July 1996*, UN GAOR, 51st sess., Supp. (No. 10), p. 88, UN Doc. A/51/10 (1996).

The Commission's reference to "massive criminal conduct" is evidently to the "massive" character of the intent, rather than to the sub-paragraph act, which need not be against large numbers of persons.

In the Yugoslavia tribunal, the Jelisic trial chamber did refer to hatred towards the group as if it must be proved as an element:

> By killing an individual member of the targeted group, the perpetrator does not thereby only manifest his hatred of the group to which his victim belongs but also knowingly commits this act as part of a wider-ranging intention to destroy the national, ethnical, racial or religious group of which the victim is a member.[12]

The appeals chamber in the Jelisic case specifically disagreed with the trial chamber on the issue of hatred. Referring to the need to distinguish the intent required by Article II from motive, it stated:

> The personal motive of the perpetrator of the crime of genocide may be, for example, to obtain personal economic benefits, or political advantage or some form of power. The existence of a personal motive does not preclude the perpetrator from also having the specific intent to commit genocide.[13]

A genocide defendant may well act out of hatred for the target group, but hatred need not be proved by the prosecution. An actor may participate in violence against members of a group protected under Article II, with intent to destroy that group, not out of hatred for the group, but because the actor hopes thereby to please certain authorities, or even to avoid negative consequences to himself. Many of those who participated in mass killings in Rwanda characterized their motivation as lying in such practical concerns.

Persons who take part in committing genocide may do so to enhance their political standing, or to avoid being fired from their job. They may act out of concern that if they do not help others commit atrocities, they may be suspected of disloyalty, or of sympathizing with the victim group. These motives do not negate the intent required by Article II.

Motive, writes Alicia Gil Gil, is irrelevant in a genocide prosecution. It matters not, she says, that the aim to destroy the group was based on motives political, economic, or xenophobic, or even out of revenge.[14] It suffices that the actor committed one of the enumerated acts with the intent to destroy the group "as such" in whole or in part. Joe Verhoeven, calling the motives "irrelevant," writes, "It is enough that the will to

---

12 Prosecutor v. Jelisic, Case No. IT-95-10-T, Judgment, 14 December 1999, para. 79.

13 Prosecutor v. Jelisic, Case No. IT-95-10-A, Decision, 5 July 2001, para. 49.

14 Gil Gil, A. (1999), *Derecho Penal Internacional: Especial Consideración del Delito de Genocidio*, p. 178, Editorial Tecnos, Madrid.

destroy a group is present; the precise reasons, for example ideological or economic, that may explain it have no importance in establishing the crime of genocide."[15]

The absence of a motive requirement may seem at odds with the origins of the concept of genocide. Matthew Lippman, focusing on the origins, has written that "the requisite intent to commit genocide must be accompanied by proof of motive."[16] Henri Donnedieu de Vabres found it inherent in the idea of genocide that one acts by reason of the nationality or other characteristic of the victims, and thus that, contrary to the general approach in penal law, a motive is encompassed within the definition of the offense.[17] As authority for this position, Donnedieu de Vabres relied on Raphael Lemkin, not on the text of Article II. Those who argue that Article II implies a motive requirement must read it into the text, relying on the phrase "as such."

The Third Reich attacked population groups on the basis of a philosophy that denigrated them. One group was superior to others. Hitler's theory of Aryan superiority provided a rationale for killing other groups. "The Aryan," wrote Adolf Hitler in his 1925 book *Mein Kampf*, is "greatest ... in the extent of his willingness to put all his abilities in the service of the community. In him the instinct of self-preservation has reached the noblest form, since he willingly subordinates his own ego to the life of the community and, if the hour demands, even sacrifices it."[18] To this superior race, Hitler contrasted the Jews. "The mightiest counterpart to the Aryan is represented by the Jew," he wrote. They lacked the sense of sacrifice found in Aryans: "If the Jews were alone in this world, they would stifle in filth and offal."[19]

Even though a developed theory of racial superiority underlay the atrocities that gave rise to the Genocide Convention, the text requires no proof of motive. The phrase "as such" meant that the intent must be directed against the group, but without a requirement of a finding of a particular motive.[20]

---

15 Verhoeven, J. (1991), 'Le crime de génocide: originalité et ambiguïté,' *Revue belge de droit international* 24, no. 1, p. 5, p. 19.

16 Lippman, M. (1985), 'The Drafting of the 1948 Convention on the Prevention and Punishment of the Crime of Genocide,' *Boston University International Law Journal* 3, p. 1, p. 41 (1985).

17 Donnedieu de Vabres, H. (1950), 'De la Piraterie au Génocide ... les Nouvelles Modalités de la Répression Universelle,' in *Le Droit Privé Français au Milieu du XXe Siècle: Études offertes à Georges Ripert*, vol. 1, p. 226, p. 245, Librarie générale de droit et de jurisprudence, Paris.

18 Hitler, A. (1971), *Mein Kampf*, p. 297, Houghton-Mifflin, Boston.

19 Ibid., p. 300 and 302.

20 Ratner, S. and J.S. Abrams (1997), *Accountability for Human Rights Atrocities in International Law: Beyond the Nuremberg Legacy*, p. 3, Clarendon Press, Oxford and New York.

Destroying for Practical Ends

The issue of motive has emerged in connection with hypothetical or real examples of a government undertaking economic development in a forested area, resulting in the death of inhabitants. Roger Clark, setting forth a hypothetical inspired by the situation of the Ache Indians of Paraguay, and similar situations in Brazil, posits a road being built to open up a uranium mine in a Latin American country, through territory occupied by an indigenous Indian group:

> As a result of building the road and related industrial activities, the ecology of the forest is changed, the Indian food supply shrinks, and most of the Indians die of starvation or diseases brought in by non-Indians against which the Indians have no natural immunity.[21]

These examples raise a general question about motive in relation to genocide. Could the Netherlands, a NATO State sued in the ICJ for the 1999 NATO bombing of Yugoslavia, argue that even if it intended to destroy the population of Yugoslavia, it did not do so out of a purpose to discriminate against that population? Could the actors in the uranium mine example successfully defend by asserting that their intent was to raise the gross national product, and that they were not acting with the aim of bringing harm to the indigenous population?

The answer is clearly in the negative. Criminal conduct is assessed in relation to acts and mental state in relation to the victim or victims. An example used in domestic penal law is that of the hypothetical airplane designer who plants a bomb on a competitor's test aircraft, setting the bomb to detonate while the test aircraft is in flight. The designer's aim is to prevent the competitor from testing the aircraft, and thereby to improve his own chances for commercial success. If the bomb detonates and kills the pilot, the designer cannot successfully defend on the ground that his aim was only to destroy the aircraft, and that he had no interest in killing the pilot.

This issue may be relevant in a number of situations in which genocide is charged. If an actor kills members of a group to frighten other members of the group into evacuating their home areas, he might assert that he only wanted the group to move away, and that killing some members was only a means to that end. Nonetheless, the prosecution might argue that the actor intended to destroy the group, at least in part, even if only as a means to a further end of securing its departure.

Another example comes from allegations that have been made of genocide in Paraguay. Individuals have allegedly killed members of the Ache indigenous group, for the purpose of taking their children as slaves. According to the allegations, the actors would "hunt" for Ache children, who would typically be found in the company of their parents. The actors would be able to get the children only by killing their

---

21 Clark, R. (1981), 'Does the Genocide Convention Go Far Enough? Some Thoughts on the Nature of Criminal Genocide in the Context of Indonesia's Invasion of East Timor,' *Ohio Northern University Law Review* 8, p. 321, p. 326.

parents and therefore did so. The result was the deaths of a substantial number of adult Ache.[22]

The fact that killing parents was only a means to a further end would not exculpate. An actor could be found to have intended to destroy the Ache as a group, even though indifferent as to whether the parents lived or died. The Ache case was taken to the Inter-American Human Rights Commission, as an allegation of genocide against Paraguay as a state, since the Commission has jurisdiction only over allegations against states. The Commission decided "provisionally" that Paraguay itself had not committed genocide but indicated its concern over "possible abuses by private persons in remote areas of the territory of Paraguay." The Commission did not parse the genocide definition.[23]

Another example is killing indigenous people to secure access to their land or its minerals, as in the case of the Brazilian gold prospectors described in Chapter 6. If an actor interested in access to land or resources kills in order to gain that access, but understands that by so doing he is destroying the group, he may be guilty of genocide even if his killing was only a means to the further end of securing access.

The actor may characterize the action as directed towards an aim having nothing to do with harm to the alleged victim group. When Yugoslavia sued the NATO states, they replied that their intent was to force a policy change on the part of Yugoslavia's government, not to destroy any population group.[24] That assertion, in and of itself, is insufficient as a response to an allegation of genocidal intent. Focus must be on the actor's attitude in regard to the victim group, even if the actor is pursuing an aim that has nothing to do with the group.

Destroying for Benign Reasons

An actor may even characterize conduct that appears to constitute genocide as helpful to the victim group. One possible means of committing genocide, under Article II, is "forcibly transferring children of the group to another group." A government that takes children from an indigenous population and arranges adoptions by families of the dominant population might violate this prohibition. The government might view its policy as helpful to the children by improving their economic well-being. Matthew Storey takes as an example the assimilationist policies of the Australian government in the 1930s in relation to Australia's aboriginal population: "The fact that this act is committed with a beneficial motive is apparently irrelevant. Genocide

---

22 Münzel, M. (1976), *Manhunt*, in R. Arens (ed.), *Genocide in Paraguay*, p. 19, p. 38, Temple University Press, Philadelphia.

23 Inter-American Commission on Human Rights, *Informe anual 1975*, para. 13.

24 Legality of Use of Force (Yugoslavia v. Belgium), ICJ, oral argument, 10 May 1999 (Mr. Ergec, Belgium).

does not require malice; it can be (misguidedly) committed 'in the interests of' a protected population."[25]

Croatia alleged genocide against Yugoslavia for encouraging Croatian nationals of Serb ethnicity to evacuate the Knin region of Croatia in 1995. Yugoslavia had captured the region in 1991 and held it until 1995, when Croatia was able to re-take it. Croatia did not allege that Yugoslavia harmed these Croatian nationals of Serb ethnicity. Yugoslavia said it was acting to protect these persons from anticipated Croatian reprisals once Croatia re-took the territory. Yet Croatia alleged genocide: "this action is a deliberate and calculated program designed by the Belgrade Government to clear an ethnic population, and constitutes 'ethnic cleansing' and genocide."[26]

Destroying One's Own Group

The fact that motive is not required as an element of proof of genocide is relevant to an issue that has proved controversial: whether the perpetrator can be of the same group as the victims. The case that raised the issue most prominently was that of Cambodia. Many Khmer Rouge atrocities were committed against members of groups constituting minorities within Cambodia, but the bulk of the atrocities were against members of the majority Khmer population. Even as the United Nations, through the 1990s, urged the Cambodian government to agree to an internationalized adjudication of Khmer Rouge atrocities, the UN equivocated on whether atrocities committed against Khmers would qualify as genocide. The UN General Assembly referred to the Cambodian atrocities in a way that suggested genocide may have been committed, when it called for UN assistance in investigating them, "including responsibility for past international crimes, such as acts of genocide."[27]

An expert group appointed by the UN Secretary-General to explore possible fora for a trial said that "the Khmer people of Cambodia do constitute a national group within the meaning of the Convention. However, whether the Khmer Rouge committed genocide with respect to part of the Khmer national group turns on complex interpretive issues, especially concerning the Khmer Rouge's intent with respect to its non-minority-group victims." The experts said that any tribunal hearing these cases would have to resolve the issue, if prosecutors were to charge Khmer Rouge officials with genocide for acts against Khmers.[28]

---

25 Storey, M. (1998), 'Kruger v The Commonwealth: Does Genocide Require Malice?,' *University of New South Wales Law Journal* 21, p. 224, pp. 228-230.

26 Application of the Convention on the Prevention and Punishment of the Crime of Genocide (Croatia v. Yugoslavia), Application, para. 24, 2 July 1999.

27 GA Res. 52/135, UN GAOR, 52nd sess., 12 December 1997, UN Doc. A/RES/52/135 (1997).

28 *Report of the Group of Experts for Cambodia Established Pursuant to General Assembly Resolution 52/135*, UN GAOR, 53rd sess., UN Doc. A/53/850, UN Doc. S/1999/231, annex,

Although the Khmers might be characterized as a national or ethnic group, the bulk of victims in Cambodia were not of a group identified by Article II that would distinguish them from the alleged perpetrators. Jason Abrams stated, "While the Cambodian people clearly constitute a national group, it would appear that the Khmer Rouge targeted their non-minority Cambodian victims as members of political, professional, or economic groups, which were not protected groups under the definition of genocide, rather than as members of a national group."[29]

Abrams' objection focuses precisely on the issue mentioned by the UN group of experts, namely that of intent. The issue is whether an actor can intend to destroy a group of which the actor is a part. To some analysts, this seems an impossibility. William Schabas said that "the fundamental difficulty with using the term genocide to describe the Cambodian atrocities lies with the group that is the victim of genocide. Destruction of Khmers by Khmers simply stretches the definition too much."[30] As Abrams pointed out, those Khmer targeted fell into certain strata within the Khmer group. If they were targeted because of the fact of being, for example, a professional person, perhaps the intent involved is something other than an intent to destroy the Khmer national group, or a part of it.

The drafting history of Article II is not instructive on the issue. The past atrocities cited by various delegates involved acts by persons who were not members of the victim group: by Japanese against Chinese when Japan was in occupation of China in the 1930s, or by Germans against Jews.[31] The issue was not debated, however. In principle, there would seem to be no reason why one could not intend to destroy his own group, or a part of it, and the text of Article II imposes no requirement that the victims be of a group different from that of the perpetrator. "[T]he definition does not exclude cases where the victims are part of the violator's own group," wrote Ben Whitaker in his UN study on genocide.[32] Schabas elsewhere agrees with this conclusion, stating, "Nothing prevents the offender from being a member of the targeted group."[33] A UN rapporteur, Abdelwahab Bouhdiba, examining the Khmer Rouge atrocities, recited acts of the Khmer Rouge directed against the majority

para. 65 (1999).

29 Abrams, J.S. (2001), 'The Atrocities in Cambodia and Kosovo: Observations on the Codification of Genocide,' *New England Law Review* 35, p. 303, p. 307.

30 Schabas, W.A. (2001d), 'Problems of International Codification – Were the Atrocities in Cambodia and Kosovo Genocide?,' *New England Law Review* 35, p. 287, p. 291.

31 UN GAOR, 3rd sess., Part 1, *Summary Records of Meetings 21 September - 10 December 1948*, p. 175, UN Doc. A/C.6/SR.81 (Mr. Li, China).

32 *Revised and updated report on the question of the prevention and punishment of the crime of genocide prepared by Mr. B. Whitaker*, 2 July 1985, Commission on Human Rights, UN Doc. E/CN.4/Sub.2/1985/6, p. 16.

33 Schabas, W.A. (2001b), 'The Crime of Genocide in the Jurisprudence of the International Criminal Tribunals for the Former Yugoslavia and Rwanda,' in H. Fischer, C. Kress and S. Luder (eds), *International and National Prosecution of Crimes Under International Law*, p. 447, p. 464, Berlin Verlag, Berlin.

population of Cambodia and called it "autogenocide."[34] By this term, Bouhdiba meant that Khmer on Khmer acts constituted genocide. In a later report, Bouhdiba similarly made it clear that he applied the term "genocide" to acts affecting the population of Cambodia generally. He referred to the Khmer Rouge atrocities as "barbaric genocide, millions dead, millions maimed, hundreds of thousands of children scarred, probably for the rest of their lives, millions of families destroyed, famine, disease, etc."[35]

Although accusations of genocide have generally been against persons not of the same group as the victims, in 1982 Israel charged Iraq with genocide for killings of Iraqis in an Iraqi village. It characterized as genocide acts by Iraq in the town of Ad Dujayl (near Baghdad) that allegedly resulted in the deaths of 150 Iraqi civilians. The group intended to be destroyed, according to Israel's accusation, was the population of the town of Ad Dujayl, which was about 2000 persons in total. The number allegedly killed was 150.[36] The accusation reflects an assumption that Iraq could be responsible for intending to destroy a group of Iraqis.

The key to resolving the issue of whether perpetrators need be of a group different from that of the victims is the absence of a requirement of motive. Hurst Hannum, who says that the Khmer on Khmer atrocities in Cambodia did constitute genocide, points out that if one intends to destroy a protected group, it is not necessary that one do so out of a motivation related to the distinguishing feature of the group. Thus, "destruction of a geographically distinct racial group as such in order to secure national borders would constitute genocide, as would destruction of a religious group because it was considered to wield too much economic power or because its members were considered heretics."[37]

The experts appointed by the United Nations to analyze the Khmer Rouge atrocities with a view to trials also held open the possibility of genocide involving Khmer non-minority victims:

> As for atrocities committed against the general Cambodian population, some commentators have asserted that the Khmer Rouge committed genocide against the Khmer national group, intending to destroy a part of it. The Khmer people of Cambodia do constitute a national group within the meaning of the Convention. However, whether the Khmer Rouge committed genocide with respect to part of the Khmer national group turns on complex interpretive issues, especially concerning the Khmer Rouge's intent with respect to its non-minority-group victims. The Group does not take a position on this issue, but believes that any tribunal

34 Commission on Human Rights, 35th sess., 1510th meeting, *Question of the violation of human rights and fundamental freedoms in any part of the world*, p. 7, UN Doc. E/CN.4/SR.1510 (1979).

35 Commission on Human Rights, 37th sess., *The situation of human rights in Kampuchea*, p. 4, UN Doc. E/CN.4/1437 (1981).

36 UN GAOR, 37th sess., 108th plenary meeting, 16 December 1982, p. 1832, UN Doc. A/37/PV.108 (1986) (Yehuda Blum, Israel).

37 Hannum, H. (1989), 'International Law and Cambodian Genocide: The Sounds of Silence,' *Human Rights Law Quarterly* 11, p. 82, p. 108.

will have to address this question should Khmer Rouge officials be charged with genocide against the Khmer national group.[38]

By making intent the problematic issue, the experts implicitly affirmed the possibility of genocide against one's own group. If genocidal intent can be shown, by their analysis, then genocide is present.

It is the intent to destroy the group, or a part of it, that is critical. Thus, even if the victim group is not distinct from the perpetrator, genocide can be present because it is not necessary that the perpetrator be acting on the basis of the distinguishing feature. A Khmer would not need to hate Khmer in order to be guilty of genocide. A Khmer need not intend to destroy the Khmer group because he hates Khmers. It suffices if he intends to destroy the Khmer group, or a part of it, for whatever reason.

Abrams sees an obstacle in the fact that the Khmer perpetrators focused on particular strata within the Khmer group, and that those strata are not mentioned in Article II, namely officials of the prior regime, intellectuals, and professional people.[39] Yet one can intend to destroy a group by destroying only certain strata. The absence of a reference to these groups in Article II does not negative genocidal intent. Nothing in Article II, or in its intent requirement, precludes liability for acts against a group of which the perpetrator is a member.

If the actor must be of a different group, it could have curious implications. Hitler may have had Jewish ancestry. Hitler's paternal grandmother, unmarried, was a domestic worker in the household of a Jewish family in Graz, Austria. When Hitler's father was born to her, no man acknowledged paternity. At the time, a son in the family in Graz was nineteen years of age. The family paid child support for Hitler's father to age fourteen.[40] Into adulthood, Hitler's father was known by the surname of his mother.[41] Some biographers of Hitler think that Hitler's father was fathered by the nineteen-year-old son.[42] If so, Hitler would have had Jewish parentage.

Were Hitler prosecuted for genocide, the fact, if it were so, of his being Jewish would not seem relevant. Since any motive will do for genocide, a person who commits sub-paragraph acts against immediate victims, with the intent to destroy their group, commits genocide.

---

38 Identical letters dated 15 March 1999 from the Secretary-General to the President of the General Assembly and the President of the Security Council, UN Doc. A/53/850, S/1999/231, 16 March 1999, Annex: Report of the Group of Experts for Cambodia established pursuant to General Assembly resolution 52/135, p. 20.

39 Abrams (2001), p. 306.

40 Payne, R. (1973), *The Life and Death of Adolf Hitler*, p. 6, Praeger, New York.

41 Bullock, A. (1952), *Hitler: A Study in Tyranny*, p. 18, Harper, New York.

42 Toland, J. (1977), *Adolf Hitler*, pp. 2-3, Ballantine, New York. Stierlin, H. (1976), *Adolf Hitler: A Family Perspective*, pp. 20-21, Atcom, New York.

Chapter 19

The Intent of Others

Applying the intent element of genocide is complicated by the fact that the acts may be carried out by a group, like a military organization or a government. Not all actors stand in the same relationship to the conduct, and not all may have the same state of mind about it. Some actors may be charged on the rationale that they took part in the acts of others.

Some individuals may personally inflict violence on victims. Others may organize their activity. Still others may plan the activity. In a case tried by the Rwanda tribunal, Samuel Musabyimana, a local bishop in Rwanda, was charged with facilitating killing by paying the Hutu militia who killed Tutsi, and by compiling lists of refugees by ethnicity. According to the prosecution's evidence, Hutu militia used these lists to identify Tutsis and then to kill them.[1]

Hierarchical structures, like armies or police forces, are often the context for acts by one person that relate to the genocidal acts of another. A superior may be charged for acts of a subordinate. A subordinate may be charged for acts of a superior. The Genocide Convention facilitates the charging of anyone whose conduct is related in a culpable way to genocide committed by others. Article III lists acts punishable under the Convention as: genocide, conspiracy to commit genocide, direct and public incitement to commit genocide, attempt to commit genocide, and complicity in genocide.

With genocide being charged in such situations, proof of intent is problematic. Since motive need not be proved, not all participants must act out of the same motive. The Genocide Convention does not expressly indicate whether all participants must harbor genocidal intent, or whether some may be convicted on the basis of the genocidal intent of others.

Liability of Superiors for Intent of Subordinates

The intent element presents itself differently depending on where the actor stands in relation to the conduct. Figures at different levels of authority may be involved. Adolf Eichmann held a high position in the government of the Third Reich, but below the top leadership level. A number of persons charged with genocide have occupied posts that allowed them to organize atrocities by others. Jan Kambanda, who pleaded guilty to genocide before the Rwanda tribunal, was prime minister of

---

1   Prosecutor v. Musabyimana, Case No. ICTR-01-62, Indictment, 15 March 2001.

Rwanda and thus stood atop a governmental hierarchy; he acknowledged directing others to kill.[2] In Cambodia, Pol Pot and Ieng Sary were the primary governmental policy-makers and were charged with formulating a policy of destroying groups and with overseeing its implementation. Slobodan Milosevic was president of Yugoslavia and was indicted for acting in a similar capacity in relation to destroying groups in Bosnia.[3]

Primary policy-makers may bear penal responsibility for acts committed by the structure generally. If central directives call for genocidal conduct, the policy-makers are responsible, at least so long as they are cognizant of what is being done. A Cambodian court convicted Pol Pot and Ieng Sary of genocide, finding the requisite intent: "After examining the criminal acts committed by the accused, the tribunal can conclude that Pol Pot and Ieng Sary committed these crimes with genocidal intent."[4] The pair was responsible for political doctrine being followed by local functionaries. Mass killings were carried out in many parts of the country in similar fashion, a fact that the court took to show central direction.[5] The Phnom Penh court that convicted Pol Pot and Ieng Sary did so on the basis of circumstances suggesting central direction to the killing.

Some years later, memoranda were found, written to the leadership by Khmer Rouge functionaries, detailing how they had carried out killings, and thus providing evidence that the leaders knew about them.[6] Interviews with former functionaries suggested a strong chain of command linking the leadership to atrocities.[7]

With Radovan Karadzic and Ratko Mladic, a trial chamber of the Yugoslavia tribunal characterized the responsibility of the two men as "command responsibility." The two men were, respectively, the political and military leaders of a political-military group. For them, as we saw in Chapter 17, the trial chamber said, "the intent may be inferred from a certain number of facts such as the general political doctrine which gave rise to the acts possibly covered by the definition in Article 4."[8] Article 4 of the Statute of the International Criminal Tribunal for the Former Yugoslavia is identical to Article II of the Genocide Convention. The trial chamber considered the espousal of a political doctrine leading to acts prohibited by Article II as manifesting

---

2   Prosecutor v. Kambanda, Case No. ICTR 97-23-S, Judgment and Sentencing, 4 September 1998.

3   Prosecutor v. Milosevic, Case No. IT-02-54, Indictment, 21 April 2004.

4   De Nike, H., J. Quigley and K. Robinson (eds) (2000), *Genocide in Cambodia: Documents from the Trial of Pol Pot and Ieng Sary*, p. 541, University of Pennsylvania Press, Philadelphia.

5   Ibid., p. 541.

6   Becker, E., 'New links in Khmer Rouge chain of death: detailed reports show leaders knew of underlings' atrocities,' *New York Times*, 16 July 2001, p. A6.

7   Mydans, S., 'Researchers piece together Khmer Rouge's story,' *New York Times*, 15 September 2002, p. A6.

8   Prosecutor v. Karadzic & Mladic, Cases No. IT-95-5-R61, IT-95-18-R61, Review of Indictment Pursuant to Rule 61, 11 July 1996, para. 94.

the intent to destroy a group. "The conditions for the responsibility of superiors," said the chamber, "that is those constituting criminal negligence of superiors, have unquestionably been fulfilled."[9]

Article III of the Genocide Convention, by extending genocide liability to complicity and conspiracy, provides a route to conviction of superiors for acts of subordinates. In one war crimes prosecution arising out of World War II, a superior was convicted for the acts of subordinates, even absent a showing that he shared their intent. The Supreme Court of the United States upheld the conviction of Japanese General Tomoyuki Yamashita for war crimes against civilians and prisoners in the Philippines, while Yamashita was military and political commander there. There was no evidence that Yamashita had ordered any atrocities. The US Supreme Court upheld a death sentence against Yamashita, saying that he had "an affirmative duty to take such measures as were within his power and appropriate in the circumstances to protect prisoners of war and the civilian population."[10]

The ILC cited the *Yamashita* decision in support of its draft provision that military commanders are responsible for the conduct of subordinates "if they knew or had reason to know, in the circumstances at the time, that the subordinate was committing or was going to commit such a crime and if they did not take all necessary measures within their power to prevent or repress the crime."[11] Adolfo Miaja de la Muela read the Genocide convention to achieve the same result, namely that a commander who is aware of and tolerates genocidal acts of subordinates is also guilty of genocide.[12]

The UN Security Council, in adopting statutes for the Yugoslavia and Rwanda tribunals, included a detailed provision on the issue, applicable to all crimes within the jurisdiction of those tribunals, including genocide. According to the Statute of the Yugoslavia tribunal, a superior is criminally responsible "if he knew or had reason to know that the subordinate was about to commit such acts or had done so and the superior failed to take the necessary and reasonable measures to prevent such acts or to punish the perpetrators thereof."[13] Nearly identical language was written into the statute for the Rwanda tribunal.[14] The provision was particularly important, because

---

9   Ibid., para. 82.

10   In re Yamashita, USA, Supreme Court, 327 U.S. 1 (1946).

11   Draft Code of Crimes against the Peace and Security of Mankind, art. 6, *Report of the International Law Commission on the work of its forty-eighth session 6 May - 26 July 1996*, UN GAOR, 51st sess., Supp. (No. 10), p. 34, UN Doc. A/51/10 (1996).

12   Miaja de la Muela, A. (1951-52), 'El genocidio, delito internacional,' *Revista española de derecho internacional* 4, p. 363, pp. 387-388.

13   Statute of the International Criminal Tribunal for the Former Yugoslavia, art. 7, appended to SC Res. 827, UN SCOR, 48th sess., 3217th meeting, UN Doc. S/RES/827 (1993).

14   Statute of the International Criminal Tribunal for Rwanda, art. 6, appended to UN SC Res. 955, art. 1, UN SCOR, 49th sess., 3453rd meeting, UN Doc. S/RES/955 (1994).

the two tribunals were set up to concentrate on the prosecution of persons at higher levels of responsibility.[15]

The two statutes impose an obligation on superiors to take measures to prevent genocide by subordinates. One possible situation is that in which subordinates are committing genocide, and the superior aids them, but without sharing their genocidal intent. A trial chamber of the Rwanda tribunal said that complicity liability can rest on a reduced level of mental culpability in such a situation. In a case involving the liability of the director of a tea factory for genocide committed by his employees, the trial chamber said

> that an accused is liable for complicity in genocide if he knowingly and voluntarily aided or abetted or instigated a person or persons to commit genocide, while knowing that such a person or persons were committing genocide, even though the accused himself did not have the specific intent to destroy, in whole or in part, a national, ethnical, racial or religious group, specifically targeted as such.[16]

Liability of Subordinates for Intent of Superiors

The prosecutor for the Yugoslavia tribunal filed charges in connection with the mass killing in 1995 of Bosnian Muslims at the town of Srebrenica. She charged genocide against Ratko Mladic, the military commander in charge of the operation. She charged complicity with Mladic against Dragan Obrenovic, who commanded a brigade that, according to the allegation, carried out much of the killing. The indictment alleged that Obrenovic carried out acts in violation of sub-paragraphs (a) and (b) (killing and causing serious bodily or mental harm), and that he did so "with knowledge that they were initiated, organised and ordered by General Ratko Mladic and others, with knowledge that Ratko Mladic and others had the intent to destroy, in whole or in part, a national, ethnical, racial or religious group, as such."[17]

Obrenovic thus was not alleged to have had genocidal intent himself, but nonetheless was charged with complicity in genocide. The prosecutor's theory of liability thus holds a subordinate liable for the intent of a superior on the same terms as a superior is held liable for the intent of a subordinate. Obrenovic, under the prosecutor's theory, is guilty of complicity in genocide even if he did not harbor an intent to destroy Bosnian Muslims or a part thereof, as such, so long as he was aware that he was killing and causing harm to Bosnian Muslims in pursuance of a plan by Mladic to destroy Bosnian Muslims or a part of that group.

The appeals chamber affirmed Krstic's conviction for his role at Srebrenica on the basis of aiding and abetting, using a standard like that seen in the Obrenovic

---

15 Boelaert-Suominen, S. (2001), 'Prosecuting Superiors for Crimes Committed by Subordinates: A Discussion of the First Significant Case Law Since the Second World War,' *Virginia Journal of International Law* 41, p. 747, p. 784.

16 Prosecutor v. Musema, Case No. ICTR-96-13-T, Judgment, 27 January 2000, para. 887.

17 Prosecutor v. Obrenovic, Case No. IT-01-43, Indictment, 16 March 2001, para. 12.

indictment. Although concluding that genocidal intent could not be proved against Krstic, the appeals chamber upheld his conviction as one for complicity in genocide, on the theory that he "had knowledge of the genocidal intent of some of the Members of the VRS Main Staff."[18] It said that aiding and abetting is proved against an accused "if he assists the commission of the crime knowing the intent behind the crime. This principle applies to the Statute's prohibition of genocide."[19]

The question of how a subordinate knows the genocidal intent of a superior was addressed by the German Constitutional Court. It suggested that subordinates might be liable on the basis of statements by leaders. Convicting Jorgic, a Bosnian Serb, and a low-level actor, for genocide, it said: "It suffices if the actor internalizes the intent regarding the elements held by a structurally organized central formation, and if applicable with respect to only a part of the group. The intent of the central figures can be taken from their political statements."[20]

The ILC provided in a draft article on superior orders that acting pursuant to an order does not relieve a person of criminal responsibility.[21] Explaining this provision, the ILC gave an example of how it would apply in a genocide prosecution:

> a governmental official who plans or formulates a genocidal policy, a military commander or officer who orders a subordinate to commit a genocidal act to implement such a policy or knowingly fails to prevent or suppress such an act and a subordinate who carries out an order to commit a genocidal act contribute to the eventual commission of the crime of genocide. Justice requires that all such individuals be held accountable.[22]

The ILC was not specific about the mental culpability required. Clearly a governmental official who "plans or formulates a genocidal policy" entertains the intent required by Article II.

Obrenovic was a commander. A foot soldier acting under Obrenovic who actually carries out the killings may also be held for genocide. Under the prosecutor's theory in the Obrenovic case, the foot soldier would be liable if aware of the intent on the part of Mladic to destroy Bosnian Muslims as a group.

Complicity under the Genocide Convention

Liability of accomplices on lesser mental culpability than that required for a principal is not unknown in domestic law. Complicity is sometimes said to require that the accomplice share the intent of the principal. A principal commits an offense, and the

---

18 Prosecutor v. Krstic, Case No. IT-98-33-A, Judgment, 19 April 2004, para. 137.

19 Ibid., para. 140.

20 Case of Jorgic, Bundesverfassungsgericht, 12 December 2000, 2 BvR 1290/99, Absatz-Nr. (1-49), para. 20.

21 Draft Code of Crimes against the Peace and Security of Mankind, art. 5.

22 Draft Code of Crimes against the Peace and Security of Mankind, art. 5 (commentary) p. 31.

accomplice facilitates the offense, sharing the principal's intent that the offense be committed.[23] One finds, however, prosecutions involving a lesser culpability level on the part of the accomplice. If a principal is charged with purposeful conduct, another party may be charged for conduct that facilitates the principal's act, with knowledge that the principal's act would thereby be facilitated. For example, one who provides an instrumentality, knowing that the recipient intends to use it in crime, may be held guilty as an accomplice, even absent a desire that the principal carry out the crime. In one French case, a person who supplied the principal with a gun, knowing that the principal would use it to commit a robbery, was convicted of complicity.[24] The appeals chamber in Krstic referred to French law, and domestic law elsewhere, in support of its conclusion that Krstic could be convicted on the basis of his knowledge of the genocidal intent of others.[25]

Such cases can present difficult problems of proof, as there are many possible variations in the level of awareness on the part of the alleged accomplice as to the principal's intent. It may be that the principal is standing over the victim, menacing the victim, and declaring an intent to kill the victim, and asks the alleged accomplice to provide a weapon for the principal to use then and there to kill the victim. On the other hand, in a situation in which no victim is present, the principal might ask for a weapon, stating that he is thinking about killing someone with it. The alleged accomplice might not believe the principal or might think that the principal will use the weapon for some other purpose. In the case of the immediate victim, it is easier to conclude that the alleged accomplice knew that the principal would use the weapon for purposes of crime.

International practice finds complicity liability absent a sharing of the intent, on the basis of knowledge of the intent, accompanied by an act that helps to carry out the intent of the other. In finding Krstic guilty of complicity in genocide, the Yugoslavia tribunal's appeals chamber wrote: "The conviction for aiding and abetting genocide upon proof that the defendant knew about the principal perpetrator's genodical intent is permitted by the State and case-law of the Tribunal." The appeals chamber cited a similar approach in "[m]any domestic jurisdictions, both common and civil law."[26] The possibility of complicity liability based on the genocidal intent of either a subordinate or a superior expands the potential reach of the crime of genocide.

Liability on too low a level of mental culpability, however, should be avoided. Alicia Gil Gil suggested using the standards found in domestic penal law for omission liability, which are arguably higher than what is provided in the Yugoslavia

---

23 Dressler, J. (2001), *Understanding Criminal Law*, pp. 471-472, Matthew Bender, New York.

24 France, Penal Code (1810), art. 60(2), applied in Case of Garici Said, France, Cour de Cassation, Chambre Criminelle, 17 May 1962, *Recueil Dalloz de doctrine, de jurisprudence et de législation*, p. 473 (1962).

25 Prosecutor v. Krstic, Case No. IT-98-33-A, Judgment, 19 April 2004, para. 141.

26 Ibid., paras. 140-141.

and Rwanda tribunal statutes.[27] Mirjan Damaska expressed concern that "specialists in public international law have labored in acoustic isolation from their brethren working the vein of municipal criminal law."[28] Damaska fears that in their quest to stop atrocities, the international lawyers may impose penal responsibility in inappropriate circumstances. International judges, he fears, may allow "the minimum threshold of negligence" to "shade into liability without culpability." The risk is that commanders will be convicted as scapegoats for conduct they could not have prevented.[29]

Damaska's warning should be heeded. It was an important advance in the law to establish that commanders and rulers are not exempt from liability. At the same time, if superiors are held too strictly accountable, the traditional philosophical basis for criminal responsibility disappears. Similarly with subordinates, there may be various levels of awareness of the genocidal intent of the superior. No person should be convicted of a crime so serious as genocide absent a sufficient finding of mental culpability.

---

27 Gil Gil, A. (1999), *Derecho Penal Internacional: Especial Consideración del Delito de Genocidio*, p. 283, Editorial Tecnos, Madrid.

28 Damaska, M. (2001), 'The Shadow Side of Command Responsibility,' *American Journal of Comparative Law* 49, p. 455, p. 495.

29 Ibid., p. 481.

PART FIVE
THE VICTIMS OF GENOCIDE

Chapter 20

The Numbers Game

By limiting genocide to acts intended to affect only certain types of groups, the drafters of the Genocide Convention created more complexity than they realized. The very existence of a group may be disputed. Even if the group is found to exist, an accused may deny that fact, thereby casting doubt on whether he had an intent to destroy it. Or an accused may act against persons thinking they belong to a group that in fact does not exist.

There may also be difficulty determining, as to particular victims, whether they were members of a given group. The drafters did not address situations in which a victim is, in the actor's perception, a member of a certain group but in fact is not. Nor did they address situations in which the victim is a member of a given group but the actor did not so realize.

Defining genocide based on an intent to destroy a group also raised the question of whether the actor must intend the destruction of the group in its entirety. As the drafting proceeded, some participants worried that persons accused of genocide might argue that they did not intend to destroy the entire group, but only a portion of it. So the drafters added the phrase "in whole or in part." But in solving one problem, the drafters created another. The phrase "in part" has eluded precise application. By one reading, it imports a minimum numerical requirement.

Part Five examines these questions of identifying the groups to which genocidal intent may run. This chapter analyzes the phrase "in whole or in part." Chapter 21 examines the drafters' choice of the types of groups to protect. Chapter 22 asks how the existence of a given group can be determined. Chapter 23 asks how it is determined whether particular victims are members of a given group.

Drafting History

The terms "in part" or "partially" appeared in early drafts of the Genocide Convention.[1] The Secretary-General's draft used the phrase "in whole or in part" to modify "destroying" of groups.[2] It was recognized early on that conviction for genocide was appropriate where the actor intended to kill only a part of a group.

---

1   Schabas, W.A. (2000), *Genocide in International Law: The Crime of Crimes*, pp. 230-232, Cambridge University Press, Cambridge.

2   UN ECOSOCOR, 2nd sess., Secretary-General, Draft Convention on the Crime of Genocide (Report of Secretary-General, 26 June 1947), UN Doc. E/447, p. 5.

In the Sixth Committee, a draft definition of genocide proposed by the USSR also included the formula "in whole or in part" in describing genocidal intent.[3] However, in the definitional language then under primary consideration, such language was lacking. That absence evoked concern from Venezuela that "there was reference to the destruction of groups without specifying whether that reference was to total or partial destruction." Its delegate thought that "it should be stated that destruction of part of a group also constituted genocide."[4]

Responding to these concerns, Norway drew the phrase "in whole or in part" from the Soviet proposal and introduced it as an amendment to the Article II language then under consideration.[5] Norway proposed this language at a time when France advocated a definition of genocide that would have had no sub-paragraphs enumerating acts, and no clause about intent regarding a group. France would have defined genocide as "an attack on the life of a human group or of an individual as a member of such group, particularly by reason of his nationality, race, religion or opinions."[6]

France's proposal was criticized both on the basis that the concept "attack on the life" was unclear, and because conviction would have been possible even of persons who acted without an intent against the group. Thus, Egypt stated,

> the idea of genocide could hardly be reconciled with the idea of an attack on the life of a single individual. He felt that the aim of the French amendment would be met if the Committee adopted the Norwegian proposal [A/C.6/228] to insert the words "in whole or in part" after the words "with the intent to destroy."[7]

Little discussion followed of the meaning of the phrase "in whole or in part." The *Columbia Law Review* said that Norway explained in the Sixth Committee that it was proposing the words "in whole or in part" to show "that it was not necessary to kill all the members of a group in order to commit genocide."[8] However, Norway's statement related not to the intent element but to the act element of genocide.

---

3 UN GAOR, 3rd sess., Part 1, *Annexes to the Summary Records of Meetings*, pp. 16-18 (*Union of Soviet Socialist Republics: amendments to the draft convention on genocide (E/794)*), UN Doc. A/C.6/215/Rev.1 (1948).

4 UN GAOR, 3rd sess., Part 1, *Summary Records of Meetings 21 September - 10 December 1948*, p. 58, UN Doc. A/C.6/SR.69 (Mr. Pérez Peroso, Venezuela).

5 Ibid., p. 61 (Mr. Wikborg, Norway).

6 UN GAOR, 3rd sess., Part 1, *Annexes to the Summary Records of Meetings*, pp. 13-14 (France: Draft convention on genocide), UN Doc. A/C.6/211 (1948).

7 UN GAOR, 3rd sess., Part 1, *Summary Records of Meetings 21 September - 10 December 1948*, p. 92, UN Doc. A/C.6/SR.73 (Mr. Raafat, Egypt).

8 'Note: Rethinking Genocidal Intent: The Case for a Knowledge-Based Interpretation,' *Columbia Law Review* 99, p. 2259, p. 2290 (1999). The cited language of Norway appears at UN GAOR, 3rd sess., Part 1, *Summary Records of Meetings 21 September - 10 December 1948*, p. 93, UN Doc. A/C.6/SR.73 (Mr. Wikborg, Norway). The *Note* erroneously cites this statement as being at p. 97.

Norway's point was the obvious one that the act element does not require killing all members of a group. The Sixth Committee proceedings yield little learning on the phrase "in part."

"In Part" as Requiring a Minimum Number or Proportion

In the United States, however, the phrase "in whole or in part" drew attention. When the US Senate Foreign Relations Committee considered the Genocide Convention, it opined that "the reference to 'in part' means to a substantial number of individual group members. An act must be intended to destroy the group as a viable entity to qualify as genocide."[9] When the United States ratified, it entered an "understanding" of the phrase "in part" that uses the modifier "substantial." It said that Article II requires "the specific intent to destroy, in whole or in substantial part, a national, ethnical, racial or religious group as such."[10] No other ratifying state entered a written "understanding" on the point.

When the Genocide Convention was written into US domestic law as a penal offense, the US Congress explained "substantial part" even further, as "a part of a group of such numerical significance that the destruction or loss of that part would cause the destruction of the group as a viable entity within the nation of which such group is a part."[11]

This "viable entity" approach focuses not on how many, or what percentage, an actor intends to destroy, but rather on how many, or what percentage, an actor intends not to destroy. An actor would presumably not be guilty of genocide who intends to leave enough group members to sustain the group.

Other efforts at interpreting the phrase "in part" have focused on how many an actor intends to destroy. According to the ILC, genocide "by its very nature requires the intention to destroy at least a substantial part of a particular group."[12] Ben Whitaker, reporting to the UN Commission on Human Rights about the law of genocide, suggested that the phrase "in part" must mean a "reasonably significant number, relative to the total of the group as a whole, or else a significant section of a group such as its leadership."[13]

---

9 Committee on Foreign Relations, United States Senate, *Report on the International Convention on the Prevention and Punishment of the Crime of Genocide*, 99th Cong., 1st sess., Exec. Rpt. No. 99-2, p. 22 (1985).

10 *Multilateral Treaties Deposited with the Secretary-General: Status as at 31 December 2003*, p. 126, UN Doc. ST/LEG/SER.E/22 (2003).

11 US Code 18, §1093(8).

12 Draft Code of Crimes against the Peace and Security of Mankind (commentary), *Report of the International Law Commission on the work of its forty-eighth session 6 May - 26 July 1996*, UN GAOR, 51st sess., Supp. (No. 10), p. 89, UN Doc. A/51/10 (1996).

13 *Revised and updated report on the question of the prevention and punishment of the crime of genocide prepared by Mr. B. Whitaker*, 2 July 1985, Commission on Human Rights, UN

Trial chambers in both the Rwanda and Yugoslavia tribunals have also suggested a quantitative minimum. The Jelisic trial chamber, citing Whitaker, said that "the intention to destroy must target at least a substantial part of the group."[14] The Sikirica trial chamber said that a "reasonably substantial" number is required.[15] The Kayishema trial chamber said that "in part" requires an intention to destroy "a considerable number of individuals who are part of the group."[16] That formulation seems to refer to some absolute minimum number.

The Sikirica trial chamber said that substantiality would be determined by taking the number of immediate victims as a percentage of the total population of the group. Applying that approach, it said that Sikirica victimized the Bosnian Muslims detained in the prison camp where he worked, numbering between 1,000 and 1,400. The total number of Bosnian Muslims in the municipality was 49,351. Thus, Sikirica victimized between 2 per cent and 2.8 per cent of the Bosnian Muslims of the municipality, a percentage that the trial chamber said was not a "reasonably substantial" part of the entirety.[17] The only other way an intent to destroy the group could be proved, it said, was to show an intent to destroy a leadership segment of the group. Targeting leadership is examined in Chapter 27.

Hazards of Setting a Minimum Number or Proportion

The Sikirica trial chamber's methodology is dubious. If an actor victimizes a high percentage of the members of the relevant group, that fact may evidence an intent to destroy the group. However, the trial chamber appeared to require the actual victimization of some minimum percentage. That approach is inconsistent with Article II, which does not require victimization on any particular scale.

Even as to the intent to destroy, the need for a minimum absolute number, or a minimum percentage, is questionable. The variety of approaches at construing the phrase "in part" reflects the difficulty of the enterprise. None of the suggested approaches is satisfactory. Least satisfactory is the gloss reflected in the US legislation that would require an intent to destroy the group as a viable entity. That approach would significantly limit the scope of the crime of genocide. It would mean that the actor's destructive intent would need to run to nearly the totality of the group. As Jordan Paust has suggested, this gloss might require exoneration where the group

---

Doc. E/CN.4/Sub.2/1985/6, p. 16.

14 Prosecutor v. Jelisic, Case No. IT-95-10-T, Judgment, 14 December 1999, para. 82.

15 Prosecutor v. Sikirica, Case No. IT-95-8, Judgment on Defence Motions to Acquit, 3 September 2001, para. 65.

16 Prosecutor v. Kayishema & Ruzindana, Case No. ICTR-95-1-T, Judgment, 21 May 1999, para. 97.

17 Prosecutor v. Sikirica, Case No. IT-95-8, Judgment on Defence Motions to Acquit, 3 September 2001, paras. 69-72.

intended to be destroyed numbers thirty million, but the actor seeks to kill twenty-nine million.[18]

Paust expressed doubt that Article II requires an intent to destroy a large part of a group. He writes that "[g]enocide *can* occur with the specific intent to destroy a small number of a relevant group. Nothing in the language of the Convention's definition, containing the phrase 'or in part,' requires such a limiting interpretation."[19] Paust was criticizing a proposed interpretation that was suggested during the drafting of the Statute of the International Criminal Court that "in part" should mean that the actor intends "to destroy more than a small number of individuals who are members of a group."[20] The phrase "or in part," to be sure, establishes no minimum, since a part of a whole may be any part of the whole. The suggested gloss on the words "or in part" was not included in the Statute of the International Criminal Court.

The various attempted phrasings of a quantitative requirement suffer from vagueness and thus may be of little use. The US-suggested construction, "substantial part," has no clear meaning. It probably does not mean a majority, although even that might be debated. Whitaker's formulation that "in part" means a "reasonably significant number, relative to the total of the group as a whole," similarly provides little guidance.

Another difficulty with any effort at definition of the phrase "in part" is that it may not be meaningful as an indicator of the actor's state of mind. One may feel comfortable believing that Adolf Hitler intended to kill a "substantial part" of the Jews of the world, or at least of those in Germany or the countries the Third Reich occupied. If an actor kills a member of a group because he would like to see the group reduced in numbers, it may be difficult, if not impossible, to determine what percentage of the group he intended to destroy.

Persons who victimize members of a group may not conceptualize their conduct in the way envisaged by Article II. In India in recent years, to take one example, groups of men have periodically killed groups of Dalits (Untouchables). The men who kill Dalits may do so when an opportunity presents itself but may not think conceptually about all the Dalits. They may think only of "killing Dalits."

---

18 Paust, J. (2000), 'Problematic U.S. Sanctions Efforts in response to Genocide, Crimes Against Humanity, War Crimes, and Other Human Rights Violations,' *Waseda Proceedings of Comparative Law* 3, p. 96, pp. 102-103, Institute of Comparative Law, Waseda University, Tokyo.

19 Paust, J. (1998), 'Commentary on Parts 1 and 2 of the Zutphen Intersessional Draft,' in L. Sadat Wexler (ed.), *13bis Nouvelles études pénales: Observations on the Consolidated ICC Text Before the Final Session of the Preparatory Committee*, p. 27, Association Internationale de Droit Pénal.

20 Report of the Intersessional Meeting from 19 to 30 January 1998 in Zutphen, The Netherlands, in L. Sadat Wexler (ed.), *13bis Nouvelles études pénales: Observations on the Consolidated ICC Text Before the Final Session of the Preparatory Committee*, Association Internationale de Droit Pénal, p. 121 (1998).

Nazi officials could not legitimately defend against genocide charges by arguing that their plans did not involve killing Jews on a worldwide basis.[21] The District Court of Jerusalem, trying Adolf Eichmann, said that he shared the intent embodied in the "Final Solution" plan, to destroy the Jewish people. The court referred to evidence showing, on Eichmann's part, "a desire for biological extermination, directed against an entire people."[22] The court referred to "an entire people" even though, as the Attorney General framed the matter and the court apparently accepted, Eichmann's intent ran only to those Jews "within the area of German influence," meaning, presumably, in Germany and in German-occupied territory.[23]

The US Congress' formulation has not yet been tested in practice, but it may be impossible to apply. In its phrase "the nation of which such group is a part," "nation" is not defined but presumably refers to a nation-state. Thus, if the group is one that spans boundaries, like the Kurds, who inhabit portions of Turkey, Iran, Iraq, and Syria, intending to destroy the Kurds in one of these countries only might be genocide, whereas intending to destroy small percentages in each of the four countries might not. Moreover, a court trying to determine how many members are required for a group to remain "viable" would find little guidance.

Appropriate Construction of "In Part"

The drafting history provides no support for a reading of "part" as meaning "substantial part." As explained in this chapter, the phrase "in part" was not explained in floor debate. In the debates, no one was thinking in quantitative terms. The rationale for the phrase "in part" was simply that intent to destroy a group need not run to the entirety of the group. No lower limit was discussed.

As a matter of logic the effort to require that part be a "substantial" part fails, even if one can ascertain the meaning of "substantial." Take as an example the citizenry of China, numbering approximately one billion. Assume that the actor declares an intent to kill 100,000 Chinese. This number would constitute only one ten thousandth of the Chinese population. Such a small fraction would probably not constitute a "substantial" part of the Chinese population. Killing that number would not destroy the Chinese as a "viable entity."

The concern behind the adoption of the phrase "in part" was that actors should not be exonerated because their intent did not run to the entirety of a group. The efforts to read "in part" as setting a lower limit are at odds with the drafters' aim.

The killing of a large number may create an inference of an intent to destroy a group, even if it is not required as an element. A trial chamber of the Yugoslavia

---

21 Schabas (2000), p. 235.

22 Attorney-General of the Government of Israel v. Eichmann, District Court of Jerusalem, 12 December 1961, *International Law Reports* 36, p. 23, p. 228.

23 Attorney-General of the Government of Israel v. Eichmann, District Court of Jerusalem, p. 230.

tribunal suggested, "The number of the victims selected only because of their membership in a group would lead one to the conclusion that an intent to destroy the group, at least in part, was present."[24] If an actor kills one or two members of a group, but not more, significant evidence would be needed to show an intent to destroy the group. On the other hand, if an actor kills five thousand, the act itself provides evidence that the actor intended to destroy the group.

---

24 Prosecutor v. Karadzic & Mladic, Cases No. IT-95-5-R61, IT-95-18-R61, Review of Indictment Pursuant to Rule 61, 11 July 1996, para. 94.

Chapter 21

Identifying a Group

In a criminal prosecution for genocide, a prosecutor must allege the existence of a group. An indictment must recite that the accused performed an act against a member of a named group, with intent to destroy that group. Article II seems to regard the existence of a victim group as an objective matter. The drafters gave no indication that they anticipated difficulty in determining the existence of a group. They specified four types of groups as the objects of genocide—"national, ethnical, racial or religious"—but did not define these four terms. They did not indicate whether the actor would have to understand that the group is one that qualifies as one of the four types.

In a development that might surprise the drafters of the Genocide Convention, the identification of victim groups has been a major issue of controversy. The Rwanda and Yugoslavia tribunals have faced defense arguments that the groups specified in indictments do not exist.

Stable Groups

In Rwanda, genocide charges have involved acts against immediate victims identified by the prosecution as Tutsi, with intent to destroy the Tutsi as a group. But the trial chambers have not found it obvious that such a group as the Tutsi existed. Although Article II of the Genocide Convention appears to require that a protected group exist as a matter of fact, the first trial chamber of the Rwanda tribunal to hear a genocide case, that of Akayesu, said that "the Tutsi population does not have its own language or a distinct culture from the rest of the Rwandan population."[1] Language and culture are two typical features said to distinguish a group. Neither language nor culture provided a distinction of Tutsi from other Rwandans. The trial chamber was hard pressed to find objective criteria on which to conclude that the Tutsi were a group covered by Article II.[2]

In addition to questioning whether the Tutsi are a group, the Akayesu trial chamber asked itself whether the Tutsi might be a group, but one not falling into one of the four categories of groups specified in Article II. The chamber said that in determining which groups to include in Article II, the drafters had sought those that

---

1   Prosecutor v. Akayesu, Case No. ICTR-96-4-T, Judgment, 2 September 1998, para. 170.

2   Drumbl, M.A. (1998), 'Rule of Law Amid Lawlessness: Counseling the Accused in Rwanda's Domestic Genocide Trials,' *Columbia Human Rights Law Review*, p. 545, p. 578.

have a certain stability. The chamber reasoned that any group reflecting stability may qualify, even if it does not fall into one of the four named types of group.

> [T]he question that arises is whether it would be impossible to punish the physical destruction of a group as such under the Genocide Convention, if the said group, although stable and membership is by birth, does not meet the definition of any one of the four groups expressly protected by the Genocide Convention. In the opinion of the Chamber, it is particularly important to respect the intention of the drafters of the Genocide Convention, which according to the *travaux préparatoires* [drafting history - J.Q.], was patently to ensure the protection of any stable and permanent group.[3]

In convicting Akayesu of genocide, the trial chamber found that "the Tutsi did indeed constitute a stable and permanent group and were identified as such by all."[4] The reasoning of the Akayesu trial chamber was that when the drafters listed the four types of groups, their focus had been not so much on those four types of groups as on trying to find terms to depict groups of a "stable and permanent" type.

This conclusion by the Akayesu trial chamber was taken by commentators as a major innovation in the meaning of genocide. Paul Magnarella said that the chamber "has significantly expanded the kinds of populations that will be protected" by the Genocide Convention.[5] The *Harvard Law Review* expressed concern that the divergence between the Akayesu trial chamber on this point and other trial chambers, which limited themselves to the four enumerated categories, "has created the potential for inconsistent protection."[6]

Despite its statement that any stable and permanent group is covered, the Akayesu trial chamber referred to evidence about ethnicity. It said of the Tutsi:

> that there are a number of objective indicators of the group as a group with a distinct identity. Every Rwandan citizen was required before 1994 to carry an identity card which included an entry for ethnic group (*ubwoko* in Kinyarawanda and *ethnie* in French), the ethnic group being Hutu, Tutsi or Twa [Twa is a third group in Rwanda - J.Q.]. The Rwandan Constitution and laws in force in 1994 also identified Rwandans by reference to their ethnic group. Article 16 of the Constitution of the Rwandan Republic, of 10 June 1991, reads, "All citizens are equal before the law, without any discrimination, notably, on grounds of race, colour, origin, ethnicity, clan, sex, opinion, religion or social position." Article 57 of the Civil Code of 1988 provided that a person would be identified by "sex, ethnic group, name, residence and domicile." Article 118 of the Civil Code provided that birth certificates would include "the year, month, date and place of birth, the sex, the ethnic group, the first and last name of the

---

3   Prosecutor v. Akayesu, Case No. ICTR-96-4-T, Judgment, 2 September 1998, para. 516.

4   Ibid., para. 702.

5   Magnarella, P.J. (1997), 'Some Milestones and Achievements at the International Criminal Tribunal for Rwanda: The 1998 Kambanda and Akayesu Cases,' *Florida Journal of International Law* 11, p. 517, p. 531.

6   'Developments in the Law – International Criminal Law: IV. Defining Protected Groups Under the Genocide Convention,' *Harvard Law Review* 114, p. 2007, p. 2024 (2001).

infant." The Arusha Accords of 4 August 1993 in fact provided for the suppression of the mention of ethnicity on official documents ...[7]

This last reference was to a 1993 agreement, unsuccessful as it turned out, to end the civil hostilities in Rwanda between the Hutu-led government and Tutsi-led insurgency. In the 1993 agreement, the government agreed to stop noting ethnicity on documents relating to an individual, because the Tutsi viewed these notations as facilitating discrimination against them.

Based on this review of Rwandan practice, the Akayesu trial chamber found that:

> the identification of persons as belonging to the group of Hutu or Tutsi (or Twa) had thus become embedded in Rwandan culture. The Rwandan witnesses who testified before the chamber identified themselves by ethnic group, and generally knew the ethnic group to which their friends and neighbours belonged. Moreover, the Tutsi were conceived of as an ethnic group by those who targeted them for killing.[8]

At the end of its opinion, the Akayesu trial chamber, curiously, stated its conclusion as if the standard were that any stable and permanent group would qualify, but referred prominently to the cited evidence of the Tutsi as an ethnic group. The chamber wrote:

> In light of the facts brought to its attention during the trial, the Chamber is of the opinion that, in Rwanda in 1994, the Tutsi constituted a group referred to as "ethnic" in official classifications. Thus, the identity cards at the time included a reference to "*ubwoko*" in Kinyarwanda or "*ethnie*" in French which, depending on the case, referred to the designation Hutu or Tutsi, for example. The Chamber further noted that all the Rwandan witnesses who appeared before it invariably answered spontaneously and without hesitation the questions of the Prosecutor regarding their ethnic identity. Accordingly, the Chamber finds that, in any case, at the time of the alleged events, the Tutsi did indeed constitute a stable and permanent group and were identified as such by all.[9]

As Leila Sadat has pointed out, the Akayesu trial chamber spoke of the Tutsi being regarded in Rwanda as an ethnic group, and not simply as a stable group.[10] Other judges of the Rwanda tribunal have read the Akayesu trial chamber's opinion in this way and have found it to be authority for the proposition that the Tutsi are an ethnic group. The Kayishema-Ruzindana trial chamber wrote: "In *Akayesu*, Trial Chamber I found that the Tutsis are an ethnic group, as such. Based on the evidence presented

---

7   Prosecutor v. Akayesu, Case No. ICTR-96-4-T, Judgment, 2 September 1998, para. 170.

8   Ibid., para. 171.

9   Ibid., para. 702.

10   Sadat, L. (2002), *The International Criminal Court and the Transformation of International Law: Justice for the New Millennium*, p. 144, Transnational Publishers, Ardsley NY (referring to Prosecutor v. Akayesu, Case No. ICTR-96-4-T, Judgment, 2 September 1998, para. 702).

in the present case, this Trial Chamber concurs."[11] The Kayishema-Ruzindana trial chamber apparently read the statement that the Tutsi are a "stable and permanent group" to mean that the Tutsi are a stable and permanent ethnic group. The Akayesu trial chamber itself, when it later heard the Musema case, referred to Musema having had the intent to destroy the "Tutsi ethnic group."[12]

Four Types as a Single Type

In the Yugoslavia tribunal, the Krstic trial chamber suggested a reading of Article II that would characterize the types of groups in yet another way. Citing the Genocide Convention's drafting history, it said that the listing of categories "was designed more to describe a single phenomenon, roughly corresponding to what was recognised, before the second world war, as 'national minorities,' rather than to refer to several distinct prototypes of human groups. To attempt to differentiate each of the named groups on the basis of scientifically objective criteria would thus be inconsistent with the object and purpose of the Convention."[13]

Diane Amann took this statement to mean that the Krstic trial chamber viewed the four adjectives describing categories of groups as representing not four independent categories of groups, but rather a single category, with the four adjectives providing differing ways to identify it. She writes that the chamber found Bosnian Muslims to constitute simply a "group" protected under Article II, but not a group that can be identified as "national," "ethnical," "racial," or "religious."[14]

The Krstic trial chamber, although it referred to the drafting history, did not cite any specific interchange among the drafters. Amann appropriately doubts that the drafters thought they were defining a single type of group, rather than four types.[15] Even if the drafters did have in mind the national minorities of inter-war central and eastern Europe, the terms they used did not characterize such groups only. To consider the four adjectives to describe a single category of group would be inconsistent with the text, which, by listing four categories in the disjunctive, indicates that genocidal intent can be directed against a group falling into any single one. If a putative "group" is one that can be distinguished from others only by its religion, it clearly qualifies as a protected group.

Moreover, as Amann notes, when the Krstic trial chamber came to characterizing the Bosnian Muslims, it said that they had at one time been viewed as a religious

---

11 Prosecutor v. Kayishema & Ruzindana, Case No. ICTR-95-1-T, Judgment, 21 May 1999, para. 526.

12 Prosecutor v. Musema, Case No. ICTR-96-13-T, Judgment, 27 January 2000, para. 934.

13 Prosecutor v. Krstic, Case No. IT-98-33-T, Judgment, 2 August 2001, para. 556.

14 Amann, D.M. (2002), 'Group Mentality, Expressivism, and Genocide,' *International Criminal Law Review* 2 (2002), p. 93, pp. 111-112.

15 Ibid., pp. 111-112.

group, but later as a national group.[16] The trial chamber thus appeared to conclude that the Bosnian Muslims constituted a "national" group. As a result, the Krstic trial chamber seems to have acted like the Akayesu trial chamber in that it posited a construction of Article II that would depart from the concept of four distinct types of groups but yet found the putative group in question to fall within one of those types of groups.

Permanency of a Group

The criteria of stability and permanency referenced by the Akayesu trial chamber had, to be sure, been a consideration for the Sixth Committee as it decided which types of groups to include in Article II. The delegates, however, mentioned stability and permanency not as independent sufficient criteria, but as criteria to justify the inclusion of particular types of groups. A number of delegates assumed that the types of groups they specified would not change over time, and that this factor made it appropriate to include them, but to exclude others. Poland, arguing against the inclusion of political groups, said that "[g]enocide was basically a crime committed against a group of people who had certain stable and characteristic features in common."[17] Brazil, supporting Poland's objection to the inclusion of political groups, said that genocide "could only be perpetrated against groups which were stable and permanent."[18] The drafting history suggests that only those types of groups specified in Article II could be victim groups in genocide.

The religion category is problematic from this perspective. Membership in a religious group is not permanent, as individuals may separate themselves from a religious group. For this reason, the inclusion of religious groups was questioned in the Sixth Committee.[19] On the other hand, in some parts of the world, a person's religion is akin to ethnicity, that is, a person is considered to be of the religion of her or his parents, or even of the dominant religion of her or his society, regardless of actual adherence. In the Muslim world, for example, a European may be regarded as Christian, simply by the fact of being European.

The nationality category is problematic as well. The term "national" carries two distinct meanings. In one meaning, it is a group sharing a history and culture, and in this sense the term "nation state" came into being, namely a state that is composed of persons who are members of a single nation. Alicia Gil Gil refers to "persons

---

16 Prosecutor v. Krstic, Case No. IT-98-33-T, Judgment, 2 August 2001, para. 559.

17 UN GAOR, 3rd sess., Part 1, *Summary Records of Meetings 21 September - 10 December 1948*, p. 19, UN Doc. A/C.6/SR.64 (Mr. Lachs, Poland).

18 UN GAOR, 3rd sess., Part 1, *Summary Records of Meetings 21 September - 10 December 1948*, p. 57, UN Doc. A/C.6/SR.69 (Mr. Amado, Brazil).

19 UN GAOR, 3rd sess., Part 1, *Summary Records of Meetings 21 September - 10 December 1948*, p. 106, UN Doc. A/C.6/SR.74 (Mr. Kaeckenbeeck, Belgium).

belonging to a single nationality in a material sense, that is, to the same people even if the people is not identified with a state."[20]

As Gil Gil notes, the term "nationality" is also used to indicate affiliation with a state, akin to the concept of citizenship. By this understanding, a person's nationality changes if the person renounces a nationality upon being naturalized into another. Moreover, a person may have more than one nationality, as reflected in the practice of dual nationality.

It was in this sense that Yugoslavia used the term "national" in its 1999 suit alleging genocide against the NATO states for the bombing of Yugoslavia. By Yugoslavia's claim, the group that the NATO states intended to destroy was the collectivity of persons sharing Yugoslav nationality in the sense of citizenship.

One NATO state, Italy, argued that "national" did not mean "citizen." Italy said that the term "group" is used in Article II rather than "people," and that the latter term would have been used had the citizenry of a state been intended. Further, Italy argued, if "group" could mean the citizenry, then any use of armed force in an international conflict "would automatically become a case of genocide."[21]

Italy's position is questionable. The term "national" is typically used to mean those affiliated with a state via citizenship. Moreover, Italy's argument that any use of armed force against a state would become genocide is ill conceived. A use of force against a state would not automatically become genocide. It would be genocide only if genocidal intent were present.

Historical and subjective circumstances may play a role. An expert witness testifying in the Akayesu trial chamber noted that identifying Rwandans as Hutu, Tutsi or Twa in official documents began in the 1930s, when Rwanda was under Belgian administration. The Belgian administration required the population to register according to ethnic group. This registration requirement may have contributed to a sense that Hutu and Tutsi were different one from another. According to the expert witness:

The categorisation imposed at that time is what people of the current generation have grown up with. They have always thought in terms of these categories, even if they did not, in their daily lives have to take cognizance of that. This practice was continued after independence by the first Republic and the Second Republic in Rwanda to such an extent that this division into three ethnic groups became an absolute reality.[22]

Race is similarly problematic in that it may depend on perception, and the perception may vary over time, or even from place to place. In the United States in the nineteenth century, a person of fifteen sixteenths European descent and one sixteenth African descent was deemed to be African. If such a person had migrated

---

20 Gil Gil, A. (1999), *Derecho Penal Internacional: Especial Consideración del Delito de Genocidio*, p. 184, Editorial Tecnos, Madrid.

21 Legality of Use of Force (Yugoslavia v. Italy), ICJ, oral argument, 11 May 1999, para. 3B (Mr. Leanza, Italy).

22 Prosecutor v. Akayesu, Case No. ICTR-96-4-T, Judgment, 2 September 1998, para. 172.

to Africa, she or he would have been considered a European. In South Africa under apartheid, a racial classification of "colored" included both persons of African-European parentage and the descendants of migrants from India. Thus, two disparate groups were in a single racial category.

Chapter 22

A Group in the Eye of the Beholder

Difficulty over ascertaining the existence of a group has led courts to inquire whether the group must be determined to exist as an objective matter, or whether the critical question is whether the group was perceived to exist by relevant parties.

Rwanda Tribunal Trial Chambers

The Kayishema-Ruzindana trial chamber gave more play to subjective factors than had the Akayesu trial chamber. The Kayishema-Ruzindana chamber took expert testimony and decided that it could fairly characterize the Tutsi as an ethnic group.[1] It defined "ethnic group" broadly, to conclude that the Tutsi were an ethnic group either on objective criteria, or on community perception. The chamber said that an ethnic group is "one whose members share a common language and culture; or, a group which distinguishes itself, as such (self identification); or, a group identified as such by others, including perpetrators of the crimes (identification by others)."[2] This tripartite definition included, first, objective criteria, then self-perception of the victim group, and finally, the perception of others. If the Tutsi qualified on any of the three, they would be an ethnic group.

To the Kayishema-Ruzindana trial chamber, the second of the three factors allowed it to conclude that the Tutsi were an ethnic group. Self-identification by the Tutsi was key. To establish that the Tutsi self-identified, the chamber referred to much of the same evidence as the Akayesu trial chamber. Since 1931, it noted, Rwandans were required to carry an identity card that listed ethnicity, the three options being Hutu, Tutsi, or Twa.[3] Like the Akayesu trial chamber, the Kayishema-Ruzindana trial chamber referred to the 1993 agreement. The issue of ethnicity was so prominent in Rwanda, the trial chamber said, that this peace agreement had determined to eliminate the practice of noting ethnicity on identity cards.[4]

The Kayishema-Ruzindana trial chamber also relied on the perception of Tutsi who happened to appear before it as witnesses. Rwandans who testified at the Kayishema-Ruzindana trial, the chamber said, identified themselves to the chamber

---

1   Prosecutor v. Kayishema & Ruzindana, Case No. ICTR-95-1-T, Judgment, 21 May 1999, para. 523.

2   Ibid., para. 98.

3   Ibid., para. 523.

4   Ibid., para. 524.

as Tutsi and said that persons they saw killed were Tutsi.[5] If the trial chamber were to rely on self-perception, it might have sought a more scientific means of ascertaining whether there is a self-perception of a Tutsi ethnicity. The chamber apparently felt comfortable relying on the self-perception of these witnesses. Based on indicators of self-identification of some Rwandans as Tutsi, the Kayishema-Ruzindana trial chamber found "beyond a reasonable doubt that the Tutsi victims of the massacres were an ethnical group."[6]

The same trial chamber that had heard the Akayesu case heard the case of Rutaganda. In the Rutaganda case, the chamber said:

> membership of a group is, in essence, a subjective rather than an objective concept. The victim is perceived by the perpetrator of genocide as belonging to a group slated for destruction. In some instances, the victim may perceive himself/herself as belonging to the said group.[7]

But, said the chamber, "a subjective definition alone is not enough to determine victim groups, as provided for in the Genocide Convention."[8] Here, however, the chamber did not recite any objective criteria but confined itself to saying that the drafters had excluded economic and political groups on the rationale that such groups are not stable and permanent. Thus, it was saying that Article II sets limits on what perpetrators may perceive to be protected groups. The trial chamber concluded, as it had in the Akayesu case, that "the Tutsi group is a protected group under the Convention on genocide."[9]

Yugoslavia Tribunal Trial Chambers

Like the Rwanda trial chambers, the trial chambers of the Yugoslavia tribunal have taken subjective factors into account in deciding whether a given group exists. The issue was addressed in the Jelisic and Krstic cases. Bosnia presented a delicate identification problem. The three commonly identified groups—Croats, Serbs, and Muslims—spoke what was essentially the same language, although some variation could be identified. As for culture, the three were more readily distinguishable one from another than were Hutus from Tutsis.

Nonetheless, the Yugoslavia trial chambers appeared wary of having their genocide decisions rest on the chamber's ability to determine, as an objective matter, that these groups qualified as one of the four types identified in Article II. The Jelisic trial chamber stated:

---

5   Ibid., para. 525.

6   Ibid., para. 526.

7   Prosecutor v. Rutaganda, Case No. ICTR 96-3-T, Judgment, 6 December 1999, para. 56.

8   Ibid., para. 57.

9   Ibid., para. 402.

Although the objective determination of a religious group still remains possible, to attempt to define a national, ethnical or racial group today using objective and scientifically irreproachable criteria would be a perilous exercise whose result would not necessarily correspond to the perception of the persons concerned by such categorisation. Therefore, it is more appropriate to evaluate the status of a national, ethnical or racial group from the point of view of those persons who wish to single that group out from the rest of the community. The Trial Chamber consequently elects to evaluate membership in a national, ethnical or racial group using a subjective criterion. It is the stigmatisation of a group as a distinct national, ethnical or racial unit by the community which allows it to be determined whether a targeted population constitutes a national, ethnical or racial group in the eyes of the alleged perpetrators.[10]

In the Krstic case, the same trial chamber said that "[a] group's cultural, religious, ethnical or national characteristics must be identified within the socio-historic context which it inhabits. ... the Chamber identifies the relevant group by using as a criterion the stigmatisation of the group, notably by the perpetrators of the crime, on the basis of its perceived national, ethnical, racial or religious characteristics."[11] Thus, the trial chambers in both the Rwanda and Yugoslavia tribunals have focused on perception by relevant population groups. This approach avoids the need for objective identification of a group, an undertaking that, as the trial chambers suggest, is often difficult.

Relevance of Objective Factors

Neither the text of Article II, nor its drafting history, offers much assistance to a court in determining how to place particular putative groups within the four categories. On its face, Article II appears to treat the "group" element as objective, that is, a given group would need to be found to exist as a fact, an element commonly characterized as an attendant circumstance of an actor's conduct. Offense elements are divided into action elements and attendant circumstances. If, to take an example, a statute prohibits "stealing a cow," then "steal" is the action element and "cow" the attendant circumstance.

As regards genocide, groups in the four categories are not as readily ascertainable as was apparently assumed by the Sixth Committee in 1948. The interpretative approach taken by the various trial chambers involves subjectivity—on the part of the perpetrators as well as on the part of the victims and the general community—to construe the meaning of the four types of groups listed in Article II. This approach is an analytical innovation not obvious from the text of Article II.

Despite their focus on subjectivity in the identification of a group, the trial chambers have identified objective factors, in particular, in regard to Rwanda, the identity cards that specified ethnicity. It seems doubtful that the trial chambers would find a purported group to exist without objective factors. Although the trial

---

10 Prosecutor v. Jelisic, Case No. IT-95-10-T, Judgment, 14 December 1999, para. 70.
11 Prosecutor v. Krstic, Case No. IT-98-33-T, Judgment, 2 August 2001, para. 557.

chambers refer to perception, they evidently do not mean a perception held by a single perpetrator. It is a perception of the groups involved.

The UN Security Council's commission of inquiry into atrocities in the Darfur region of Sudan similarly resorted to the subjective perception on the part of the victim group, as it analyzed whether genocide might be present. The "African" villagers, it said, viewed themselves as being attacked by militias of "Arab tribes." The two groups shared the Islamic faith and the Arabic language, although the "Africans" spoke Arabic only as a second language. High levels of inter-marriage made physical differences between the two difficult to ascertain. The commission concluded that the two are not, objectively speaking, different ethnic groups, but that for purposes of the Genocide Convention the perception of the victims sufficed that they were being attacked by "persons belonging to another and hostile group."[12]

Like the trial chambers, the commission of inquiry focused on the perception not of an individual member of the victim or perpetrator group, but of the community of persons inhabiting the relevant territory. Thus, the Jelisic trial chamber, when it said that stigmatization by the perpetrators was key, said, as we saw, that it means stigmatization "by the community." The criterion is not as subjective as it might appear. If an entire community perceives a group to exist, that perception is a fact that can be ascertained by a court.

---

12 *Report of the International Commission of Inquiry on Darfur to the United Nations Secretary-General pursuant to Security Council Resolution 1564 of 18 September 2004*, 25 January 2005, para. 511.

Chapter 23

Genocide by Mistake

Another hurdle in making out a case of genocide, once it is established that the group exists, is to establish that the victims were members. Here too the question arises whether the determination is objective or subjective. Is the immediate victim's membership in the group a matter of fact to be determined on objective criteria? Or is a court's conclusion dependent on what the actor perceived?

In criminal law analysis, the element of the group identity of the immediate victims is an attendant circumstance, a category we encountered in Chapter 22. Culpability requirements may differ for the two kinds of elements. The action element may require higher culpability. To revert to the example used in Chapter 22, "steal" requires that an actor seek to deprive the owner. Hence, an actor who takes a cow, mistakenly believing it to be his, is not guilty of stealing.

As for the attendant circumstance, the mental element may be handled variously, depending on the legislature's preference. "Cow" may require only that the actor be aware that the object is a cow, rather than that the actor intend to steal the object because it is a cow. The legislature may provide liability even if the actor was not aware that the object was a cow but, based on circumstances known to him, should have understood that the object was a cow.

With genocide, the element of intent to destroy a group would seem to require that the actor at least be aware that the victim is a member of the group. Take the case of an actor who kills a victim, and the victim is a member of a group that the actor intends to destroy, yet the actor was not aware that the victim was a member of the group. This actor would not be guilty of genocide, because it is hard to conclude that he intended, by the act of killing this victim, to destroy the group.

The issue of an actor's perception as to group identity can also arise when an actor perceives a victim to be a group member even though the victim is not. An actor intends to destroy the group of which he believes the victim to be a member and kills the victim with that intent. This scenario raises the question of whether one can commit genocide even if the victim is not a member of the target group.

The Possibility of Mistake

In some cases of possible genocide, the fact of the victim's group membership and the actor's awareness of that fact may be clear. It may not be contested by the accused. In other cases, this fact may be far from obvious. If the group is a religious group, the actor may have taken the victim to be a member if the victim was participating in a ritual peculiar to the group, or was wearing symbols particular to the group. If the group is an ethnic or racial group, the actor may rely on the victim's facial appearance, or mode of dress.

The possibility of such mistakes is not merely hypothetical. One day in 1994 in Rwanda, Hutu soldiers were loading Tutsi refugees onto a truck. According to the Rwanda tribunal prosecutor, the soldiers were taking the Tutsi to another location to execute them. Present was an Anglican bishop whom the prosecutor later charged with genocide for identifying Tutsis to be killed. Looking into the truck, the bishop recognized a young Hutu man in the group being loaded. As recounted by the prosecutor, the soldiers "had mistaken [the young man] for Tutsi and loaded [him] onto the vehicle to be killed with the others." When the bishop told the soldiers of their mistake, they let the young man off the truck. Then, according to the prosecutor, "the other Tutsi refugees were led away to be killed."[1]

Mistakes about the group identity of intended victims may well occur in situations of mass disorder. In Rwanda the risk of error was high, since the difference between Hutu and Tutsi was not always obvious. One Rwandan charged with genocide was, additionally, charged with complicity in murder on an allegation that he pointed out Tutsi houses to military personnel, who were looking for Tutsi to kill.[2] The military personnel evidently needed a local person familiar with the particular neighborhood to distinguish Tutsi from Hutu.

Ambiguity about a Victim's Membership

Apart from identifying a particular individual as a group member, there may be ambiguity as to whether a given person is a member of a given group. One of those convicted in Rwanda, as mentioned in Chapter 5, was Froduald Karamira, who was, from the evidence, born a Tutsi. However, because of discrimination against Tutsi in Rwanda, many Tutsi assimilated as Hutu and even underwent a process, recognized by local custom, to "convert" to Hutu. Karamira apparently "converted" to Hutu.[3] In a situation in which persons are able to switch from one group to another, an actor might well take a particular individual to be a member of a group of which that person is not in fact a member.

A group may experience difficulty in determining which persons are members. In Israel, litigation has been initiated and legislation has been adopted to determine who is a Jew. In Israeli law, the original standard was Jewish religious law, according to which a person born to a Jewish mother is a Jew. In one case, a man born to a Jewish mother became a Roman Catholic, by conversion, but still claimed to be

1   Prosecutor v. Musabyimana, Case No. ICTR-01-62, Indictment, 1 March 2001, para. 15.

2   Public Ministry v. Ntaganda, Case No. RPA 01/R1/RUH, Court of Appeal of Ruhengeri, 24 June 1998.

3   'Rwanda's Lord Haw-Haw dies,' *Irish Times*, 25 April 1998, p. 14.

a Jew. The Supreme Court of Israel said he was not.[4] According to the Supreme Court, being religious was not necessary to be a Jew, that is, an atheist born to a Jewish mother was a Jew, but a Jew who became an adherent of a religion other than Judaism was not.

Israel's parliament decided that the matter should be decided by legislation, and it adopted a statute affirming the Supreme Court's view, defining "Jew" as "a person who was born of a Jewish mother or has become converted to Judaism and who is not a member of another religion." However, the parliament thought this definition too narrow for determining who is Jewish for purposes of migrating to Israel as of right. For that purpose, it adopted a provision stating that the rights "are also vested in a child and a grandchild of a Jew, the spouse of a Jew, the spouse of a child of a Jew and the spouse of a grandchild of a Jew, except for a person who has been a Jew and has voluntarily changed his religion."[5] Thus, in the immigration context, a broader range of persons is deemed to be Jewish.

The criteria for membership in a group can change over time, the criteria can vary for different purposes, and litigation may be required to determine group affiliation. That being the case, one can well imagine error by those targeting members of a group. If members of a group experience difficulty figuring out who belongs, outsiders may as well.

Group Identity in "Hate Crime" Statutes

Although the issue of mistakenly identifying a victim as a member of a particular group is not addressed in Article II of the Genocide Convention, it is addressed in US statutes aimed at protecting groups. Under a California "hate crime" statute, anyone who commits a felony offense against another person is eligible for a higher penalty if the offense was committed "because of the victim's race, color, religion, nationality, country of origin, ancestry, disability, gender, or sexual orientation, or because [the actor] perceives that the victim has one or more of those characteristics."[6] Wisconsin's "hate crime" statute provides for penalty enhancement if the actor selects the victim "in whole or in part because of the actor's belief or perception regarding the race, religion, color, disability, sexual orientation, national origin or ancestry of that person ... whether or not the actor's belief or perception was correct."[7] These statutes penalize an actor who mistakenly thinks that the victim was a group member but does not penalize an actor who acts against a group member unaware of the victim's membership in the group.

---

4   Oswald Rufeisen v. Minister of the Interior, High Court Case No. 72/62, *Piskei din* 16, p. 2428, in *Selected Judgments of the Supreme Court of Israel*, Special Volume (1971), p. 1.

5   Law of Return (Amendment No. 2), *Laws of the State of Israel* 24, p. 28 (1970).

6   California Penal Code §422.75.

7   Wisconsin Statutes Annotated §939.645.

Mistake as Attempted Genocide

Article II has no comparable language about an actor's perception of group identity. The question of liability where the actor mistakenly believes the victim to be a member of a target group must, therefore, be resolved by construing the text of Article II, in light of general principles of law.

Article II, in its sub-paragraphs, requires an act against members of the target group. If the victim is not in fact a member of that group, one would have no such act, even if the actor thought he was committing such an act. Hence, the "act" element of genocide is not present. The result contemplated by the California and Wisconsin statutes would not obtain. An actor who intends to destroy a group and who kills persons who are not members, believing them erroneously to be so, is not guilty of genocide.

The issue could arise, however, whether such an actor may be guilty of an attempt at genocide, which is punishable under Article III of the Genocide Convention. In some situations in penal law, an actor who performs an act directed at the offense can be held for attempt even though, as a result of the actor's misperception, the crime could not be carried out. Thus, a person who puts his hand in another's pocket, to steal money, but finds the pocket empty, is guilty of attempted theft.

This principle has been employed by courts when the offense definition contemplates a victim of a particular class and where the actor performed the prohibited act against a person, believing the person to be of that class, but where the person in fact is not. According to Henri Donnedieu de Vabres, the issue has troubled the courts of France, but the predominant approach is to convict. Attempt liability lies, says Donnedieu de Vabres, "whenever acts have been performed that, in the thinking of the actor, should complete the offense that he had in mind. It does not matter that, as result of a circumstance independent of his will, the offense was not committed."[8]

In penal policy, there is a plausible argument for liability. One who intends to commit a given offense and who commits an act thought to contain the elements of the offense, but which as a result of a misperception did not, represents as much danger to society as one who did everything required for liability. A Hutu who is out to kill Tutsis, with the intent of destroying Tutsis as a group, but who kills a Hutu believing him to be a Tutsi, is as much a menace as a Hutu who killed a Tutsi, intending to destroy Tutsis as a group. As explained by Donnedieu de Vabres: "From the standpoint of social defense, the repression of an impossible crime seems to be compelling. ... The accused has demonstrated that he is immoral and dangerous to society; ..."[9]

Wayne LaFave, a US analyst, finds the same policy in US judicial decisions on attempts:

---

8   Donnedieu de Vabres, H. (1947), *Traité de droit criminel et de législation pénale comparée*, p. 142, Librarie de Recueil Sirey, Paris.

9   Ibid., p. 139.

the defendant's mental state was the same as that of a person guilty of the completed crime, and by committing the acts in question he has demonstrated his readiness to carry out his illegal venture. He is therefore deserving of conviction and is just as much in need of restraint and corrective treatment as the defendant who did not meet with the unanticipated events which barred successful completion of the crime.[10]

To date, no prosecutions have been brought for attempted genocide on this basis. However, convictions for attempted genocide in cases of misperceived group identity would be possible, on the same rationale as found in domestic law.

---

10 LaFave, W.R. (2000), *Criminal Law*, p. 555, West Group, St. Paul.

PART SIX
THE SCALE OF GENOCIDE

Chapter 24

Retail Genocide

Genocide may be alleged in situations like that in Rwanda, where atrocities were widespread. It may also be alleged in situations like that in Bolivia, where there was only a handful of victims. Part Six examines the question of whether harm inflicted on a modest scale may qualify as genocide. Genocide is sometimes characterized as a "mass" crime. The inspiration for the Genocide Convention—the atrocities of World War II—were the product of a philosophy of racial inferiority and involved victims numbering in the millions. The philosophy had been outlined by Adolf Hitler in *Mein Kampf*, and the power of the German state propelled the acts.

Article II of the Genocide Convention did not limit genocide to situations involving these elements. Nonetheless, most prosecutions and suits for genocide have involved situations of widespread depredations. The acts alleged have typically been directed against victims over an extensive geographic area, and have not been limited to victims of a particular social status. Based on this practice, and on the origins of the Genocide Convention, some analysts find mass action to be implied in Article II as a requirement for genocide liability, even though it is not stated.

Part Six examines this question. On occasion, genocide has been alleged when the acts have been limited. Part Six inquires whether genocide can be committed against a victim group in only a small geographic area, leaving the bulk of the group unmolested. It inquires whether genocide is present when the acts are directed against a defined stratum of people within a victim group, where the actor identifies the stratum as critical to the group's existence. This chapter, and the one following, inquire whether genocide can be committed by an isolated actor whose acts against victims are modest in scope, and who has little realistic possibility of destroying the relevant victim group.

A Master Plan Requirement as Viewed by Analysts

By one view, genocide requires the backing of a state or some similarly powerful entity. "It is virtually impossible for the crime of genocide to be committed without some direct or indirect involvement on the part of the State given the magnitude of this crime," wrote Virginia Morris and Michael Scharf.[1] And William Schabas:

---

1   Morris, V. and M. Scharf (1998), *The International Criminal Tribunal for Rwanda*, vol. 1, p. 168, Transnational Publishers, Irvington-on-Hudson NY.

Because of the scope of genocide, it can hardly be committed by an individual, acting alone. Indeed, while exceptions cannot be ruled out, it is virtually impossible to imagine genocide that is not planned and organized either by the State itself or by some clique associated with it. This is another way of saying that, for genocide to take place, there must be a plan, even though there is nothing in the Convention that explicitly requires this.[2]

George Fletcher and J.D. Ohlin argue that "the historical paradigm of genocide is the clash of embattled groups, i.e., the attempt by one ethnicity to wipe out the population of another group." Citing Article 5 of the Statute of the International Criminal Court, they write, "While it may be theoretically possible for one individual to engage in a genocidal attack, there is no reason to think that such a mass murder would be one of 'the most serious crimes of concern to the international community as a whole'."[3]

Analysts who take this view acknowledge that such a limitation is not directly reflected in Article II, or in domestic statutes modeled on Article II. Alicia Gil Gil, one such analyst, wrote: "This limitation is not found literally in the typical text, but it is manifest, nevertheless, from the idea of the value that is legally protected, from the very concept of an international offense, and from the idea of subsidiarity of international penal law."[4] By "subsidiarity," Gil Gil was referring to the concept that international penal law is concerned only with major offenders.

Other analysts find no requirement of a master plan or state direction, even by implication. Article II, they say, is directed at individual perpetrators. Joe Verhoeven writes that since "intent is decisive, nothing in principle keeps genocide from being committed when only a single person has been an immediate victim."[5] Albin Eser, in his commentary on the genocide provision in the German penal code, writes: "The perpetrator may be a single individual. A connection to a larger, powerful group is not required."[6] Eser notes the utility of a connection to an organization in proving intent but says that intent may be proved in other ways, as the appeals chamber found in Jelisic's case. Eser writes, "This intent can be provided not only by mass actions, but also by a single act, so long as the will of the perpetrator is directed towards the destruction of a group."[7]

---

2 Schabas, W.A. (2000), *Genocide in International Law: The Crime of Crimes*, p. 207, Cambridge University Press, Cambridge.

3 Fletcher, G.P. and J.D. Ohlin (2005), 'Reclaiming Fundamental Principles of Criminal Law in the Darfur Case,' *Journal of International Criminal Justice* 3, p. 537, 546.

4 Gil Gil, A. (1999), *Derecho Penal Internacional: Especial Consideración del Delito de Genocidio*, p. 203, Editorial Tecnos, Madrid.

5 Verhoeven, J. (1991), 'Le crime de génocide: originalité et ambiguïté,' *Revue belge de droit international* 24, no. 1, p. 5, p. 18.

6 Eser, A. (1997), in A. Schönke and H. Schröder (eds), *Strafgesetzbuch: Kommentar,* p. 1597, C.H. Beck'sche Verlagsbuchhandlung, Munich.

7 Ibid., p. 1597.

The UN Security Council's commission of inquiry into atrocities in the Darfur region of Sudan accepted the foregoing analysis when it asked itself whether genocide was being committed in Darfur. It concluded that Sudan as a state lacked genocidal intent but said that, nevertheless, it was possible that particular individuals, even perhaps government officials, involved in the situation may have had such intent, and that if they did, they could be guilty of genocide.[8] This analysis implies that even though there might not be an overall plan of genocide, individuals might still be guilty of genocide.

Most early analysts of the Genocide Convention similarly concluded that Article II covers an isolated actor. Adolfo Miaja de la Muela referred to genocide by an isolated actor as involving "impulsive acts."[9] Hans-Heinrich Jescheck wrote:

> As a rule to be sure one thinks of genocide as an effort by state organs against a group, but the elements of the violation would be fulfilled as well by a killing or serious bodily injury in today's Germany against a Jew with the aim of destroying the group today inhabiting Germany. The protective aim of the prescription requires the inclusion of an isolated act.[10]

Kurt Stillschweig, writing about lynchings in the American South, said: "One who, for example, lynches a Negro, in order to eliminate colored people from the world, should, according to the interpretation prevailing in the General Assembly have committed genocide, ..."[11] Racial lynchings were perpetrated by *ad hoc* gangs when an African-American was suspected of committing a crime.[12] They were also perpetrated by locals who resented particular African-Americans who had achieved economic success.[13]

A.A. Smith, a Texas lawyer, thought that Article II might apply to race riots, as occurred from time to time in Texas. A physical assault by whites on a group of Negroes might, he feared, be considered as undertaken to destroy at least a part of

---

8   *Report of the International Commission of Inquiry on Darfur to the United Nations Secretary-General pursuant to Security Council Resolution 1564 of 18 September 2004*, 25 January 2005, para. 520.

9   Miaja de la Muela, A. (1951-52), 'El genocidio, delito internacional,' *Revista española de derecho internacional* 4, p. 363, p. 382.

10 Jescheck, H.-H. (1954), 'Die internationale Genocidium-Konvention vom 9. Dezember 1948 und die Lehre vom Völkerstrafrecht,' *Zeitschrift für die gesamte Strafrechtswissenschaft*, p. 193, pp. 212-213.

11 Stillschweig, K. (1949), 'Das Abkommen zur Bekämpfung von Genocide,' *Die Friedens-Warte* 49, p. 93, p. 99, Blätter für internationale Verständigung und zwischenstaatliche Organisation, H. Wehberg (ed.).

12 Chadbourn, J.H. (1933), *Lynching and the Law*, pp. 4-12, University of North Carolina Press, Chapel Hill.

13 Barclay, D., T. Lewan and A.G. Breed, 'Land often the motive for attacks on blacks, lynchings,' Associated Press, 4 December 2001.

a race.[14] Concern that Article II covered race riots and lynchings was a factor in the US Senate's refusal to consent to the ratification of the Genocide Convention when President Harry Truman submitted it.[15]

A Master Plan Requirement before the Courts

When atrocities have been committed with central backing, prosecutors have, to be sure, stressed that point in making out a case of genocide against individual defendants. In both the Yugoslavia and Rwanda tribunals, prosecutors charging genocide have sought to link the actions of the defendant to similar actions occurring elsewhere in the country. In Yugoslavia a Bosnian Serb military-political apparatus organized attacks on Muslims and Croats, while in Rwanda, the Hutu-led government promoted attacks on the Tutsi. Indictments for genocide issued in the Rwanda tribunal routinely began with a recitation of the atrocities against Tutsi committed all over Rwanda, before listing acts charged against the particular defendant. The concerted character of the anti-Tutsi depredations have helped prosecutors in proving the intent of a particular accused.[16]

The issue has come before the appeals chamber, which hears appeals from both the Rwanda and Yugoslavia trial chambers. In the case of Kayishema and Ruzindana, the trial chamber had said "a specific plan to destroy does not constitute an element of genocide."[17] The appeals chamber found as a fact that a plan for killing Tutsi was formulated and promoted by the government in Rwanda in 1994. Reacting to the statement of the trial chamber, it said a plan might be relevant to show the actor's intent:

> The first-instance chamber thought, and the appeals chamber shares this view, that even if "the existence of a plan of genocide is not a necessary element of the crime of genocide, the existence of such a plan would demonstrate conclusively the presence of the specific intent required for the crime of genocide."[18]

One month later, the appeals chamber heard the prosecutor's appeal from the acquittal of Jelisic on a genocide charge. Jelisic had argued in the trial chamber

---

14 White, A.A. (1949), 'Tomorrow One May Be Guilty of Genocide,' *Texas Bar Journal* 12, p. 203, p. 227.

15 LeBlanc, L.J. (1991), *The United States and the Genocide Convention*, p. 34, Duke University Press, Durham and London.

16 Aptel, C. (2002), 'The Intent to Commit Genocide in the Case Law of the International Criminal Tribunal for Rwanda,' *Criminal Law Forum* 13, p. 273, p. 291.

17 Prosecutor v. Kayishema & Ruzindana, Case No. ICTR-95-1-T, Judgment, 21 May 1999, para. 94.

18 Kayishema & Ruzindana v. Prosecutor, Case No. ICTR-95-1-A, Decision, 1 June 2001, para. 138 (translation by author from French text).

that he could be convicted only if he acted pursuant to a plan coming from higher authority. The trial chamber replied:

> it is *a priori* possible to conceive that the accused harboured the plan to exterminate an entire group without this intent having been supported by any organisation in which other individuals participated.[19]

The Jelisic trial chamber referred to the drafting history of the Genocide Convention, and specifically to the rejection by the Sixth Committee of a requirement of a showing of premeditation. Had the Sixth Committee considered that a master plan was required, the trial chamber reasoned, it would have required premeditation as an element of genocide.[20]

On the appeal in Jelisic's case, the appeals chamber similarly rejected Jelisic's argument that he could be convicted of genocide only if he acted pursuant to a plan. The appeals chamber said that it was "of the opinion that the existence of a plan or policy is not a legal ingredient of the crime."[21] On the facts of Jelisic's case, the appeals chamber disagreed with the trial chamber, which had acquitted Jelisic for lack of intent. The appeals chamber found that Jelisic did have genocidal intent. It cited evidence of statements by Jelisic that he hated Muslims and wanted to kill them all, that he wanted to rid the world of Muslims, that Muslim women should be sterilized to prevent an increase in the Muslim population, that Muslim men should be killed to prevent procreation, that he referred to himself as "Adolf the Second," and that he would comment on how many Muslims he had killed.[22] This evidence relating to his attitude sufficed, the appeals chamber said, to establish his intent to destroy Bosnian Muslims. It was not necessary that he be shown to be carrying out a plan developed by higher authority.

A Master Plan Requirement in the Sixth Committee

The appeals chamber did not refer to the drafting history of Article II. The trial chamber, as noted, had cited the rejection of premeditation by the Sixth Committee as indicating a lack of a requirement of state backing. Even more compelling in the drafting history is the fact that the Sixth Committee specifically rejected a proposal to require state backing as an element of genocide.

France at one point suggested adding the following language in Article II: "It [genocide] is committed, encouraged or tolerated by the heads of a State."[23] Delegates

---

19 Prosecutor v. Jelisic, Case No. IT-95-10-T, Judgment, 14 December 1999, para. 100.

20 Ibid., para. 100.

21 Prosecutor v. Jelisic, Case No. IT-95-10-A, Decision, 5 July 2001, para. 48.

22 Ibid., paras. 62 and 67.

23 UN GAOR, 3rd sess., Part 1, *Summary Records of Meetings 21 September - 10 December 1948*, p. 165, UN Doc. A/C.6/SR.80 (1948).

speaking against the amendment explained that genocide could be committed by individuals absent government backing.

The Netherlands complained that the French amendment "excluded from the field of the convention genocide committed by individuals when it was neither encouraged nor tolerated by rulers."[24] The Philippines objected that such a limitation would hamper domestic enforcement of the prohibition against genocide: "If the French point of view were adopted, domestic laws would not punish private individuals for committing crimes of genocide, but merely for crimes punishable under the ordinary law, even in cases of obvious intent to destroy a particular group. ... Genocide might be committed with the support or the tolerance of the State, but it might also be committed by private individuals without the active intervention or connivance of the rulers."[25] The French amendment was put to a vote in the Sixth Committee and was rejected.[26] This rejection suggests that, to the drafters, state backing was not an element of genocide.

Genocide as a Preparatory Offense

As quoted above, Morris and Scharf refer to "the magnitude of this crime" and Schabas to "the scope of genocide" in a way that suggests that the harm caused by the actor must be great in scope. This analysis confuses the "scope" or "magnitude" of the harm caused with the "scope" or "magnitude" of the intent. It is the intent that must be wide in scope. There is no such requirement regarding the act.

Nehemiah Robinson, an early commentator, understood that distinction. Robinson wrote that genocide "must involve the planned destruction of a group. To carry such a program to successful completion would almost necessarily require active or silent support of the State having territorial jurisdiction of the offense."[27] Completing the destruction of a group is far different, however, from entertaining an intent to do so.

As we saw in Chapter 2, genocide differs from crimes against humanity, which do require widespread or systematic acts. This distinction reinforces the conclusion that genocide need not involve mass depredations. On trial for genocide before a trial chamber of the Rwanda tribunal, George Rutaganda objected that it was improper to convict him of both genocide and a crime against humanity for the same conduct. Crimes against humanity have an explicit element of being committed in a widespread or systematic manner. If genocide too must be committed in a widespread or systematic manner, Rutaganda argued, then the two offenses are too

---

24 Ibid., p. 171 (Mr. de Beus, Netherlands).

25 Ibid., p. 166 (Mr. Paredes, Philippines).

26 UN GAOR, 3rd sess., Part 1, *Summary Records of Meetings 21 September - 10 December 1948*, p. 170, UN Doc. A/C.6/SR.82 (1948).

27 'Genocide: A Commentary on the Convention,' *Yale Law Journal* 58, p. 1142, p. 1147 (1949).

similar to convict a person of both. The trial chamber found no problem, however, with convicting Rutaganda of both genocide and crimes against humanity. The trial chamber said that crimes against humanity require many victims, whereas with genocide the number may be small.[28]

Although the mass killings of World War II inspired the Genocide Convention, its text encompasses conduct that constitutes only a modest step towards mass killings. In that way, Article II went beyond the concept of crimes against humanity, which focus on actual harm.[29] Genocide is an offense that seeks to "nip crime in the bud." The harm the drafters feared was mass harm, but they defined the offense to encompass conduct that fell well short of that end, hoping thereby to stop the conduct before mass harm resulted. Otto Triffterer finds the origin of this approach in an effort to prevent a repetition of Hitler. Had the Genocide Convention been in effect at that time, Hitler would have been guilty of genocide upon committing the initial atrocities.[30]

The Article II definition is satisfied, even if the individual in question does not, realistically, have the capability to carry out mass killings. Article II contains no implied requirement of the involvement of a state, or an organization of similar strength.

---

28 Prosecutor v. Rutaganda, Case No. ICTR-96-3-T, Judgment, 6 December 1999, paras. 114-115.

29 Donnedieu de Vabres, H. (1950), 'De la Piraterie au Génocide . . . les Nouvelles Modalités de la Répression Universelle,' in *Le Droit Privé Français au Milieu du XXe Siècle: Études offertes à Georges Ripert*, vol. 1, p. 226, pp. 245-246, Librarie Générale de droit et de jurisprudence, Paris.

30 Triffterer, O. (2001), 'Genocide, Its Particular Intent to Destroy in Whole or in Part the Group as Such,' *Leiden Journal of International Law* 14, p. 399, pp. 401-402.

Chapter 25

Wholesale Genocide

The question of the context in which the actor operates, in the crime of genocide, surfaced in connection with the creation of an International Criminal Court. As indicated in Chapter 8, genocide was included as an offense within the jurisdiction of the court. A Preparatory Commission for the International Criminal Court was tasked with drafting offense definitions. For genocide, the commission tracked Article II of the Genocide Convention but added the following: "The conduct took place in the context of a manifest pattern of similar conduct directed against that group or was conduct that could itself effect such destruction." The Assembly of States Parties to the Rome Statute of the International Criminal Court confirmed this language.[1] Although this language did not require participation by a state, it would limit genocide prosecutions to situations involving a pattern of activity directed against a group.

The "Context" Element

Elaborating on this "context" element, the Preparatory Commission wrote a definition of "manifest," stating that it is "an objective qualification." The phrase "in the context of," it explained, "would include the initial acts in an emerging pattern."[2] Schabas takes the Preparatory Commission's "context" element as reflecting "an implied element in the definition of genocide."[3] Some of the members of the Preparatory Commission viewed the "context" element that way. Roger Clark, who served on the commission, reported that certain delegates thought that this limitation was "part of the concept of genocide." Other delegates saw the limitation as "a reasonable way to distinguish those killings and other depredations which are of international

---

1   Assembly of States Parties to the Rome Statute of the International Criminal Court, *Official Records*, 1st sess., 3-10 September 2002, p. 113, UN Doc. ICC-ASP/1/3 (2002).

2   Preparatory Commission for the International Criminal Court, *Finalized draft text of the Elements of Crimes*, 2 November 2000, art. 6, UN Doc. PCNICC/2000/1/Add.2 (2000), confirmed by Assembly of States Parties to the Rome Statute of the International Criminal Court, *Official Records*, 1st sess., 3-10 September 2002, p. 113, UN Doc. ICC-ASP/1/3 (2002).

3   Schabas, W.A. (2001c), 'The *Jelisic* Case and the *Mens Rea* of the Crime of Genocide,' *Leiden Journal of International Law* 14, p. 125, p. 137.

dimensions from those which belong solely in domestic courts."[4] On this second rationale, the "context" element limits the International Criminal Court to handling only certain cases of genocide, and reflects a view that genocide can be committed by an isolated actor.[5] An isolated actor who carries out genocide would be tried in domestic courts, not in the International Criminal Court.

The proceedings in the Preparatory Commission thus revealed one body of opinion that views genocide as requiring some connection to a larger pattern of activity, but another that does not. The two groups agreed only that prosecutions in the International Criminal Court for genocide should be limited to instances in which the conduct was part of a larger pattern.

Appropriateness of the "Context" Element

The Preparatory Commission's "context" element has yet to be applied in practice before the International Criminal Court. However, the "context" element faces a significant hurdle. The production of "elements of crimes" was ordered by Article 9 of the court's Statute. Article 9 specifies that such elements "shall be consistent with this Statute." Thus, if an element written by the Preparatory Commission is inconsistent with the Statute, the court would appropriately disregard it. Otto Triffterer finds it to be an additional element, and therefore in violation of Article 9.[6]

Deciding whether the "context" element is inconsistent with the Statute will present a certain complexity. Article 6 of the Statute defines genocide without a "context" element. If the International Criminal Court were to say, along with the appeals chamber of the Rwanda and Yugoslavia tribunals, that genocide can be committed by an isolated actor, then it might say that the "context" element violates Article 6. On the other hand, Article 1 of the Statute states that the court is to exercise jurisdiction only for the most serious crimes of international concern, and that the court shall be complementary to domestic courts.[7] Relying on Article 1, the court might say that the Preparatory Commission read the Statute's genocide definition in light of the requirement that the court limit itself to only the most serious cases. Thus, the Preparatory Commission would have carved out of the universe of genocide cases a smaller number to be subject to the court's jurisdiction.

---

4   Clark, R. (2001), 'The Mental Element in International Criminal Law: The Rome Statute of the International Criminal Court and the Elements of Offenses,' *Criminal Law Forum* 12, no. 3, p. 291, p. 326.

5   Ruckert, W., and G. Witschel (2001), 'Genocide and Crimes Against Humanity in the Elements of Crimes,' in H. Fischer, C. Kress and S. Luder (eds), *International and National Prosecution of Crimes Under International Law*, p. 59, p. 66, Berlin Verlag, Berlin.

6   Triffterer, O. (2001), 'Genocide, Its Particular Intent to Destroy in Whole or in Part the Group as Such,' *Leiden Journal of International Law* 14, p. 399, p. 407.

7   Statute of the International Criminal Court, art. 1, UN Doc. A/CONF.183/9, 17 July 1998, *International Legal Materials* 37, p. 999 (1998).

Ambiguity of the "Context" Element

Even if the International Criminal Court decides to consider the "context" requirement valid, it may have difficulty applying it. The definition, unfortunately, is far from clear. Even though the proposed definition characterizes "manifest" as "an objective qualification," it addresses the question of whether the actor must know by stating: "the appropriate requirement, if any, for a mental element regarding this circumstance will need to be decided by the Court on a case-by-case basis."[8] This requirement of a mental element contradicts the characterization of the context requirement as an "objective qualification." Moreover, it violates the basic principle of penal law that the law should be decided in advance, by a legislative body, and not *ad hoc* by a court trying a person brought before it.[9]

The requirement of acting within a "context" is in any event quite vague. The term implies that some activity is already being directed against the protected group, but the proposed definition states, as indicated, that it includes "the initial acts in an emerging pattern." Hence, no pattern is actually required at the time of the actor's conduct. "Delegations agreed," wrote analysts, "that, especially given the particular danger and gravity of an initial act ('igniting the genocide'), the perpetrator should not go free due to the fact that there cannot be any genocidal context for the first act."[10]

The provision for a mental element is equally complicated and would further render the definition meaningless. The provision states, as indicated, that the question of whether there is an accompanying mental element for this circumstance is to be decided on a case-by-case basis. That would mean that a court trying a case is to decide whether there is a requirement that the actor be aware of the "context." It violates the concept of trying persons only for crimes previously defined by law, to let the court trying a case determine an offense element. There either should, or should not be, a mental element for this circumstance.

Grades of Genocide

The view of at least some members of the Preparatory Commission that genocide not involving a pattern of atrocities be left for domestic prosecution recalls a 1951 proposal for two "grades" of genocide. The Spanish jurist Adolfo Miaja de la Muela suggested two grades for punishment purposes. He said that genocide may consist either of acts by an isolated actor, or of acts pursuant to a master plan of a state or

---

8   Preparatory Commission for the International Criminal Court, *Finalized draft text of the Elements of Crimes*, 2 November 2000, art. 6, UN Doc. PCNICC/2000/1/Add.2 (2000), confirmed by Assembly of States Parties to the Rome Statute of the International Criminal Court, *Official Records*, 1st sess., 3-10 September 2002, p. 113, UN Doc. ICC-ASP/1/3 (2002).

9   Triffterer (2001), p. 407.

10   Ruckert and Witschel (2001), p. 66.

other organization. Although the Genocide Convention, he wrote, did not require "a genocide committed *en masse*," it

> would have been especially desirable in the case of genocide to differentiate premeditated, even scientifically developed acts of the type our generation has known, from impulsive acts, even if brutal, that, at any time period, people of the masses have perpetrated, being deranged in their moral sense, under impulse of whatever type of fanaticism. Even when persons who are part of the masses have a genocidal intent, that is, to destroy the persecuted group, the moral profile of these people of the masses is obviously different from those who have made satanic genocidal plans and have used the force that political power affords in order to implement them.
>
> Also, this defect—quite serious from the human viewpoint—appears attenuated in a Convention that, by not fixing penalties for the acts rendered culpable, allows a broad discretion to the tribunals that are to apply it. In any event, there is [in the Convention] no scale of circumstances aggravating or mitigating penal responsibility that would provide a tribunal a guide to judge one set of facts or another with different severity.[11]

Miaja de la Muela read the Genocide Convention to cover any individual who commits one of the acts listed in the sub-paragraphs of Article II with genocidal intent, and suggested distinguishing between such a person and one who devised a plan to destroy a given population group and is able to use a state or an organ of similar strength to implement that plan. Miaja de la Muela thought that a Hitler deserved greater punishment than an isolated actor.

The Genocide Convention left the penalty issue open, for resolution by individual states, or by such international tribunals as might gain jurisdiction to try for genocide. To date, no grading along the lines suggested by Miaja de la Muela has been attempted, either by states, or by international tribunals. Judges, however, might well take this circumstance into account in sentencing a particular defendant.

---

11 Miaja de la Muela, A. (1951-52), 'El genocidio, delito internacional,' *Revista española de derecho internacional* 4, p. 363 pp. 382-383.

Chapter 26

Local Genocide

Some genocide indictments have involved conduct in a single town. In the Rwanda and Yugoslavia tribunals, a number of those prosecuted have been local officials, whose conduct was confined to their locality. Some of these defendants have objected that their intent ran at most to only a small fraction of the entire membership of the group, and therefore that they did not intend to destroy the group. As we saw in Chapter 20, there is no unanimity on the meaning of "in part" as it appears in Article II. If "in part" means, as some suggest, a substantial part, and if a group inhabits more than one locality, then an official whose conduct is limited to one locality might not entertain an intent that runs to enough of the group to constitute genocide.

Nonetheless, the Rwanda and Yugoslavia tribunals have readily entered convictions when the acts were limited to a small geographic area.[1] Jean-Paul Akayesu was mayor of a town, and the acts alleged against him all related to Tutsi in that single town, yet the trial chamber convicted.[2]

Despite consistently convicting on such facts, the trial chambers have not been consistent in how they have characterized the actor's intent, as regards the scope of the group intended to be destroyed. If an actor acted against victims in a locality only, one may say that he intended to destroy only those members of the protected group of that locality. Applying Article II, Alicia Gil Gil says that the actor intends to destroy a part of the group, and on this basis has the intent required by Article II.[3] Nehemiah Robinson, similarly, says that an actor who intends to destroy group members in a locality only would intend to destroy the group "in part." Genocide is committed, he said, even if the persons intended to be destroyed "constitute only part of a group either within a country or within a region or within a single community, provided the number is substantial."[4]

Another possible analysis is that the actor intends to destroy the group generally but victimizes only those to whom he has access. Whatever evidence may be found of the actor's intent likely pertains to the group generally. For example, if there is

1 Zimmermann, A. (1998), 'The Creation of a Permanent International Criminal Court,' *Max Planck Yearbook of United Nations Law* 2, p. 169, p. 172.

2 Prosecutor v. Akayesu, Case No. ICTR-96-4-T, Judgment, 2 September 1998, paras. 3-23.

3 Gil Gil, A. (1999), *Derecho Penal Internacional: Especial Consideración del Delito de Genocidio*, p. 182, Editorial Tecnos, Madrid.

4 Robinson, N. (1960), *The Genocide Convention: A Commentary*, p. 63, Institute of Jewish Affairs, New York.

evidence of derogatory references by the actor, they are likely to be references to group members generally, not to those in a particular locality only. If one takes this approach, one would say that the actor intended to destroy the group in its entirety, even though his acts were limited geographically.

Intent to Destroy Only in a Locality

In the Yugoslavia tribunal, the Nikolic trial chamber approved an indictment that charged an intent to destroy Bosnian Muslims, even though the prosecutor alleged that the actor intended to destroy Bosnian Muslims only in one region of Bosnia.[5] The prosecutor appeared to take the view that Nikolic intended to destroy only a geographically limited segment of the Bosnian Muslims. The Jelisic trial chamber similarly said that genocidal intent may extend to group members in a particular locality only:

> In view of the object and goal of the Convention and the subsequent interpretation thereof, the Trial chamber thus finds that international custom admits the characterisation of genocide even when the exterminatory intent only extends to a limited geographic zone.[6]

The Jelisic trial chamber cited in support a UN General Assembly resolution characterizing as genocide the mass killings at the Sabra and Shatila Palestinian refugee camps in Beirut in September 1982, the killing having been limited to these two camps.[7] Although the General Assembly did not analyze the intent involved, the trial chamber assumed that it was directed only to those Palestinians inhabiting the two camps, who numbered in the thousands, rather than to Palestinians generally, who numbered in the millions.

The killing in the Sabra and Shatila camps was also characterized as genocide, despite the geographical limitation, by the UN Commission on Human Rights. The commission "condemn[ed] in the strongest terms the large-scale massacre of Palestinian civilians in the Sabra and Shatila refugee camps for which the responsibility of the Israeli Government has been established" and "decid[ed] that the massacre was an act of genocide."[8] The commission did not elaborate, to explain whether it regarded the group intended to be destroyed as Palestinians generally, or only those Palestinians in the two refugee camps.

---

5   Prosecutor v. Nikolic, Case No. IT-94-2-R61, Review of Indictment Pursuant to Rule 61, 20 October 1995, para. 34.

6   Prosecutor v. Jelisic, Case No. IT-95-10-T, Judgment, 14 December 1999, para. 83.

7   Prosecutor v. Jelisic, Case No. IT-95-10-T, Judgment, 14 December 1999, para. 83, citing Res. 37/123D, 16 December 1982, para. 2.

8   *The right of peoples to self-determination and its application to peoples under colonial or alien domination or foreign occupation*, Commission on Human Rights, Res. 1983/3, 15 February 1983, UN ECOSOCOR, Supp. (No. 3), p. 118, UN Doc. E/1983/13, E/CN.4/1983/60 (1983).

Germany's Constitutional Court, in reviewing a conviction for genocide against a Bosnian Serb for ethnic cleansing in Bosnia, said that the element of intent to destroy could be satisfied by proof of intent to destroy persons in a limited geographic area. The court appeared to take the genocidal intent as running only to the Bosnian Muslims inhabiting the locality.[9]

In 1982, as noted in Chapter 18, Israel characterized as genocide acts by Iraq in a town near Baghdad. Israeli UN ambassador Yehuda Blum said that Iraq had committed genocide, when Iraqi authorities went from house to house killing about 150 inhabitants. The targeted group, according to Israel's accusation, was the population of the town.[10] Iraq denied the allegation generally and did not give a reply referring to the elements of genocide. Irrespective of what actually may have occurred, the charge reflected Israel's understanding that acts directed against the population of a single town may constitute genocide.

Intent to Destroy a Group Generally

In the Milosevic case, a trial chamber of the Yugoslavia tribunal, ruling on a motion to dismiss after conclusion of the prosecution case, found that the prosecution had presented evidence that Milosevic shared with others an "intent to destroy a part of the Bosnian Muslims as a group in that part of the territory of Bosnia and Herzegovina which it was planned to include in the Serbian state."[11]

The most detailed analysis of the issue, however, came in the Krstic case. Krstic commanded the Bosnian Serb force in the town of Srebrenica in 1995, and those forces, the trial chamber found, executed 7,500 persons. Krstic's command responsibility extended only to that geographic area. He was charged with no acts outside that locality.

The trial chamber was hard pressed to identify which Bosnian Muslims Krstic intended to destroy. So too was the prosecutor, who characterized the group at different times in three different ways. The trial chamber chided the prosecutor:

> Whereas the indictment in this case defined the targeted group as the Bosnian Muslims, the Prosecution appeared to use an alternative definition in its pre-trial brief by pleading the intention to eliminate the "Bosnian Muslim population of Srebrenica" through mass killing and deportation. In its final trial brief, the Prosecution chose to define the group as the Bosnian

---

9 Case of Jorgic, Bundesverfassungsgericht, 12 December 2000, 2 BvR 1290/99, Absatz-Nr. (1-49), para. 20.

10 UN GAOR, 37th sess., 108th plenary meeting, 16 December 1982, p. 1832, UN Doc. A/37/PV.108 (1986).

11 Prosecutor v. Milosevic, Case No. IT-02-54-T, Decision on Motion for Judgment of Acquittal, 15 June 2004, para. 288.

Muslims of Srebrenica, while it referred to the Bosnian Muslims of Eastern Bosnia in its final arguments.[12]

The prosecution thus identified the group variously as Bosnian Muslims, Bosnian Muslims of Srebrenica, and Bosnian Muslims of eastern Bosnia.

Krstic's attorneys took a more consistent position. They argued "that the Bosnian Muslims of Srebrenica did not form a specific national, ethnical, racial or religious group," and that "one cannot create an artificial 'group' by limiting its scope to a geographical area."[13] Krstic's attorneys contended that "part" means "substantial" part, and that the 7,500 killed were not a substantial part of the 40,000 Bosnian Muslims then inhabiting Srebrenica, if one were to confine the intent to that local group, and even less a substantial part of the 1.4 million Muslims in Bosnia.[14]

The trial chamber decided that the relevant group was Bosnian Muslims. It said that the protected group "must be defined, in the present case, as the Bosnian Muslims. The Bosnian Muslims of Srebrenica or the Bosnian Muslims of Eastern Bosnia constitute a part of the protected group."[15]

The trial chamber did not specifically address the defense contention that the part intended to be destroyed must be a substantial part. However, in finding Krstic guilty, it deemed the Bosnian Muslims of Srebrenica to be a part of the Bosnian Muslims and implicitly accepted that 40,000 was "part" of 1.4 million. Thus, the number in Srebrenica constituted less than 3 per cent of the total number of Bosnian Muslims.

The appeals chamber, in approving the trial chamber's analysis, acknowledged that the Bosnian Muslims of Srebrenica amounted to only 2.9 per cent of the Muslims of Bosnia. But it said that "part" is determined not only by numbers: "Although this population constituted only a small percentage of the overall Muslim population of Bosnia and Herzegovina at the time, the importance of the Muslim community of Srebrenica is not captured solely by its size." The chamber then recited that ridding eastern Bosnia of Muslims was central to the project of creating a Serb-populated area contiguous with Serbia: "Without Srebrenica, the ethnically Serb state of Republica Srpska they sought to create would remain divided into two disconnected parts, and its access to Serbia proper would be disrupted."[16]

By analyzing in this way, the appeals chamber was taking an approach similar to that we will see in the next chapter, relating to the targeting of leadership. If the targeting of a small number that is viewed as critical to a group's survival can qualify as genocidal intent, then one must doubt if the destruction is a physical destruction.

---

12 Prosecutor v. Krstic, Case No. IT-98-33-T, Judgment, 2 August 2001, para. 558 (citations to prosecution submissions omitted).

13 Ibid., para. 558 (citations to defense submissions omitted).

14 Ibid., para. 593.

15 Ibid., para. 560.

16 Prosecutor v. Krstic, Case No. IT-98-33-A, Judgment, 19 April 2004, para. 15.

The appeals chamber in the Krstic case further relied on what one might call the moral significance of the Bosnian Muslim population of Srebrenica as a factor showing that, although a small part, it was a substantial part: "Srebrenica was important due to its prominence in the eyes of both the Bosnian Muslims and the international community. The town of Srebrenica was the most visible of the 'safe areas' established by the UN Security Council in Bosnia. By 1995 it had received significant attention in the international media." A guarantee of protection for the Muslims of Srebrenica, moreover, had been given by the UN Protection Force, such that "[t]he elimination of the Muslim population of Srebrenica ... would serve as a potent example to all Bosnian Muslims of their vulnerability and defenselessness in the face of Serb military forces."[17]

The appeals chamber did not elaborate further, but it was following an approach that departs from the quantitative. It was admitting that the 3 per cent was not "substantial," but nonetheless the 3 per cent qualified as a "part" of the Bosnian Muslims. This analysis reveals perhaps the futility of importing a substantiality requirement. Had the media not focused on Srebrenica, had the UN not declared it a "safe area," the targeting of the Bosnian Muslims of Srebrenica would seem no less to be the targeting of a "part" of the Bosnian Muslims.

"Part" as a "Distinct" Part

The Krstic trial chamber, deciding that a local segment of a larger group may constitute a "part" of a group, added one additional qualification, namely that the part must be a "distinct" part, at least in the subjective perception of the actor:

> [T]he intent to destroy a group, even if only in part, means seeking to destroy a distinct part of the group as opposed to an accumulation of isolated individuals within it. Although the perpetrators of genocide need not seek to destroy the entire group protected by the Convention, they must view the part of the group they wish to destroy as a distinct entity which must be eliminated as such. A campaign resulting in the killings, in different places spread over a broad geographical area, of a finite number of members of a protected group might not thus qualify as genocide, despite the high total number of casualties, because it would not show an intent by the perpetrators to target the very existence of the group as such. Conversely, the killing of all members of the part of a group located within a small geographical area, although resulting in a lesser number of victims, would qualify as genocide if carried out with the intent to destroy the part of the group as such located in this small geographical area. Indeed, the physical destruction may target only a part of the geographically limited part of the larger group because the perpetrators of the genocide regard the intended destruction as sufficient to annihilate the group as a distinct entity in the geographic area at issue.[18]

In this section of its analysis, the trial chamber did not mention the fact, though mentioned elsewhere in its Judgment, that the 40,000 Bosnian Muslims who

---

17 Ibid., para. 16.

18 Prosecutor v. Krstic, Case No. IT-98-33-T, Judgment, 2 August 2001, para. 590.

inhabited the Srebrenica area before the killings and deportation of 1995 were not permanent residents of Srebrenica. As the trial chamber well knew, Srebrenica had been designated a "safe area" by the United Nations and thus was temporary home to Bosnian Muslims from a wide sector of Bosnia who were fearful of remaining in their home areas. To this extent, one wonders how the trial chamber could characterize the Bosnian Muslims of Srebrenica as a "distinct part" of the Bosnian Muslims, rather than as "an accumulation of isolated individuals." One wonders whether the trial chamber would have considered Krstic guilty of genocide if the Bosnian Serb army had intercepted and deported these refugees as they were entering Srebrenica from their home areas, but before they had taken up temporary residence there.

A distinction between the two situations hardly seems warranted. The Krstic trial chamber's effort to limit "part" to "distinct part" is fraught with difficulty of application. The trial chamber thinks it less likely that one who targets group members across a broad geographical area intends to destroy the group. In principle, however, as suggested in Chapter 20, one who targets group members in small numbers across a broad geographical area may nonetheless harbor the intent to destroy the group.

Chapter 27

Targeting Important Persons

Allegations of genocide have been made for violence not against group members generally, but against only a sub-group, such as the group's political leadership, intelligentsia, or military. Two levels of intent are possible. The actor may intend to destroy only the sub-group, or may intend to destroy the sub-group as a means towards destroying the entirety of the group. An actor who directs intent only at a sub-group arguably does not intend to destroy the group "as such." On the other hand, the sub-group could be viewed as a part of the group, leading to culpability for an intent to destroy the group "in part."

Leaders or Intellectuals as a Sub-group

The sub-group that has figured most prominently in genocide allegations is the political leadership stratum. Albin Eser wrote that acts against the leadership with intent to destroy it may constitute genocide: "A group can also be destroyed (in part) if the leadership is eliminated."[1] Hans-Heinrich Jescheck argued that a group could be destroyed by the elimination of its leadership, at least if the group's cohesiveness would be jeopardized. Jescheck read the term "destroy" to extend beyond biological or physical destruction. Jescheck wrote "that the general subjective unlawful element of genocide is construed in the broad sense and includes as well the destruction of the group as a social entity in its particularity, so that an intent to eliminate the leadership of a group without exterminating the broader masses of the group would also suffice."[2]

The German Constitutional Court read the German penal code's genocide provision in this way, viewing it as protecting the social existence of the group. "The text of the law," it said in the Jorgic case, "does not therefore compel the interpretation that the culprit's intent must be to exterminate physically at least a substantial number of the members of the group."[3] Taking up Jescheck's analysis that an intent

---

1   Eser, A. (1997), in A. Schönke and H. Schröder (eds), *Strafgesetzbuch: Kommentar,* p. 1597, C.H. Beck'sche Verlagsbuchhandlung, Munich.

2   Jescheck, H.-H. (1954), 'Die internationale Genocidium-Konvention vom 9. Dezember 1948 und die Lehre vom Völkerstrafrecht,' *Zeitschrift für die gesamte Strafrechtswissenschaft,* p. 193, p. 213.

3   Case of Jorgic, Bundesverfassungsgericht, 12 December 2000, 2 BvR 1290/99, Absatz-Nr. (1-49), para. 3(4)(a)(aa).

to destroy a group encompasses its destruction as a social unit, the court said that the intent must be directed at "the destruction of the group, or of a geographically limited part of the group, as a distinct social unit, and is not necessarily confined to its physical or biological elimination." Giving examples of how a group may be destroyed as a social unit, the court said that this could be accomplished by acts not specified in the genocide provision itself. "Possible additional means," it said, "may be incarceration in inhumane conditions, destruction or plundering of houses or of buildings important for the group, or expulsion of members of the group."[4]

Some genocide charges have involved allegations of targeting a group's intellectuals, as a sub-group that was viewed as a threat to government policy. President Macias was accused of killing the intellectuals of Equatorial Guinea, apparently because of the potential they held for opposing his polices, and his tenure as president. In Cambodia, the Khmer Rouge leaders Pol Pot and Ieng Sary were accused of killing Khmer intellectuals, because of the potential they held for opposing the reform of society envisioned by the Khmer Rouge.

The leadership or intellectuals, in a literal sense, are "part" of the group. If the aim of the Genocide Convention is to protect the enumerated groups, however, such actors do not intend to destroy them. The issue of motive may be relevant. If the Genocide Convention requires something like race hatred, then one who intends to kill only the leadership or intellectuals is not guilty. However, as we saw in Chapter 18, a hate motive is not needed, so that one who intends to kill the leadership may well violate Article II.

A factual question may remain in these examples as to whether the actors intended to destroy only the intellectuals, or whether they killed intellectuals as a way of destroying the group. An intent to destroy the group is probably clearer for Cambodia, where the Khmer Rouge sought to break down the society in order to reconstitute it according to new principles, than for Equatorial Guinea, where Macias simply sought to protect his own tenure by eliminating opposition intellectuals.

Leadership elements or intellectuals may be targeted because they have particular importance for the group, and their elimination may destroy the group. This latter possibility has been posited in several cases decided by the Yugoslavia tribunal. The Jelisic trial chamber, although it acquitted Jelisic, found a possibility of establishing an intent to destroy in situations in which the actor's victims are from the leadership only. The Jelisic trial chamber cited an example given by a Commission of Experts appointed by the UN Security Council to analyze the situation in Bosnia:

> The Commission of Experts specified that "[i]f essentially the total leadership of a group is targeted, it could also amount to genocide. Such leadership includes political and administrative leaders, religious leaders, academics and intellectuals, business leaders and others – the totality per se may be a strong indication of genocide regardless of the actual numbers killed. A corroborating argument will be the fate of the rest of the group. The character of the attack on the leadership must be viewed in the context of the fate or what happened to the rest of the group. If a group has its leadership exterminated, and at the same time or in the wake of that,

---

4   Ibid., para. 20.

has a relatively large number of the members of the group killed or subjected to other heinous acts, for example deported on a large scale or forced to flee, the cluster of violations ought to be considered in its entirety in order to interpret the provisions of the Convention in a spirit consistent with its purpose."[5]

On that basis, the Jelisic trial chamber concluded:

Genocidal intent may therefore be manifest in two forms. It may consist of desiring the extermination of a very large number of the members of the group, in which case it would constitute an intention to destroy a group en masse. However, it may also consist of the desired destruction of a more limited number of persons selected for the impact that their disappearance would have upon the survival of the group as such. This would then constitute an intention to destroy the group "selectively."[6]

On this analysis, the actor selects individual victims on the rationale that their elimination will destroy the group. The actor's intent to destroy runs to the entire group, and the means chosen for destroying the group is to destroy the leadership stratum. One would not say that the actor intends to destroy the group only in part. The actor intends to destroy the entire group, and victimizing the leadership is a means to that end.

The Yugoslavia tribunal's appeals chamber lent support to this analysis. In the Krstic case, it said that targeting a particular sub-group might suffice for genocidal intent. The numbers of the targeted portion, it said, need not be high if the loss of that portion threatens the group as a whole: "In addition to the numeric size of the targeted portion, its prominence within the group can be a useful consideration. If a specific part of the group is emblematic of the overall group, or is essential to its survival, that may support a finding that the part qualifies as substantial within the meaning of Article 4."[7]

Soldiers as a Sub-group

Military personnel may constitute a leadership group whose targeting evidences genocidal intent. In the Sikirica case in the Yugoslavia tribunal, the prosecution asked the trial chamber to view Bosnian Muslims who had taken an active role in defending their villages from Bosnian Serb attack as a leadership group. The trial chamber refused, saying that to do so "would necessarily involve a definition of leadership so elastic as to be meaningless." The trial chamber seemed concerned as

---

5 Prosecutor v. Jelisic, Case No. IT-95-10, Judgment, 14 December 1999, para. 82, quoting *Final Report of the Commission of Experts established pursuant to Security Council resolution 780*, para. 94, UN Doc. S/1994/674 (1994).

6 Prosecutor v. Jelisic, Case No. IT-95-10-T, Judgment, 14 December 1999, para. 82.

7 Prosecutor v. Krstic, Case No. IT-98-33-A, Judgment, 19 April 2004, para. 12.

well that the number of such persons victimized was too low to "have a significant impact on the survival of the Muslim population."[8]

The issue surfaced as well in the Krstic prosecution. At Srebrenica, the troops commanded by Krstic killed nearly all the males of military age among the Bosnian Muslims they found there, while forcibly evacuating the rest of the population. The defense argued that the aim of the killing was simply to eliminate the possibility of military resistance from the Bosnian Muslims. The killing thus bespoke no intent against the Bosnian Muslims as a group. According to Krstic's attorneys, "had the VRS [the Bosnian Serb military of which Krstic was commander at Srebrenica] actually intended to destroy the Bosnian Muslim community of Srebrenica, it would have killed all the women and children, who were powerless and already under its control, rather than undertaking the time and manpower consuming task of searching out and eliminating the men of the column." Krstic's lawyers argued "that the VRS forces intended to kill solely all potential fighters in order to eliminate any future military threat. The wounded men were spared."[9]

Krstic's prosecutor, to the contrary, took the killing of the males of military age in the context of the forcible evacuation of the rest of the population as indicating an intent to destroy the group. The prosecutor argued that "by killing the leaders and defenders of the group and deporting the remainder of it, ... General Krstic had assured that the Bosnian Muslim community of Srebrenica and its surrounds would not return to Srebrenica nor would it reconstitute itself in that region or indeed, anywhere else."[10] The trial chamber accepted the prosecutor's view. It said that the wounded had been spared "only because of the presence of UNPROFOR [UN military force]," a suggestion by the trial chamber that the VRS would have killed the wounded but was deterred by the UN presence.[11]

The Krstic trial chamber in its analysis connected the two facts of the killing of military-age males and the deportation of the rest, viewing the deportation as an indication that the killing of the military-age males bespoke an intent to destroy, as argued by the prosecution, rather than simply an intent to gain a military advantage, as argued by the defense. Here the Krstic trial chamber followed the lead of the Jelisic trial chamber, quoting the work of the Commission of Experts appointed by the UN Security Council who analyzed Bosnia. The Krstic trial chamber said that the commission's report:

> considered that an intent to destroy a specific part of a group, such as its political, administrative, intellectual or business leaders, "may be a strong indication of genocide regardless of the actual numbers killed." The report states that extermination specifically directed against law enforcement and military personnel may affect "a significant section of a group in that it renders the group at large defenceless against other abuses of a similar or other nature."

---

8 Prosecutor v. Sikirica, Case No. IT-95-8, Judgment on Defence Motions to Acquit, 3 September 2001, paras. 80-81.

9 Prosecutor v. Krstic, Case No. IT-98-33-T, Judgment, 2 August 2001, para. 593.

10 Ibid., para. 592.

11 Ibid., para. 594.

However, the Report goes on to say that "the attack on the leadership must be viewed in the context of the fate of what happened to the rest of the group. If a group suffers extermination of its leadership and in the wake of that loss, a large number of its members are killed or subjected to other heinous acts, for example deportation, the cluster of violations ought to be considered in its entirety in order to interpret the provisions of the [Genocide] Convention in a spirit consistent with its purpose."[12]

The trial chamber applied this analysis to Srebrenica, taking the deportation as an indication that the killing of the military-age males was done with the intent to destroy the group.

The Krstic prosecution, as we saw in Chapter 26, involved action in one locality only. Thus, Krstic's victims were part of a part of the Bosnian Muslims. Nonetheless, the trial chamber's analysis seems appropriate. The trial chamber viewed the Bosnian Muslims of Srebrenica as a "part" of the Bosnian Muslims and then found an intent to destroy that part by the killing of the military-age males. The appeals chamber accepted this aspect of the trial chamber's analysis.[13]

---

12 Ibid., para. 587, citing *Final Report of the Commission of Experts established pursuant to Security Council resolution 780*, para. 94, UN Doc. S/1994/674 (1994).

13 Prosecutor v. Krstic, Case No. IT-98-33-A, Judgment, 19 April 2004, para. 20.

Chapter 28

Targeting Political Opponents

Political opponents of a government have frequently been the target of repression. Although early drafts of the Genocide Convention included political groups in the list of types of groups protected, the final text omitted them. One contention against including political groups was that their membership is changeable.[1] Nonetheless, as we saw in Chapter 3, a number of states included political groups in their genocide provisions. As we saw in Chapter 6, genocide has been charged with political opponents as the victims.

Political Groups as a Sub-group

The case that has yielded the most extensive judicial analysis of the issue of political groups was initiated in Spain. Criminal charges were instituted against Argentinean and Chilean military officers for atrocities committed in Argentina and Chile during the 1970s and 1980s. The context of the events was the so-called "dirty war" against domestic insurgencies, and the alleged victims of genocide were persons who had opposed the government.

In 1996, formal charges of genocide were issued against these officers for detaining and secretly killing, or, in the parlance of the era, "forcibly disappearing" them. In 1998, the judicial orders issued in these two cases were appealed to the Supreme Court of Spain. The accused argued that even if the allegations of fact were true, they had not committed genocide, because the groups allegedly targeted were not national, ethnical, racial, or religious. They said that the allegations showed repression that was politically motivated.

The Supreme Court of Spain disagreed and found the genocide charges proper.[2] Spain's genocide provision, as we saw in Chapter 3, mirrors Article II in the enumeration of types of groups protected and thus omits "political" groups. The

---

1   UN GAOR, 3rd sess., Part 1, *Summary Records of Meetings 21 September - 10 December 1948*, p. 19, UN Doc. A/C.6/SR.64 (Mr. Lachs, Poland). UN GAOR, 3rd sess., Part 1, *Summary Records of Meetings 21 September - 10 December 1948*, p. 57, UN Doc. A/C.6/SR.69 (Mr. Amado, Brazil).

2   Auto de la Sala de lo Penal de la Audiencia Nacional confirmando la jurisdicción de España para conocer de los crímenes de genocidio y terrorismo cometidos durante la dictadura argentina, Spain, Supreme Court, Criminal Chamber, 4 November 1998. Auto de la Sala de lo Penal de la Audiencia Nacional confirmando la jurisdicción de España para conocer de los

Supreme Court found the victims to fall within a "national" group. Regarding the Argentina charges, the court said that the victims comprised "a group of Argentineans or residents of Argentina capable of being distinguished and that, doubtless, was distinguished by the practitioners of persecution and harassment." This group, said the court, was "a definite sector of the population, a group quite heterogeneous, but distinguishable." The group consisted, the court said, of "those citizens who were not of the type contemplated by the promoters of the repression as appropriate to the new order to be instituted in the country. It included citizens opposed to the regime, but as well citizens who were indifferent to the regime."[3]

Referring to the purpose of the Genocide Convention, the Supreme Court of Spain said that the expressed need to prevent and punish genocide

> requires that the term "national group" not mean "a group comprising persons who belong to one nation," but, simply, a national human group, a distinguishable human group characterized by something, and which is a segment of a larger collectivity. The restrictive interpretation of the elements of genocide proposed by the appellants would preclude characterizing as genocide acts so odious as the systematic elimination, by a government or by a faction, of AIDS sufferers as a distinguishable group, or of the elderly, also as a distinguishable group, or of foreigners residing in a country, who, despite being of different nationalities, can be taken to be a national group in relation to the country in which they are living, distinguishable precisely for not being nationals of that state. This social conception of genocide, as felt, as understood by society, and on which its rejection of and horror at the crime is based, would not allow exclusion of the groups indicated [AIDS sufferers, the elderly, foreigners - J.Q.].[4]

The victims, said the court, "made up a distinguishable group within the nation."[5]

Destruction of a Sub-group

Predictably, the court drew criticism for its focus on a sub-group within a group of the type listed in Article II. Alicia Gil Gil said that the accused lacked an intent to destroy the nationals of Argentina.[6] Basing her view on the phrase "as such" in the genocide definition, Gil Gil said that intending to destroy only those Argentine nationals of a given political persuasion did not amount to intending to destroy

---

crímenes de genocidio y terrorismo cometidos durante la dictadura chilena, Spain, Supreme Court, Criminal Chamber, 5 November 1998; both accessible at www.derechos.org/nizkor.

3 Auto de la Sala de lo Penal de la Audiencia Nacional confirmando la jurisdicción de España para conocer de los crímenes de genocidio y terrorismo cometidos durante la dictadura argentina, Spain, Supreme Court, Criminal Chamber, 4 November 1998, para. 5, accessible at www.derechos.org/nizkor.

4 Ibid., para. 5.

5 Ibid., para. 5.

6 Gil Gil, A. (1999), *Derecho Penal Internacional: Especial Consideración del Delito de Genocidio*, p. 185, Editorial Tecnos, Madrid.

Argentine nationals.[7] The Supreme Court of Spain, she wrote, "confuses crimes against humanity with genocide."[8] With crimes against humanity, as we saw in Chapter 2, the target may be any civilian population.

Gil Gil appropriately criticized the Supreme Court of Spain for resorting to a "social" understanding of genocide: "If by 'social concept' is meant a non-legal or popular concept of genocide, the argument is surprising."[9] An understanding of genocide not found in the text cannot be used to construe the text.

The Supreme Court of Spain might have used other modes of analysis to reach its conclusion. It might have tried, as the Akayesu trial chamber tentatively did, to expand beyond the four types of groups listed. The court might have tried to discover a definition of genocide in customary law that would include political groups. Genocide is generally understood to be prohibited by customary law, even apart from the Genocide Convention, and, by one view, political groups are protected under the customary law definition of genocide.[10] Political groups and "other" groups were included by the UN General Assembly in a 1947 resolution declaring genocide to be a crime under international law. "Many instances," read the resolution, "of such crimes of genocide have occurred when racial, religious, political, and other groups have been destroyed, entirely or in part."[11] Still another approach would have been to rely on the phrase "in part" in the genocide definition. That phrase does not figure in the court's analysis. The court could have said that the group it identified was "part" of the larger group of nationals of Argentina. Genocide does not require intending to destroy the entirety of one of the types of groups listed. The court could have said that a distinguishable sub-group is "part" of a group.

These three possible modes of analysis all run the risk of expanding the definition of genocide beyond what was intended, in particular in light of the rule of lenity that cautions prudence in construing penal legislation. An analysis based on the "in part" language would be the strongest of the three. Article II does not require the "part" to be a particular kind of part. As we saw in Chapter 26, courts have found group members inhabiting a particular locality to be a "part" of a group. Other courts have found leadership elements, or intellectuals, or potential soldiers can be a "part," as we saw in Chapter 27. The logic of finding genocidal intent in the targeting of such sub-groups is strongest when the group holds a particular importance for a society, so that its elimination will harm the group as a whole. With political opponents, that logic holds.

---

7   Ibid., pp. 182-183.

8   Ibid., p. 187.

9   Ibid., p. 187.

10   Van Schaack, B. (1997), 'The Crime of Political Genocide: Repairing the Genocide Convention's Blind Spot,' *Yale Law Journal* 106, p. 2259.

11   Draft convention on genocide, GA Res. 180, preamble, UN GAOR, 2nd sess., *Resolutions*, p. 129, UN Doc. A/519 (1948).

PART SEVEN
TECHNIQUES OF GENOCIDE

Chapter 29

Ethnic Cleansing and Genocidal Intent

Genocide has been alleged to be committed by a variety of techniques. The individuals or states cited have typically denied genocidal intent, even if their acts could fall within the sub-paragraphs of Article II. Part Seven examines genocidal intent in four situations: ethnic cleansing, destruction of human habitat, aerial bombardment, and nuclear attack.

The term "ethnic cleansing" came into vogue in the 1990s to describe the forced removal of Muslims and Croats in Bosnia. The term does not appear in treaties or statutes. When facts relating to ethnic cleansing have been alleged, other legal categories have been invoked. Forced removal of population, and the degradation that typically accompanies it, may constitute a crime against humanity.

Intent to Expel as Inconsistent with Genocide

Radislav Krstic was convicted for killings committed, as the trial chamber found, less by a desire to see Muslims dead than to see them gone, so that Srebrenica would be left Serb-dominated. Commenting on the Krstic conviction, journalist Georgie Anne Geyer wrote: "The question of the specific and stunning charge of genocide is an interesting one indeed. For no one alleges that all Bosnian Muslims were to be killed."[1] William Schabas, thinking along the same lines, finds the intent behind ethnic cleansing inconsistent with the intent required for genocide. Ethnic cleansing involves "displacing a population in order to change the ethnic composition of a given territory," whereas genocide "is directed at the destruction of the group."[2]

Schabas points out that the District Court of Jerusalem acquitted Adolf Eichmann for acts of expulsion of Jews prior to 1941, when Germany allowed emigration of Jews, but convicted him for acts against Jews after 1941, when Germany no longer let them emigrate.[3] Eichmann was tried under a statute that incorporated most of the elements of genocide. The conclusion Schabas draws is that the Israeli court viewed an intention to expel as inconsistent with the intention required for genocide.

---

1   Geyer, G.A., 'Following orders?; Genocide charges raise complex questions of command responsibility,' *Tulsa World*, 9 August 2001.

2   Schabas, W.A. (2000), *Genocide in International Law: The Crime of Crimes*, pp. 199-200, Cambridge University Press, Cambridge.

3   Ibid., p. 200.

The Eichmann ruling, however, is not quite so clear. The District Court acquitted Eichmann for acts of expulsion prior to 1941, not because an intent to expel was inconsistent with an intent to destroy, but because it could not find evidence that Eichmann understood, before 1941, that the expellees would be killed. The Supreme Court of Israel found that Eichmann organized expulsions "with complete disregard for the health and lives of the deported Jews," and that the death of many Jews resulted. "We have pondered very carefully," the court said, "whether or not the accused foresaw the murderous consequences of these deportations and desired them. But ultimately a doubt remains in our minds whether there was here that specific intention to exterminate, required for proof of a crime against the Jewish people, ..."[4] The implication is that had Eichmann foreseen deaths, he would have been guilty of genocide for organizing expulsions. The Eichmann case thus reflects a view that expulsion is not inconsistent with an intent to destroy.

Expulsion as Viewed During the Drafting

Forced removal was not directly proposed in the Sixth Committee as an act that might constitute genocide, but Syria proposed adding a category as follows: "imposing measures intended to obligate members of a group to abandon their homes in order to escape the threat of subsequent ill-treatment."[5] Syria argued that if destruction of a human group constituted genocide, then a threat of such destruction must as well.[6] Although Syria's proposed language focused on measures imposed on a group, not on forced removal as such, the ensuing debate elicited views on forced removal.

Yugoslavia supported Syria, citing "an instance in which the Nazis had dispersed a Slav majority from a certain part of Yugoslavia in order to establish a German majority there. That action was tantamount to the deliberate destruction of a group. Genocide could be committed by forcing members of a group to abandon their homes."[7]

Disagreeing, the United Kingdom told the Sixth Committee that forced expulsion "did not fall within the definition of genocide."[8] Cuba said that it "did not seem to come within the definition of the crime of genocide, which was, essentially, the destruction of a human group."[9] Egypt abstained on the Syrian proposal, stating that it "went beyond the accepted idea of genocide in that it did not concern the

---

4   Attorney-General of the Government of Israel v. Eichmann, Supreme Court of Israel, 29 May 1962, *International Law Reports* 36, p. 230.

5   UN GAOR, 3rd sess., Part 1, *Summary Records of Meetings 21 September - 10 December 1948*, p. 176, UN Doc. A/C.6/SR/81 (1948).

6   UN GAOR, 3rd sess., Part 1, *Summary Records of Meetings 21 September - 10 December 1948*, p. 187, UN Doc. A/C.6/SR.82 (Mr. Tarazi, Syria).

7   Ibid., p. 184 (Mr. Bartos, Yugoslavia).

8   Ibid., p. 185 (Mr. Fitzmaurice, UK).

9   Ibid., p. 185 (Mr. Dihigo, Cuba).

destruction of human groups. The act referred to in the amendment created displaced persons."[10]

Several states that opposed the proposal acknowledged the possibility of links between forced expulsion and genocide. The USSR said that the proposal fell outside the scope of the definition of genocide, but it hastened to say that forced migration might be a consequence of the commission of genocide, since people might flee because of the commission of genocide.[11]

The United States said that the proposal "deviated too much from the original concept of genocide"[12] but left it unclear whether it opposed including forced removal as a form of genocide, or whether it found Syria's particular language inadequate. It said that "[t]he wording of the Syrian amendment was too indefinite to allow of strict interpretation: for example, the time factor came into play in the term 'subsequent ill treatment'."[13] The US view thus implied that if a demand were made to depart under threat of immediate harm, genocide might be present.

The Syrian proposal was defeated 29 votes to 5 with 8 abstentions.[14] As a result, no language about expulsion appears in Article II. Schabas asserts that the drafters could not have contemplated that expulsion might constitute genocide, because, he says, the use of force or intimidation to terrorize a population to flight was not understood to be a human rights violation until "the late twentieth century."[15] To support his thesis that ethnic cleansing was not unlawful at mid-century, Schabas recounts a 1952 discussion of the legality of ethnic cleansing at the Institute of International Law. Schabas states that the Institute's rapporteur on the issue found ethnic cleansing consistent with international law.[16] In fact, the rapporteur said that the Universal Declaration of Human Rights "excludes rather clearly any form of pressure or threat to convince a population to abandon the territory on which it is located. And more generally," he continued, "modern international law forbids any forced transfer."[17] The Universal Declaration of Human Rights, which was adopted by the UN General Assembly within days of the Genocide Convention, guarantees a right to return to one's country, a proposition that effectively forbids

---

10 Ibid., p. 186 (Mr. Raafat, Egypt).

11 Ibid., p. 185 (Mr. Morozov, USSR).

12 Ibid., p. 185 (Mr. Maktos, USA).

13 Ibid., p. 187 (Mr. Maktos, USA).

14 Ibid., p. 186.

15 Schabas (2000), p. 195.

16 Ibid., pp. 195-196.

17 'Rapport présenté par M. Giorgio Balladore Pallieri,' *Annuaire de l'institut de droit international* 44(2), p. 138, p. 146 (1952).

forced removal.[18] By mid-century, customary international law prohibited states from expelling population.[19]

The drafters of the Genocide Convention gave no hint that they thought that expulsion was a lawful activity. Even as regards its possible characterization as genocide, the defeated Syrian proposal did not directly address it. Such statements as were made against expulsion as genocide were premised on removal of a population group from one place to another, with no consideration of the circumstances of harm that might be involved. That would not be the case if the consequence of being removed was serious physical harm to the expellees.

Expulsion in More Recent International Practice

The issue of expulsion as genocide has been revisited by subsequent drafters tasked with formulating a genocide definition. They have found that, despite the failure of Syria's proposal, the language the drafters did include in the sub-paragraph acts leaves ample room to characterize expulsion, at least as it has occurred in many circumstances, as genocide. The ILC prepared a Draft Code of Crimes Against the Peace and Security of Mankind and included a provision on genocide, tracking closely Article II of the Genocide Convention. In a commentary, the commission said that its sub-paragraph on creating conditions of life, which was taken *verbatim* from Article II of the Genocide Convention, "covered deportation when carried out with the intent to destroy the group in whole or in part."[20]

The Preparatory Commission for the International Criminal Court also viewed the sub-paragraph on "creating conditions of life" to include forced removal. Breaking genocide down into separate elements, the Commission included:

> Element #4: The conditions of life were calculated to bring about the physical destruction of that group, in whole or in part.[21]

In a note to Element #4, the commission explained that the term "conditions of life" may include "systematic expulsion from homes."[22]

UN organs found genocide to have been committed in Bosnia in the context of ethnic cleansing. The UN General Assembly referred to ethnic cleansing, as practiced

---

18 Universal Declaration of Human Rights, GA Res. 217A, art. 13, para. 2, UN Doc. A/810, p. 71 (1948).

19 Quigley, J. (1997), 'Mass Displacement and the Individual Right of Return,' *British Year Book of International Law* 68, p. 65.

20 Draft Code of Crimes against the Peace and Security of Mankind (commentary), *Report of the International Law Commission on the work of its forty-eighth session 6 May - 26 July 1996*, UN GAOR, 51st sess., Supp. (No. 10), p. 92, UN Doc. A/51/10 (1996).

21 Preparatory Commission for the International Criminal Court, *Finalized draft text of the Elements of Crimes*, 2 November 2000, art. 6, UN Doc. PCNICC/2000/1/Add.2 (2000).

22 Ibid.

in Bosnia, as "a form of genocide."[23] A commission of experts appointed by the UN Security Council to investigate the situation in Bosnia said that acts constituting ethnic cleansing could "fall within the meaning of the Genocide Convention."[24] The UN Commission on Human Rights noted that the states involved in the Bosnia conflict were parties to the Genocide Convention and called on them to fulfill their obligations under the Convention.[25] In another resolution on Bosnia, the Commission called on the states involved to consider "the extent" to which the acts occurring in Bosnia amounted to genocide.[26]

An intent to expel, far from contradicting an intent to destroy a group, may help prove such an intent. An intent to expel individuals belonging to a given group makes it clear that the acts directed against them are undertaken based on the membership of those individuals in the group, and with intent to cause harm to the group. Like other analysts, Lori Damrosch concluded that ethnic cleansing, as carried out in Bosnia in 1991-93, constituted genocide.[27]

The UN Security Council's commission of inquiry on atrocites in the Darfur region of Sudan concluded that Sudan was not responsible for genocide for absence of genocidal intent. It found that Sudan organized killings of "African" villagers to force the villagers to flee. However, the aim was to drive them out "primarily for purposes of counter-insurgency warfare." The commission said that this intent was inconsistent with an intent to destroy the villagers as a group.[28]

---

23 The situation in Bosnia and Herzegovina, GA Res. 47/121, preambular para. 9, 18 December 1992, UN Doc. A/RES/47/121 (1993).

24 Letter dated 9 February 1993 from the Secretary-General addressed to the President of the Security Council, Annex, *Interim Report of the Commission of Experts Established Pursuant to Security Council Resolution 780 (1992)*, 26 January 1993, p. 16, UN Doc. S/25274 (1993).

25 Commission on Human Rights, Res. 1992/S-1/1, para. 10, 14 August 1992, *Report of the Commission on Human Rights on its First Special Session*, UN Doc. E/CN.4/1992/84/ Add.1, E/1992/22/Add.1 (1992).

26 Commission on Human Rights, Res. 1992/S-2/1, para. 12, 3 December 1992, *Report of the Commission on Human Rights on its Second Special Session, Annex* (resolution of Subcommission on Prevention of Discrimination and Protection of Minorities), UN Doc. E/ CN.4/1992/84/Add.2, E/1992/22/Add.2 (1992).

27 Damrosch, L.R. (1998), 'Genocide and Ethnic Conflict,' in D. Wippman (ed.), *International Law and Ethnic Conflict*, p. 256, p. 267 note 37.

28 *Report of the International Commission of Inquiry on Darfur to the United Nations Secretary-General pursuant to Security Council Resolution 1564 of 18 September 2004*, 25 January 2005, para. 518.

Chapter 30

Ethnic Cleansing in the Courts

Whether the activity that has come to be termed ethnic cleansing constitutes genocide has also been considered by courts. In Brazil, as recounted in Chapter 6, the Superior Tribunal of Justice convicted prospectors for genocide. The prospectors killed indigenous Yanomami to remove them from an area. The prospectors killed some Yanomami, to frighten larger numbers to depart. The defendants may not have harbored ill will towards those they killed. They simply wanted them out of the way so that prospecting work might proceed.

The Superior Tribunal found the act to be genocide by focusing on the manner in which the prospectors killed. It stressed that the prospectors killed all the Yanomami they met—men, women and children. They did not choose victims because of any prior interaction with a particular person, hence not on the basis of animus towards a particular individual. The prospectors killed, the court said, solely because the individuals were Yanomami.[1] That circumstance, which allowed a conclusion that the defendants intended to kill Yanomami "as such," was different from the circumstances of the case of Novislav Djajic, which we saw in Chapter 6, in which a German court acquitted of genocide because it found that Djajic killed Bosnian Muslims in revenge for a prior attack. In any event, killing to force the Yanomami out, in the view of the Superior Tribunal, constituted genocide.

Yugoslavia Tribunal

Bosnia, the situation that gave rise to the term "ethnic cleansing," has generated the most copious case law on ethnic cleansing as genocide. As in Brazil, violence was used in Bosnia to set groups to flight. Courts in Germany and Croatia, as we saw in Chapter 6, have convicted of genocide for acts of violence that were part of an ethnic cleansing campaign. They did not find an intent to expel inconsistent with an intent to destroy. A court in Kosovo refused to find genocidal intent on similar facts.

The issue has generated detailed analysis in the Yugoslavia tribunal. A trial chamber of the Yugoslavia tribunal asked a prosecutor to amend the Nikolic indictment to add a count of genocide, because, it said, the acts of ethnic cleansing alleged against Nikolic amounted to genocide:

---

1 Brazil, Superior Tribunal of Justice, Recurso Especial No. 222,653 (Roraima) (1999/0061733-9), 22 May 2001, p. 12.

It emerged on the basis of the record that the policy of discrimination implemented at Vlasenica, of which Dragan Nikolic's acts formed a part, was specifically aimed at "cleansing" the region of its Muslim population. In this instance, the policy of "ethnic cleansing" took the form of discriminatory acts of extreme seriousness which tend to show its genocidal character. For instance, the Chamber notes the statements by some witnesses which point, among other crimes, to mass murders being committed in the region. ... The chamber considers that the Tribunal may possibly have jurisdiction in this case under Article 4 of the Statute [of the International Tribunal, defining genocide in the same way as genocide is defined in the Genocide Convention - J.Q.].[2]

In later indictments, the Yugoslavia tribunal prosecutor charged genocide based on ethnic cleansing. Biljana Plavsic and Momcilo Krajisnik were charged with genocide, on an allegation that they killed, caused serious bodily and mental harm, and detained under conditions calculated to bring about destruction. The indictment stated that Plavsic acted to take over areas of Bosnia, and that, in order to attain this objective, she

> initiated and implemented a course of conduct which included the creation of impossible conditions of life, involving persecution and terror tactics, that would have the effect of encouraging non-Serbs to leave those areas; the deportation of those who were reluctant to leave; and the liquidation of others. By 31 December 1992, this course of conduct resulted in the death or forced departure of a significant portion of the Bosnian Muslim, Bosnian Croat and other non-Serb groups ... [3]

The first genocide conviction in the Yugoslavia tribunal was of Radislav Krstic, for killing several thousand Bosnian males of military age at Srebrenica. Examining the context of the killings, the trial chamber said that Srebrenica was a Bosnian Muslim enclave in territory otherwise predominantly Bosnian Serb, and that the killings were committed

> at a time when the forcible transfer of the rest of the Bosnian Muslim population was well under way. The Bosnian Serb forces could not have failed to know, by the time they decided to kill all the men, that this selective destruction of the group would have a lasting impact upon the entire group. Their death precluded any effective attempt by the Bosnian Muslims to recapture the territory. Furthermore, the Bosnian Serb forces had to be aware of the catastrophic impact that the disappearance of two or three generations of men would have on the survival of a traditionally patriarchal society, an impact the chamber has previously described in detail. The Bosnian Serb forces knew, by the time they decided to kill all of the military aged men, that the combination of those killings with the forcible transfer of the women, children and elderly would inevitably result in the physical disappearance of the Bosnian Muslim population at Srebrenica. Intent by the Bosnian Serb forces to target the Bosnian Muslims of Srebrenica as a group is further evidenced by their destroying homes

---

2   Prosecutor v. Nikolic, Case No. IT-94-2-R61, Review of Indictment Pursuant to Rule 61, 20 October 1995, para. 34.

3   Prosecutor v. Plavsic, Case No. IT-00-40-I, Indictment, 3 April 2000; Prosecutor v. Krajisnik, Case No. IT-00-39-I, Amended Indictment, 21 March 2000.

of Bosnian Muslims in Srebrenica and Potocari and the principal mosque in Srebrenica soon after the attack.[4]

Thus, the aim of the killings, in the trial chamber's analysis, was to facilitate the ethnic cleansing of Srebrenica. The trial chamber's reference to the survival of a traditionally patriarchal society is to evidence that with males in the middle years all dead, it was unlikely that the remainder of the population could re-establish itself in their home areas around Srebrenica.

The trial chamber's factual analysis, however, does not rely on the specifics of Bosnian Muslim society but involves gender roles typical of many societies. The trial chamber said that the women would have difficulty finding employment, and in taking over family businesses, should they attempt a mass return to Srebrenica.[5]

In saying that Krstic's acts would result in "the physical disappearance of the Bosnian Muslim population at Srebrenica," the trial chamber viewed the disappearance of Bosnian Muslims in Srebrenica as destruction of the group. The trial chamber did not require a physical destruction in order to find genocidal intent. Their removal from Srebrenica sufficed.

A contrary view of ethnic cleansing and genocidal intent was taken by another trial chamber of the Yugoslavia tribunal. The Stakic trial chamber found ethnic cleansing inconsistent with genocidal intent: "It does not suffice to deport a group or a part of a group. A clear distinction must be drawn between physical destruction and mere dissolution of a group. The expulsion of a group or a part of a group does not in itself suffice for genocide."[6]

When Krstic's case was taken to the appeals chamber in 2004, that chamber was thus faced with conflicting analyses by two trial chambers. The appeals chamber found that Krstic himself did not undertake the forced removal of population from Srebrenica as a means to killing them, and that he sought to protect those being removed.[7] On the issue of principle, however, the appeals chamber sided with the Krstic trial chamber. "As the trial chamber explained," it said, "forcible transfer could be an additional means by which to ensure the physical destruction of the Bosnian Muslim community in Srebrenica. The transfer completed the removal of all Bosnian Muslims from Srebrenica, thereby eliminating even the residual possibility that the Muslim community in the area could reconstitute itself."[8]

In a passage that reflected a rejection of the approach of the Stakic trial chamber, the appeals chamber said, "The fact that the forcible transfer does not constitute in and of itself a genocidal act does not preclude a Trial Chamber from relying on it as evidence of the intentions of members of the VRS Main Staff. The genocidal

4 Prosecutor v. Krstic, Case No. IT-98-33-T, Judgment, 2 August 2001, para. 595.
5 Prosecutor v. Krstic, Case No. IT-98-33-T, Judgment, 2 August 2001, paras. 90-94.
6 Prosecutor v. Stakic, Case No. IT-97-24-T, Judgment, 31 July 2003, para. 519.
7 Prosecutor v. Krstic, Case No. IT-98-33-A, Judgment, 19 April 2004, para. 132.
8 Ibid., para. 31.

intent may be inferred, among other facts, from evidence of 'other culpable acts systematically directed against the same group'."[9]

When it said that ethnic cleansing was inconsistent with genocidal intent, the Stakic trial chamber had cited in support the ruling of the German Federal High Court in the Kusljic case. According to the trial chamber, the German courts "have found that the expulsion of Bosnian Muslims from the areas in which they lived did not constitute genocide."[10] While expulsion, as we have seen, constitutes a distinct offense as a crime against humanity, the German courts have convicted individual Bosnian Serbs for complicity in genocide as well. The German Federal High Court in fact found Kusljic guilty of complicity in genocide.[11]

International Court of Justice

The ICJ also suggested that ethnic cleansing as practiced in Bosnia may constitute genocide. Bosnia, suing Yugoslavia for genocide for promoting the ethnic cleansing being carried out in Bosnia by Bosnian Serb militias, asked for an injunction against Yugoslavia. The court granted the injunction, calling on Yugoslavia to "take all measures within its power to prevent commission of the crime of genocide." The court stated that Yugoslavia

> should in particular ensure that any military, paramilitary or irregular armed units which may be directed or supported by it, as well as any organizations and persons which may be subject to its control, direction or influence, do not commit any acts of genocide, of conspiracy to commit genocide, of direct and public incitement to commit genocide, or of complicity in genocide, whether directed against the Muslim population of Bosnia and Herzegovina or against any other national, ethnical, racial or religious group.[12]

Although the court did not expressly say that Yugoslavia was perpetrating genocide, Judge Tarassov, who wrote a separate opinion, said that the quoted language was "open to the interpretation that the Court believes that the Government of the Federal Republic of Yugoslavia is indeed involved in such genocidal acts."[13] Writing separately, Judge *ad hoc* Lauterpacht wrote:

---

9 Ibid., para. 33.

10 Prosecutor v. Stakic, Case No. IT-97-24-T, Judgment, 31 July 2003, para. 519, citing Case of Kusljic, Bundesgerichtshof, Third Criminal Chamber, 21 February 2001, 3 StR 244/00, *Neue Juristische Wochenschrift*, Book 37, p. 2732 (2001).

11 Case of Kusljic, Bundesgerichtshof, Third Criminal Chamber, 21 February 2001, 3 StR 244/00, *Neue Juristische Wochenschrift*, Book 37, p. 2732, p. 2734 (2001).

12 Application of the Convention on the Prevention and Punishment of the Crime of Genocide (Bosnia and Herzegovina v. Yugoslavia (Serbia and Montenegro)), Order of 8 April 1993, 1993 ICJ Rep., p. 24.

13 Application of the Convention on the Prevention and Punishment of the Crime of Genocide (Bosnia and Herzegovina v. Yugoslavia (Serbia and Montenegro)), Order of 8 April

[I]t is difficult to regard the Serbian acts as other than acts of genocide in that they clearly fall within categories (a), (b) and (c) of the definition of genocide ..., they are clearly directed against an ethnical or religious group as such, and they are intended to destroy that group, if not in whole certainly in part, to the extent necessary to ensure that that group no longer occupies the parts of Bosnia-Herzegovina coveted by the Serbs.[14]

Expulsion Resulting in Death or Serious Harm

Genocide may be present in a forcible deportation as a result of harm caused in the course of the deportation itself. The trial chamber of the Yugoslavia tribunal that reviewed the Mladic-Karadzic indictment focused on the causing of serious bodily or mental harm as the section of Article II that is violated by ethnic cleansing. The chamber stated, "the causing of serious bodily or mental harm to the member or members of the group or groups occurred through inhumane treatment, torture, rape and deportation."[15] Bodily harm is often caused in the course of expulsions. In many instances of expulsions one would find mental harm, in that the way of life of the expellees is being altered, and they are under compulsion and do not know what violence may be inflicted upon them while they are being forcibly transported.

The Mladic-Karadzic trial chamber was of the view that deporting people might cause bodily or mental harm and thus constitute the act required for genocide. The trial chamber thought that genocidal intent might also be demonstrated by acts of deportation that would result in bodily or mental harm to the deportees.

Forced removal may as well be followed by death or great harm, where the removal is undertaken as a prelude to killing. The District Court of Jerusalem, as indicated, focused on the harm following upon forced removal in convicting Eichmann. Such harm might be human-inflicted, or the result of circumstances. Harm might be readily foreseeable, for example, when indigenous peoples are forcibly re-settled so that their land can be used for development projects. Conditions are difficult to replicate elsewhere for indigenous populations. Russel Barsh has written, "The systematic removal of indigenous peoples from their land, and disruption of their traditional means of subsistence, almost inevitably results in malnutrition, nutrition-related disabilities, and decreased resistance to infectious disease, if not outright starvation as well."[16]

1993, 1993 ICJ Rep., p. 26 (declaration, Tarassov).

14 Application of the Convention on the Prevention and Punishment of the Crime of Genocide (Bosnia and Herzegovina v. Yugoslavia (Serbia and Montenegro)), Order of 13 September 1993, 1993 ICJ Rep., p. 325, p. 431 (separate opinion, Lauterpacht).

15 Prosecutor v. Karadzic & Mladic, Cases No. IT-95-5-R61 & IT-95-18-R61, Review of Indictment Pursuant to Rule 61, 11 July 1996, para. 93.

16 Barsh, R.L. (1987), 'Arctic Nutrition and Genocide,' *Nordic Journal of International Law* 56, p. 322.

Germany's Constitutional Court

Germany's Constitutional Court, in a case noted in Chapter 6, analyzed expulsion as genocide. Nikola Jorgic, a Bosnian Serb, was convicted of genocide by the State Supreme Court of Dusseldorf, on allegations that he engaged in ethnic cleansing of Bosnian Muslims. The German Supreme Court, on appeal, stated that, "systematic expulsion" can be taken as an indication of intent to destroy. On constitutional review, the Constitutional Court approved this view.[17] These German courts said that intent may be present on the part of an actor engaging in ethnic cleansing.

Confirming the construction given in the case by the trial court, and on review by the Federal Supreme Court, the German Federal Constitutional Court stated that the intent to destroy is satisfied by an intent to destroy a protected group "as a social unit," even if there is no intent to destroy it physically or biologically. The Federal Constitutional Court said that a variety of specific acts could be the "means of destroying." It said:

> The State Supreme Court [of Dusseldorf - J.Q.] and the Federal Supreme Court find that Penal Code §220a protects the group; they are in agreement in viewing the intent involved in Penal Code §220a as the destruction of the group, or of a geographically limited part of the group, as a distinct social unit, and is not necessarily confined to its physical or biological elimination. Both courts thus find that the actor must have in mind using, as a means of destruction, primarily the acts identified in Penal Code §220a, para. 1, sub-paragraphs 1 through 5, either himself or through others. Possible additional means may be incarceration in inhumane conditions, destruction or plundering of houses or of buildings important for the group, or expulsion of members of the group.[18]

What the German court had in mind is that deportation may, in many situations, have the same impact as transferring the children or preventing births. If a group is dispersed so that members of the group no longer reproduce with each other, the group dies out. In that situation, it is difficult to distinguish deportation from transfer of children or birth prevention. Nonetheless, the German court insisted on acts specified in the sub-paragraphs before characterizing the conduct as genocide.

---

17 Case of Jorgic, Bundesverfassungsgericht, 12 December 2000, 2 BvR 1290/99, Absatz-Nr. (1-49), para. 25.

18 Ibid., para. 20.

Chapter 31

Human Habitat

Inflicting conditions of life calculated to destroy a group is, as we have seen, genocide, so long as it is done with the requisite intent. With regard to the preservation of species of animals, it is customary to speak of their habitat, and the need to preserve it. If the habitat of a species is eliminated, the species may die out. The same can occur with humans. Indigenous peoples are at risk if the natural environment on which they rely is threatened. Urbanized peoples are at risk if the modern infrastructure on which they rely is threatened. Just as forcing a group out of its home area may destroy it, so too may rendering it impossible for the group to sustain itself.

Destroying Physical Environment

In Chapter 18, we saw an example proposed by Roger Clark but based on situations that have actually arisen. Clark posited the construction of a road through the territory of indigenous peoples, under circumstances that the food supply would be damaged and large numbers would die.[1] A number of indigenous peoples in South America have been threatened with extinction in such circumstances.

To date there has been little implementation of the genocide prohibition in such circumstances. Sub-paragraph (c) may cover conduct that harms only indirectly. Depriving a group of life necessities, like water, if the group had no other access to water, might qualify. The sub-paragraphs on killing and causing bodily or mental harm might also apply.

Still, intent to destroy the group would need to be shown. Clark, writing in 1981, feared that the road builders might not be guilty of genocide, for lack of an intent to destroy.[2] However, as we saw in Chapter 17, the *ad hoc* tribunals have said that Article II intent is present if the actor understood or should have understood the deadly consequences of contemplated actions. Moreover, there need be no proof that the actor bore ill will to the victims as a group, as we saw in Chapter 18. A government minister promoting commercial development of a rain forest, who is aware of facts from which he should conclude that the indigenous population

---

1   Clark, R. (1981), 'Does the Genocide Convention Go Far Enough? Some Thoughts on the Nature of Criminal Genocide in the Context of Indonesia's Invasion of East Timor,' *Ohio Northern University Law Review* 8, p. 321, p. 326.

2   Ibid., p. 327.

will not survive, might be considered to know, or should have known the deadly consequence.

Destroying Infrastructure

Modern societies are dependent on infrastructural facilities to maintain normal life. In 1991, Iraq charged that in the bombing of its territory by the US-led forces, vibrations and shock waves cracked water and sewer mains throughout Baghdad. No water purification capacity remained functional. Bombers targeted and destroyed the city's electrical generating capacity. The lack of electricity and potable water brought infant diarrhea and other disease.[3] An investigating UN team confirmed the extent of the damage:

> The recent conflict has wrought near-apocalyptic results upon the economic infrastructure of what had been, until January 1991, a rather highly urbanized and mechanized society. Now, most means of modern life support have been destroyed or rendered tenuous. Iraq has, for some time to come, been relegated to a pre-industrial age, but with all the disabilities of post-industrial dependency on an intensive use of energy and technology.[4]

Such damage might not permanently render territory uninhabitable, as when the territory of an indigenous group is denuded of flora or fauna, yet the group might experience significant deterioration in its ability to sustain itself for an extended period.

Further harm to Iraq's economy flowed from economic sanctions that were maintained by the UN Security Council for the next decade. Economic sanctions were said to have led to mass malnutrition and death from disease.[5] The elements of genocide were arguably present.[6] In a letter of complaint to the UN Secretary-General, Iraq charged genocide:

---

3   'Health Crisis in Baghdad,' *Record* (Physicians for Human Rights) 4, p. 1 (spring 1991); 'Increased Activity in Northern Iraq,' *Bulletin* (ICRC), no. 184, p. 1 (May 1991).

4   Letter dated 20 March 1991 from the Secretary-General addressed to the President of the Security Council, UN SCOR, 46th sess., UN Doc. S/22366 (1991), Annex: Report to the Secretary-General on humanitarian needs in Kuwait and Iraq in the immediate post-crisis environment by a mission to the area led by Mr Martti Ahtisaari, Under-Secretary-General for Administration and Management, dated 20 March 1991, p. 5. 'Excerpts from U.N. Report on Need for Humanitarian Assistance in Iraq,' *New York Times*, 23 March 1991, p. A5. Lewis, P., 'UN Survey Calls Iraq's War Damage Near-Apocalyptic,' *New York Times*, 22 March 1991, p. A1.

5   Simons, G. (1998), *The Scourging of Iraq: Sanctions, Law, and Natural Justice*, p. 223, St. Martin's Press, New York. Bisharat, G.E. (2001), 'Sanctions as Genocide,' *Transnational Law & Contemporary Problems* 11, p. 379, p. 381.

6   Bisharat (2001), pp. 411-424.

The comprehensive sanctions that have been maintained against Iraq for more than 10 years, the constant military aggression against Iraqi territory since 1991 that has devastated the country's civilian infrastructure, and the enforcement of the unlawful no-flight zones that intimidate the civilian inhabitants, especially children and women, and inflict large-scale losses in human and material terms—all of these have prevented the people of Iraq from enjoying the exercise of its economic, social, cultural, civil and political rights, chief among them the right to life and the right to development. This is to be considered as tantamount to genocide, whose perpetrators are to be punished by the international community under the terms of the 1948 Convention on the Prevention and Punishment of the Crime of Genocide.[7]

Bolstering Iraq's case, the deaths being caused by the sanctions were widely known, even as the UN Security Council repeatedly voted to extend sanctions. In response, the United States attributed the deaths not to the sanctions, but to the Iraqi government, which, it said, could have ensured an adequate food and water supply and health care despite sanctions.

Causation

That line of defense raises an issue that will often be present when genocide is charged for destruction of environment or infrastructure. The deaths that may flow from such acts do not occur as directly as deaths from, say, military massacres. Moreover, acts on the part of the victims themselves and the governing authorities may play a role. Deaths perhaps could have been averted. Causation in penal law, however, need not always be direct. An accused who inflicts a serious wound may be deemed to cause death, even if the victim could have taken action to avert death.

One of the allegations made in regard to economic exploitation of the Amazon is that indigenous peoples, like the Yanomami, have committed suicide in significant numbers, out of despair over their inability to sustain their lives. In penal law, even if a victim brings about his own death, the original actor may be responsible, if the original act put the victim in an untenable position.[8]

It will be recalled from Chapter 15, that, in the Sixth Committee, China insisted on covering mental injury, in particular to deal with the promotion of opium use. Appropriate language was included in Article II sub-paragraph (b) to cover mental injury. This language was adopted despite the fact that it would be the victim who directly brings on the harm. Promotion of opium use would cause harm only through an act taken by the victim, but presumably in response to the situation created by the putative perpetrator of genocide.

---

7   Response of the Government of Iraq to the interim report of the Special Rapporteur, p. 3, *Annex to the letter dated 2 November 2000 from the Permanent Representative of Iraq to the United Nations addressed to the Secretary-General*, UN Doc. A/C.3/55/5 (2000).

8   Dressler, J. (2001), *Understanding Criminal Law*, pp. 193-194, Matthew Bender, New York.

Chapter 32

Aerial Genocide

Wartime offers opportunity to kill in large numbers. Yet if genocide applies in wartime, potentially all wartime killing is genocide. Enemies are typically of a different nationality, therefore members of a protected group. A warring party might be viewed as entertaining the intent to destroy the group as such. The state would be liable for genocide, and the commanders would be prosecutable.

Concern was expressed in the Sixth Committee that genocide might be charged even where military action was lawfully initiated. New Zealand raised the example of "a defensive war, especially a war undertaken on instructions from the Security Council." It said:

> Modern war was total, and there might be bombing which might destroy whole groups. If the motives for genocide were not listed in the convention, such bombing might be called a crime of genocide; but that would obviously be untrue. It was, therefore, essential to include the enumeration of the motives for genocide in article II.[1]

The United Kingdom, which opposed a listing of motives, replied that intending to destroy a group, even in a defensive war, would constitute genocide:

> The representative of New Zealand had brought forward the strongest argument against the United Kingdom amendment. Taking issue with the example which he had given, Mr. Fitzmaurice pointed out that the fact that a war was defensive was not sufficient reason for permitting the destruction of an entire group. Even if in that case there were no intent to destroy the whole group, it would be genocide.[2]

No listing of motives was included, but Article I specified that genocide can be committed in wartime: "The Contracting Parties confirm that genocide, whether committed in time of peace or in time of war, is a crime under international law which they undertake to prevent and to punish." The atrocities most prominent in the minds of the drafters of the Genocide Convention had occurred in wartime, namely during World War II.

Adoption of the text of the Genocide Convention, even with this clear language in Article I, did not put the issue to rest. One early analyst of the Genocide Convention suggested solving the problem by interpreting Article II not to apply in wartime.

---

1   UN GAOR, 3rd sess., Part 1, *Summary Records of Meetings 21 September - 10 December 1948*, pp. 119-120, UN Doc. A/C.6/SR.75 (Mr. Reid, New Zealand).
2   Ibid., pp. 120-121 (Mr. Fitzmaurice, UK).

Adolfo Molina said that Article II(a) should be read to exclude the killing of foreign nationals. Otherwise, he said, "war itself would be a continuing offense of genocide, and even more so atomic bombing, or other bombing, and all attacks on the civilian population of the belligerent countries."[3]

The United States too was concerned that Article II might cover wartime killing generally. But instead of denying the applicability of the Genocide Convention in wartime, it followed the lead suggested by the UK in the Sixth Committee and focused on "intent to destroy." When it ratified the Genocide Convention, the United States filed with the UN Secretary-General an interpretive understanding: "That acts in the course of armed conflicts committed without the specific intent required by Article II are not sufficient to constitute genocide as defined by this Convention."[4] Technically, the understanding is superfluous, since an act committed without the Article II intent would not be genocide in any event.[5]

State practice confirms the position that genocide can be committed in wartime, and in particular that necessities of war may not be invoked to justify genocide. Lori Damrosch has written, "Wartime exigencies" are "no defense against a charge of genocide, whether committed by the initiator of aggression or by a party acting in self-defense."[6]

Domestic genocide legislation is typically silent on this topic. One penal code, that of Romania, prescribes a more severe penalty for genocide committed in wartime and thereby reflects Romania's understanding that wartime genocide is prohibited. Death was made the only possible penalty for wartime genocide, whereas either the death penalty or imprisonment could be used for peacetime genocide.[7] UN bodies have found genocide to be committed in wartime. Allegations of genocide were raised against Israel during its 1982 invasion of Lebanon, when a large number of Palestinians in refugee camps in Beirut were killed in an episode of mass assaults. Three UN bodies condemned these killings as genocide.[8]

---

3   Molina, A. (1950), 'El delito de genocidio en la legislación Guatemalteca,' *Revista de la Facultad de Ciencias Jurídicas y Sociales de Guatemala*, p. 25, p. 31.

4   *Multilateral Treaties Deposited with the Secretary-General: Status as at 31 December 2003*, p. 126, UN Doc. ST/LEG/SER.E/22 (2003).

5   Damrosch, L.R. (1998), 'Genocide and Ethnic Conflict,' in D. Wippman (ed.), *International Law and Ethnic Conflict*, p. 256, p. 268.

6   Ibid., p. 267.

7   *Penal Code of the Romanian Socialist Republic* (1976), art. 357, Fred B. Rothman, Hackensack NJ and Sweet & Maxwell Ltd., London.

8   GA Res. 37/123D, UN GAOR, 36th sess., 16 December 1982. Commission on Human Rights, Res. 1983/3, 15 February 1983; Subcommission on the Prevention of Discrimination and Protection of Minorities, *Question of the Violation of Human Rights and Fundamental Freedoms including Policies of Racial Discrimination and Segregation and of Apartheid, in All Countries, with Particular Reference to Colonial and Other Dependent Countries and Territories: Report of the Sub-Commission under Commission on Human Rights Resolution 8 (XXIII)*, 25 August 1983, UN Doc. E/CN.4/Sub.2/1983/L.9 (1983).

State Practice on Genocide by Bombing

The devastation that can be caused by aerial bombardment was well known to the drafters of the Genocide Convention. The United States had used nuclear bombs in Hiroshima and Nagasaki. The Allied bombing of Dresden and Tokyo with conventional weaponry killed thousands. Leo Kuper has suggested that these bombing raids constituted genocide.[9] By the twenty-first century, satellite targeting and long-distance bombardment made it even easier to kill large numbers with minimal risk to pilots.

A number of states have charged genocide over a military bombardment. In Lebanon in 1989, when Syria shelled sectors of Beirut inhabited by Maronite Christians, Israel's Prime Minister Itzhak Shamir charged: "we are witnessing genocide at the hands of the Syrians and no one is lifting a finger."[10] Pope John Paul II made the same accusation of genocide against Syria.[11]

In 1983, Chad made a charge of genocide against Libya in the UN Security Council, alleging indiscriminate bombing by Libya of a Chad city. Libya, declared Chad, "launched a veritable genocide against the civilian population of Faya-Largeau through the night of 1 August 1983 by stepping up aerial bombing. The number of civilian victims in the town of Faya-Largeau which was razed has reached very startling and dramatic proportions." Chad charged that Libya sought "to exterminate the people of Chad, destroy and occupy the country."[12] Chad told the Security Council that Libya was waging "a war of extermination, a war of genocide."[13] Libya denied the facts alleged by Chad and did not address the elements of genocide.[14] Nor did Security Council delegates, who instead took Chad's complaint as an allegation of aggression.[15]

Two elements of genocide raise potential obstacles to an allegation of genocide by aerial bombardment. One is the fact that bombing typically is of military objectives and does not focus on a particular population group. When Yugoslavia sued ten

---

9   Kuper, L. (1985), *The Prevention of Genocide*, pp. 13-14, Yale University Press, New Haven.

10   'Consul-General of Israel in Los Angeles,' PR Newswire, 17 August 1989.

11   Haberman, C., 'Pope, Addressing Syrians, Labels the Shelling of Beirut "Genocide",' *New York Times*, 16 August 1989, p. A10.

12   Letter dated 2 August 1983 from the representative of Chad to the President of the Security Council, UN SCOR, Supp. for July, August and September 1983, p. 40, UN Doc. S/15902 (1983).

13   UN SCOR, 38th sess., 2463rd meeting, Provisional Verbatim Record, 11 August 1983, p. 3, UN Doc. S/PV.2463 (1983).

14   Letter dated 2 August 1983 from the representative of the Libyan Arab Jamahiriya to the President of the Security Council, UN SCOR, 38th sess., Supp. for July, August and September 1983, p. 41, UN Doc. S/15903 (1983).

15   UN SCOR, 38th sess., 2464th meeting, Provisional Verbatim Record, 11 August 1983, UN Doc. S/PV.2464 (1983).

NATO states in 1999 for bombing densely populated areas of Yugoslavia, Italy, a defendant state, told the court that

> the crime of genocide must involve acts directed against a national, ethnic, racial, or religious group. To the contrary, the facts and situations alleged by the Federal Republic of Yugoslavia refer to acts affecting a state's territory and, as a consequence, its population taken as a whole. The Federal Republic of Yugoslavia in effect has never maintained that the target of NATO acts might be one or another group within the Yugoslav population.[16]

Italy appeared to be asserting that no group within the meaning of Article II was the alleged victim. It thought that Yugoslavia would have to allege that the group intended to be destroyed was some group within the Yugoslav population that would qualify under Article II. Yugoslavia, however, apparently viewed the relevant group as nationals of Yugoslavia. In its Application, it referred to "the obligation contained in the Convention on the Prevention and Punishment of the Crime of Genocide not to impose deliberately on a national group conditions of life calculated to bring about the physical destruction of the group."[17] Yugoslavia chose "national" rather than "ethnical," "racial," or "religious" to characterize the group. Italy may have considered "population taken as a whole" as more inclusive than "nationals," on the rationale that resident aliens and visitors would have been present during the bombing.

The population of a given state is, to be sure, different from "nationals" of that state. Article II does not address the issue of a group that may include non-members. It would seem, however, that Italy could, in principle, intend to destroy nationals of Yugoslavia even though others might suffer along with them. Italy's possible intent to destroy nationals of Yugoslavia would not be negated by the fact that Italy might harm others in the process.

The Intent Behind Bombing

Critical to whether those who bomb commit genocide is the intent issue. An actor who launches bombs will typically assert that the aim was to strike certain targets of military significance, and that there was no intent to harm civilians, hence no intent to destroy the group of which those civilians are a part. The actor may assert that the intent was to pressure a government to alter a policy, rather than to harm civilians.

The intent issue was central to the defense asserted against Yugoslavia by Italy and the other NATO states. Yugoslavia alleged that the NATO states were targeting civilian objectives and using weaponry that caused pollution of soil, air, and water, the destruction of the country's economy, and long-term health risks from depleted uranium on missile tips. Yugoslavia relied on Article II(c), alleging a deliberate

---

16 Legality of Use of Force (Yugoslavia v. Italy), ICJ, oral argument, 11 May 1999, para. 3B (translated by author from French text).

17 Legality of Use of Force (Yugoslavia v. Italy), ICJ, Application, 29 April 1999.

creation of conditions of life calculated to bring about the physical destruction of a national group, namely, the nationals of Yugoslavia.[18]

The NATO states responded by denying any intent to destroy a group.[19] The United Kingdom said, "There is no plausible evidence, nor could there be, that the United Kingdom has the intent required by the Convention."[20] "Genocide is the intended destruction of a national, ethnical, racial or religious group," said Germany. "We have no such intentions."[21] Belgium argued that the NATO bombing involved no "intent to destroy all or part of an ethnic, racial or religious [group]."[22]

Canada made an argument to the court that recalled the Sixth Committee point raised by New Zealand. It expressed concern that unless the ICJ demanded that Yugoslavia prove the Article II intent, it could be held for genocide for force of a type that parties normally employ in warfare. Canada said:

> The suggestion [by Yugoslavia] is that by taking part in the air operations, with the collateral damages and casualties a military campaign inevitably entails, Canada is *automatically* engaged in that form of genocide referred to in Article II(c), the deliberate infliction of conditions of life calculated to destroy a national group in whole or in part. On this view, any use of force and any act of war is automatically equated with genocide.[23]

France, denying it had the intent required by Article II, declared, "Without this element of intent, the idea of genocide would be confused with the use of force causing the loss of human life, and as a result the Convention of 1948 would be deprived of its object."[24]

The Netherlands, another NATO defendant, said that Yugoslavia had failed to allege a "discriminatory purpose" in the NATO bombing.[25] If the Netherlands was suggesting that it was responsible for genocide only if it subjectively sought to discriminate against a particular protected group in Yugoslavia, it was reading the genocide definition too narrowly.

---

18 Legality of Use of Force (Yugoslavia v. Belgium), Order, 1999 ICJ, pp. 136-137.

19 Legality of Use of Force (Yugoslavia v. Belgium), ICJ, oral argument, 10 May 1999 (Mr. Ergec, Belgium).

20 Legality of Use of Force (Yugoslavia v. UK), ICJ, oral argument, 11 May 1999 (Mr. Greenwood, UK).

21 Legality of Use of Force (Yugoslavia v. Germany), ICJ, oral argument, 12 May 1999 (Mr. Hilger, Germany).

22 Legality of Use of Force (Yugoslavia v. Belgium), Order, 1999 ICJ Rep., p. 124, p. 137.

23 Legality of Use of Force (Yugoslavia v. Canada), ICJ, oral argument, 10 May 1999, para. 33 (Mr. Kirsch, Canada).

24 Legality of Use of Force (Yugoslavia v. France), ICJ, oral argument, 12 May 1999 (Mr. Abraham, France).

25 Legality of Use of Force (Yugoslavia v. Netherlands), ICJ, oral argument, 11 May 1999, paras. 29 & 31 (Mr. Lammers, Netherlands).

Yugoslavia sought an injunctive order against the NATO bombing. The court denied the injunction, for lack of proof of genocidal intent: "it does not appear at the present stage of the proceedings that the bombings which form the subject of the Yugoslav Application indeed entail the element of intent, towards a group as such."[26]

Aerial Bombardment as Genocide

The court did not elaborate on how one would determine whether genocidal intent were present in a military bombardment. Portugal argued to the court that aerial bombardment can never show genocidal intent. It said, "airplane bombings are clearly inadequate to the commitment of a crime (genocide) that would require a selective effort in the choice of victims, incompatible with the contingent effect of the employed means."[27]

That position has been rejected, however, by the Yugoslavia tribunal, where shelling and bombardment have figured in genocide indictments. A trial chamber of the Yugoslavia tribunal reviewing the Mladic-Karadzic indictment said that bombardment of a populated area may constitute genocide precisely on the grounds charged by Yugoslavia against the NATO states, namely, by creating conditions of life calculated to bring about the destruction of a group. The trial chamber found that the facts of the case provisionally supported the charge: "the deliberate inflicting on the group [of] conditions of life calculated to bring about its physical destruction in whole or in part was put into effect ... through the siege and shelling of cities and protected areas."[28]

---

26 Legality of Use of Force (Yugoslavia v. Belgium), Order, 1999 ICJ Rep., p. 138.

27 Legality of Use of Force (Yugoslavia v. Portugal) (1999), ICJ, oral argument, 11 May 1999, para. 2.1.2.2.2 (Mr. Martins, Portugal).

28 Prosecutor v. Karadzic & Mladic, Cases No. IT-95-5-R61 & IT-95-18-R61, Review of Indictment Pursuant to Rule 61, 11 July 1996, para. 93.

Chapter 33

Nuclear Genocide

The issue of nuclear weaponry as genocide was argued before the International Court of Justice when the UN General Assembly asked for an advisory opinion on the legality of using nuclear weapons. In a case styled Legality of the Threat or Use of Nuclear Weapons, the court considered a number of legal bases on which the use of nuclear weapons might be unlawful, including genocide.

Some states urged the court to say that in some, or all, instances of use of nuclear weapons, genocide would be committed. The court summarized the argument:

> It was maintained before the Court that the number of deaths occasioned by the use of nuclear weapons would be enormous; that the victims could, in certain cases, include persons of a particular national, ethnic, racial or religious group; and that the intention to destroy such groups could be inferred from the fact that the user of the nuclear weapon would have omitted to take account of the well-known effects of the use of such weapons.[1]

The court answered by reference to genocidal intent:

> the prohibition of genocide would be pertinent in this case if the recourse to nuclear weapons did indeed entail the element of intent, towards a group as such, required by the provision quoted above [Article II]. In the view of the Court, it would only be possible to arrive at such a conclusion after having taken due account of the circumstances specific to each case.[2]

Thus, the court was unwilling, without having specific facts, to say whether intent would be present.[3]

Two of the court's judges thought that the court should have devoted more attention to the issue of whether a nuclear launch is genocide. Judges Weeramantry and Koroma, like the states mentioned by the court, stressed the large number of victims one might anticipate. "Nuclear weapons used in response to a nuclear attack," said Judge Weeramantry, "especially in the event of an all-out nuclear response, would be likely to cause genocide by triggering off an all-out nuclear

---

1   Legality of the Threat or Use of Nuclear Weapons (adv. op.), 1996 ICJ Rep., p. 66, pp. 226 & 240.

2   Ibid., p. 240.

3   Gowlland-Debbas, V. (1999), 'The Right to Life and Genocide: The Court and International Public Policy,' in L. Boisson de Chazournes and P. Sands (eds), *International Law, the International Court of Justice and Nuclear Weapons*, p. 315, p. 331, Cambridge University Press, Cambridge.

exchange, ..." A use of nuclear weapons in self-defense, he explained, would "result in all probability in all-out nuclear war" and thus "is even more likely to cause genocide than the act of launching an initial strike. If the killing of human beings, in numbers ranging from a million to a billion, does not fall within the definition of genocide, one may well ask what will."[4]

Defensive Use of Nuclear Weapons

Judge Weeramantry's conclusion about defensive use of nuclear weapons as being more clearly genocide is based on his analysis that an actor launching nuclear weapons in response to a first use would act quickly and on the basis of information that might well be inaccurate. In such circumstances, he says, there would be a high probability of mistake.[5]

Judge Weeramantry wrote that the launch of even a single nuclear warhead could constitute genocide, but that the number launched in a defensive response would likely be higher:

> Even a single "small" nuclear weapon, such as those used in Japan, could be instruments of genocide, judging from the number of deaths they are known to have caused. If cities are targeted, a single bomb could cause a death toll exceeding a million. If the retaliatory weapons are more numerous, on WHO's [Worth Health Organization] estimates of the effects of nuclear war, even a billion people, both of the attacking State and of others, could be killed. This is plainly genocide and, whatever the circumstances, cannot be within the law.[6]

Next, Judge Weeramantry addressed the intent element of genocide, and the question of whether the victims would constitute a protected group within the meaning of Article II. Both elements he found would be satisfied by a nuclear launch:

> When a nuclear weapon is used, those using it must know that it will have the effect of causing deaths on a scale so massive as to wipe out entire populations. Genocide, as defined in the Genocide Convention (Art. II), means any act committed with intent to destroy, in whole or in part, a national, ethnical, racial or religious group, as such. ... In discussions on the definition of genocide in the Genocide Convention, much play is made upon the words "as such." The argument offered is that there must be an intention to target a particular national, ethnical, racial or religious group qua such group, and not incidentally to some other act. However, having regard to the ability of nuclear weapons to wipe out blocks of population ranging from hundreds of thousands to millions, there can be no doubt that the weapon targets, in whole or in part, the national group of the State at which it is directed.[7]

　　4　Legality of the Threat or Use of Nuclear Weapons (adv. op.), 1996 ICJ Rep., p. 226, p. 517 (dissenting opinion, Weeramantry).

　　5　Ibid., p. 515.

　　6　Ibid., p. 501.

　　7　Ibid., p. 502.

Certainly, Judge Weeramantry is correct in saying that the fact that an act is undertaken for a purpose other than to destroy a protected group does not prevent it from being genocide. So long as group destruction is foreseeable, genocide could be present. An actor who launches a defensive nuclear strike would presumably say that the purpose was to protect a domestic population. That purpose is not, however, inconsistent with entertaining an intent to destroy a protected group.

Regarding the protected group, Judge Weeramantry says that the victims would be a group consisting of nationals of the state into whose territory the nuclear weapon is launched. Clearly, "nationals" in Article II means those who hold a given nationality, and in most imaginable scenarios of a nuclear launch, the victims would be predominantly of a given nationality. There need not be a negative animus to the victim group in the sense of race hatred before Article II is satisfied. The victim group here is similar to what Yugoslavia was alleging to be the victim group in the NATO bombing of Yugoslavia.

Defensive or Offensive Use of Nuclear Weapons

Judge Koroma also finds that the launching of nuclear weapons constitutes genocide, although he does not distinguish first use from responsive use. Judge Koroma referred to the court's statement in the Reservations case that genocide involves a denial of the existence of human groups:

> The Court cannot therefore view with equanimity the killing of thousands, if not millions, of innocent civilians which the use of nuclear weapons would make inevitable, and conclude that genocide has not been committed because the State using such weapons has not manifested any intent to kill so many thousands or millions of people. Indeed, under the Convention, the quantum of the people killed is comprehended as well. It does not appear to me that judicial detachment requires the Court (to refrain) from expressing itself on the abhorrent shocking consequences that a whole population could be wiped out by the use of nuclear weapons during an armed conflict, and the fact that this could tantamount [*sic*] to genocide, if the consequences of the act could have been foreseen. Such expression of concern may even have a preventive effect on the weapons being used at all.[8]

Judge Koroma, like Judge Weeramantry, focused on the foreseeability of the result. They say that genocide might be found even absent a purpose to destroy a protected group, so long as the actor understands that by launching a nuclear weapon, the result, either as a result of the weapon launched by the actor, or as a result of weapons that may be launched in response, will be the destruction of a protected group.

Article II intent may be present where the actor knew or should have known the consequences of an action. Bombing with conventional weapons, or nuclear bombing, will typically be done for a military aim. Even so, if it is done under circumstances

---

8   Ibid., p. 577 (dissenting opinion, Koroma).

that make it obvious that an Article II-protected group will be destroyed, genocide may be present.

PART EIGHT
GENOCIDE BY A STATE

Chapter 34

Opting Out

Suits for genocide have been filed in the International Court of Justice. It has been controversial, however, whether the court has jurisdiction to hear a genocide suit. Even if it does, some state parties to the Genocide Convention have sought to exempt themselves from the court's jurisdiction by filing a reservation to their acceptance of the Genocide Convention.

Reservations to Submission Clauses

The ICJ is a court of limited jurisdiction. All UN member states are automatically parties to the court's Statute and hence potentially subject to its jurisdiction. However, the fact that a state is a party to the Statute does not in and of itself allow other states to sue it in the court. When the Statute was drafted, states were reluctant to subject themselves to suit, so they preserved for themselves the right to determine the circumstances in which they could be sued.

States may accept the court's jurisdiction by filing a declaration with the court, declaring that other states may sue on any issue of international law. Most states have not filed such declarations. Additionally, the parties to a treaty may provide for dispute resolution in the ICJ. The treaty will specify that a state party alleging breach by another state party may sue.

Such a provision is called a submission clause. States agree in advance that they will respond to a suit and comply with whatever decision the court makes. Typically, however, some states that are party to a treaty are unwilling to submit themselves in advance to the court's jurisdiction.

When the United Nations began sponsoring the adoption of multilateral treaties on various issues, the hope was that states would ratify them in totality. If states were to pick and choose provisions of treaties to accept, then the prospect was reduced for effective law at the international level.

Reservations to Article IX

The Genocide Convention contains a submission clause, as Article IX:

> Disputes between the Contracting Parties relating to the interpretation, application or fulfilment of the present Convention, including those relating to the responsibility of a State

for genocide or for any of the other acts enumerated in article III, shall be submitted to the International Court of Justice at the request of any of the parties to the dispute.

When this clause was debated in the Sixth Committee, India worried aloud that mandatory jurisdiction over state-perpetrated genocide "would make it possible for an unfriendly State to charge, on vague and unsubstantiated allegations, that another State was responsible for genocide within its territory."[1] The worry is not unfounded, as the ICJ has not distinguished itself as a fact-finder. In the Bosnia case, Yugoslavia objected that the evidence submitted by Bosnia consisted in substantial measure of media accounts.[2] Although the court is empowered to hear experts, or even to appoint a fact-finder, it typically does not engage in extensive fact-finding to verify the veracity of information presented by a party.

When the Genocide Convention was opened for ratification, a number of states, mainly the socialist bloc, reserved to Article IX. The bloc states viewed the ICJ as Western-dominated and therefore biased against them. Commenting on these reservations, Manley Hudson expressed concern that this practice "would seriously restrict the role of the Court in the interpretation and application of international legislative instruments."[3]

Some ratifying states, concerned over the reservations to Article IX, filed documents in which they objected to them. The legal significance was unclear, nor was it clear that reservations to Article IX were valid. Adolfo Miaja de la Muela, noting the reservations filed to Article IX, wrote: "Some governments filed objections to these reservations, thereby yielding a situation of such chaos as to make it difficult to figure out the effect of the Convention against genocide for the reserving states and the objecting states."[4]

The UN Secretary-General, designated in Article XI as the depositary agency for the Genocide Convention, was uncertain whether to accept reservations to Article IX to be valid. To resolve the confusion, the UN General Assembly asked the ICJ for an advisory opinion. In *Reservations to the Genocide Convention*, the court gave its opinion, deciding that reservations are, in principle, permissible so long as they are not inconsistent with the object and purpose of a treaty. That standard has since been incorporated into the Vienna Convention on the Law of Treaties as the criterion for determining the permissibility of a reservation. But both under the court's analysis in the Reservations case, and under the Vienna Convention, the positing of the question

---

1   UN GAOR, 3rd sess., Part 1, *Summary Records of Meetings 21 September - 10 December 1948*, pp. 437-438, UN Doc. A/C.6/SR.103 (1949) (Mr. Sundaram, India).

2   Application of the Convention on the Prevention and Punishment of the Crime of Genocide (Bosnia and Herzegovina v. Yugoslavia (Serbia and Montenegro)), Order of 13 September 1993, 1993 ICJ Rep., p. 325, p. 357 (separate opinion, Shahabuddeen).

3   Hudson, M.O. (1951), 'The Twenty-Ninth Year of the World Court,' *American Journal of International Law* 45, p. 1, p. 34.

4   Miaja de la Muela, A. (1951-52), 'El genocidio, delito internacional,' *Revista española de derecho internacional* 4, p. 363 p. 407.

of whether a particular reservation is consistent with the object and purpose of the treaty appears to be an objective matter, that is, a particular reservation either is or is not consistent.

The Vienna Convention states that a state may formulate a reservation unless "the reservation is incompatible with the object and purpose of the treaty."[5] The only procedure, however, provided in the Vienna Convention leaves the matter to individual determination by each other state party. Other states may file in return if they object and may, in addition, indicate whether they desire to be bound by the treaty with respect to the reserving state.[6] In the Reservations case, the court did not specifically address the question of whether a reservation to Article IX is contrary to the object and purpose of the Genocide Convention.

Reaction to Reservations to Article IX

By the turn of the century, primarily as a result of the end of the Cold War, most of the socialist bloc states that reserved to Article IX upon ratification had withdrawn these reservations.[7] Of the 138 states currently party to the Genocide Convention, sixteen have reservations to Article IX: Algeria, Bahrain, Bangladesh, China, India, Malaysia, Morocco, Rwanda, Singapore, Spain, UAE, USA, Venezuela, Vietnam, Yemen, and Yugoslavia. Five of these – Algeria, China, Rwanda, Spain, and UAE – phrase their reservations to say they are not bound by Article IX. The others phrase their reservations to say that their consent, or that of all parties to a dispute, is required.[8]

A number of other state parties filed formal objections to these reservations. Mexico and the Netherlands characterized the reservations as incompatible with the object and purpose of the Genocide Convention.[9] The UK said that "this is not the kind of reservation which intending parties to the Convention have the right to make."[10]

Despite their objections, most of these states did not specify that the reservations would keep the Convention from entering into force between them and the reserving state. As the USA noted in its oral argument in the ICJ,[11] the Netherlands did take that extra step. In objecting to the USA reservation to Article IX, the Netherlands

---

5 Vienna Convention on the Law of Treaties, art. 19(c), UNTS 1155, p. 331.

6 Ibid., art. 21, para. 1.

7 *Multilateral Treaties Deposited with the Secretary-General: Status as at 31 December 2003*, pp. 131-132, UN Doc. ST/LEG/SER.E/22 (2003). And see www.un.org.

8 Ibid., pp. 124-127.

9 Ibid., p. 128.

10 Ibid., p. 129.

11 Legality of Use of Force (Yugoslavia v. USA), ICJ, oral argument, 11 May 1999, para. 2.21 (Mr. Crook, USA).

recited, "the Government of the Kingdom of the Netherlands does not consider the United States of America a party to the Convention."[12]

The rationale behind the position that a reservation to Article IX is incompatible with the object and purpose of the Genocide Convention is that state-perpetrated genocide was already prohibited by customary international law, apart from the Genocide Convention, and thus the obligation to submit to the court's jurisdiction, which is not found in customary law, is the critical element of the Convention.

Validity of Reservations to Article IX

Yugoslavia's 1999 filing against ten NATO states represented the first time that any state that was sued for genocide on the basis of Article IX had reserved to it. Yugoslavia invoked the Genocide Convention as a basis of jurisdiction over the ten states, all of which were parties to the Genocide Convention. Of the ten, however, two of them, Spain and the USA, had reservations to Article IX on file with the UN Secretary-General.

Spain's reservation reads: "With a reservation in respect of the whole of article IX (jurisdiction of the International Court of Justice)."[13] The USA reservation reads: "That with reference to article IX of the Convention, before any dispute to which the United States is a party may be submitted to the jurisdiction of the International Court of Justice under this article, the specific consent of the United States is required in each case."[14] On the strength of the two reservations, the court dismissed Yugoslavia's Genocide Convention claims against both Spain[15] and the USA.[16]

Spain's reservation, by simply stating that Spain is not bound by Article IX, clearly frees it of an obligation to submit to the court's jurisdiction. The USA reservation is more nuanced than a simple outright rejection of Article IX, as a result of which the USA felt it necessary to make an argument that it should apply. In oral proceedings in the case filed against it by Yugoslavia, the USA told the court that "[t]he United States reservation is clear and unambiguous. The United States has not given the specific consent it requires. It will not do so. Thus, there is no jurisdiction, prima facie or otherwise."[17]

The USA, apparently concerned that the court might take it upon itself to decide as an objective matter that a reservation to Article IX is inconsistent with the object and purpose of the Genocide Convention, argued that its reservation

---

12 *Multilateral Treaties Deposited with the Secretary-General: Status as at 31 December 2003*, p. 128.

13 Ibid., p. 126.

14 Ibid., p. 126.

15 Legality of Use of Force (Yugoslavia v. Spain), Order, 1999 ICJ Rep., p. 761, p. 772.

16 Legality of Use of Force (Yugoslavia v. USA), Order, 1999 ICJ Rep., p. 916, p. 924.

17 Legality of Use of Force (Yugoslavia v. USA), ICJ, oral argument, 11 May 1999, para. 2.10 (Mr. Crook, USA).

is not contrary to the Convention's object and purpose. The possibility of recourse to this Court for settlement of disputes is not central to the overall system of the Convention, which has as its essential elements the definition of the crime of genocide and the creation of obligations to try and punish those responsible for genocide.[18]

In support of its position that Article IX is not central, the USA pointed out that other states maintained reservations to Article IX, and that still others had previously done so but later withdrew their reservations.[19]

The court dismissed Yugoslavia's claim against the USA because of the USA reservation. The court said that "the said reservation had the effect of excluding that Article from the provisions of the Convention in force between the Parties."[20] That conclusion is imprecise, however, because the reservation does not purport to exclude Article IX from the Genocide Convention as it is in force between the USA and other contracting parties.

Spain's reservation is straightforward in its import, but the USA reservation does not automatically exclude application of Article IX. As the court noted, Yugoslavia submitted no argument to the court concerning the USA reservation to Article IX. Thus, the matter was not the subject of serious analysis in the proceedings before the court.[21] The USA reservation indicates that Article IX may indeed be the basis for jurisdiction, so long as "the specific consent of the United States" is given.

The USA did not do what would have made the reservation "clear and unambiguous," namely to make it read, "The USA reserves to Article IX." The reservation must mean something different from such a simple statement of reservation. The reservation may mean that although the specific consent of the USA is required before Article IX confers jurisdiction on the court, the USA, given its status as a party to the Genocide Convention, is obliging itself to act in good faith if sued by another state party and to give its consent, absent some compelling reason to the contrary. If that is the meaning, then the court could determine whether the USA were, in a specific case, acting in good faith in withholding consent.

The court did not make it clear whether it ruled in favor of the United States because it was up to other states to decide on a reservation's validity, or because the USA reservation was consistent with the object and purpose of the Genocide Convention. A reservation to Article IX does, however, seem to run counter to the object and purpose of the Genocide Convention. Subjecting states to accountability was a central feature of the Genocide Convention. The fact that a number of states have withdrawn their reservations to Article IX has lessened the problem, yet the number of reservations remains sufficiently high to threaten the ability of the ICJ to enforce the Genocide Convention.

---

18 Ibid., para. 2.17 (Mr. Crook, USA).

19 Ibid., para. 2.18 (Mr. Crook, USA).

20 Legality of Use of Force (Yugoslavia v. USA), Order, 1999 ICJ Rep., p. 916, p. 924.

21 Ibid., p. 924.

Chapter 35

The Convention's Curious Omission

There is no disagreement that Article IX allows suit for failing to punish genocide perpetrated by others. If, for example, a person accused by State A of committing genocide flees to State B, and State A asks State B to extradite, State B must do so, as long as State A can produce evidence of guilt. Article VII of the Genocide Convention requires extradition. If State B refuses to extradite, State A could sue under Article IX.

When Bosnia sued Yugoslavia in 1993, invoking Article IX as the basis of jurisdiction, it alleged something quite different: that Yugoslavia had participated in the actual perpetration of genocide.[1] Yugoslavia objected that Article IX does not cover the perpetration of genocide by a state: "The duties prescribed by the Convention relate to 'the prevention and punishment of the crime of genocide' when this crime is committed by individuals."[2]

Yugoslavia pointed out that the provisions of the Genocide Convention defining genocide contained no mention that genocide could be committed by anyone other than individuals. As a result, it said, Article IX, in referring disputes over compliance to the ICJ, covers only disputes over whether a state carried out its duty to punish individuals. Bosnia replied that state responsibility for the perpetration of genocide is apparent from the text of Article IX. It traced the drafting history of Article IX to argue that states are responsible before the court for their own perpetration of genocide, not only for failing to punish individuals.[3]

When the court in 1993 issued an injunctive order against Yugoslavia, Nina Jorgensen took it not to refer to perpetration of genocide by Yugoslavia, but to preventing and punishing genocide by others. She said that the court must have been

---

1   Application of the Convention on the Prevention and Punishment of the Crime of Genocide (Bosnia and Herzegovina v. Yugoslavia (Serbia and Montenegro)), Order of 8 April 1993, 1993 ICJ Rep., p. 1.

2   Application of the Convention on the Prevention and Punishment of the Crime of Genocide (Bosnia and Herzegovina v. Yugoslavia), Preliminary Objections, Memorial of Yugoslavia, June 1995, p. 130.

3   Application of the Convention on the Prevention and Punishment of the Crime of Genocide (Bosnia and Herzegovina v. Yugoslavia (Serbia and Montenegro)), 1994 ICJ (memorial of Bosnia and Herzegovina, typescript, pp. 200-204).

referring to the Convention's Article I, "which imposes an obligation on states to prevent and punish the crime of genocide."[4]

Although the court's order is more appropriately read as ordering Yugoslavia not to perpetrate genocide itself, the odd fashion in which the Genocide Convention treats state responsibility left room for debate. The specific duties imposed on states in the Genocide Convention relate only to preventing and punishing. States must enact legislation against genocide and provide penalties (Article V), and try individuals who commit genocide (Article VI), or extradite them to other countries (Article VII). The articles that impose duties on states nowhere specify that a state must refrain from perpetrating genocide. Marcel Sibert noted the Convention's "silence" on this matter.[5]

The UK's Effort to Insert State Responsibility

This "silence" was a product of contentious debate. In the Sixth Committee, the United Kingdom tried repeatedly to insert language on state responsibility for committing genocide, but was rebuffed.[6] It urged that the Convention should

> contain a direct reference to the type of genocide which was most likely to occur, i.e. genocide committed by a State or a Government. Since it was to be assumed that individuals acting on behalf of the State would not be punished by the courts of that State, it was essential to insert into the convention provisions to the effect that such acts would constitute a violation of the convention.[7]

The UK argued that it might be impossible to secure the legal accountability of high officials, since trial was to be conducted in the territory where the acts were committed, and since heads of state, under local law, often enjoyed immunity from prosecution. Therefore, it said,

> the only provision that could be made was to arraign Governments guilty of genocide before the only existing international court: the International Court of Justice, which would not

---

4   Jorgensen, N. (2000), *The Responsibility of States for International Crimes*, p. 265, Oxford University Press, Oxford.

5   Sibert, M. (1951), *Traité de droit international public. Le droit de la paix*, vol. 1, p. 446.

6   UN GAOR, 3rd sess., Part 1, *Summary Records of Meetings 21 September - 10 December 1948*, p. 314, UN Doc. A/C.6/SR.93 (Mr. Fitzmaurice, UK). Jørgensen, N. (1999), 'State Responsibility and the 1948 Genocide Convention,' in G. Goodwin-Gill and S. Talmon (eds), *The Reality of International Law: Essays in Honour of Ian Brownlie*, p. 273, p. 276, Clarendon Press, Oxford.

7   UN GAOR, 3rd sess., Part 1, *Summary Records of Meetings 21 September - 10 December 1948*, p. 344, UN Doc. A/C.6/SR.95 (Mr. Fitzmaurice, UK).

pronounce sentence, but would order the cessation of the imputed acts, and the payment of reparation to the victims.[8]

Article I requires a state to prevent and punish genocide. The UK suggested that this obligation implied an obligation not to perpetrate genocide, but that a more explicit statement would be in order:

> Some delegations had stated that it was implicit in the convention that an act of genocide committed by a State or Government would be contrary to the terms of the convention. While he agreed that article I implied that the Governments themselves would not commit acts of genocide, Mr. Fitzmaurice thought it would be better to say so clearly, ...[9]

The UK ultimately succeeded in getting a more explicit mention of state responsibility, but only in the submission clause (Article IX). The states were willing to write state responsibility into that provision. This left the unusual situation of a treaty that refers one type of violation to international adjudication even though the violation is not identified in the provisions specifying obligations.

The Court's Judgment on Jurisdiction

In 1996, the ICJ responded to Yugoslavia's objection to jurisdiction and, for the first time, rendered an opinion on whether a state may be sued under Article IX for perpetrating genocide. The court noted that, by Yugoslavia's argument, Article IX "would only cover the responsibility flowing from the failure of a State to fulfil its obligations of punishment and prevention as contemplated by Articles V, VI and VII; on the other hand, the responsibility of a State for an act of genocide perpetrated by the State itself would be excluded from the scope of the Convention." The court rejected this argument in a single paragraph, stating "that the reference in Article IX to 'the responsibility of a State for genocide or for any of the other acts enumerated in Article III' does not exclude any form of State responsibility."[10]

On this reasoning, the court decided, by thirteen votes to four, that Article IX gave it jurisdiction to hear an allegation of state-perpetrated genocide. Since the court was responding to Yugoslavia's argument that Article IX covers only the obligation to prevent and punish, the court's mention of "any form of State responsibility" was an evident reference to preventing and punishing as one form, and to perpetrating as another form. Judges Shi, Vereshchetin, Kreca, and Oda disagreed. They said that a state may not be sued, under Article IX, for perpetrating genocide. Unlike

---

8   Ibid., p. 342 (Mr. Fitzmaurice, UK).

9   UN GAOR, 3rd sess., Part 1, *Summary Records of Meetings 21 September - 10 December 1948*, p. 352, UN Doc. A/C.6/SR.96 (Mr. Fitzmaurice, UK).

10   Application of the Convention on the Prevention and Punishment of the Crime of Genocide (Bosnia and Herzegovina v. Yugoslavia), Preliminary Objections, Judgment, 1996 ICJ Rep., p. 595, p. 616.

the majority, which did not elaborate extensively on its position, these four judges explained their views in detail.

Views of Judges Shi, Vereshchetin, Kreca, and Oda

Judges Shi and Vereshchetin, writing a joint opinion, said:

> [W]e are disquieted by the statement of the Court ... that Article IX of the Genocide Convention "does not exclude any form of State responsibility." It is this disquiet that we wish briefly to explain.
>
> The Convention on Genocide is essentially and primarily directed towards the punishment of persons committing genocide or genocidal acts and the prevention of the commission of such crimes by individuals. The *travaux préparatoires* [drafting history - J.Q.] show that it was during the last stage of the elaboration of the Convention that, by a very slim majority of 19 votes to 17 with 9 abstentions, the provision relating to the responsibility of States for genocide or genocidal acts was included in the dispute settlement clause of Article IX, without the concurrent introduction of necessary modifications into other articles of the convention. As can be seen from the authoritative commentary to the Convention, published immediately after its adoption, "there were many doubts as to the actual meaning" of the reference to the responsibility of States (Nehemiah Robinson, *The Genocide Convention. Its Origin(s) and Interpretation*, New York, 1949, p. 42.) As to the creation of a separate civil remedy applicable as between States, the same author observes that "since the Convention does not specifically refer to reparation, the parties to it did not undertake to have accepted the Court's compulsory jurisdiction in this question" (*ibid.*, p. 43).[11]

Judge Kreca had been appointed to sit on the case by Yugoslavia under a procedure that allows a state with no national of its own on the bench to appoint a judge for the particular case. Whereas Judges Shi and Vereshchetin focused on the drafting history, Judge Kreca focused on the text. Judge Kreca reasoned that the Genocide Convention addresses penal responsibility and said that penal responsibility attaches to individuals, but not to states. Like Judges Shi and Vereshchetin, Judge Kreca noted that the Genocide Convention's provisions defining genocide do not mention the responsibility of a state for the perpetration of genocide. Therefore, he concluded, the reference to state responsibility in Article IX cannot encompass responsibility for the perpetration of genocide by the state itself. Judge Kreca cited Article IV, which states, "Persons committing genocide or any of the other acts enumerated in article III shall be punished, whether they are constitutionally responsible rulers, public officials or private individuals." In Article IV Judge Kreca found "a negative meaning—contained in the exclusion of criminal responsibility of States, governments or State authorities and the rejection of the application of the doctrine of the act of the State in this matter."

Since, Judge Kreca reasoned, criminal responsibility for perpetration of genocide is limited to individuals, states are not responsible under Article IX for

---

11 Ibid., p. 631 (joint declaration, Shi, Vereshchetin).

the perpetration of genocide. Rather, the responsibility of a state under Article IX is limited to preventing and punishing genocide perpetrated by individuals.[12]

Like Judge Kreca, Judge Oda focused on the text of the Convention. Unlike Judge Kreca, however, Judge Oda said that the state responsibility clause of Article IX addresses the perpetration of genocide by a state. To this extent, Judge Oda agreed with the majority. But Judge Oda found an obstacle to a suit by another state party. Article IX gives the court jurisdiction over "disputes" between two state parties. The injured party in genocide, he said, is not another state, but rather the individual victims. Bosnia, as a state, was not injured by the acts allegedly committed by Yugoslavia. Thus, he said, there was no "dispute" between Bosnia and Yugoslavia.

Judge Oda said that the Genocide Convention "is essentially directed *not* to the rights and obligations of States *but* to the protection of rights of individuals and groups of persons which have become recognized as universal."[13] He wrote:

> Yugoslavia might have been responsible for certain instances of genocide or genocidal acts committed by its public officials or surrogates in the territory of Bosnia and Herzegovina, but this fact alone does not mean that there is a "dispute" between the States relating to the responsibility of a State, as Yugoslavia did not violate the rights bestowed upon Bosnia and Herzegovina by the Convention. I would like to repeat and to emphasize that what should be protected by the Convention is *not* the particular rights of any individual State (Bosnia and Herzegovina in this case) *but* the status of human beings with human rights and the universal interest of the individual in general.
>
> What Bosnia and Herzegovina did in its Application was to point to certain facts tantamount to genocide or genocidal acts which had allegedly been committed within its territory by the Government of Yugoslavia or by its agents or surrogates, and to submit claims alleged to have arisen out of these acts. This cannot be taken to indicate the existence of an inter-State dispute relating to the responsibility of a State which could have been made a basis for the Court's jurisdiction.[14]

Like Judges Kreca, Shi, and Vereshchetin, Judge Oda stressed that the Convention in its definitional provisions addresses the obligation of individuals not to perpetrate genocide, rather than any obligation of states not to do so. He thought that if state-perpetrated genocide were to occur, it would not give rise to a "dispute" between the state in default and a potential plaintiff state, since, in his view, the potential plaintiff state has no rights that would be violated by the genocide.

---

12 Ibid., pp. 767-771 (dissenting opinion, Kreca).

13 Ibid., p. 626 (declaration, Oda).

14 Ibid., pp. 628-629.

Chapter 36

States as Criminals

A theme of the opinions of these four judges was the penal character of the Genocide Convention, and whether that precluded liability on the part of a state. This issue had come up in the Sixth Committee. Pakistan "was doubtful as to the advisability of dealing with civil responsibility in a document which referred solely to a criminal matter."[1] Even the UK, the proponent of a provision explicitly holding states accountable for committing genocide, used penal-law terminology when it said, as we saw in the last chapter, that a state committing genocide should be "arraigned" before the ICJ. Delegates were confused over the character of the state responsibility the UK was suggesting. Canada could not understand whether Article IX would impose liability of a civil or penal character, or perhaps both.[2] A number of states shared Canada's confusion.[3]

Judges Shi and Vereshchetin, as we saw in the last chapter, cited this drafting history in concluding that Article IX does not cover state-perpetrated genocide. They referred to a commentary by Nehemiah Robinson, who said, accurately, that during the drafting doubts were expressed as to the meaning of this phrase "responsibility of a state" as it appeared in the draft of what became Article IX.[4]

The Character of Responsibility in Article IX

Judges Shi and Vereshchetin took Robinson's reference to doubts about the meaning as doubts whether the Article IX language covered state-perpetrated genocide. But the doubts Robinson meant were doubts about whether the responsibility for state-perpetrated genocide would put states in the position of being criminals. The delegates understood that the language being proposed for the submission clause would cover state perpetration of genocide. The confusion, rather, was whether the contemplated state responsibility for the perpetration of genocide was civil or penal.

---

1   UN GAOR, 3rd sess., Part 1, *Summary Records of Meetings 21 September - 10 December 1948*, p. 438, UN Doc. A/C.6/SR.103 (Mr. Agha Shahi, Pakistan).

2   Ibid., pp. 438-439 (Mr. Lapointe, Canada).

3   Drost, P.N. (1959), *The Crime of State: Penal Protection for Fundamental Freedoms of Persons and Peoples: Book II: Genocide: United Nations Legislation on International Criminal Law*, pp. 67-70, A.W. Sythoff, Leiden.

4   Robinson, N. (1960), *The Genocide Convention: A Commentary*, pp. 101-102, Institute of Jewish Affairs, New York.

And some opposed the draft language on that basis, namely because they did not understand how one could equate a state with a criminal.

The Genocide Convention spoke of genocide as a crime, which is not the kind of responsibility that states normally bear at the international level. The ICJ, to which cases might, under Article IX, be referred, was an institution with powers comparable to those of a domestic court exercising civil jurisdiction between parties. It is not surprising, therefore, that there was confusion about whether the liability of a state would be civil or penal in character.[5]

Iran objected when the UK proposed adding a reference to state responsibility in what became Article IV. Iran did not oppose the inclusion of state responsibility for the perpetration of genocide, but it did not want the reference to appear to call state-perpetrated genocide a crime. Iran

> could not support the United Kingdom amendment in the form in which it was drafted although, in principle, he was in agreement with the two ideas it contained: first, the civil responsibility of States and secondly, the necessity of utilizing the existing International Court of Justice in the field of genocide. However, the wording used presupposed that a State or government might commit a crime, a theory with which the Iranian delegation was not in agreement.[6]

As described by Robinson, the uncertainty to which he refers on the part of the drafters related to this confusion over the legal character of a state's liability.[7] But Robinson said that the drafters had no doubt that Article IX provided jurisdiction over an allegation of perpetration of genocide by a state. Robinson, in fact, specifically stated, on the page quoted by Judges Shi and Vereshchetin, that "such disputes [in Article IX] may relate to the responsibility of a State for acts of Genocide or any of the other punishable acts."[8]

Manley Hudson also understood Article IX in this sense. He wrote:

> the "responsibility of a State" referred to in Article IX is not criminal liability. Instead it is limited to the civil responsibility of a state, and such responsibility is governed, not by any provisions of the Convention, but by general international law.[9]

Adolfo Miaja de la Muela took the same view. He wrote that the phrase "including those relating to the responsibility of a State for genocide"

---

5   Schabas, W.A. (2000), *Genocide in International Law: The Crime of Crimes*, p. 423, Cambridge University Press, Cambridge.

6   UN GAOR, 3rd sess., Part 1, *Summary Records of Meetings 21 September - 10 December 1948*, p. 351, UN Doc. A/C.6/SR.96 (Mr. Abdoh, Iran).

7   Robinson, N. (1949), *The Genocide Convention: Its Origins and Interpretation*, pp. 42-43, Institute of Jewish Affairs, New York.

8   Ibid., p. 43.

9   Hudson, M.O. (1951), 'The Twenty-Ninth Year of the World Court,' *American Journal of International Law* 45, p. 1, pp. 33-34.

might raise the issue of whether this responsibility is civil or penal, but the enumeration of those presumptively responsible, in Article 4, which does not include a State, dispels any doubt; moreover, the Court will have to decide on the basis of the legal sources listed in Article 38 of its Statute, and by them one cannot conclude that a state bears penal responsibility.[10]

Analyzing Article IV, Miaja de la Muela thus concluded that since it does not list "state" among those not excluded from penal liability, the liability of a state must be civil in character. His reference to the ICJ Statute is to its Article 38, which lists the sources of law the court is to use in deciding cases, principal of which are treaties, customary norms, and the general principles of law. His point was that one did not find in international law a concept of penal responsibility of a state, and thus that the responsibility of a state under Article IX was civil in character.

States ratifying treaties on occasion indicate their understanding of a provision by filing an explanatory statement. Only one state has entered a formal "understanding" about the meaning of the state responsibility phrase of Article IX. The Philippines said, "With further reference to article IX of the Convention, the Philippine Government does not consider said article to extend the concept of State responsibility beyond that recognized by the generally accepted principles of international law."[11]

In the Sixth Committee, the Philippines had opposed adding the state responsibility clause to Article IX, arguing that one could not "stigmatize a whole state for acts for which only its officials or rulers are responsible."[12] This statement and the Philippine "understanding" confirm the analysis of Robinson that the confusion over the state responsibility language of Article IX related to whether one could speak of state responsibility in a treaty that provided for a crime. By its "understanding," the Philippines was expressing its view that the state responsibility envisaged by Article IX could not be penal.

Recent Confusion over the Civil-Penal Issue

The character of the responsibility contemplated by Article IX was raised when the ILC debated its Draft Articles on State Responsibility. In a 1998 discussion, the commission considered the question of whether a distinction should be drawn in state responsibility between a criminal-type responsibility and a civil-type responsibility. Some members who advocated the concept of penal responsibility of states referred to the ICJ analysis of Article IX in the Bosnia case as indicating that the court thought that the state responsibility for genocide in Article IX is penal. Citing both the pleadings and the court's statement, quoted above, "that the reference

---

10 Miaja de la Muela, A. (1951-52), 'El genocidio, delito internacional,' *Revista española de derecho internacional* 4, p. 363, p. 400.

11 *Multilateral Treaties Deposited with the Secretary-General: Status as at 31 December 2003*, pp. 125-126, UN Doc. ST/LEG/SER.E/22 (2003).

12 UN GAOR, 3rd sess., Part 1, *Summary Records of Meetings 21 September - 10 December 1948*, p. 433, UN Doc. A/C.6/SR.103 (Mr. Inglés, Philippines).

in Article IX to 'the responsibility of a state for genocide or for any of the other acts enumerated in Article III', does not exclude any form of State responsibility," they argued that "any form" includes criminal-type responsibility.[13]

In reply, other commission members said that nothing in the Bosnia case, or in Article IX, suggested that the responsibility of a state for genocide was penal. They said that the drafting history showed that Article IX did not refer to the criminal responsibility of states. They said that the type of state responsibility to which the court referred in the Bosnia case was of the civil type, which would, for example, include redressing the injuries suffered by the victims of genocide.[14] James Crawford, the commission's special rapporteur on the law of state responsibility, shared this view. Referring specifically to the Genocide Convention, he said that Article IX did not envisage State crime or the criminal responsibility of States.[15]

The civil-penal issue also troubled Judge Weeramantry, when Yugoslavia filed a counter-claim against Bosnia, alleging state-perpetrated genocide by Bosnia. Most of the court's judges did not see anything in the legal nature of state responsibility for genocide that might preclude a counter-claim. Judge Weeramantry, however, referred to genocide as a crime and concluded on that basis that no counter-claim could be made:

> [T]he concept of a counter-claim is a concept of the civil, as opposed to the criminal, law, for while civil acts and claims may be set off one against another, the intrinsic nature of a criminal wrong prevents the set-off of one criminal act against another. The impact of crime stretches far beyond the party actually injured, and the concept of one crime being set off or used as a counter-claim to another crime is totally alien to modern jurisprudence, domestic or international. ... An act of genocide by the applicant cannot be a counter-claim to an act of genocide by the respondent. Each act stands untouched by the other, in drawing upon itself the united condemnation of the international community.[16]

State Responsibility as Civil Responsibility

It is, of course, possible, that given conduct can give rise to both penal and civil liability. In domestic law, it is not uncommon that an assault may be treated both as a crime and as a subject of suit by the victim. However, the state responsibility contemplated by Article IX is civil in nature. The 1998 discussion in the ILC reflected the views of commission members both that Article IX contemplates the responsibility of a

---

13 *Report of the International Law Commission to the General Assembly on the work of its fiftieth session 20 April - 12 June 1998, 27 July - 14 August 1998*, UN GAOR, 53rd sess., Supp. (No. 10), p. 124, UN Doc. A/53/10 (1998).

14 Ibid., p. 124.

15 Ibid., p. 120.

16 Application of the Convention on the Prevention and Punishment of the Crime of Genocide (Bosnia and Herzegovina v. Yugoslavia), Counter-claims, Order, 1997 ICJ Rep., p. 243, pp. 291-292 (dissenting opinion, Weeramantry).

state for perpetrating genocide, and that the responsibility contemplated is civil in character. Rapporteur Crawford and those commission members who asserted that the court in the Bosnia case viewed the state responsibility referenced in Article IX as civil responsibility had the better side of this argument. The court, as noted in the last chapter, made its statement that Article IX does not exclude any form of state responsibility in responding to Yugoslavia's argument that under Article IX a state is responsible only for failing to prevent or punish genocide perpetrated by others. Thus, the court is handling genocide allegations just as it does any other allegation of an international-law violation, on the basis of the powers it has as an adjudicatory body.

In its 1996 decision in the Bosnia case, the ICJ did not suggest that the state responsibility contemplated by Article IX was penal in character. Nor did the contending parties. The court has no authority to impose economic, diplomatic, or military sanctions, the remedies associated with penal liability of states.

There is a theoretical possibility of the Security Council invoking penal-type sanctions to enforce a judgment of the court. According to Article 94 of the UN Charter, "If any party to a case fails to perform the obligations incumbent upon it under a judgement rendered by the Court the other party may have recourse to the Security Council, which may, if it deems necessary, make recommendations or decide upon measures to be taken to give effect to the judgement." This provision has remained practically a dead letter, however. Despite a number of instances of states disregarding judgments, the Security Council has never imposed a sanction. The court has no bailiff or a sheriff tasked with enforcing its judgments through any coercive process. Moreover, the existence of coercive mechanisms to enforce a court's order in a civil case does not convert the case into a criminal case.

The court may be empowered to award so-called "moral damages" or "punitive damages," in excess of actual monetary losses.[17] An international arbitral tribunal ordered the United States in one case to pay $25,000 to Canada, not for monetary loss but "as a material amend in respect of the wrong."[18] In domestic law, even where such damages are permitted, the case is still considered civil, rather than criminal, in nature.

State responsibility in a treaty clause referring jurisdiction to the court can only be responsibility involving those remedies the court is empowered to utilize. "Any possible doubts on the non-penal nature of this responsibility," wrote Antonio Planzer of Article IX, "are dissipated, in view of the fact that the International Court of Justice would have to decide disputes on the basis of Article 38 of its Statute."[19] Article 38 enumerates the sources of international law applicable in suits between states. Josef L. Kunz drew the same conclusion about Article IX:

17 Shelton, D. (1999), *Remedies in International Human Rights Law*, pp. 126-132, Oxford University Press, Oxford and New York.

18 I'm Alone, Arbitral Award of 5 January 1935, *UN Reports of International Arbitral Awards* 3, p. 1609, p. 1618.

19 Planzer, A. (1956), *Le Crime de Génocide*, p. 127, F. Schwald AG, St. Gallen.

Individuals are criminally liable for genocide in a domestic court under domestic law, but they are not internationally liable. States alone are, under the general conditions of state responsibility, internationally responsible, but under international law, not under criminal law; only this international state responsibility includes—and here lies the innovation—genocide committed by a state against its own citizens.[20]

By "the general conditions of state responsibility," Kunz meant the remedies traditionally used in international claims. As to whether that responsibility is of a civil or penal character, the question so hotly debated during the drafting, the matter would seem to be irrelevant. Article IX calls for submission to the ICJ. The submission therefore is to whatever remedies the court has at its disposal. A state in breach of a treaty must cease its violation and may be required to commit not to repeat the violation in the future. Or it can be required to make "reparation," which may include restitution of the prior existing situation and compensation for harm caused, as well as an apology.[21]

Jørgensen has suggested that even if the responsibility contemplated by the drafters in 1948 was civil, the development in customary law since that date of the concept of penal responsibility of states may be used to re-interpret Article IX as calling for penal responsibility. She refers to the ICJ statement in its 1996 judgment in the Bosnia-Yugoslavia case that Article IX does not exclude any form of state responsibility.[22]

As of 1948, there had been no analysis in international law of the acts of a state under the rubric "crime." Some years later, the ILC wrote the Draft Articles of State Responsibility and did include, as Article 19, a provision that suggests that some wrongful acts committed by states are crimes, rather than being wrongful acts as traditionally conceived in state to state relations, namely, wrongs to which only civil-type remedies attach. The commission used genocide as an example of a wrong that falls into the category of "crime" that can be committed by a state.[23]

However, the proposed concept of state crime was much criticized for its ambiguity. It was not clear what the difference might be between an "ordinary" wrongful act by a state and one that might be denominated a crime. Before it finalized its work on state responsibility, the ILC deleted the concept of "state crime" as a

---

20 Kunz, J.L. (1949), 'The United Nations Convention on Genocide,' *American Journal of International Law* 43, p. 738, p. 746.

21 UN GAOR, International Law Commission, 53rd sess., 23 April-1 June and 2 July-10 August 2001, *State Responsibility*, arts. 30-31, 34-37, UN Doc. A/CN.4/L.602/Rev.1 (2001).

22 Jørgensen, N. (2000), *The Responsibility of States for International Crimes*, p. 271, Oxford University Press, Oxford.

23 Draft Articles on State Responsibility, *Report of the International Law Commission to the General Assembly on the work of its thirty-second session (5 May - 25 July 1980)*, UN GAOR, 35th sess., Supp. (No. 10), p. 59, UN Doc. A/35/10 (1980), also in *Year Book of the International Law Commission*, p. 30 (1980, vol. 2), UN Doc. A/CN.4/SER.A/1980/Add.1 (Part 2).

special form of state responsibility.[24] Whether a concept of "state crime" is found in international law, Article IX does not provide for penal responsibility. The ICJ is limited to the types of remedies at its disposal.

---

24 UN GAOR, International Law Commission, 53rd sess., 23 April-1 June and 2 July-10 August 2001, *State Responsibility*, UN Doc. A/CN.4/L.602/Rev.1 (2001).

Chapter 37

States as Perpetrators of Genocide

The character of the Genocide Convention as penal understandably created confusion as to whether it prohibits genocide perpetrated by a state. So too did the omission of any reference to state responsibility, save in the submission clause. Over and against these factors stands Article IX, with its reference to a state's responsibility for genocide. A proper reading must account for all factors.

Article IV and States

Judges Shi and Vereshchetin focused on the omission of any mention of states in Article IV of the Genocide Convention. Article IV stipulates that government officials are not exempt from prosecution for genocide: "Persons committing genocide or any of the other acts enumerated in article III shall be punished, whether they are constitutionally responsible rulers, public officials or private individuals."

Johan van der Vyver reads Article IV as an exhaustive list of parties that can be responsible for genocide. Liability under the Genocide Convention, he wrote, referring to Article IV, is "confined to those who have something in common with those categories, i.e., natural persons."[1] Van der Vyver invoked in support of this conclusion the maxim of statutory construction *ejusdem generis*.[2] By this maxim, if a catch-all category follows a specific item or a series of items, one reads the catch-all category to include only items having something in common with those enumerated.[3]

In the Bosnia case, the ICJ addressed Article IV before coming to its conclusion that the Genocide Convention applies to states that perpetrate genocide. The court wrote, contrary to van der Vyver, that the Convention does not exclude the responsibility of a state for genocide. After stating that Article IX "does not exclude any form of State responsibility," the court continued, "Nor is the responsibility of a State for acts of its organs excluded by article IV of the Convention, which contemplates the commission of an act of genocide by 'rulers' or 'public officials'."[4]

---

1   van der Vyver, J.D. (1999), 'Prosecution and Punishment of the Crime of Genocide,' *Fordham International Law Journal* 23, p. 286, p. 290.

2   Ibid., p. 290.

3   *Black's Law Dictionary* (1999).

4   Application of the Convention on the Prevention and Punishment of the Crime of Genocide (Bosnia and Herzegovina v. Yugoslavia), Preliminary Objections, Judgment, 1996

The court's implication is that there is no reason to read Article IV as limiting the Convention's applicability for perpetration of genocide to individuals. Nothing in Article IV purports to limit liability to individuals. The purpose of Article IV was to ensure that individuals not escape responsibility by virtue of their position in a government. Article IV thus applies to individuals as parties responsible under the Genocide Convention. The fact that the Convention extends liability to natural persons regardless of their status does not mean that liability under the Convention is limited to natural persons.

The maxim *ejusdem generis*, invoked by van der Vyver, has, to be sure, been used in the interpretation of treaties.[5] However, that maxim applies only to situations in which a list of categories appears in a statute. It is "[a] canon of construction that when a general word or phrase follows a list of specific persons of things, the general word or phrase will be interpreted to include only persons or things of the same type as those listed."[6]

Article IV contains no catch-all category. As a result, the maxim *ejusdem generis* is inapplicable. Article IV merely means that as among individuals who may be charged with genocide, immunity is not enjoyed by public officials or constitutionally responsible rulers. Article IV does not exclude entities other than individuals from responsibility for perpetrating genocide.

The Intent of a State

The requirement in Article II of an intent may seem to limit liability to individuals. William Schabas has argued that intent is a concept relating to the mind of a person accused of crime and thus cannot apply to a state. Therefore, he said, a state should not be understood as an entity that can be responsible for genocide under the Genocide Convention.[7] Many instances of a state's responsibility under international law, however, rest on the state's attitude towards an act it commits. Moreover, states act through individual officials, and those officials can act with a certain intent. In international law, "the conduct of any State organ shall be considered an act of that State," and "an organ includes any person or entity which has that status in accordance with the internal law of the State."[8]

If persons whose conduct is attributable to the state entertain the requisite intent, then the state is responsible. It need not be found that the state, as a collectivity,

ICJ Rep., p. 595, p. 616.

5   McNair, A. (1961), *The Law of Treaties*, pp. 393-399, Clarendon Press, Oxford.

6   *Black's Law Dictionary* (1999).

7   Schabas, W.A. (2000), *Genocide in International Law: The Crime of Crimes*, p. 444, Cambridge University Press, Cambridge.

8   UN GAOR, International Law Commission, 53rd sess., 23 April-1 June and 2 July-10 August 2001, *State Responsibility*, art. 4, UN Doc. A/CN.4/L.602/Rev.1 (2001).

entertained the requisite intent. Moreover, as noted in Chapter 17, even as to individuals, intent can be inferred from acts.

Genocide, as we saw in Chapter 11, is prohibited in customary international law, so the same issue of a state's intent arises there. If the intent requirement negated state responsibility, there would be no state responsibility for genocide in customary law. Since there is such responsibility, the intent requirement is no obstacle.

The issue of a state's intent arose, as we saw in Chapter 32, when Yugoslavia alleged genocide against NATO states. Yugoslavia alleged that the NATO states targeted civilian objectives, and that they used cluster bombs, which are specifically designed to kill human beings, as well as depleted uranium, which has long-lasting adverse effects on humans.[9] Yugoslavia asked the court to determine that bombing of such objectives and with such weaponry revealed genocidal intent. The NATO states replied that they did not expose civilians to dangers beyond what is inevitable in warfare.[10] The two sides in the litigation differed on their view of whether genocidal intent was present, but the court was able to resolve the issue.

The Plain Meaning of Article IX

Article IX, by referring to a state's responsibility "for genocide or for any of the other acts enumerated in article III," makes it plain that a state may perpetrate genocide, including conspiracy, incitement, attempt, and complicity. The reference to Article III is to the ancillary acts of conspiracy, incitement, complicity, and attempt and thus says that a state may be responsible for those acts, as well as for genocide itself. "That a state may incur international responsibility for genocide is clearly borne out by Article IX of the Genocide Convention," writes Daniel Nsereko.[11]

There is stylistic awkwardness here, to be sure. Article III says, "The following acts shall be punishable," and then lists "genocide" plus the ancillary acts. The term "punishable" is directed at individuals, as a term of penal law. As indicated in the last chapter, the drafters conceived a state's liability for committing genocide as civil in character. Thus, one would not say that a state is "punishable" under Article III. Rather, from the wording of Article IX, one would say that a state is liable ("responsibility of a state") for genocide.

It is hard to avoid the conclusion that Article IX imposes liability on a state for its own perpetration of genocide. Any doubt that might be thought to emanate from

---

9   Legality of Use of Force (Yugoslavia v. Belgium), Order, 1999 ICJ Rep., p. 124, p. 127.

10 Legality of Use of Force (Yugoslavia v. Belgium), ICJ, oral argument, 10 May 1999 (Mr. Ergec, Belgium).

11 Nsereko, D.D.N. (2000), 'Genocide: A Crime Against Mankind,' in G.K. McDonald and O. Swaak-Goldman (eds), *Substantive and Procedural Aspects of International Criminal Law: The Experience of International and National Courts*, vol. 1, p. 113, p. 135, Kluwer, The Hague.

the English-language text is dispelled by reference to the text in the other official languages of the Genocide Convention, in particular the Russian text.

When a treaty is concluded in more than one language, "[t]he terms of the treaty are presumed to have the same meaning in each authentic text."[12] Article X of the Genocide Convention recites that the text is equally authentic in its Chinese, English, French, Russian and Spanish versions.

Where the English text of Article IX reads "for genocide," the French text uses "*en matière de génocide*," and the Spanish text "*en materia de genocidio*." These two texts mean something like "in respect of genocide." They read similarly to the English "for genocide" in stating that what is at issue is the responsibility of a state for perpetrating genocide.

The Russian and Chinese texts differ slightly from the other three. The Russian text reads "for the commission of genocide." Thus, the Russian text adds a noun that does not appear in the English, French, or Spanish texts. The Russian noun used—"*sovershenie*"—means "commission" or "perpetration."[13] This noun appears in Russian penal legislation to refer to the commission of a criminal act.[14] By adding the word "commission," the Russian text spells out what is strongly implied in the English "for genocide," the French "*en matière de génocide*," and the Spanish "*en materia de genocidio*," namely that "for genocide" means "for the commission of genocide."

The Chinese text uses a different syntax from the other four texts and, curiously, omits the term "genocide" altogether. It reads: "the responsibility of a state including responsibility for harming a race of people."[15] Thus, where the other four texts use the term "genocide," the Chinese uses "harming a race of people." In the Chinese text, "harming" obviously refers to a state as the actor.

The Genocide Convention's definitional clauses characterize genocide in penal law terms and make no reference to the responsibility of a state for perpetrating genocide. However, Article IX provides for jurisdiction in the ICJ for claims against a state for genocide. A principle of treaty construction is a presumption that all language found in a treaty has some significance. If one were to limit the phrase "including those relating to the responsibility of a State for genocide" to failures to prevent and punish genocide, then the phrase would be duplicative of the prior section of that sentence, which refers to disputes "relating to the interpretation, application or fulfilment." The latter language covers a failure to prevent and punish. There would have been no need to add the phrase "including those relating to the responsibility of a State for genocide."

---

12 Vienna Convention on the Law of Treaties, art. 33, para. 3, UNTS 1155, p. 331.

13 *Russko-angliiskii slovar'. Russian-English Dictionary* (A. I. Smirnitskii, ed., 1959).

14 Russia, *Ugolovnyi kodeks RSFSR* [Criminal Code of the Russian Soviet Federated Socialist Republic], art. 8 (1960) (*sovershenie prestupleniia umyshlenno* [Commission of a crime intentionally]).

15 Author's approximation of the Chinese text based on consultation with Chinese-speaking lawyers.

Consensus on State Perpetration

Litigation in the ICJ subsequent to the court's 1996 decision suggests that the issue of jurisdiction over state-perpetrated genocide may no longer be contested. In 1997, when it filed its counter-memorial on the merits of Bosnia's case, Yugoslavia reversed course and asserted its own genocide allegation against Bosnia. Yugoslavia asserted a counter-claim, alleging that Bosnia had committed genocide in the course of the same hostilities.[16] "Bosnia and Herzegovina," wrote Yugoslavia, "is responsible for the acts of genocide committed against the Serbs in Bosnia and Herzegovina."[17] Under the court's rules of procedure, a counter-claim is admissible only if jurisdiction is proper. Yugoslavia claimed jurisdiction over Bosnia under Article IX. Bosnia urged the court to reject the counter-claim, arguing that Yugoslavia would be expanding the case to include new factual issues.[18]

Yugoslavia insisted that the counter-claim be considered nonetheless,[19] and the court decided to allow it.[20] Without discussion, the court noted that "Bosnia and Herzegovina recognizes that these claims meet the jurisdiction requirement."[21] By accepting the counter-claim, the court reaffirmed its 1996 position that Article IX permits a suit for the perpetration of genocide.

In 2001, Yugoslavia withdrew its counter-claim against Bosnia, without explanation.[22] But in 1999, it sued ten NATO states for perpetrating genocide. Also in 1999, Croatia sued Yugoslavia for perpetrating genocide, alleging the killing of Croatian nationals during the hostilities of 1993. Croatia sought no interim order, and to date no ruling on jurisdiction has resulted. Yugoslavia, however, asked for interim orders against the NATO bombing of its territory, so the court was forced to consider whether it had jurisdiction.

In its 1999 filing, Yugoslavia asserted, consistent with the court's 1996 judgment in Bosnia's case, that a state can be sued under the Genocide Convention for the

---

16 Application of the Convention on the Prevention and Punishment of the Crime of Genocide (Bosnia and Herzegovina v. Yugoslavia), Counter-memorial of Yugoslavia, 23 July 1997, p. 2, pp. 349-1077 (Chapter 7: Crime of Genocide Against the Serbs in Bosnia and Herzegovina).

17 Application of the Convention on the Prevention and Punishment of the Crime of Genocide (Bosnia and Herzegovina v. Yugoslavia), Counter-memorial of Yugoslavia, 23 July 1997, p. 1084.

18 Letter of Bosnia-Herzegovina to Registrar, dated 9 October 1997, received 10 October 1997.

19 Letter of Yugoslavia to Registrar, dated 23 October 1997, received 24 October 1997.

20 Application of the Convention on the Prevention and Punishment of the Crime of Genocide (Bosnia and Herzegovina v. Yugoslavia), Counter-claims, Order, 1997 ICJ Rep., p. 243, p. 260.

21 Ibid., p. 258.

22 Application of the Convention on the Prevention and Punishment of the Crime of Genocide (Bosnia and Herzegovina v. Yugoslavia), President, Order, 2001 ICJ Rep., p. 572, p. 573.

perpetration of genocide. Spain and the USA, the two of the ten NATO states that had reserved to Article IX, contested jurisdiction, but the other eight did not. The court said, as it had in 1996, that Article IX covers state perpetration of genocide. In its decision on Yugoslavia's request for an interim order against Belgium, the court said:

> [I]t is not disputed that both Yugoslavia and Belgium are parties to the Genocide Convention without reservation; and whereas Article IX of the Convention accordingly appears to constitute a basis on which the jurisdiction of the Court might be founded to the extent that the subject-matter of the dispute relates to "the interpretation, application or fulfilment" of the Convention, including disputes "relating to the responsibility of a State for genocide or for any of the other acts enumerated in article III" of the said Convention.[23]

Only one judge took the view that state-perpetrated genocide is outside the court's jurisdiction. Judges Kreca, Shi, and Vereshchetin, who had taken that position in 1996, did not address the matter. Only Judge Oda did, and he held to his 1996 view. Judge Oda wrote that Yugoslavia was not a state whose rights under the Genocide Convention were affected, even if the NATO states were committing genocide in Yugoslavia:

> Even if, as alleged, the respondent States are responsible for certain results of the bombing or armed attacks by NATO armed forces in the territory of the Federal Republic of Yugoslavia, this fact alone does not mean that there is a "dispute relating to the interpretation, application or fulfilment of the Convention," as the respondent States did not violate the rights conferred upon the Federal Republic of Yugoslavia by the Convention. What is protected by the Convention is *not* the particular rights of any individual State (the Federal Republic of Yugoslavia in this case) *but* the status of human beings with human rights and the universal interest of the individual in general.[24]

Judge Oda remained the only member of the court to insist that Article IX does not provide jurisdiction over a state that perpetrates genocide.

---

23 Legality of Use of Force (Yugoslavia v. Belgium), Order, 1999 ICJ Rep., p. 124, p. 137.

24 Ibid., p. 157 (separate opinion, Oda).

Chapter 38

Other Routes to Jurisdiction

The Genocide Convention is not the only international instrument aimed at stopping atrocities. Other mechanisms are potentially available that might give the ICJ jurisdiction over conduct that could be characterized as genocide. If such mechanisms are widely available, or if they become widely available in the future, states may have other ways to gain ICJ jurisdiction over a state that commits acts that might be characterized as genocide, but might as well be characterized as violations of other human rights obligations. This chapter inquires whether other mechanisms are available, in order to determine how critical a role the Genocide Convention plays.

Three other routes to ICJ jurisdiction are possible: jurisdiction by consent of the state accused, compulsory jurisdiction, and jurisdiction under treaties other than the Genocide Convention.

Consent for the Particular Case

The acts constituting genocide might involve violations of other international obligations, such as the right to life, or the prohibition against inhuman or degrading treatment. Suit can be brought in the ICJ on any international-legal issue if the defendant state consents to being sued. Under Article 36 of the Statute, a state may sue another if the latter consents to jurisdiction in the particular case. If consent of the defendant state is a likely route to jurisdiction, then the Genocide Convention with its submission clause may not be necessary.

No state has, however, succeeded in convincing another state to allow itself to be sued over alleged atrocities. States are never pleased to have atrocity allegations made against them and are not likely to want to litigate over them. Yugoslavia tried this basis of jurisdiction, among others, when it sued ten NATO states in 1999. Yugoslavia sought, for example, the consent of France to be sued. However, France refused, and the court found that Yugoslavia had not established jurisdiction on this basis.[1] Yugoslavia's only route to jurisdiction over France was the Genocide Convention.

---

1 Legality of Use of Force (Yugoslavia v. France), Order, 1999 ICJ Rep., p. 363, p. 373.

Compulsory Jurisdiction

Another possibility is to sue on the basis of consent previously given, under an ICJ procedure called compulsory jurisdiction. Article 36 invites state parties to the Statute to file a declaration in which they subject themselves to suit by any other state party that files a similar declaration. Such a declaration could subject a state to the court's jurisdiction for "the interpretation of a treaty" or "any question of international law." A state party that has filed such a declaration could be sued only by another state party that itself has filed such a declaration.[2]

"Any question of international law" could include genocide as a norm of customary international law. Thus, under compulsory jurisdiction, even a state that is not party to Genocide Convention could be sued for genocide. Also, a state that is party to the Genocide Convention but which has reserved to Article IX could be sued for genocide.

Beyond genocide, a state that can establish compulsory jurisdiction over another state could sue for violation of a variety of norms in humanitarian law or human rights law. These could include the right to life, or the prohibition against inhuman or degrading treatment. The availability of compulsory jurisdiction as a jurisdictional base is, however, limited. Most state parties to the Statute have failed to file a declaration, and some that filed a declaration later withdrew it. At present, only 66 states have a declaration on file with the court.[3] Moreover, both the potential plaintiff state and the potential defendant state must have filed such a declaration, so the circle of states that potentially may sue each other is small.

In discussion in the Sixth Committee in 1948, the United Kingdom noted that compulsory jurisdiction was likely to be of limited utility and used that fact as an argument for including state-perpetrated genocide in Article IX. It said, "The Court's jurisdiction was compulsory only for a limited number of States which, in accordance with Article 36 of the Statute of the Court, had recognized it by official declaration."[4]

To make matters worse, many of the states filing declarations wrote in exceptions that exempt the state from the court's jurisdiction in particular situations, one such situation being military action.[5] Thus, a potential defendant state may have exempted itself from suit on the issue the potential plaintiff state seeks to raise.

A rare instance of a suit over atrocities against civilians, based on compulsory jurisdiction, was filed by Congo in 1999. Congo sued Uganda for armed intervention

---

2   Case of Certain Norwegian Loans (France v. Norway), Judgment, 1957 ICJ Rep., p. 9.

3   *Multilateral Treaties Deposited with the Secretary-General: Status as at 31 December 2003*, pp. 11-12, UN Doc. ST/LEG/SER.E/22 (2003).

4   UN GAOR, 3rd sess., Part 1, *Summary Records of Meetings 21 September - 10 December 1948*, p. 430, UN Doc. A/C.6/SR.103 (1949) (Mr. Fitzmaurice, UK).

5   *Multilateral Treaties Deposited with the Secretary-General: Status as at 31 December 2003*, pp. 12-27, UN Doc. ST/LEG/SER.E/22 (2003).

in Congo, and for the victimization of Congolese civilians in Congo. Congo alleged that Ugandan troops had massacred Congolese civilians. Congo was able to base jurisdiction on the compulsory procedure, because both Congo and Uganda had filed Article 36 declarations subjecting themselves to the court's jurisdiction.[6]

Yugoslavia, however, failed when it tried to gain compulsory jurisdiction over some of the NATO states it sued in 1999. Yugoslavia cited the declarations recognizing compulsory jurisdiction that had been filed by these states. Yugoslavia itself had filed such a declaration, but only on 25 April 1999, four weeks after the commencement of NATO bombing, which began on 24 March 1999. In its declaration Yugoslavia specified that it consented to ICJ jurisdiction only for disputes arising after the date of its declaration.

The potential defendant states, which contested jurisdiction, invoked this limitation in Yugoslavia's declaration. Since a state may sue on the basis of compulsory jurisdiction only if it itself has filed a declaration, a potential defendant state is entitled to rely on any reservation or limitation that the potential plaintiff state has written into its declaration. Yugoslavia had subjected itself to suit only for a dispute arising after 25 April 1999. The NATO states invoked that limitation against Yugoslavia. They argued that the dispute arose on 24 March 1999.[7] The court accepted this argument, deciding that the dispute arose on 24 March 1999, and therefore did not fall within the terms of Yugoslavia's acceptance of compulsory jurisdiction. On this basis, the court ruled that it had no jurisdiction over the NATO states under the compulsory jurisdiction procedure.[8]

Jurisdiction under Human Rights Treaties

A state alleging genocide might be able to establish ICJ jurisdiction under some other human rights category. In addition to the Genocide Convention, three human rights treaties with widespread adherence contain submission clauses providing for jurisdiction in the court: the International Convention on the Elimination of All Forms of Racial Discrimination,[9] the Convention on the Elimination of All Forms

---

6   Armed Activities on the Territory of the Congo (Congo v. Uganda), 1999 ICJ, Application, 23 June 1999.

7   Legality of Use of Force (Yugoslavia v. Canada), oral argument, ICJ, 10 May 1999, para. 17 (Mr. Kirsch, Canada).

8   Legality of Use of Force (Yugoslavia v. Belgium), Order, 1999 ICJ Rep., p. 124, pp. 134-135.

9   International Convention on the Elimination of All Forms of Racial Discrimination, art. 22, UNTS 660, p. 195.

of Discrimination against Women,[10] and the Convention against Torture and Other Cruel, Inhuman or Degrading Treatment or Punishment.[11]

A number of state parties to these treaties have, however, reserved to their submission clauses. To date, the only state to invoke them has been Congo, when it sued neighboring states that intervened militarily and occupied Congolese territory. In 1999, at the same time as it filed against Uganda on the basis of compulsory jurisdiction, Congo filed against Burundi and Rwanda, using the Convention against Torture and Other Cruel, Inhuman or Degrading Treatment or Punishment as its jurisdictional base. As in its filing against Uganda, Congo alleged massacres of Congolese civilians.[12] In 2002, Congo filed again against Rwanda, using both the Convention on the Elimination of All Forms of Discrimination against Women, and the International Convention on the Elimination of All Forms of Racial Discrimination, to allege "large-scale human slaughter" by Rwanda.[13] Rwanda, however, had filed a reservation to the submission clause in the latter Convention.

On one earlier occasion, another state nearly filed an atrocity allegation under the International Convention on the Elimination of All Forms of Racial Discrimination. After Bosnia sued Yugoslavia for genocide under the Genocide Convention, it publicly declared its intent to sue the United Kingdom for genocide on the ground that the UK failed to prevent genocide in Bosnia by maintaining an arms embargo against Bosnia. Additionally, Bosnia said that it would sue the UK for violating the International Convention on the Elimination of All Forms of Racial Discrimination by proposing solutions to the Bosnia conflict that were racially discriminatory.[14] In the event, Bosnia did not file against the UK.[15]

---

10 Convention on the Elimination of All Forms of Discrimination against Women, art. 29, UNTS 1249, p. 13.

11 Convention against Torture and Other Cruel, Inhuman or Degrading Treatment or Punishment, art. 30, UNTS 1465, p. 85.

12 Armed Activities on the Territory of the Congo (Democratic Republic of Congo v. Burundi), 1999 ICJ, Application, 23 June 1999. Armed Activities on the Territory of the Congo (Democratic Republic of Congo v. Rwanda), 1999 ICJ, Application, 23 June 1999.

13 Armed Activities on the Territory of the Congo (Congo v. Rwanda), 2002 ICJ, Application, 28 May 2002.

14 Statement of Intention by the Republic of Bosnia and Herzegovina to Institute Legal Proceedings Against the United Kingdom before the International Court of Justice, 15 November 1993, in Boyle, F.A. (1996), *The Bosnian People Charge Genocide: Proceedings at the International Court of Justice Concerning* Bosnia v. Serbia *on the Prevention and Punishment of the Crime of Genocide*, p. 365, Aletheia Press, Amherst.

15 Joint Statement by the Government of Bosnia-Herzegovina and the United Kingdom of Great Britain and Northern Ireland, 20 December 1993, ibid., p. 368.

The Court's Caution in Exercising Jurisdiction

In its 1993 suit against Yugoslavia, Bosnia, in addition to asserting jurisdiction under the Genocide Convention, attempted to ground jurisdiction on a treaty that contained human rights guarantees. Bosnia argued that the ICJ had jurisdiction under a 1919 treaty. A minority protection treaty concluded between the World War I allies and Yugoslavia, which then was known as the Serb-Croat-Slovene Kingdom, required the latter to "assure full and complete protection of life and liberty to all inhabitants of the Kingdom without distinction of birth, nationality, language, race or religion."[16] The treaty called for submission of cases, in the event of a dispute, to the Permanent Court of International Justice.[17] As successor to the Permanent Court of International Justice, the ICJ gains jurisdiction under submission clauses that refer cases to the Permanent Court.

When Bosnia's case reached the preliminary objections stage, it withdrew this claim for jurisdiction, deciding to confine itself to the Genocide Convention alone for jurisdiction over Yugoslavia. The parties did not brief the issue to the court. Nonetheless, in ruling in 1996 on Yugoslavia's objections to jurisdiction, the court addressed the issue and decided that the 1919 treaty did not give Bosnia jurisdiction over Yugoslavia. The 1919 treaty, the court said, applied to Yugoslavia's treatment of minorities only within Yugoslavia's borders. The atrocities alleged by Bosnia occurred in Bosnia, after Bosnia seceded from Yugoslavia in 1992. Therefore, said the court, the 1919 treaty did not cover them.[18]

The ICJ may be forced to re-visit this issue in future cases, given the possibility of renewed unrest in the Balkans. Although the 1919 treaty referred to the treatment of minorities in state territory, the unique circumstances presented by Bosnia's suit made application appropriate. The 1919 treaty required Yugoslavia to protect those minorities that inhabited its territory. In the early 1990s, several of these minorities, including the Bosnian Muslims and Croats, split off to form separate states. Yugoslavia refused to recognize those states. According to Bosnia's allegations, Yugoslavia used its army, still stationed on the territory of Bosnia after Bosnia's secession, to kill Bosnian Muslims and Croats. Thus, the alleged victims were the very minorities the 1919 treaty protected.

The issue concerns not only the 1919 treaty applicable to Yugoslavia, but similar minority protection treaties that were concluded at Versailles between the World War I allies and various states of eastern Europe. Even under the limited view of

---

16 Treaty between the Allied and Associated Powers and the Kingdom of the Serbs, Croats and Slovenes (Protection of Minorities), 10 September 1919, art. 2, British Treaty Series, no. 17 (1919), reprinted in Hudson, M.O. (1931), *International Legislation: A Collection of the Texts of Multipartite International Instruments of General Interest*, vol. 1, p. 312.

17 Ibid., art. 11.

18 Application of the Convention on the Prevention and Punishment of the Crime of Genocide (Bosnia and Herzegovina v. Yugoslavia), Preliminary Objections, Judgment, 1996 ICJ p. 595, pp. 619-620.

territorial reach taken by the ICJ, the court may have jurisdiction over a range of human rights atrocities in eastern Europe under the submission clauses in these minority protection treaties,[19] in post-World War I peace treaties,[20] and in League-era unilateral declarations promising fair treatment for minorities.[21]

Human rights treaties other than the Genocide Convention hold some potential for ICJ suits against a state that commits atrocities. Compulsory jurisdiction holds modest potential as well. In many instances, however, as the UK predicted in the Sixth Committee, a state unable to establish jurisdiction under the Genocide Convention has no other jurisdictional basis on which to sue.

---

19 Treaty between the Allied and Associated Powers and Poland, 28 June 1919, art. 12, *British Foreign & State Papers*, vol. 112 (1922), p. 232. Treaty between the Allied and Associated Powers and Czechoslovakia, 10 September 1919, art. 14, *British & Foreign State Papers*, vol. 112 (1922), p. 502. Treaty between the Allied and Associated Powers and Rumania, 9 December 1919, art. 12, LNTS 5, p. 335. Treaty on the Protection of Minorities in Greece, 10 August 1920, art. 16, LNTS 28, p. 243.

20 Treaty of Peace between the Allied and Associated Powers and Austria, 10 September 1919, art. 69, reprinted in Israel, F. (ed.) (1967), *Major Peace Treaties of Modern History 1648-1967*, p. 1535. Treaty of Peace between the Allied and Associated Powers and Bulgaria, 27 November 1919, art. 57, ibid., p. 1727. Treaty of Peace Between the Allied and Associated Powers and Hungary, 4 June 1920, art. 60; ibid., p. 1863. Treaty of Peace between the British Empire, France, Italy, Japan, Greece, Roumania, the Serb-Croat-Slovene State and Turkey, 24 July 1923, art. 44, LNTS 28, p. 11.

21 Declaration concerning the Protection of Minorities in Albania, 2 October 1921, art. 7(3) in Hudson (1931), vol. 1, p. 733. Declaration Concerning the Protection of Minorities in Lithuania, 12 May 1922, art. 9, LNTS 22, p. 393.

Chapter 39

States as Intermeddlers

If states can be sued for committing genocide, as the ICJ has said they can under Article IX of the Genocide Convention, the door is open to other states to file. Typically, only a state with a strong connection to a situation will sue. But genocide is the concern of the international community as a whole. That, after all, is why a treaty was concluded on genocide. That concept opens the possibility that states having no direct connection to an instance of genocide might nonetheless seek to sue. When human rights guaranteed by treaty are violated, "there is a common interest in accomplishing the objectives of the treaty, a collective interest in the integrity of the commitments involved," writes Dinah Shelton, therefore a "public action in favour of the treaty system" may be provided.[1]

In 1949, Kurt Stillschweig posed the issue the ICJ would need to resolve:

> State responsibility was mentioned in Article IX, which speaks of a general "responsibility of a state for Genocide." These words were added by an English-Belgian amendment and indicate only "civil responsibility," as the English delegate expressly stated and the majority of the Sixth Commission accepted.
>
> Article IX is, however, only procedural in character and does not specify the exact contours of material responsibility. That issue will have to be resolved in individual cases by the Hague court, and it is a difficult problem, especially as concerns the obligation for damages of a state that commits genocide against its own nationals.[2]

Genocide and "Non-involved" States

When Yugoslavia asserted a counter-claim of genocide against Bosnia, Judge *ad hoc* Lauterpacht worried aloud that genocide suits may present novel complexities:

> The closer one approaches the problems posed by the operation of the judicial settlement procedure contemplated by Article IX of the Genocide Convention, the more one is obliged to recognize that these problems are of an entirely different kind from those normally confronting an international tribunal of essentially civil, as opposed to criminal, jurisdiction.

---

1   Shelton, D. (1999), *Remedies in International Human Rights Law*, p. 103, Oxford University Press, Oxford and New York.

2   Stillschweig, K. (1949), 'Das Abkommen zur Bekämpfung von Genocide,' *Die Friedens-Warte* 49, p. 93, p. 103, Blätter für internationale Verständigung und zwischenstaatliche Organisation, Hans Wehberg (ed.).

The difficulties are systemic and their solution cannot be rapidly achieved, whether by the Court or, perhaps more appropriately, by the Parties to the Genocide Convention.[3]

An issue yet to be addressed by the court is whether a "non-involved" state may sue. In Bosnia's case against Yugoslavia, in Yugoslavia's case against the NATO states, and in Croatia's case against Yugoslavia, the victims were, in the main, nationals of the plaintiff state, and the alleged acts occurred in the territory of the plaintiff state. Yugoslavia's counter-claim against Bosnia was based on harm allegedly caused in Bosnia to Bosnian Serbs, that is, to inhabitants of Bosnia who were Serb and thus had an ethnic connection to Yugoslavia.

One can ask, however, whether it would have been open to Uruguay, for example, to sue Yugoslavia over its alleged genocide in Bosnia, even if no Uruguayan nationals were among the victims. Uruguay might have considered itself to have a "dispute" with Yugoslavia simply because, in Uruguay's opinion, Yugoslavia was committing genocide. UN member states have an obligation, under Article 56 of the UN Charter, to act in cooperation with the UN to promote human rights. The Genocide Convention was a project of the United Nations. A state in Uruguay's position might view itself as fulfilling its UN Charter obligation by suing Yugoslavia. Uruguay might argue that any state party to the Genocide Convention may sue for state-perpetrated genocide and may even be legally required to do so.[4]

Yugoslavia might object that no "dispute" exists between it and Uruguay regarding genocide in Bosnia because of Uruguay's lack of a direct connection. Uruguay might respond in turn that Article IX posits that a dispute may exist between a state perpetrating genocide and any other state party.

The United States has shown concern that "non-involved" states might sue for genocide. In 1949, US President Harry Truman asked the US Senate to consent to the ratification of the Genocide Convention. In transmitting the Convention to the Senate, President Truman referred to an interpretation of Article IX that had recently been written by the US Department of State. According to the Department, the Convention did not apply to a state's treatment of its own nationals. Adopting that view, Truman suggested that the Senate approve the Genocide Convention

with the understanding that article IX shall be understood in the traditional sense of responsibility to another state for injuries sustained by nationals of the complaining state in violation of principles of international law, and shall not be understood as meaning that a state can be held liable in damages for injuries inflicted by it on its own nationals.[5]

---

3 Application of the Convention on the Prevention and Punishment of the Crime of Genocide (Bosnia and Herzegovina v. Yugoslavia), Counter-claims, Order, 1997 ICJ Rep., p. 243, pp. 285-286 (separate opinion, Lauterpacht).

4 Frowein, J.A. (1994), 'Reactions by Not Directly Affected States to Breaches of Public International Law,' *Recueil des Cours* (Hague Academy of International Law) 248, vol. 4, p. 345, pp. 397-398.

5 'The President's Letter of Transmittal: Report of the Secretary of State,' *Department of State Bulletin* 21, p. 844, p. 846 (1949).

248 The Genocide Convention

Under this interpretation, the only state entitled to sue would be one whose nationals were injured.

The US Senate did not give President Truman its consent to ratification, and so it did not act on his proposed statement of understanding. When, however, the US Senate once again considered the Genocide Convention in the 1980s, the Senate Foreign Relations Committee issued a report that repeated *verbatim* the Truman interpretation. Explaining the state responsibility clause in Article IX, the committee said: "This is to be understood in the traditional sense of responsibility to another state for injuries sustained by nationals of the complaining state in violation of principles of international law."[6] When the United States ratified the Convention, as we saw in Chapter 34, it filed a reservation to Article IX and thus had no need to express its understanding of the meaning of Article IX. No other state entered any "understanding" that would limit suit to states whose nationals were victims.

Weight of Opinion on "Non-involved" States as Plaintiffs

William Schabas has said that only a state whose nationals are injured is an "injured state" for purposes of suit under Article IX, hence only such a state may sue.[7] Adolfo Molina assumed that "only when genocide affects nationals of another state may an international tribunal intervene." He thought that "responsibility of a State" in Article IX referred to responsibility towards another state for harm to nationals of that state.[8] Pieter Drost also accepted the Truman view, based on the fact that the Genocide Convention made no provision for claims by individuals:

> In the absence of any specific stipulation as to the right of redress and reparation of individuals, be they either aliens or nationals, against the state for acts of genocide committed within its territory, a claim of compensation and restitution can only be brought before the Court under the Convention *juncto* the Statute of the Court by a state whose nationals have suffered damage by acts of genocide, against the state where the cases of genocide took place. No international claim could be put forward with respect to damage inflicted upon non-nationals of the claimant state, in particular upon nationals of the defendant state.[9]

The fact that the Genocide Convention creates no cause of action for individuals does not, however, restrict the circle of states that may sue.

---

6 'Genocide Convention,' US Senate Executive Report No. 2, 99th Cong., 1st sess., p. 12 (1985).

7 Schabas, W.A. (2000), *Genocide in International Law: The Crime of Crimes*, p. 445, Cambridge University Press, Cambridge.

8 Molina, A. (1950), 'El delito de genocidio en la legislación Guatemalteca,' *Revista de la Facultad de Ciencias Jurídicas y Sociales de Guatemala*, p. 25, p. 32.

9 Drost, P.N. (1959), *The Crime of State: Penal Protection for Fundamental Freedoms of Persons and Peoples: Book II: Genocide: United Nations Legislation on International Criminal Law*, pp. 67-70, A.W. Sythoff, Leiden.

A more convincing analysis was provided by ICJ Judge Philip Jessup, who read Article IX to allow any state party to sue. Jessup had served as Deputy US Representative to the UN Security Council in 1948, when the Genocide Convention was being drafted. "For over a century," he explained, "treaties have specifically recognized the legal interests of States in general humanitarian causes and have frequently provided procedural means by which States could secure respect for these interests." Jessup cited the inter-war minorities treaties, which allowed any member of the Council of the League of Nations to sue a state in the Permanent Court of International Justice for violating the rights of its own nationals who were members of minority groups.[10] Jessup cited the court's advisory opinion in Reservations to the Genocide Convention, where the court stated, "In such a convention the contracting States do not have any interests of their own; they merely have, one and all, a common interest, namely the accomplishment of those high purposes which are the raison d'être of the convention."[11]

Thus, Jessup understood Article IX to mean that any state could sue, and the precedent he cites involved suits against a state violating the rights of its own nationals.

André de Hoogh, in his study of the international responsibility of states, concludes that Article IX gives any state party to the Genocide Convention a legal interest to sue another state party for perpetration of genocide.[12]

The Truman view has been portrayed by Nina Jørgensen, who has analyzed the issue in detail, as reflecting the accepted meaning of Article IX. Jørgensen writes, "Both the literature contemporaneous with the adoption of the Genocide Convention and subsequent doctrine conform to this standpoint." Jørgensen cited seven authorities who, she says, regard the Truman view as reflecting the proper meaning of Article IX.[13]

---

10 South West Africa Cases (Ethiopia v. S. Africa, Liberia v. S. Africa), Preliminary Objections, 1962 ICJ Rep., p. 319, pp. 425-426 (separate opinion, Jessup).

11 Reservations to the Convention on the Prevention and Punishment of the Crime of Genocide (adv. op.), 1951 ICJ Rep., p. 15, p. 23.

12 de Hoogh, A. (1996), *Obligations Erga Omnes and International Crimes: A Theoretical Inquiry into the Implementation and Enforcement of the International Responsibility of States*, p. 42, Kluwer, The Hague and Boston.

13 Jørgensen, N. (1999), 'State Responsibility and the 1948 Genocide Convention,' in G. Goodwin-Gill and S. Talmon (eds), *The Reality of International Law: Essays in Honour of Ian Brownlie*, p. 273, p. 278 note 28, Clarendon Press, Oxford, citing the following: 'Genocide: A Commentary on the Convention,' *Yale Law Journal* 58, pp. 1142-1160 (1949); Kunz, J.L. (1949), 'The United Nations Convention on Genocide,' *American Journal of International Law* 43, pp. 738-746; Graven, J. (1950), 'Les crimes contre l'humanité,' *Recueil des Cours* (Hague Academy of International Law) 76, vol. 1, p. 429, pp. 507-511; Hudson, M.O. (1951), 'The Twenty-Ninth Year of the World Court,' *American Journal of International Law* 45, p. 1, pp. 33-34; Sibert, M. (1951), *Traité de droit international public. Le droit de la paix*, vol. 1, p. 446; Robinson, N. (1960), *The Genocide Convention: A Commentary*, pp. 99-106, Institute

However, none of the seven analysts cited by Jørgensen accepts the Truman view. A Yale commentary she cites does not mention the issue.[14] Marcel Sibert criticizes the Genocide Convention for not addressing state responsibility in its substantive provisions but does not discuss Article IX.[15] M.N. Shaw reports that the view among the drafters was that the liability was of a civil character but finds nothing definitive in the drafting history about compensation of a state's own nationals: "The question," he wrote, "of States having to compensate their own nationals under an international legal rule also caused some interest in this connection, but without clarification or determination."[16] Jean Graven says only that the type of liability understood by the drafters in Article IX was civil rather than penal but does not address the issue of which states may sue.[17] Manley Hudson insists that Article IX provides for civil-type liability only, and while he mentions Truman's view, he does not state a position on it.[18]

Two of the seven analysts cited by Jørgensen specifically refute the Truman view. Josef Kunz writes: "States alone are, under the general conditions of state responsibility, internationally responsible, but under international law, not under criminal law; only this international state responsibility includes—and here lies the innovation—genocide committed by a state against its own citizens."[19]

Nehemiah Robinson, in his 1949 book on the Genocide Convention, did accept the Truman view that only the state of nationality of the victims could sue under Article IX. Relying on the general rule that states sue on behalf only of their own nationals, he said, "the question of compensation could arise only if the respondent State were responsible for such action in the territory of another State or against citizens of the claimant state. No compensation could be claimed for the benefit of the citizens of the defendant State or other persons not protected by a claimant State because in international law the holder of a right in all international disputes is the State."[20] However, in his 1960 book, the one cited by Jørgensen, Robinson took the contrary position, writing that Article IX "goes beyond the generally accepted rules of international law" on the question of who may sue. He explained why that approach was appropriate for the Genocide Convention:

---

of Jewish Affairs, New York; Shaw, M.N. (1989), 'Genocide and International Law,' in Y. Dinstein (ed.), *International Law at a Time of Perplexity*, p. 797, p. 818, Martinus Nijhoff Publishers, Dordrecht.

14 'Genocide: A Commentary on the Convention,' p. 1148.
15 Sibert (1951) vol. 1, p. 446.
16 Shaw (1989), p. 818.
17 Graven (1950), p. 511 note 2.
18 Hudson (1951), p. 34.
19 Kunz (1949), p. 746.
20 Robinson, N. (1949), *The Genocide Convention: Its Origins and Interpretation*, p. 43, Institute of Jewish Affairs, New York.

If Genocide is a crime under an international convention and if such crimes, when committed by a government in its own territory against its own citizens, are a matter of international concern, why should not the State responsible for acts of Genocide against its own nationals be liable for the reparation of the civil damages caused, just as it is responsible for the criminal prosecution of those who have perpetrated these acts against nationals of another State? This would seem to be the logical conclusion of the civil responsibility of the State.[21]

Whether State Genocide Gives Rise to a "Dispute"

Shabtai Rosenne, a leading analyst of ICJ jurisdiction, read the drafting history to mean that a state having a dispute with another over fulfilment is limited to states specially affected by a violation. He cited:

> the refusal of the negotiating States in the General Assembly to accept a compromissory clause which would have allowed, and possibly obliged, any State party to the Convention to institute proceedings, and the decision to limit the right to seise the Court to a State party to a dispute concerning the interpretation, application or fulfilment of the Convention.[22]

Rosenne recounted the drafting history as follows: "India introduced an amendment to the joint Belgian/British amendment. It was to replace 'at the request of any of the High Contracting Parties' by 'at the request of any of the parties to the dispute.' This was adopted."[23] India made the proposal at the Sixth Committee's 103rd meeting,[24] and it was adopted at the 104th meeting.[25]

Rosenne regarded the addition of the term "dispute" as showing that the circle of states entitled to sue was being narrowed from all state parties to only those who particularly suffer injury as a result of harm to their nationals. Rosenne drew the conclusion:

> this shuts out the slight opening that the unamended texts might have given to the idea of an actio popularis in relation to the erga omnes obligations of the Genocide Convention, initiated by a third State as an original party. It may go further, and weaken any idea that those obligations are obligations erga omnes, as that expression is gaining currency in international law.[26]

---

21 Robinson (1960), p. 104.

22 Rosenne, S. (1996), 'War Crimes and State Responsibility,' in Y. Dinstein and M. Tabory (eds), *War Crimes in International Law*, p. 65, p. 81.

23 Ibid., p. 80.

24 UN Doc. A/C.6/260, introduced at UN GAOR, 3rd sess., Part 1, *Summary Records of Meetings 21 September - 10 December 1948*, p. 437, U.N. Doc. A/C.6/SR.103 (1949) (Mr. Sundaram, India).

25 UN GAOR, 3rd sess., Part 1, *Summary Records of Meetings 21 September - 10 December 1948*, p. 447, U.N. Doc. A/C.6/SR.104 (1949).

26 Rosenne (1996), p. 81.

By "*actio popularis*," which means, "popular action," Rosenne refers to the possibility of a legal action instituted by a party that has not suffered injury. By "*erga omnes*," which means "among all," he refers to the concept that the obligations of the Genocide Convention are owed to the international community generally, and not simply to persons directly injured.

Rosenne's recitation of the drafting history on the meaning of the term "dispute" is questionable. By his account of India's amendment and its acceptance into the text, the rejected Belgian/British language would have allowed any state party to sue even if it had no dispute with the state alleged to be the author of genocide. Thus, Rosenne makes it appear that a proposal to allow any state party to sue was replaced by one that would allow only a state party with a dispute to sue. That was not the case. The Belgian/British proposed language read:

> Any dispute between the High Contracting Parties relating to the interpretation, application or fulfilment of the present Convention, including disputes relating to the responsibility of a State for any of the acts enumerated in articles II and IV, shall be submitted to the International Court of Justice at the request of any of the High Contracting Parties.[27]

The Belgian/British language thus included reference to a "dispute." India objected to this language only because it could be read to mean that if there is a dispute between State A and State B, then suit could be filed by State C. What India, by proposing its amendment, sought to clarify was that the phrase "any of the High Contracting Parties" referred to the state identified in the beginning of the sentence as having a dispute with the state in default.

Belgium and the UK, indeed, had only shortly before proposed another formulation of what became Article IX that had expressly limited suit to a state having a dispute. This earlier language read: "all disputes between the High Contracting Parties relating to the interpretation or application of the Convention shall, at the request of any party to the dispute, be referred to the International Court of Justice."[28] When India asked that Belgium and the UK return to their own earlier formulation, the UK readily agreed and India's proposed language was incorporated.[29] Nothing in the drafting of this language suggests that a "dispute" exists only with a state party whose nationals are harmed by genocide.

---

27 UN GAOR, 3rd sess., Part 1, *Annexes to the Summary Records of Meetings 1948*, p. 28, UN Doc. A/C.6/258 (1948).

28 UN GAOR, 3rd sess., Part 1, *Annexes to the Summary Records of Meetings 1948*, p. 24, UN Doc. A/C.6/236 (1948).

29 UN GAOR, 3rd sess., Part 1, *Summary Records of Meetings 21 September - 10 December 1948*, p. 447, U.N. Doc. A/C.6/SR.104 (1949) (Mr. Fitzmaurice, UK).

Chapter 40

A Legal Interest in Genocide

The possibility of a legal action instituted by a state not directly affected is not unique to the Genocide Convention. To be sure, with most international obligations, only a state directly injured may sue. If State A's state-owned fishing fleet fishes without permission in the territorial waters of State B, only State B may seek cessation of the breach, or make a demand for damages.[1]

Some obligations, however, run to more than one state. With a multilateral treaty on disarmament, for example, a breach injures the rights of all parties, since the obligation of each to disarm is premised on an obligation by all the others similarly to disarm. These have been characterized as "integral obligations."[2] The same is true of human rights violations, despite the circumstance that with a human rights violation an individual person is the ultimate victim.

States on occasion even take countermeasures, unilaterally or collectively, to protest human rights violations, where none of their own nationals have been injured. Several states, for example, revoked the landing rights of Yugoslav aircraft, as a reaction to Yugoslavia's treatment of Albanian-minority nationals of Yugoslavia.[3] The conceptual underpinning of this approach is the one indicated by Judge Jessup, namely that the obligation to observe human rights serves the general welfare.

A potential obstacle to allowing a non-connected state to take up the cause of the victim of a human rights violation is that, in traditional theory, if a state takes up the claim of its national, the claim becomes its own. When a state sues on behalf of a national, the claim is considered to be that of the state, even though the individual is the true party in interest.[4] In a case brought before the Permanent Court of International Justice, Greece sued the UK, alleging violation of the economic interests of a Greek national named Mavrommatis. The Permanent Court said "that the dispute was at first between a private person and a State—i.e. between M. Mavrommatis and the UK. Subsequently, the Greek Government took up the case. The dispute then entered

---

1   Kamminga, M.T. (1992), *Inter-State Accountability for Violations of Human Rights*, p. 165, University of Pennsylvania Press, Philadelphia.

2   UN GAOR, International Law Commission, 52nd sess., 1 May-9 June and 10 July-18 August 2000, *Third report on State responsibility by Mr. James Crawford, Special Rapporteur*, UN Doc. A/CN.4/507, p. 40 (2000).

3   Reid, T.R., 'Yugoslavia loses landing rights: Six G-8 nations vote new sanction to halt Kosovo offensive,' *Washington Post*, 13 June 1998, p. A17.

4   *Third report on State responsibility by Mr. James Crawford, Special Rapporteur*, p. 39.

upon a new phase; it entered the domain of international law, and became a dispute between two States."[5]

If a given group is the victim of genocide, it might not seem possible that multiple states could make the claim their own. The concept that the claim in such a situation is that of the state is, however, something of a fiction, because the claim is actually that of the individual. The state is only taking up the individual's cause. If, during the time the state was pursuing the matter, the individual were to settle the claim with the host state, the matter would be ended.

The same is true with human rights obligations. If a state raises a claim of violation by another state of the human rights of an individual, but then the individual resolves the claim, the state that raised the claim would have nothing further to maintain. Conversely, if the state raising the claim does not prevail, the individual may pursue it in whatever forum may be available.[6] If the state that raised the claim agrees to accept an apology (without compensation), the individual may pursue compensation by other means. If the individual prefers to seek a particular form of reparation, wrote Crawford, a state entitled to raise the claim is in no position to "countermand that preference."[7]

Obligations Owed to All

A number of human rights treaties recognize the role of a non-connected state by providing for state-to-state complaints, regardless of the nationality of the victims. Under the International Covenant on Civil and Political Rights, a party may initiate a complaint against another state party.[8] This is sometimes called an obligation *erga omnes partes* (among all the parties). The other state is not considered to have suffered a direct injury, yet it is entitled to raise a claim.[9]

The same is true in the European human rights system. The European Commission of Human Rights heard a complaint filed against Greece by Norway, Sweden, Denmark, and the Netherlands, alleging that Greece had violated rights of Greek nationals in Greece. The complaining states had no connection to the victims by nationality or otherwise. Yet the Commission acted on their complaint.[10]

Under the rules of warfare, to take another example, a state may raise a violation, even if it is not directly affected. The four Geneva humanitarian conventions require

---

5   Mavrommatis Palestine Concessions, 1924 PCIJ Rep. (ser. A, no. 2), p. 12.

6   Rosenne, S. (1985), *The Law and Practice of the International Court*, p. 130, Martinus Nijhoff Publishers, Dordrecht.

7   *Third report on State responsibility by Mr. James Crawford, Special Rapporteur*, p. 42.

8   International Covenant on Civil and Political Rights, art. 41, UNTS 999, p. 171.

9   de Hoogh, A. (1996), *Obligations* Erga Omnes *and International Crimes: A Theoretical Inquiry into the Implementation and Enforcement of the International Responsibility of States*, pp. 53-54, Kluwer, The Hague and Boston.

10 Greek Case, *Year Book of the European Convention on Human Rights* 12(2) (1969).

every state party to take appropriate action to ensure that other state parties comply with their wartime obligations.[11] According to Article One, common to the four conventions, "The High Contracting Parties undertake to respect and to ensure respect for the present Convention in all circumstances."[12] The UN Security Council has said that common Article One requires state parties to take appropriate action against a non-complying state.[13]

In the *Barcelona Traction* case, the ICJ explained that human rights obligations differ from other international obligations, in that the legal interest of all states is at stake. The court stated:

> [A]n essential distinction should be drawn between the obligations of a State towards the international community as a whole, and those arising vis-à-vis another State in the field of diplomatic protection. By their very nature the former are the concern of all States. In view of the importance of the rights involved, all States can be held to have a legal interest in their protection; they are obligations *erga omnes*. Such obligations derive, for example, in contemporary international law, from the outlawing of acts of aggression and of genocide, and also from the principles and rules concerning the basic rights of the human person, including protection from slavery and racial discrimination. Some of the corresponding rights of protection have entered into the body of general international law; others are conferred by international instruments of a universal or quasi-universal character.[14]

The European Court of Human Rights used a similar analysis when Ireland sued the United Kingdom over the alleged violation of human rights by the United Kingdom in Northern Ireland. Regarding Ireland's standing to raise such a claim, the court stated:

> Unlike international treaties of the classic kind, the [European human rights] Convention comprises more than mere reciprocal engagements between contracting States. It creates, over and above a network of mutual, bilateral undertakings, objective obligations which, in the words of the Preamble, benefit from a "collective enforcement". ... [T]he Convention allows Contracting States to require the observance of those obligations without having to justify an interest deriving, for example, from the fact that a measure they complain of has prejudiced one of their own nationals.[15]

---

11 Frowein, J.A. (1994), 'Reactions by Not Directly Affected States to Breaches of Public International Law,' *Recueil des Cours* (Hague Academy of International Law) 248, vol. 4, p. 345, pp. 395-397.

12 Convention Relative to the Treatment of Civilian Persons in Time of War, art. 1, 12 August 1949, UNTS 75, p. 287 (1950).

13 SC Res. 681, UN SCOR, 45th sess., *Resolutions & Decisions*, p. 8, UN Doc. S/INF/46 (1991).

14 Barcelona Traction, Light & Power (Belgium v. Spain), Judgment, 1970 ICJ Rep., p. 3, p. 32.

15 Ireland v. United Kingdom, European Court of Human Rights, Judgment of 18 January 1978, vol. 25 (Ser. A), pp. 90-91.

Other State Parties as "Injured" States

The position of non-connected states, sometimes termed "third states," was addressed by the ILC, which drafted norms on the law of state responsibility. That body of law contains norms that spell out the consequences of the breach of an international obligation, including the modalities for redress. The Commission's Draft Articles on State Responsibility defined the term "injured state" as its way of identifying those states that may bring a claim in the event of a violation of the law of state responsibility. According to the 1996 draft, "if the right infringed by the act of a State arises from a multilateral treaty or from a rule of customary international law," then the term "injured state" means "any other State party to the multilateral treaty or bound by the relevant rule of customary international law, if it is established that ... the right has been created or is established for the protection of human rights and fundamental freedoms."[16] Thus, if a human rights norm in a multilateral treaty, like the Genocide Convention, is violated, "any other State party" would be deemed injured.[17]

The "Legal Interest" of Other States

Reacting to the ILC draft, some states questioned whether third states are correctly viewed as being "injured" by a human rights violation.[18] So too did James Crawford, as the commission's rapporteur on state responsibility. Beginning from the obvious point that human rights norms protect individuals, and thus that it is they who are the right holders, Crawford wrote:

> a distinction should ... be drawn between the rights of the victims and the responses of States. Otherwise the effect of article 40(2)(e)(iii) is to translate human rights into States' rights, ... The States concerned may be representing the victims, but they are not to be identified with them, and they do not become the right-holders because they are recognized as having a legal interest in the author State's compliance with its human rights obligations.[19]

Crawford thus distinguished the individual victim, a right-holder, from a state that seeks to force compliance. In drawing this distinction, Crawford relied on the ICJ reference in the *Barcelona Traction* case to the individual victim as the right-holder, and to third states as having a "legal interest" in the protection of the rights of the victim.[20] A state with a "legal interest" would not be entitled to seek reparations for

---

16 Draft Articles on State Responsibility, art. 40, *Report of the International Law Commission on the work of its forty-eighth session 6 May - 26 July 1996*, UN GAOR, 51st sess., Supp. (No. 10), p. 140, UN Doc. A/51/10 (1996).

17 de Hoogh (1996), pp. 52-53.

18 *Third report on State responsibility by Mr. James Crawford, Special Rapporteur*, p. 34.

19 Ibid., pp. 38-39.

20 Ibid., p. 43.

itself but could seek cessation of the offensive conduct, plus reparation to injured parties.[21]

The *Restatement of the Foreign Relations Law of the United States* follows this approach, allowing other states to raise a claim, but not viewing them as being "injured":

> The customary law of human rights protects individuals subject to each state's jurisdiction, and the international obligation runs equally to all other states, with no state a victim of the violation more than any other. Any state, therefore, may make a claim against the violating state. Where the complaining and the accused states have agreed to means for settling disputes between them generally—for example, by accepting the jurisdiction of the International Court of Justice or submitting to arbitration—such means are available ...[22]

Elsewhere, the *Restatement* indicates, with respect to human rights norms: "When a state has violated an obligation owed to the international community as a whole, any state may bring a claim ... without showing that it suffered any particular injury."[23] The term "particular" implies that a third state suffers injury in a general sense, namely that the regime of human rights observance works to the benefit of all states.

What "international community as a whole" means is not entirely clear. In the ILC some thought it referred to the states of the world, while others thought it included other parties, such as individuals and non-governmental organizations.[24] The term, in any event, includes states and thus suffices to give other states an interest in a law violation by another state.

The ILC accepted Crawford's analysis.[25] The drafting committee decided not to use an article defining "injured state" to identify those states entitled to raise a claim.[26] It limited its definition of "injured state" to states suffering particular injury.[27] It added a provision titled "Invocation of responsibility by States other than the injured State," specifying that "any State other than an injured State is entitled to invoke the responsibility of another State if: (a) The obligation breached is owed to a group of States including that State, and is established for the protection of a collective interest; (b) The obligation breached is owed to the international community as a whole."[28] This provision embodies the *actio popularis* approach that permits any

---

21 Ibid., pp. 34-35.

22 *Restatement (Third): Foreign Relations Law of the United States* (1987), '703, Reporters' note 3, American Law Institute, St. Paul.

23 Ibid., §902 comment (a).

24 *Report of the International Law Commission on the work of its fifty-second session 1 May - 9 June and 10 July - 18 August 2000*, UN GAOR, 55th sess., Supp. (No. 10), p. 41, UN Doc. A/55/10 (2000).

25 Ibid., p. 40.

26 Ibid., pp. 42-43.

27 Draft Articles on State Responsibility, art. 43, *Report of the International Law Commission on the work of its fifty-second session 1 May - 9 June and 10 July - 18 August 2000*, p. 135.

28 Draft Articles on State Responsibility, art. 49(1), ibid., p. 137.

state to invoke state responsibility for certain types of violations. As explained by Crawford, "other states, by virtue of their participation in a multilateral regime or as a consequence of their membership in the international community, have a legal interest in the performance of certain multilateral obligations."[29]

Some analysts have questioned whether states have a "legal interest" in each and every human rights violation. David Bederman criticized Article 40(2)(e)(iii) of the ILC 1996 Draft Articles on State Responsibility for allowing any state to sue for any human rights violation, even a violation of lesser gravity.[30] In the ILC, similarly, "The view was expressed that the category of obligations *erga omnes* should be reserved for fundamental human rights deriving from general international law and not just from a particular treaty regime."[31] Some commission members, however, expressed concern about any attempt to distinguish fundamental human rights from others: "any distinction would be difficult to apply in practice and would go against the current trend towards a unified approach to human rights."[32] Even if such a distinction is made, however, genocide would be numbered among the more serious of rights violations.

In its state responsibility document as finalized in 2001, the ILC followed the 2000 draft, providing broad scope for claims by non-connected states. Any state may invoke the responsibility of another state if

(a) The obligation breached is owed to a group of States including that State, and is established for the protection of a collective interest of the group; or
(b) The obligation breached is owed to the international community as a whole.[33]

This article avoided the phrase "legal interest," apparently out of concern that an injured state also has a legal interest, and thus that factor would not distinguish an injured state from others entitled to sue.[34] The UN General Assembly, by resolution, commended the commission's state responsibility document to the attention of states.[35]

---

29 Crawford, J., P. Bodeau and J. Peel (2000), 'The ILC's Draft Articles on State Responsibility: Toward Completion of a Second Reading,' *American Journal of International Law* 94, p. 660, p. 667.

30 Bederman, D. (1998), 'State Responsibility in a Multiactor World,' *American Society of International Law Proceedings* 92, p. 291, p. 294.

31 *Report of the International Law Commission on the work of its fifty-second session 1 May - 9 June and 10 July - 18 August 2000*, pp. 40-41.

32 Ibid., pp. 40-41.

33 Responsibility of States for Internationally Wrongful Acts, art. 48, International Law Commission, *Report of the International Law Commission on the work of its fifty-third session*, UN GAOR, 56th sess., Supp, (No. 10), p. 43, UN Doc. A/56/10 (2001).

34 Crawford, J. (2002), *The International Law Commission's Articles on State Responsibility: Introduction, Text and Commentaries*, pp. 276-277, Cambridge University Press, Cambridge.

35 Responsibility of States for Internationally Wrongful Acts, G.A. Res. 56/83, UN Doc. A/RES/56/83 (2001).

If it were not for third-state remedies, genocide could be committed by a state against its own nationals, and no state would be in a position to sue. As Jonathan Charney has written, "third state remedies" are necessary "to meet the needs of the international society. ... One type of situation in which the need may arise is when no directly injured state would have traditional standing to seek a remedy. For example, this may be presented when a government commits genocide against its own nationals."[36]

---

36 Charney, J.I. (1989), 'Third State Remedies in International Law,' *Michigan Journal of International Law* 10, p. 57, p. 95.

Chapter 41

Compensation for Victims

Once an episode of genocide has ended, financial compensation may be one way of aiding the victims. In the Sixth Committee, concern was expressed whether a non-connected plaintiff state could properly seek damages on behalf of genocide victims. According to Iran [paraphrase]:

> In international law, a State asked for reparation of damages inflicted on its nationals by another State; but in the case of genocide, it was a question of injuries inflicted on citizens by citizens of the same State. Mr. Abdoh [Iran - J.Q.] wondered how the civil responsibility of the State would arise. Reparations could be paid to a State when its citizens had been the victims of an act of genocide in another State, but in some of the cases envisaged in the convention, it was difficult to determine which State would have the right to damages.[1]

Greece said that if civil liability of a state for genocide were contemplated,

> the result would be that in a number of cases the State responsible for genocide would have to indemnify its own nationals. But in international law the real holder of a right was the State and not private persons. The State would thus be indemnifying itself.[2]

The UK, as the proponent of Article IX, thought that this matter could be resolved as cases arose. It said that the ICJ "would order the cessation of the imputed acts, and the payment of reparation to the victims."[3] It found no obstacle to the court ordering payment on behalf of nationals of the defendant state. The matter was not, however, addressed in detail during the drafting meetings. Stillschweig, commenting on the Genocide Convention, identified the issue as one that the court would need to resolve.[4]

By specifying that any state party may sue, Article IX contemplates that a plaintiff state may seek whatever remedies are appropriate. This might include damages for

---

1   UN GAOR, 3rd sess., Part 1, *Summary Records of Meetings 21 September - 10 December 1948*, p. 443, UN Doc. A/C.6/SR.104 (Mr. Abdoh, Iran).

2   UN GAOR, 3rd sess., Part 1, *Summary Records of Meetings 21 September - 10 December 1948*, p. 433, UN Doc. A/C.6/SR.103 (1949) (Mr. Spiropoulos, Greece).

3   UN GAOR, 3rd sess., Part 1, *Summary Records of Meetings 21 September - 10 December 1948*, p. 342, UN Doc. A/C.6/SR.95 (1949) (Mr. Fitzmaurice, UK).

4   Stillschweig, K. (1949), 'Das Abkommen zur Bekämpfung von Genocide,' *Die Friedens-Warte* 49, p. 93, p. 103, Blätter für internationale Verständigung und zwischenstaatliche Organisation, Hans Wehberg (ed.).

injury to the state itself if, for example, a state in perpetrating genocide damages property of another state or requires that state to make expenditures to deal with the consequences of the genocide. As well, According to the ILC, a state may sue on behalf of "the beneficiaries of the obligation."[5]

Financial Compensation for Non-nationals

There is no reason that the ICJ may not order a state to pay monetary compensation to a plaintiff state on behalf of the victims, regardless of their nationality. In the case brought against Greece by four European states, recounted in Chapter 40, the four states alleged and proved that Greece had tortured a number of named Greek nationals. The European Commission of Human Rights proposed that compensation be awarded for the benefit of those Greek nationals.[6] The European Commission had no difficulty with this claim by states for victims not their nationals, even where, as in that case, the victims were nationals of the defendant state.

The ILC followed this approach. In its provision titled "Invocation of responsibility by States other than the injured State," the drafting committee specified what a state other than the injured state may seek: "A State entitled to invoke responsibility under paragraph 1 may seek from the responsible State: (a) cessation of the internationally wrongful act, and assurances and guarantees of non-repetition in accordance with article 30; (b) performance of the obligation of reparation ... in the interest of the injured State or of the beneficiaries of the obligation breached."[7]

The typical situation in international claims, to be sure, involves a state seeking compensation for its own nationals. If the plaintiff state files based on injury to its nationals, it is understood that, although the plaintiff state has the international claim, the recovery is for the benefit of the injured nationals. The measure of damages is the loss to the injured nationals. When a state brings an action for the wrongful death of a national, the measure of damages is loss to surviving heirs of the deceased.[8] The state must turn any monetary recovery over to them.

"The national," writes Marjorie Whiteman, has "an expectancy coupled with an interest that the state espousing his claim will collect it and pay him the indemnity thus collected."[9] The ILC draft, by specifying that third states may sue on behalf of

---

5   Responsibility of States for Internationally Wrongful Acts, art. 48(2), *Report of the International Law Commission on the work of its fifty-third session*, UN GAOR, 56th sess., Supp. (No. 10), p. 43, UN Doc. A/56/10 (2001).

6   Greek Case, *Year Book of the European Convention on Human Rights* 12(2), p. 515 (1969).

7   Responsibility of States for Internationally Wrongful Acts, art. 48(2).

8   Shelton, D. (1999), *Remedies in International Human Rights Law*, p. 112, Oxford University Press, Oxford and New York.

9   Whiteman, M. (1937), *Damages in International Law*, vol. 1, p. 275, US Government Printing Office, Washington.

beneficiaries of the obligation breached, presumably would have these principles apply. A state that sues another state for genocide against persons who are not nationals of the former would allege and prove injury to those persons, would recover on their behalf, and would be obligated to turn the monetary recovery over to them.

Practical problems may result, to be sure, if the victims are nationals of the defendant state. The defendant state may try to prevent receipt of the recovery by its nationals. Any such effort on its part would have to be viewed as a violation of the court's judgment. The UN Charter, Article 94, requires UN member states to comply with ICJ decisions, and enforcement can be sought from the UN Security Council. The UK pointed out, when urging International Court of Justice jurisdiction over states for genocide, that a plaintiff state could approach the Security Council for assistance in gaining the consent of the defendant state to the transfer of funds.[10]

For problems that arise, the ICJ would have a body of law available. The law of state responsibility contains rules on monetary compensation. Like any treaty, the Genocide Convention does not contain, within its text, all rules of law relevant to its implementation. Treaties in this sense are similar to contracts in domestic law. Two private parties may conclude a written contract for the sale of a commodity. But their contract does not include all the legal norms potentially relevant. The scope of damages for breach, for example, will not likely be reflected in the contract itself. In the event of breach, resort will be made to the law of the jurisdiction on damages.

The ICJ has said that treaties must be applied with the law of state responsibility as a base, in particular as to the consequences of a breach. On the issue of what compensation may be due for breach, the court referred to the law of state responsibility.[11] On state responsibility for genocide, the scope of a state's obligations, in the event it commits genocide, may be determined by the law of state responsibility.

Chaos in the Court?

A potential complicating circumstance, if any state party to the Genocide Convention is entitled to sue another for the perpetration of genocide, and to seek damages, is that more than one may decide to sue over the same alleged violation. The other states might even act at cross purposes to each other. As explained by ILC Rapporteur Crawford, "the term '[a]ny state' is intended to avoid any implication that these States have to act together or in unison."[12] These states might have different theories of why the target state is liable. One state might be willing to accept an assurance

10 UN GAOR, 3rd sess., Part 1, *Summary Records of Meetings 21 September - 10 December 1948*, p. 444, UN Doc. A/C.6/SR.104 (1949) (Mr. Fitzmaurice, UK).

11 Gabcikovo-Nagymaros Project (Hungary/Slovakia), Judgment, 1997 ICJ Rep., p. 7, p. 38.

12 Crawford, J. (2002), *The International Law Commission's Articles on State Responsibility: Introduction, Text and Commentaries*, p. 277, Cambridge University Press, Cambridge.

of non-repetition as a remedy. Another might insist on monetary compensation for the victims.

Such potential complexities are likely to be rare. States are typically reluctant to sue over human rights when they have no nationality-based or ethnically-based relationship to the victims. The International Covenant on Civil and Political Rights provides for the possibility of complaints filed by one state party against another state party. Although that procedure entered into force upon the filing of the tenth declaration in 1979, no state has ever filed against another.[13] The European regional human rights treaty, as indicated, provides a similar possibility, but the four-state complaint against Greece in 1968, and another against Turkey in 1982, are the only instances in which European states having no nationality or ethnic connection to the victims have filed.[14] Practice under the Genocide Convention conforms to this pattern. In the genocide cases filed to date, the plaintiff states had a connection to the alleged victims.

States may be pressed by a domestic constituency sympathetic to a group being victimized abroad to take action. Yet, addressing practice under the Genocide Convention, Lori Damrosch wrote that "states seem unwilling to undertake the burdens of a protracted litigation unless they perceive something tangible to be gained by doing so."[15] "The risk to the political and economic interests of a complainant state has proved to be a strong deterrent to the initiation of proceedings under Article IX," writes Payan Akhavan, "except in rare cases where the complainant state itself is directly affected or victimized."[16] Akhavan states that "the failure to apply Article IX in all but cases where the contracting state itself has direct interests can be explained by the reluctance of governments to put humanitarian considerations before narrow political interests. A more enlightened and principled definition of the 'common interest' does not yet find itself playing a prominent role in international relations."[17] A state that sues another for genocide may poison relations with the target state and may jeopardize other important contacts with it.

Tools Available to the Court

The ICJ could avert problems arising from multiple suits if that situation arises. One is to encourage states to file together and to adopt a common litigational strategy. If

---

13 International Covenant on Civil and Political Rights, art. 41(2), UNTS 999, p. 171.

14 Frowein, J.A. (1994), 'Reactions by Not Directly Affected States to Breaches of Public International Law,' *Recueil des Cours* (Hague Academy of International Law) 248, vol. 4, p. 345, p. 393.

15 Damrosch, L.R. (1998), 'Genocide and Ethnic Conflict,' in D. Wippman (ed.), *International Law and Ethnic Conflict*, p. 256, p. 274.

16 Akhavan, P. (1995), 'Enforcement of the Genocide Convention: A Challenge to Civilization,' *Harvard Human Rights Journal* 8, p. 229, p. 247.

17 Ibid., p. 251.

more than one state files, the court may consolidate the actions.[18] In the Greek case in the European Commission of Human Rights, Norway, Sweden, Denmark, and the Netherlands filed identical applications, and the Commission consolidated them into a single case.[19]

A state intent on pressing a state that has committed genocide could participate in a suit already filed by another state. The court is required to notify all states that are parties to a treaty if the court intends to construe that treaty: "Whenever the construction of a convention to which states other than those concerned in the case are parties is in question, the Registrar shall notify all such states forthwith."[20] The court complied with this requirement when Bosnia sued Yugoslavia under the Genocide Convention, by notifying all state parties.[21]

A state receiving such a notification may intervene: "Every state so notified has the right to intervene in the proceedings; but if it uses this right, the construction given by the judgment will be equally binding upon it."[22] Under the court's Statute, "Should a state consider that it has an interest of a legal nature which may be affected by the decision in the case, it may submit a request to the court to be permitted to intervene."[23] An intervening state is supplied copies of pleadings and may submit written pleadings of its own and participate in oral argument.[24]

These procedures reduce the likelihood that, after the court has rendered judgment, another state might file over the same facts. Since such a state would have failed to avail itself of the opportunity to intervene, the court might invoke the principle of *res judicata*, which would allow it to dismiss the case on the basis that it had already decided the matter.[25] The court has used this principle in the past.[26] That principle would apply even though the claimant state differs, because the right involved would be identical to that in the prior case.

---

18 ICJ Rules of Court (as amended 5 December 2000), art. 47.

19 Greek Case, *Year Book of the European Convention on Human Rights* 12(2), p. 11 (1969).

20 Statute of the International Court of Justice, art. 63(1).

21 Application of the Convention on the Prevention and Punishment of the Crime of Genocide (Bosnia and Herzegovina v. Yugoslavia (Serbia and Montenegro)), Order of 8 April 1993, 1993 ICJ Rep., p. 1, p. 9.

22 Statute of the International Court of Justice, art. 63(2).

23 Ibid., art. 62(1).

24 ICJ Rules of Court (as amended 5 December 2000), art. 85.

25 Rosenne, S. (1985), *The Law and Practice of the International Court*, pp. 623-628, Martinus Nijhoff Publishers, Dordrecht.

26 Corfu Channel Case, Judgment: Compensation, 1949 ICJ Rep., p. 222, p. 244 and p. 248.

PART NINE
WHY GENOCIDE?

Chapter 42

The World Court's Power

A reader who has persisted to this point may be vexed to hear the author ask whether genocide as a legal category has any great consequence. Nonetheless, the question cannot be avoided. Do other legal prohibitions render genocide redundant? Does the prohibition of genocide deter genocide? Do genocide claims and prosecutions reduce the frequency of atrocities? Part Nine asks these questions, beginning with the question of the significance of ICJ action.

If the ICJ has only minimal capacity to stop a state that is perpetrating genocide, or to deter future genocide, then genocide suits provide little protection to populations at risk of being victimized. We saw in the last chapter that states are reluctant to sue another state for genocide. Lori Damrosch has written that this reluctance limits the utility of genocide suits: "The difficulties of finding a willing applicant ... create considerable pessimism about the prognosis for relying on the strictly state-to-state mechanism of the ICJ."[1] The unwillingness of states to sue is a serious negative. At the same time, in three instances, states have sued for genocide, which means that they saw some utility in doing so.

What the Court Can Do

In the Sixth Committee, several delegates opined that the ICJ is not well positioned to stop genocide. When the UK proposed adding a reference to state responsibility in what became Article IV, Venezuela objected that ordering a state to pay compensation would achieve little:

> The only punishment which could be imposed on a State would be the exaction of material reparations. It would not, however, have the effect which was the aim of all punitive sanctions, that is, it would not serve as an example, because the State would not be touched as would a private individual in a similar situation, since the taxpayers would pay the required reparations.[2]

Forcing a state to pay may pressure it to change policy, and other states may take heed. The fact that taxpayers ultimately pay may result in domestic pressure on

---

1 Damrosch, L.R. (1998), 'Genocide and Ethnic Conflict,' in D. Wippman (ed.), *International Law and Ethnic Conflict*, p. 256, p. 275.

2 UN GAOR, 3rd sess., Part 1, *Summary Records of Meetings 21 September - 10 December 1948*, p. 345, UN Doc. A/C.6/SR.95 (1949) (Mr. Pérez Perozo, Venezuela).

a government. Over and beyond deterrence, an ICJ finding of genocide may have significance. A finding by an impartial body that atrocities were committed may influence other states and international organizations in their dealings with the state at fault.

Suit may be brought, of course, while acts of genocide are ongoing. Here the aim of the plaintiff state may be less to get damages than to stop the acts before more persons are harmed. As we have seen, one aim of defining genocide in terms of intent was to allow a finding of genocide at an early stage. One potential advantage of ICJ jurisdiction over state-perpetrated genocide is that the court may help stop the offending state.

In the Sixth Committee, however, doubts were expressed whether the court could stop ongoing genocide. The USSR said that an offending state was unlikely to observe a cease and desist order. Opposing the UK's effort at ICJ jurisdiction over state-perpetrated genocide, the USSR argued that genocide fell within the province of the UN Security Council, which had economic and military sanctions at its disposal. "[T]he Court," said the USSR, "was not the competent body to consider situations endangering the maintenance of international peace and security, since it did not have the means to prevent acts of genocide."[3] Czechoslovakia also argued that the Security Council was better positioned to take rapid action: "the human group concerned would be massacred," it said, "before the completion of proceedings instituted with the International Court of Justice."[4]

If the court orders a state to stop genocide, there is no assurance it will comply. When a state's vital interests, as it defines them, are at stake, a court order may have little impact. When the court ruled in 1974 that Iceland had to let the British and Germans fish in an offshore fishing zone that Iceland had declared, Iceland not only refused to comply but extended its fishing zone even farther out to sea.[5]

The enforcement mechanism for judgments of the court is the UN Security Council. A prevailing plaintiff state may ask the Security Council to force a non-compliant defendant state to honor the court's judgment. The Security Council has hardly been effective at this task. At the same time, a favorable ICJ order is often viewed as significant by a plaintiff state. The court enjoys a reputation for objectivity that gives weight to its orders. Its judges are drawn from countries of differing political coloration and differing legal traditions. An injunctive order calling on a state to desist from conduct that the court identifies as genocide puts pressure on the offending state. Even though an offending state may not comply immediately, the order may affect its conduct.

---

3   UN GAOR, 3rd sess., Part 1, *Summary Records of Meetings 21 September - 10 December 1948*, p. 440, UN Doc. A/C.6/SR.104 (1949) (Mr. Morozov, USSR).

4   UN GAOR, 3rd sess., Part 1, *Summary Records of Meetings 21 September - 10 December 1948*, p. 439, UN Doc. A/C.6/SR.103 (1949) (Mr. Zourek, Czechoslovakia).

5   Fisheries Jurisdiction Case, Judgment, 1974 ICJ Rep., p. 3.

The Court's Ruling in Bosnia's Case

The Bosnia case is the only one in which the ICJ has issued a desist order while alleged genocide was ongoing. In that case, each side alleged genocide against the other, and each sought a desist order. The fact that each side perceived value in gaining such an order suggests that it may have significance. The ICJ called on Yugoslavia to "take all measures within its power to prevent commission of the crime of genocide," stating that Yugoslavia

> should in particular ensure that any military, paramilitary or irregular armed units which may be directed or supported by it, as well as any organizations and persons which may be subject to its control, direction or influence, do not commit any acts of genocide, of conspiracy to commit genocide, of direct and public incitement to commit genocide, or of complicity in genocide, whether directed against the Muslim population of Bosnia and Herzegovina or against any other national, ethnical, racial or religious group.[6]

The Court appeared to be calling on Yugoslavia to desist from genocide that the court believed Yugoslavia was perpetrating. One judge, writing separately, said that the quoted language was "open to the interpretation that the Court believes that the Government of the Federal Republic of Yugoslavia is indeed involved in such genocidal acts, or at least that it may very well be so involved."[7]

Four months after gaining that order from the court, Bosnia returned to the court, because, it said, Yugoslavia was still committing genocide. The court examined the facts and concluded that

> since the Order of 8 April 1993 was made, and despite that Order, and despite many resolutions of the Security Council of the United Nations, great suffering and loss of life has been sustained by the population of Bosnia-Herzegovina in circumstances which shock the conscience of mankind and flagrantly conflict with moral law and the spirit and aims of the United Nations.[8]

The court repeated its prior order, which, it said, "should be immediately and effectively implemented."[9] Nonetheless, substantial killing for which Yugoslavia might bear responsibility continued even after the issuance of the second order. In particular, the 1995 mass execution of Bosnian Muslims at Srebrenica, which resulted in the genocide conviction of Radislav Krstic, was the largest episode of mass killing in Europe since World War II.

---

6   Application of the Convention on the Prevention and Punishment of the Crime of Genocide (Bosnia and Herzegovina v. Yugoslavia (Serbia and Montenegro)), Order of 8 April 1993, 1993 ICJ Rep., p. 24.

7   Ibid., p. 26 (declaration, Tarassov).

8   Application of the Convention on the Prevention and Punishment of the Crime of Genocide (Bosnia and Herzegovina v. Yugoslavia (Serbia and Montenegro)), Order of 13 September 1993, 1993 ICJ Rep., p. 325, p. 348.

9   Ibid., pp. 349-350.

In the Bosnia case, the court did, however, show that it can act quickly, belying the prediction in the Sixth Committee by Czechoslovakia. Even though the court typically requires several years to take a case to a final judgment, it can issue orders for interim measures in an emergency situation. In one recent case (not involving genocide), the court even issued an interim measures order on an *ex parte* basis, where it feared that delaying long enough to hold a hearing would defeat the purpose for which the order was being sought.[10]

For many years uncertainty surrounded such interim orders. It was clear from the court's Statute that states were required to carry out a final judgment, but some questioned whether the same was true of interim orders. In 2001 the ICJ ruled that such interim orders are binding.[11] The fact that the court views such orders as binding does not mean that a particular state will comply. Nevertheless, an adverse ICJ ruling may have an impact. States seek, in general, to avoid condemnation, which may lead to negative action in the form of sanctions, or of exclusion from advantageous interaction with other states.

In the Bosnia case, the United Nations was heavily involved, and an injunctive order by the court containing an implicit finding of Yugoslav responsibility may have had an effect on subsequent action by the international community. As the court mentioned in its second order of provisional measures in the Bosnia case, one week after the court issued its first order of provisional measures in that case, the UN Security Council "took note of the Court's Order of 8 April 1993 in which the Court indicated that the Federal Republic of Yugoslavia (Serbia and Montenegro) should take all measures within its power to prevent the commission of the crime of genocide."[12]

At the time Bosnia filed its case against Yugoslavia, the UN Security Council was maintaining an arms embargo on the territory of the former Yugoslavia, and that embargo prevented Bosnia from getting weaponry to defend Bosnian Muslims and Croats from the Bosnian Serb militia and the Yugoslav army. Bosnia sought to convince the Security Council to lift the embargo, and a court ruling against Yugoslavia might have carried weight with the Security Council. In the event, the Security Council did not lift the embargo, but the court's ruling may have influenced the UN and other states in actions they subsequently took to bring the hostilities in Bosnia to an end. The impact of an ICJ ruling in such a situation is often difficult to measure.

---

10 LaGrand Case (Germany v. USA), Order, 1999 ICJ Rep., p. 9, p. 16.

11 LaGrand Case (Germany v. USA), Judgment, 2001 ICJ Rep., p. 466, pp. 502-503.

12 Application of the Convention on the Prevention and Punishment of the Crime of Genocide (Bosnia and Herzegovina v. Yugoslavia (Serbia and Montenegro)), Order of 13 September 1993, 1993 ICJ Rep., p. 325, p. 348.

Chapter 43

The Need for Genocide

Under the Genocide Convention, the state-to-state mechanism works in tandem with the prosecution of individuals. The prosecution of individuals, as we have seen, may be done domestically or internationally. As a result, three potential enforcement methods are available. If any one of them were always effective, the others might not be necessary. The Genocide Convention drafters feared there might be little enforcement in any of the three ways.

As for an international penal tribunal, as of mid-century, none existed, nor was there any prospect one would soon be created. In the hope, however, that such a tribunal might be established, the drafters wrote, in Article VI, that jurisdiction would lie in "such international penal tribunal as may have jurisdiction with respect to those Contracting Parties which shall have accepted its jurisdiction."

The lack of any existing international penal tribunal was cited as a reason for ICJ jurisdiction over state-perpetrated genocide. The UK, as the primary proponent of state-to-state genocide suits, noted that there was little prospect of the early creation of a court to try individuals for genocide. The UK told the Sixth Committee that the article calling for the punishment of state officials would be of no use until an international criminal court were established, since it was unlikely they would be tried by the courts of their own states.[1]

One situation in which state responsibility may be a weaker tool than individual responsibility is that in which the government responsible for genocide is no longer in power. Under principles of state responsibility, a state is responsible for the acts of that state, regardless of changes in government. However, other states may be reluctant to sue where the government in power played no role in genocide under a prior government.

International Prosecutions

In the 1990s, significant moves were made towards the prosecution of individuals through international penal tribunals, with the creation of the *ad hoc* tribunals for Yugoslavia and Rwanda. Each of these tribunals has entered convictions for genocide. The International Criminal Court came into being in 2002, with jurisdiction to prosecute for genocide.

---

1   UN GAOR, 3rd sess., Part 1, *Summary Records of Meetings 21 September - 10 December 1948*, p. 321, UN Doc. A/C.6/SR.93 (1949) (Mr. Fitzmaurice, UK).

The ICC may, arguably, remove the need for ICJ jurisdiction over state-perpetrated genocide, or for domestic genocide prosecutions. However, the ICC, like the ICJ, will be constrained in various ways. Suspects may be located in states whose authorities will protect them from arrest. The International Criminal Tribunal for Former Yugoslavia has experienced difficulty in arresting persons it has indicted for genocide. Some arrests have required quasi-military operations and have resulted in deaths on the scene. The United States opposes the ICC and has pressured states to agree by special treaty that they will not turn US nationals over to the ICC for trial.

Moreover, the ICC does not have jurisdiction over any and all individuals, but only over those whose state of nationality has ratified the ICC Statute, and those who commit a crime in the territory of a state that has ratified. The ICC has jurisdiction only over major offenders.

More fundamentally, the ICC is jurisdictionally limited to prosecuting individuals and is not in a position to order a state to stop ongoing genocide. As indicated, genocide is often committed with participation, or condonation, by one or more states, and it is typically states that are in a position to bring genocide to a halt.

Whether Other Offenses Suffice

The utility of genocide as a charge may be undercut by the limited definition of the offense. The Genocide Convention has been criticized for taking an overly timid approach. The Convention, as Daniel Nsereko points out, includes no provisions aimed at preventing genocide before it starts. It established no international agency aimed at either prevention or punishment. Article VI did not call for universal jurisdiction over genocide but required a state to prosecute only genocide committed in its territory. "For all these weaknesses," Nsereko writes, "it is not surprising that the Convention has had little or no influence in preventing acts of genocide that have taken place across the globe since it came into force."[2] Leila Sadat levels a more fundamental criticism, questioning whether it makes sense to define offenses in terms of harm to a particular group, because "it is the very process of apportioning ourselves into groups that leads to discrimination and hate in the first place."[3] Nicolas Jacobs criticized the inclusion of the element of intent to destroy a group, as too difficult to prove.[4]

---

2   Nsereko, D.D.N. (2000), 'Genocide: A Crime Against Mankind,' in G.K. McDonald and O. Swaak-Goldman (eds), *Substantive and Procedural Aspects of International Criminal Law: The Experience of International and National Courts*, vol. 1, p. 113, p. 137, Kluwer, The Hague.

3   L. Sadat (2002), *The International Criminal Court and the Transformation of International Law: Justice for the New Millennium*, p. 146, Transnational Publishers, Ardsley NY.

4   Jacobs, N. (1969), 'A propos de la définition juridique du génocide,' *Études internationales de psycho-sociologie criminelle,* 16-17, p. 55, p. 56.

As to both international and domestic prosecution, the importance of genocide prosecutions may be undermined by the availability of other offenses that provide a readier route to conviction. Other offenses are available in both international law and domestic law. Crimes against humanity overlap to some extent with genocide. In a number of international indictments, counts have been included both for genocide and for crimes against humanity.

In the domestic setting, a full array of offenses is open to prosecutors. In Ethiopia, prosecutors charging genocide typically also charged murder, so that if they failed to prove genocide, they might still convict. "The crime of genocide," points out Joe Verhoeven, "would be absolutely indispensable if it offered the only possibility for charging for acts that would otherwise be perfectly legal, or at least not penally sanctioned. In reality it is not so. In most situations, the acts constituting genocide, and in particular murders and other assaults on the person or on families can easily be punished as such, without the need for an additional characterization."[5]

Moreover, the ambiguity surrounding the definition of genocide may deter prosecutors, who find the offense definitions of other crimes more precise, and therefore easier to prove.[6] Given the greater ease of prosecution for other offenses, one can ask why genocide would ever be charged. From a legal standpoint, states party to the Genocide Convention are obliged to prosecute when genocide is committed in their territory. From a political standpoint, a state is often at pains to show the horror of what occurred and therefore prefers to charge genocide. As indicated, domestic proceedings typically occur after a regime change, and the new regime is anxious to put the prior regime in a bad light. Thus, in the Ethiopian proceedings, it has been said that, for the new government that had overthrown the Dergue, "ample political dividend is derived from accusing the detainees of genocide—an international crime."[7]

The same was doubtless true for the government of Rwanda, which represented the Tutsi minority, and which had just overthrown the former Hutu-led government that had been responsible for anti-Tutsi atrocities. It was true as well for the government that came to power in Cambodia by overthrowing the Khmer Rouge. It had a particular reason to put the Khmer Rouge in a negative light, since the Khmer Rouge was still being recognized as the legitimate government and was still engaged in active guerrilla warfare on Cambodian soil. All three of these successor governments sought political dividends by prosecuting for genocide.

Nonetheless, it can be asked whether a trial for genocide is any more significant than a trial for the specific acts, such as murder, that typically go into a genocide charge. Must the states party to the Genocide Convention necessarily charge

---

5   Verhoeven, J. (1991), 'Le crime de génocide: originalité et ambiguïté,' *Revue belge de droit international* 24, no. 1, p. 5, p. 11.

6   Ibid., p. 8.

7   Haile-Mariam, Y. (1999), 'The Quest for Justice and Reconciliation: The International Criminal Tribunal for Rwanda and the Ethiopian High Court,' *Hastings International & Comparative Law Review* 22, p. 667, pp. 721-722.

genocide in order to "prevent and punish" genocide in their territory? Arguably, they could do so just as effectively by charging other offenses. What is important is that they prosecute. The nature of the offenses for which they prosecute may be less important.

Genocide functions as a supplement to other internationally defined offenses, those offenses falling into the category of crimes against humanity. That category includes such offenses as persecution, extermination, and deportation, although they require mass action before criminality is found. The difference with genocide is that it can be charged earlier in time, when mass atrocities have yet to be committed, but when they are contemplated. Genocide thus holds the prospect, to a greater degree than crimes against humanity, of providing a legal avenue to stopping atrocities before they occur.

Chapter 44

The Power of Domestic Courts

The capacity of domestic courts to deal effectively with genocide evokes a sharp difference of opinion. Some view it as the most effective remedy of all, because it is closer to the people who have been affected. Yet if atrocities were committed on a substantial scale, courts may be unable to process cases efficiently and fairly. Political circumstances in the country, or internationally, may affect the ability of domestic courts to prosecute for genocide.

Jurisdiction of Domestic Courts

One technical issue that may limit domestic courts is their jurisdictional reach. The Genocide Convention requires state parties to prosecute for genocide, according to Article VI, only if the genocide was committed in the state's territory. This limitation on a state's obligation has been condemned as a defect in the Genocide Convention, and the prime reason that genocide, as committed in the latter half of the twentieth century, has gone unpunished. Thus, Lee Steven writes: "Given the continued prevalence of genocide in the modern world and the concomitant lack of prosecutions, ... the Convention's most glaring weakness is its deficient implementation mechanism," by which Steven means implementation by state prosecution under Article VI, which requires states to prosecute only for genocide committed in their territory.[1]

If domestic courts prosecute only for genocide committed in their territory, their effectiveness is reduced, since governmental authorities may be implicated in the conduct and therefore reluctant to prosecute. As Sixth Committee delegates noted, governments might protect the guilty.[2] If the existing government is implicated in the conduct, its prosecutors may shy from bringing charges.[3]

---

1   Steven, L.A. (1999), 'Genocide and the Duty to Extradite or Prosecute: Why the United States is in Breach of Its International Obligations,' *Virginia Journal of International Law* 39, p. 425, p. 428.

2   UN GAOR, 3rd sess., Part 1, *Summary Records of Meetings 21 September - 10 December 1948*, pp. 349-350, UN Doc. A/C.6/SR.96 (1949) (Mr. Pescatore, Luxembourg). UN GAOR, 3rd sess., Part 1, *Summary Records of Meetings 21 September - 10 December 1948*, p. 430, UN Doc. A/C.6/SR.103 (1949) (Mr. Fitzmaurice, UK).

3   Verhoeven, J. (1991), 'Le crime de génocide: originalité et ambiguïté,' *Revue belge de droit international* 24, no. 1, p. 5, pp. 7-8.

An alternative approach for the Genocide Convention would have been to require states to prosecute any person found in their territory against whom there was credible evidence of having committed genocide, regardless of where it had been committed. Even though this approach was not taken, several countries have followed it on their own. Spain's parliament has declared universal jurisdiction over genocide,[4] and the Constitutional Tribunal of Spain has ruled that Article VI does not forbid states from exercising universal jurisdiction.[5] Israel's Supreme Court relied on universal jurisdiction to try Adolf Eichmann for acts committed in Europe. The courts of Germany said they had jurisdiction over genocide committed in Bosnia and not involving German nationals. Germany did have the connection that the defendants were residents, and were identified to German authorities by Bosnians who were also residents of Germany.

One can read Article VI as implying that states have jurisdiction only over genocide committed in their territory, and thus that a claim of universal jurisdiction is invalid. When Spain asked Mexico to extradite the Argentinean Ricardo Cavallo, to be tried, on the basis of universal jurisdiction, for genocide allegedly committed in Argentina, Mexico agreed, and the Supreme Court of Mexico found no legal impediment. Four judges (out of eleven) of the Supreme Court of Mexico dissented, insisting that Article VI limits states implementing the Genocide Convention to trying only for genocide committed in their own territory.[6]

On the other hand, Article VI may require states to prosecute genocide committed in their territory without implying that they do or do not have jurisdiction over genocide committed elsewhere. When states like Spain, Israel, and Germany have asserted universal jurisdiction of genocide, other states have not objected. The failure of other states to object suggests their acquiescence, hence their view that universal jurisdiction may be exerted over genocide.

No case on point has been decided by the ICJ. However, one case before the court involved crimes against humanity and war crimes, where the same issue arises. Not all judges expressed themselves on the issue, but three judges said that under customary international law, states are entitled to prosecute these offenses, regardless

4   Spain, Ley Organica del Poder Judicial, art. 23, para. 4(a).

5   Sentencia del Tribunal Constitucional español reconociendo el principio de jurisdicción penal universal en los casos de crímenes contra la humanidad, Spain, Constitucional Tribunal, Case No. STC 237/2005, 26 September 2005 (relating to alleged genocide in Guatemala). And see Auto de la Sala de lo Penal de la Audiencia Nacional confirmando la jurisdicción de España para conocer de los crímenes de genocidio y terrorismo cometidos durante la dictadura argentina, Spain, Supreme Court, Criminal Chamber, 4 November 1998. Auto de la Sala de lo Penal de la Audiencia Nacional confirmando la jurisdicción de España para conocer de los crímenes de genocidio y terrorismo cometidos durante la dictadura chilena, Spain, Supreme Court, Criminal Chamber, 5 November 1998; all three are accessible at www.derechos.org/nizkor.

6   Amparo en revisión 140/2002 (Ricardo Miguel Cavallo), Mexico, Supreme Court, Decision, 10 June 2003; in English (partial) in *International Legal Materials* 52, p. 888 (2003).

of where the act is committed, on the principle of universal jurisdiction.[7] Three other judges opined that there is no universal jurisdiction over these offenses.[8]

Political Factors

Political circumstances may obstruct prosecution. Khmer Rouge personnel who committed atrocities in Cambodia in the period 1975 to 1979 were insulated from prosecution through the 1980s because the Khmer Rouge government continued to be recognized internationally as the legitimate government of Cambodia after its removal from power, as it waged civil warfare from jungle redoubts. The international community was critical of the manner in which it was overthrown, in particular of Vietnam's military role, and therefore was reluctant to hold Khmer Rouge personnel to account.

Because of the difficulties of securing prompt prosecution, as reflected in the Khmer Rouge example, charges may be brought only many years after the acts in question. The efficacy of punishment long after the fact is generally thought to be much less than punishment promptly administered. Prosecutors may face the unsavory task of prosecuting an elderly individual whose physical frailty or ill health may preclude confinement in a penal institution.

"The only time states assume jurisdiction over genocide committed within their borders," writes Daniel Nsereko with much justification, "is when there has been a change of government, often by violent means."[9] As we saw in Part Two, most domestic prosecution has in fact occurred after a regime change. That scenario holds a risk, however, that the new government may be anxious to show the iniquity of the old regime and therefore may have an incentive to charge genocide on less than sufficient grounds, or to provide trials under less than due process conditions.[10]

The trial of Nicolae and Elena Ceausescu is perhaps the extreme example. They were tried for genocide, convicted, sentenced, and executed within a matter of hours, the organizers of the proceedings apparently concerned that the Ceausescus might yet mobilize supporters for a counter-coup. This political factor may do damage to the

---

7   Arrest Warrant of 11 April 2000 (Democratic Republic of the Congo v. Belgium), Judgment, 2002 ICJ Rep., p. 3, pp. 69-79 (joint separate opinion, Higgins, Kooijmans and Buergenthal).

8   Ibid., pp. 43-44 (separate opinion, Guillaume), pp. 56-58 (declaration, Ranjeva), pp. 91-94 (separate opinion, Rezek).

9   Nsereko, D.D.N. (2000), 'Genocide: A Crime Against Mankind,' in G.K. McDonald and O. Swaak-Goldman (eds), *Substantive and Procedural Aspects of International Criminal Law: The Experience of International and National Courts*, vol. 1, p. 113, p. 138, Kluwer, The Hague.

10   Kirchheimer, O. (1961), *Political Justice: The Use of Legal Proceedings for Political Ends*, Princeton University Press, Princeton.

quality of justice dispensed. "The motive," writes Daniel Nsereko, "is more likely to be revenge rather than a desire to do justice or to deter future recurrences."[11]

Prosecution after Mass Atrocities

Factors of practicality may limit the efficacy of genocide prosecution. Perhaps the most difficult situation is that in which the number of perpetrators is high. Martha Minow has appropriately suggested that the particular historical and political circumstances need to be examined before deciding whether prosecution for genocide or other crimes will be feasible or will serve a purpose.[12] The killings in Rwanda in 1994 differ from those that occurred in the Balkans in the early 1990s, or those committed by the Third Reich during World War II. In the latter two situations, killing was carried out by military and associated forces. In Rwanda, killing was carried out by broad masses of the Hutu population of Rwanda. Ordinary citizens participated in killing in a way that was not true of the other two cases.

If suspects are numerous, as in Rwanda, it may not be feasible to try them all. In Rwanda, the number of incarcerated suspects reached 10 per cent of the adult male Hutu population. In no country is the criminal justice system capable of trying so many. Thousands were held in pre-trial detention as the Rwandan courts struggled to conduct trials. By 2000, only 3,700 out of 125,000 had been tried.[13] By 2003, 100,000 remained in detention pending trial.

One means by which the Rwandan government had sought to cope with the caseload was to encourage guilty pleas by offering lower sentences.[14] The government hoped to sentence most of the suspects without a full trial. Few suspects accepted the offer, however. Having been held several years without trial, many refused to believe that if they pleaded guilty they would actually be given a reduced sentence. Moreover, because of the mass participation in the 1994 killing, many of these suspects reportedly could not view themselves as guilty, since they had done nothing that their neighbors and acquaintances had not done.[15]

A related difficulty in Rwanda in employing criminal prosecution came from the side of the victims. Criminal prosecution in normal circumstances identifies particular individuals as having violated society's norms of behavior and thereby setting themselves apart from law-abiding citizens. Victims thus are able to believe

---

11 Nsereko (2000), p. 138.

12 Minow, M. (1998), *Between Vengeance and Forgiveness: Facing History After Genocide and Mass Violence*, pp. 132-135, Beacon Press, Boston.

13 Drumbl, M.A. (2000), 'Punishment, Postgenocide: From Guilt to Shame to *Civis* in Rwanda,' *New York University Law Review* 75, p. 1221, pp. 1286-1287.

14 Rwanda, Organic Law No. 08/96 of 30 August 1996 on the Organization of the Prosecution of Infractions Constituting the Crime of Genocide or Crimes against Humanity Committed since 1 October 1990, arts. 5, 15, 16, Journal officiel, 35th year, no. 17, 1 September 1996.

15 Drumbl (2000), p. 1281 and p. 1291.

that the predators among them are being punished. In Rwanda, so many Hutus participated in the killing that the surviving Tutsis may never believe that the guilty have been punished. Moreover, surviving Tutsis feel victimized not only by those Hutu who actually killed, but by the other Hutus, few of whom did anything to stop the atrocities. Thus, criminal prosecution may not serve its purpose: to identify and stigmatize a discrete number of perpetrators, and to provide a sense that justice has been done.

One more difficulty in using criminal prosecution in Rwanda was that the government that came to power in the wake of the 1994 killings of Tutsi was Tutsi-led. Thus, the government that was trying Hutu for killing Tutsi was Tutsi-based. Hutu suspects viewed themselves as being subjected to a kind of "victor's justice," not unlike the view of Japanese and Germans who were tried after World War II.[16]

In such circumstances, argues Mark Drumbl, who served as a defense attorney in genocide trials in the Rwandan courts, procedures other than penal prosecution may more effectively mend a society torn by genocide and provide a sense of justice to survivors. In Africa, customary law processes have traditionally been used to deal with crime, with a focus less on penalization than on publicly shaming an offender, reconciling offender and victim, and reintegrating the offender into the community.[17]

In 2000, legislation was adopted in Rwanda to employ a customary law mechanism to try persons still in detention on charges stemming from the 1994 killings. Under this legislation, the bulk of the remaining suspects were to be tried not by courts, but by popular assemblies. Citizens would be elected to a group of fifty that would hear a case, and twenty of the fifty would be elected to determine a sentence. The legislation referred to this procedure as *gacaca*, a customary law mechanism for dealing with crime in Rwanda.[18] In 2001, local elections were conducted to select 260,000 persons to hear cases.[19]

Unlike the traditional *gacaca* proceedings, however, the process contemplated by the 2000 Rwanda legislation used local assemblies to establish guilt and set penalties. Even though suspects who confessed would be treated leniently, others could be given a criminal sentence by the assembly, with a right of appeal to the regular courts. The procedure was being used in part to fulfill the customary law function of shaming and reintegrating an offender, and in part to relieve the courts of the overwhelming burden they faced.[20]

---

16 Minear, R. (1971), *Victors' Justice: The Tokyo War Crimes Trial*, Princeton University Press, Princeton.

17 Drumbl (2000), pp. 1253-1263.

18 Ibid., pp. 1264-1267.

19 'Rwanda to use traditional justice in '94 killings,' *New York Times*, 7 October 2001, p. A4.

20 Drumbl (2000), p. 1266.

Jeremy Sarkin expressed concern that the judges, untrained in the law, might not dispense justice competently.[21] As an alternative, Sarkin suggested that only the major perpetrators of genocide be prosecuted, and that they be prosecuted in the regular courts. Sarkin, a South African, suggests that truth and reconciliation proceedings, as have been used in South Africa, be undertaken as well, as a supplemental means of social healing: "Only by publicly and collectively acknowledging the horror of past human rights violations will it be possible for the country to establish the rule of law and a culture of, and respect for, human rights."[22] To date, there is no consensus on how best to mend a society rent by the commission of atrocities on the scale experienced in Rwanda or Cambodia.

---

21 Sarkin, J. (2001), 'The Tension between Justice and Reconciliation in Rwanda: Politics, Human Rights, Due Process and the Role of the *Gacaca* Courts in Dealing with the Genocide,' *Journal of African Law* 45, p. 143, pp. 162-166.

22 Ibid., p. 167.

Chapter 45

The Deterrent Value of Genocide

On 22 August 1939, three weeks into the German invasion of Poland, Adolf Hitler explained to his generals his plan to depopulate Poland, in order to settle Germans there. Many Polish women and children, he said, would be sent to their deaths in the process. Hitler discounted the risk to Germany or its commanders by noting a recent historical precedent: the expulsion of the Armenians from their lands in 1915, which also involved killings in large numbers. "Who after all," Hitler reportedly told his generals, "is today speaking about the destruction of the Armenians?"[1]

Whether the atrocities of World War II could have been averted by prosecutions after World War I is not demonstrable. Two reasons are given for punishing those who commit major crimes like genocide. One is to satisfy a sense of justice in the relevant community. If genocide has been committed in the context of civil war or other mass violence, criminal punishment may help a society to heal. Absence of prosecution is said to make it difficult for victims and their relatives to live together with those responsible for crimes.

A Sense of Justice

The rationale of satisfying the public's sense of justice, sometimes termed retribution, or, more pejoratively, vengeance, is based on the concept that the public feels that persons who commit certain kinds of socially harmful acts must be punished. This rationale runs deep in penal law. In ancient China it was expressed in the idea that a criminal act violates the "cosmic order," which can be restored only by punishing the wrongdoer.[2]

In the aftermath of mass atrocities, which may be involved with the perpetration of genocide, a particular brand of the retribution concept is argued. Genocide may be committed in the context of civil conflict. Once the conflict ends, if there is no prosecution of the perpetrators of genocide, those who have committed genocide are living in the same society as the victims, and relatives of victims. The victims, it is

---

1   'Contents of the Speech by the Führer to the Chief Commanders and Commanding Generals on the Obersalzberg, August 22, 1939,' E.L. Woodward and Rohan Butler (eds), *Documents on British Foreign Policy, 1919-1939*, 3rd series, 1949-1955, vol. 7, p. 258, Great Britain, Foreign Office, London.

2   Bodde, D. and C. Morris (1967), *Law in Imperial China*, p. 4, Harvard University Press, Cambridge.

argued, cannot be expected to co-exist with perpetrators who only yesterday were, perhaps, torturing them. Social reconciliation, it is said, cannot be achieved without punishment for the perpetrators.

For a post-conflict government, the prosecution of perpetrators can be problematic. Perpetrators may occupy high positions. The conflict may have been resolved by agreement among the groups in conflict, and this agreement may have been premised, explicitly or implicitly, on a promise that no one would be prosecuted for misdeeds. Thus, a program of prosecuting for genocide may jeopardize post-conflict political stability.

Deterrence

A second reason given for holding trials for genocide is to deter future genocide. Writing in 1981, Richard Edwards reviewed allegations of mass atrocities in a number of countries since the ratification of the Genocide Convention and concluded that the Convention had not prevented genocide.[3] The Cambodia atrocities took place in the 1970s. Atrocities probably amounting to genocide occurred in that same decade in Burundi and East Pakistan, but no formal proceedings resulted. Genocide was occurring, "apparently with impunity."[4]

The deterrent value of the penal sanction has long been debated: whether the prosecution of one individual at a given point in time deters another individual at a later point in time. When one adds the factor of the episodic character of penal sanctions, the argument that deterrence is effective becomes still more difficult to sustain. Given the imperfect state of international enforcement, prosecution of individuals for genocide will necessarily be episodic, rather than systematic.

In 1998, government officials in Rwanda, explaining why they were conducting trials in the Rwandan courts for the 1994 atrocities, said they hoped to deter Hutu guerrillas, who were at the time still operating and targeting Tutsi.[5] They viewed prosecution as having a deterrent value. Pol Pot and Ieng Sary were tried *in absentia* at a time when they still controlled territory in Cambodia and were thought still to be committing atrocities. The Cambodian court issued them summonses to appear, but they did not.[6] The Cambodian government hoped to deter future atrocities.

---

3   Edwards, R. (1981), 'Contributions of the Genocide Convention to the Development of International Law,' *Ohio Northern University Law Review* 8, p. 300, p. 308.

4   Verhoeven, J. (1991), 'Le crime de génocide: originalité et ambiguïté,' *Revue belge de droit international* 24, no. 1, p. 5, p. 7.

5   McKinley Jr., J.C., 'As crowds vent their rage, Rwanda publicly executes 22,' *New York Times*, 25 April 1998, p. A1.

6   De Nike, H., J. Quigley and K. Robinson (eds) (2000), *Genocide in Cambodia: Documents from the Trial of Pol Pot and Ieng Sary*, pp. 65-66, University of Pennsylvania Press, Philadelphia.

The deterrent value of genocide as a crime cannot be considered apart from the deterrent value of any crime. In domestic law, murder is a penal offense, yet murders occur regularly. The issue as to deterrence is whether murder would occur with greater frequency in the absence of a penal sanction. Such a question cannot readily be answered, as societies have no control group against which to measure. One cannot know what level of murder would have been present in the absence of penal sanction.

Similarly with genocide, no one can prove a deterrent effect. Nonetheless, deterrence was highlighted by the UN Security Council when it established the Yugoslavia and Rwanda tribunals. In its resolution on the Rwanda tribunal, the Security Council gave as a reason "that the establishment of an international tribunal for the prosecution of persons responsible for genocide ... will contribute to ensuring that such violations are halted and effectively redressed."[7]

Domestic vs. International Courts

If deterrence works at all, domestic trials, some have argued, may have a greater impact than international trials. Yacob Haile-Mariam, comparing the international proceedings in Rwanda to the domestic proceedings in Ethiopia, suggests that the Ethiopian trials "will have a larger deterrent effect on the general population and present and future leaders of Ethiopia than the ICTR trials on the Rwandan people."[8] José Alvarez argues that trials conducted locally carry greater moral impact.[9]

International prosecutions, others say, have greater deterrent value, because they send a message to potential perpetrators around the world. Deterrence is the watchword, as in domestic penal settings. In a rationale that goes back at least to Jeremy Bentham in penology, the offender is punished in the expectation that others will be deterred from committing such offenses in the future. A subsidiary rationale, in both international and domestic penal law, is to deter the particular perpetrator from committing similar acts in the future.

Others doubt that international prosecutions can reduce atrocities. Even a permanent international criminal court, writes Makau Mutua, would not be effective, "given the large scale of abuses and the reluctance of states to punish offenders."[10] Some who perpetrate genocide, particularly those holding high governmental rank,

---

7   SC Res. 955, preamble, UN SCOR, 49th sess., 3453rd meeting, UN Doc. S/RES/955 (1994).

8   Haile-Mariam, Y. (1999), 'The Quest for Justice and Reconciliation: The International Criminal Tribunal for Rwanda and the Ethiopian High Court,' *Hastings International & Comparative Law Review* 22, p. 667, p. 744.

9   Alvarez, J. (1999), 'Crimes of State/Crimes of Hate: Lessons from Rwanda,' *Yale Journal of International Law* 24, p. 365, pp. 403-404.

10   Mutua, M. (1997), 'Never Again: Questioning the Yugoslav and Rwanda Tribunals,' *Temple International & Comparative Law Journal* 11, p. 167, p. 170.

may evade prosecution. Perpetrators may flee to a country that refuses to extradite them to states that might prosecute them for genocide.

Over and apart from whatever constraints may inhibit the work of an international criminal court, genocide is sufficiently difficult to curb that any mechanisms with a prospect of achieving results should be utilized. If maximum pressure is to be exerted against genocide, judicial mechanisms directed both against individuals and against states are in order. The two mechanisms should be viewed as complementing one another, not as competing with one another.

The effort initiated after World War II to codify an international crime of genocide grew out of concern over some of the worst atrocities ever experienced. The task that faced the drafters was daunting. They wanted to prevent the most atrocious of acts against human beings, yet they feared that if they required too much atrocious conduct, the Convention would not apply in time to stop ongoing violations.

Although the drafters focused largely on genocide as a crime for which individuals could be held accountable, they opened the possibility of suits against states, thereby creating a treaty oriented simultaneously in two directions. Suits between states may hold greater prospect of stopping genocide at an early stage. Criminal prosecution may hold greater prospect of serving as an example against future genocide.

Both prongs of the Genocide Convention have found use in recent years. Whatever the controversy about the value of genocide suits and prosecutions, one does find them continuing.

This litigation is having the effect of elaborating the meaning of genocide. If the Genocide Convention is to have any positive effect, the parameters of genocide must be understood by the courts. As new factual situations develop, the fabric of the Genocide Convention gains new richness. Despite its status as the oldest of the major human rights treaties, the Genocide Convention remains a work in progress.

Appendix

Convention on the Prevention and Punishment of the Crime of Genocide
December 9, 1948
UN Treaty Series, vol. 78, p. 277

The Contracting Parties,

Having considered the declaration made by the General Assembly of the United Nations in its resolution 96 (I) dated 11 December 1946 that genocide is a crime under international law, contrary to the spirit and aims of the United Nations and condemned by the civilized world;

Recognizing that at all periods of history genocide has inflicted great losses on humanity; and

Being convinced that, in order to liberate mankind from such an odious scourge, international co-operation is required;

Hereby agree as hereinafter provided.

Article I

The Contracting Parties confirm that genocide, whether committed in time of peace or in time of war, is a crime under international law which they undertake to prevent and to punish.

Article II

In the present Convention, genocide means any of the following acts committed with intent to destroy, in whole or in part, a national, ethnical, racial or religious group, as such:

(a) Killing members of the group; (b) Causing serious bodily or mental harm to members of the group; (c) Deliberately inflicting on the group conditions of life calculated to bring about its physical destruction in whole or in part; (d) Imposing measures intended to prevent births within the group; (e) Forcibly transferring children of the group to another group.

Article III

The following acts shall be punishable:

(a) Genocide; (b) Conspiracy to commit genocide; (c) Direct and public incitement to commit genocide; (d) Attempt to commit genocide; (e) Complicity in genocide.

Article IV

Persons committing genocide or any of the other acts enumerated in Article III shall be punished, whether they are constitutionally responsible rulers, public officials or private individuals.

Article V

The Contracting Parties undertake to enact, in accordance with their respective Constitutions, the necessary legislation to give effect to the provisions of the present Convention and, in particular, to provide effective penalties for persons guilty of genocide or any of the other acts enumerated in Article III.

Article VI

Persons charged with genocide or any of the other acts enumerated in Article III shall be tried by a competent tribunal of the State in the territory of which the act was committed, or by such international penal tribunal as may have jurisdiction with respect to those Contracting Parties which shall have accepted its jurisdiction.

Article VII

Genocide and the other acts enumerated in Article III shall not be considered as political crimes for the purpose of extradition.

The Contracting Parties pledge themselves in such cases to grant extradition in accordance with their laws and treaties in force.

Article VIII

Any Contracting Party may call upon the competent organs of the United Nations to take such action under the Charter of the United Nations as they consider appropriate for the prevention and suppression of acts of genocide or any of the other acts enumerated in Article III.

Article IX

Disputes between the Contracting Parties relating to the interpretation, application or fulfilment of the present Convention, including those relating to the responsibility of a State for genocide or for any of the other acts enumerated in Article III, shall be submitted to the International Court of Justice at the request of any of the parties to the dispute.

Article X

The present Convention, of which the Chinese, English, French, Russian and Spanish texts are equally authentic, shall bear the date of 9 December 1948.

Article XI

The present Convention shall be open until 31 December 1949 for signature on behalf of any Member of the United Nations and of any non-member State to which an invitation to sign has been addressed by the General Assembly.

The present Convention shall be ratified, and the instruments of ratification shall be deposited with the Secretary-General of the United Nations.

After 1 January 1950, the present Convention may be acceded to on behalf of any Member of the United Nations and of any non-member State which has received an invitation as aforesaid.

Instruments of accession shall be deposited with the Secretary-General of the United Nations.

Article XII

Any Contracting Party may at any time, by notification addressed to the Secretary-General of the United Nations, extend the application of the present Convention to all or any of the territories for the conduct of whose foreign relations that Contracting Party is responsible.

Article XIII

On the day when the first twenty instruments of ratification or accession have been deposited, the Secretary-General shall draw up a proces-verbal and transmit a copy of it to each Member of the United Nations and to each of the non-member States contemplated in Article XI.

The present Convention shall come into force on the ninetieth day following the date of deposit of the twentieth instrument of ratification or accession.

Any ratification or accession effected subsequent to the latter date shall become effective on the ninetieth day following the deposit of the instrument of ratification or accession.

Article XIV

The present Convention shall remain in effect for a period of ten years as from the date of its coming into force.

It shall thereafter remain in force for successive periods of five years for such Contracting Parties as have not denounced it at least six months before the expiration of the current period.

Denunciation shall be effected by a written notification addressed to the Secretary-General of the United Nations.

Article XV

If, as a result of denunciations, the number of Parties to the present Convention should become less than sixteen, the Convention shall cease to be in force as from the date on which the last of these denunciations shall become effective.

Article XVI

A request for the revision of the present Convention may be made at any time by any Contracting Party by means of a notification in writing addressed to the Secretary-General.

The General Assembly shall decide upon the steps, if any, to be taken in respect of such request.

Article XVII

The Secretary-General of the United Nations shall notify all Members of the United Nations and the non-member States contemplated in Article XI of the following:

(a) Signatures, ratifications and accessions received in accordance with Article XI; (b) Notifications received in accordance with Article XII; (c) The date upon which the present Convention comes into force in accordance with Article XIII; (d) Denunciations received in accordance with Article XIV; (e) The abrogation of the Convention in accordance with Article XV; (f) Notifications received in accordance with Article XVI.

Article XVIII

The original of the present Convention shall be deposited in the archives of the United Nations.

A certified copy of the Convention shall be transmitted to all Members of the United Nations and to the non-member States contemplated in Article XI.

Article XIX

The present Convention shall be registered by the Secretary-General of the United Nations on the date of its coming into force.

Bibliography

Abrams, J.S. (2001), 'The Atrocities in Cambodia and Kosovo: Observations on the Codification of Genocide,' *New England Law Review* 35, p. 303.

Akhavan, P. (1995), 'Enforcement of the Genocide Convention: A Challenge to Civilization,' *Harvard Human Rights Journal* 8, p. 229.

Alvarez, J. (1999), 'Crimes of State/Crimes of Hate: Lessons from Rwanda,' *Yale Journal of International Law* 24, p. 365.

Amann, D.M. (2002), 'Group Mentality, Expressivism, and Genocide,' *International Criminal Law Review* 2, p. 93.

Ambos, K. and S. Wirth (2001), 'Genocide and War Crimes in the Former Yugoslavia Before German Criminal Courts,' in H. Fischer, C. Kress and S. Luder (eds), *International and National Prosecution of Crimes Under International Law*, p. 769, Berlin Verlag, Berlin.

Ambos, K. (1998), 'Djajic,' *Neue Zeitschrift für Strafrecht* 3, p. 138.

Aptel, C. (2002), 'The Intent to Commit Genocide in the Case Law of the International Criminal Tribunal for Rwanda,' *Criminal Law Forum* 13, p. 273.

Artucio, A. (1979), *The Trial of Macias in Equatorial Guinea: The Story of a Dictatorship*, International Commission of Jurists & International University Exchange Fund, Geneva.

Barsh, R.L. (1987), 'Arctic Nutrition and Genocide,' *Nordic Journal of International Law* 56, p. 322.

Bederman, D. (1998), 'State Responsibility in a Multiactor World,' *American Society of International Law Proceedings* 92, p. 291.

Beer, D. de (1997), *The Organic Law of 30 August 1996 on the Organization of the Prosecution of Offences Constituting the Crime of Genocide or Crimes Against Humanity: Commentary*, pp. 33-34, Alter Egaux Editions, Brussels.

Berle, Jr., A.A. (1950), 'Mise hors la loi du génocide,' *Revue international de droit pénal* (no. 2), p. 147.

Bisharat, G.E. (2001), 'Sanctions as Genocide,' *Transnational Law & Contemporary Problems* 11, p. 379.

Bodde, D. and C. Morris (1967), *Law in Imperial China*, Harvard University Press, Cambridge.

Boelaert-Suominen, S. (2001), 'Prosecuting Superiors for Crimes Committed by Subordinates: A Discussion of the First Significant Case Law Since the Second World War,' *Virginia Journal of International Law* 41, p. 747.

Boyle, F.A. (1996), *The Bosnian People Charge Genocide: Proceedings at the International Court of Justice Concerning Bosnia v. Serbia on the Prevention and Punishment of the Crime of Genocide*, Aletheia Press, Amherst.

Bullock, A. (1952), *Hitler: A Study in Tyranny*, Harper, New York.

Cartner, H. (1990), 'A Rush to Appease...and to Conceal,' *Human Rights Watch/ Helsinki* 2, issue no. 6, p. 5.

Cassese, A. (2002), 'Genocide,' in A. Cassese, P. Gaeta and J. Jones (eds), *The Rome Statute of the International Criminal Court: A Commentary*, vol. 1, Oxford University Press, Oxford.

Chadbourn, J.H. (1933), *Lynching and the Law*, University of North Carolina Press, Chapel Hill.

Charney, J.I. (1989), 'Third State Remedies in International Law,' *Michigan Journal of International Law* 10, p. 57.

Chesterman, S. (2000), 'An Altogether Different Order: Defining the Elements of Crimes Against Humanity,' *Duke Journal of Comparative & International Law* 10, p. 307.

Clark, R. (2001), 'The Mental Element in International Criminal Law: The Rome Statute of the International Criminal Court and the Elements of Offenses,' *Criminal Law Forum* 12, no. 3, p. 291.

Clark, R. (2000), 'The Development of International Criminal Law,' pp. 9-10, unpublished paper presented at Conference: "Just Peace? Peace Making and Peace Building for the New Millennium," Massey University, Auckland, New Zealand, 24-28 April 2000.

Clark, R. (1981), 'Does the Genocide Convention Go Far Enough? Some Thoughts on the Nature of Criminal Genocide in the Context of Indonesia's Invasion of East Timor,' *Ohio Northern University Law Review* 8, p. 321.

Codrescu, A. (1991), *The Hole in the Flag: A Romanian Exile's Story of Return and Revolution*, William Morrow, New York.

Crawford, J. (2002), *The International Law Commission's Articles on State Responsibility: Introduction, Text and Commentaries*, Cambridge University Press, Cambridge.

Crawford, J., P. Bodeau and J. Peel (2000), 'The ILC's Draft Articles on State Responsibility: Toward Completion of a Second Reading,' *American Journal of International Law* 94, p. 660.

Dadrian, V.N. (1995), *The History of the Armenian Genocide: Ethnic Conflict from the Balkans to Anatolia to the Caucasus*, Berghahn Books, Providence.

Damaska, M. (2001), 'The Shadow Side of Command Responsibility,' *American Journal of Comparative Law* 49, p. 455.

Damrosch, L.R. (1998), 'Genocide and Ethnic Conflict,' in D. Wippman (ed.), *International Law and Ethnic Conflict*, p. 256.

Dickson, B. (1989), 'The Prevention of Terrorism (Temporary Provisions) Act 1989,' *Northern Ireland Law Quarterly* 40, p. 250.

Donnedieu de Vabres, H. (1950), 'De la Piraterie au Génocide . . . les Nouvelles Modalités de la Répression Universelle,' in *Le Droit Privé Français au Milieu du XXe Siècle: Études offertes à Georges Ripert*, vol. 1, p. 226, Librarie Générale de droit et de jurisprudence, Paris.

Donnedieu de Vabres, H. (1947), *Traité de droit criminel et de législation pénale comparée*, Librarie de Recueil Sirey, Paris.

Donnedieu de Vabres, H. (1924-1925), 'La Cour Permanente de Justice Internationale et sa Vocation en matière criminelle,' *Revue internationale de droit penal* 1 (no. 19), p. 186.

Dressler, J. (2001), *Understanding Criminal Law*, Matthew Bender, New York.

Drost, P.N. (1959), *The Crime of State: Penal Protection for Fundamental Freedoms of Persons and Peoples: Book II: Genocide: United Nations Legislation on International Criminal Law*, A.W. Sythoff, Leiden.

Drumbl, M.A. (2000), 'Punishment, Postgenocide: From Guilt to Shame to *Civis* in Rwanda,' *New York University Law Review* 75, p. 1221.

Drumbl, M.A. (1998), 'Rule of Law Amid Lawlessness: Counseling the Accused in Rwanda's Domestic Genocide Trials,' *Columbia Human Rights Law Review*, p. 545.

Edwards, R. (1981), 'Contributions of the Genocide Convention to the Development of International Law,' *Ohio Northern University Law Review* 8, p. 300.

Eser, A. (1997), in A. Schönke and H. Schröder (eds), *Strafgesetzbuch: Kommentar*, p. 1597, C.H. Beck'sche Verlagsbuchhandlung, Munich.

Fischer, H. (1998), 'Some Aspects of German State Practice concerning IHL,' *Yearbook of International Humanitarian Law* 1, p. 380, p. 385.

Fletcher, G.P. and J.D. Ohlin (2005), 'Reclaiming Fundamental Principles of Criminal Law in the Darfur Case,' *Journal of International Criminal Justice* 3, p. 537.

Fletcher, G.P. (1978), *Rethinking Criminal Law*, Little, Brown & Co., Boston.

Foregger, E. and E. Serini (eds) (1978), *Strafgesetzbuch samt den wichtigsten Nebengesetzen*, Manz Verlag, Vienna.

Forte, D.F. (1999), *Studies in Islamic Law: Classical and Contemporary Application*, Austin & Winfield, Lanham MD.

Frowein, J.A. (1994), 'Reactions by Not Directly Affected States to Breaches of Public International Law,' *Recueil des Cours* (Hague Academy of International Law) 248, vol. 4, p. 345.

Garraway, C. (2001), 'Elements of the Specific Forms of Genocide,' in R. Lee (ed.), *The International Criminal Court: Elements of Crimes and Rules of Procedure and Evidence*, p. 50, Transnational, Ardsley NY.

'Genocide: A Commentary on the Convention,' *Yale Law Journal* 58, p. 1142, p. 1147 (1949).

The Genocide and the Crimes against Humanity in Rwandan Law (1997), International Centre for the Study and the Promotion of Human Rights and Information, Editions ASSEPAC.

Gil Gil, A. (1999), *Derecho Penal Internacional: Especial Consideración del Delito de Genocidio*, Editorial Tecnos, Madrid.

Glaser, S. (1970), *Droit international pénal conventionnel*, Bruylant, Brussels.

Gorove, S. (1951), 'The Problem of "Mental Harm" in the Genocide Convention,' *Washington University Law Quarterly*, p. 174.

Gowlland-Debbas, V. (1999), 'The Right to Life and Genocide: The Court and International Public Policy,' in L. Boisson de Chazournes and P. Sands (eds),

International Law, the International Court of Justice and Nuclear Weapons, p. 315, Cambridge University Press, Cambridge.

Graven, J. (1950), 'Les crimes contre l'humanité,' *Recueil des Cours* (Hague Academy of International Law) 76, vol. 1, p. 429.

Greenawalt, A.K.A. (1999), 'Rethinking Genocidal Intent: The Case for a Knowledge-Based Interpretation,' *Columbia Law Review* 99, p. 2259.

Haile-Mariam, Y. (1999), 'The Quest for Justice and Reconciliation: The International Criminal Tribunal for Rwanda and the Ethiopian High Court,' *Hastings International & Comparative Law Review* 22, p. 667.

Hannum, H. (1989), 'International Law and Cambodian Genocide: The Sounds of Silence,' *Human Rights Law Quarterly* 11, p. 82.

Hitler, A. (1971), *Mein Kampf*, Houghton-Mifflin, Boston.

Hoogh, A. de (1996), *Obligations* Erga Omnes *and International Crimes: A Theoretical Inquiry into the Implementation and Enforcement of the International Responsibility of States*, Kluwer, The Hague and Boston.

Hudson, M.O. (1951), 'The Twenty-Ninth Year of the World Court,' *American Journal of International Law* 45, p. 1.

Hudson, M.O. (1931), *International Legislation: A Collection of the Texts of Multipartite International Instruments of General Interest*, vol. 1.

Huet, A. and R. Koering-Joulin (1994), *Droit pénal international*, p. 135, Presses Universitaires de France, Paris.

Israel, F. (ed.) (1967), *Major Peace Treaties of Modern History 1648-1967*, p.1535.

Jacobs, N. (1969), 'A propos de la définition juridique du génocide,' *Études internationales de psycho-sociologie criminelle*, 16-17, p. 55.

Jescheck, H.-H. (1954), 'Die internationale Genocidium-Konvention vom 9. Dezember 1948 und die Lehre vom Völkerstrafrecht,' *Zeitschrift für die gesamte Strafrechtswissenschaft*, p. 193.

Jørgensen, N. (2000), *The Responsibility of States for International Crimes*, Oxford University Press, Oxford.

Jørgensen, N. (1999), 'State Responsibility and the 1948 Genocide Convention,' in G. Goodwin-Gill and S. Talmon (eds), *The Reality of International Law: Essays in Honour of Ian Brownlie*, p. 273, Clarendon Press, Oxford.

Kamminga, M.T. (1992), *Inter-State Accountability for Violations of Human Rights*, University of Pennsylvania Press, Philadelphia.

Kirchheimer, O. (1961), *Political Justice: The Use of Legal Proceedings for Political Ends*, Princeton University Press, Princeton.

Kuhn, A.K. (1949), 'The Genocide Convention and State Rights,' *American Journal of International Law* 43, p. 498, p. 501.

Kunz, J.L. (1949), 'The United Nations Convention on Genocide,' *American Journal of International Law* 43, p. 738.

Kuper, L. (1985), *The Prevention of Genocide*, Yale University Press, New Haven.

LaFave, W.R. (2000), *Criminal Law*, West Group, St. Paul.

LeBlanc, L.J. (1991), *The United States and the Genocide Convention*, p. 34, Duke University Press, Durham and London.

Lemkin, R. (1944), *Axis Rule in Occupied Europe: Laws of Occupation, Analysis of Government, Proposals for Redress*, Carnegie Endowment for International Peace, Washington.

Lippman, M. (1985), 'The Drafting of the 1948 Convention on the Prevention and Punishment of the Crime of Genocide,' *Boston University International Law Journal* 3, p. 1.

Magliveras, K.D. (2002), 'The Unfinished Story of the Cambodia Criminal Tribunal: An Analysis of the Law of August 2001 and its Aftermath,' *International Enforcement Law Reporter* 18, no. 12.

Magnarella, P.J. (1997), 'Some Milestones and Achievements at the International Criminal Tribunal for Rwanda: The 1998 Kambanda and Akayesu Cases,' *Florida Journal of International Law* 11, p. 517.

Mayfield, J. (1995), 'The Prosecution of War Crimes and Respect for Human Rights: Ethiopia's Balancing Act,' *Emory International Law Review* 9, p. 553.

Mayorga R.A. (1997), 'Democracy Dignified and an End to Impunity: Bolivia's Military Dictatorship on Trial,' in A.J. McAdams (ed.), *Transitional Justice and the Rule of Law in New Democracies*, p. 61, University of Notre Dame Press, Notre Dame and London.

McNair, A. (1961), *The Law of Treaties*, Clarendon Press, Oxford.

Miaja de la Muela, A. (1951-52), 'El genocidio, delito internacional,' *Revista española de derecho internacional* 4, p. 363.

Military Trials and the Use of the Death Penalty in Equatorial Guinea, pp. 1-2, Amnesty International, New York (1987).

Minear, R. (1971), *Victors' Justice: The Tokyo War Crimes Trial*, Princeton University Press, Princeton.

Minow, M. (1998), *Between Vengeance and Forgiveness: Facing History After Genocide and Mass Violence*, Beacon Press, Boston.

Molina, A. (1950), 'El delito de genocidio en la legislación Guatemalteca,' *Revista de la Facultad de Ciencias Jurídicas y Sociales de Guatemala*, p. 25.

Morris, V. and M. Scharf (1998), *The International Criminal Tribunal for Rwanda*, Transnational Publishers, Irvington-on-Hudson NY.

Morsink, J. (1999), *The Universal Declaration of Human Rights: Origins, Drafting, and Intent*, University of Pennsylvania Press, Philadelphia.

Münzel, M. (1976), 'Manhunt,' in R. Arens (ed.), *Genocide in Paraguay*, p. 19, Temple University Press, Philadelphia.

Mutua, M. (1997), 'Never Again: Questioning the Yugoslav and Rwanda Tribunals,' *Temple International & Comparative Law Journal* 11, p. 167.

Nike, H. De, J. Quigley and K. Robinson (eds) (2000), *Genocide in Cambodia: Documents from the Trial of Pol Pot and Ieng Sary*, University of Pennsylvania Press, Philadelphia.

Nikiforov, B.S. (1963), *Nauchno-prakticheskii kommentarii ugolovnogo kodeksa RSFSR* [Scholarly and Practical Commentary to the Criminal Code of the RSFSR], Juridical Literature, Moscow.

Nowak, M. (1993), *U.N. Covenant on Civil and Political Rights: CCPR Commentary*, p. 281, N.P. Engel, Kehl, Strasbourg and Arlington.

Nsereko, D.D.N. (2000), 'Genocide: A Crime Against Mankind,' in G.K. McDonald and O. Swaak-Goldman (eds), *Substantive and Procedural Aspects of International Criminal Law: The Experience of International and National Courts*, vol. 1, p. 113, Kluwer, The Hague.

Oosterveld, V. (2001), 'The Elements of Genocide,' in R. Lee (ed.), *The International Criminal Court: Elements of Crimes and Rules of Procedure and Evidence*, Transnational, Ardsley NY.

Paust, J. (2000), 'Problematic U.S. Sanctions Efforts in response to Genocide, Crimes Against Humanity, War Crimes, and Other Human Rights Violations,' *Waseda Proceedings of Comparative Law* 3, p. 96, Institute of Comparative Law, Waseda University, Tokyo.

Paust, J. (1998), 'Commentary on Parts 1 and 2 of the Zutphen Intersessional Draft,' in L. Sadat Wexler (ed.), *13bis Nouvelles études pénales: Observations on the Consolidated ICC Text Before the Final Session of the Preparatory Committee*, p. 27, Association Internationale de Droit Pénal.

Paust, J. (1997), 'It's No Defense: *Nullum Crimen*, International Crime and the Gingerbread Man,' *Albany Law Review* 60, p. 657.

Payne, R. (1973), *The Life and Death of Adolf Hitler*, Praeger, New York.

Pérez Gonzalez, M., and M.A. Castelos (1995-96), 'Offences Against the International Community According to the Spanish Penal Code,' *Spanish Yearbook of International Law*, p. 3.

Planzer, A. (1956), *Le Crime de Génocide*, F. Schwald AG, St. Gallen.

Quigley, J. (1997), 'Mass Displacement and the Individual Right of Return,' *British Year Book of International Law* 68, p. 65.

Quintal, A.L. (1998), 'Rule 61: The "Voice of the Victims" Screams Out for Justice,' *Columbia Journal of Transnational Law* 36, p. 688.

Ratner, S. and J.S. Abrams (1997), *Accountability for Human Rights Atrocities in International Law: Beyond the Nuremberg Legacy*, Clarendon Press, Oxford and New York.

Robinson, N. (1960), *The Genocide Convention: A Commentary*, Institute of Jewish Affairs, New York.

Robinson, N. (1949), *The Genocide Convention: Its Origins and Interpretation*, Institute of Jewish Affairs, New York.

Rosenne, S. (1996), 'War Crimes and State Responsibility,' in Y. Dinstein and M. Tabory (eds), *War Crimes in International Law*, p. 65.

Rosenne, S. (1985), *The Law and Practice of the International Court*, Martinus Nijhoff Publishers, Dordrecht.

Ruckert, W., and G. Witschel (2001), 'Genocide and Crimes Against Humanity in the Elements of Crimes,' in H. Fischer, C. Kress and S. Luder (eds), *International and National Prosecution of Crimes Under International Law*, p. 59, Berlin Verlag, Berlin.

Sadat, L. (2002), *The International Criminal Court and the Transformation of International Law: Justice for the New Millennium*, Transnational Publishers, Ardsley NY.

Safferling, C.J.M. (1998), 'Public Prosecutor v. Djajic,' *American Journal of International Law* 92, p. 528.

Saldaña, Q. (1925), 'La Justice pénale internationale,' *Recueil des cours* (Hague Academy of International Law) 10, p. 369.

Salunke, S.P. (1977), *Pakistani POWs in India*, p. 104, Vikas Publishing, New Delhi.

Sarkin, J. (2001), 'The Tension between Justice and Reconciliation in Rwanda: Politics, Human Rights, Due Process and the Role of the *Gacaca* Courts in Dealing with the Genocide,' *Journal of African Law* 45, p. 143.

Saul, B. (2001), 'Was the Conflict in East Timor "Genocide" and Why Does It Matter?,' *Melbourne Journal of International Law* 2, p. 477.

Schabas, W.A. (2003), 'National Courts Finally Begin to Prosecute Genocide, the "Crime of Crimes",' *Journal of International Criminal Justice* 1, p. 39, p. 55.

Schabas, W.A. (2001a), 'Cambodia: Was It Really Genocide?,' *Human Rights Quarterly* 23, p. 470.

Schabas, W.A. (2001b), 'The Crime of Genocide in the Jurisprudence of the International Criminal Tribunals for the Former Yugoslavia and Rwanda,' in H. Fischer, C. Kress and S. Luder (eds), *International and National Prosecution of Crimes Under International Law*, p. 447, Berlin Verlag, Berlin.

Schabas, W.A. (2001c), 'The *Jelisic* Case and the *Mens Rea* of the Crime of Genocide,' *Leiden Journal of International Law* 14, p. 125.

Schabas, W.A. (2001d), 'Problems of International Codification – Were the Atrocities in Cambodia and Kosovo Genocide?,' *New England Law Review* 35, p. 287.

Schabas, W.A. (2000), *Genocide in International Law: The Crime of Crimes*, Cambridge University Press, Cambridge.

Schabas, W.A. and M. Imbleau (1997), *Introduction to Rwandan Law*, p. 35, Editions Yvon Blais, Cowansville, Québec.

Schabas, W.A. (1996), 'Justice, Democracy, and Impunity in Post-genocide Rwanda: Searching for Solutions to Impossible Problems,' *Criminal Law Forum* 7, p. 523.

Schacht, J. (1964), *An Introduction to Islamic Law*, Clarendon Press, Oxford.

Schachter, O. (1989), 'Entangled Treaty and Custom,' in Y. Dinstein (ed.), *International Law at a Time of Perplexity*, p. 717, Martinus Nijhoff Publishers, Dordrecht.

Shaw, M.N. (1989), 'Genocide and International Law,' in Y. Dinstein (ed.), *International Law at a Time of Perplexity*, p. 797, Martinus Nijhoff Publishers, Dordrecht.

Shelton, D. (1999), *Remedies in International Human Rights Law*, Oxford University Press, Oxford and New York.

Sibert, M. (1951), *Traité de droit international public. Le droit de la paix*, vol. 1, p. 446.

Simons, G. (1998), *The Scourging of Iraq: Sanctions, Law, and Natural Justice*, p. 223, St. Martin's Press, New York.

Steven, L.A. (1999), 'Genocide and the Duty to Extradite or Prosecute: Why the United States is in Breach of Its International Obligations,' *Virginia Journal of International Law* 39, p. 425.

Stierlin, H. (1976), *Adolf Hitler: A Family Perspective*, Atcom, New York.

Stillschweig, K. (1949), 'Das Abkommen zur Bekämpfung von Genocide,' *Die Friedens-Warte* 49, p. 93, Blätter für internationale Verständigung und zwischenstaatliche Organisation, H. Wehberg (ed.).

Storey, M. (1998), 'Kruger v The Commonwealth: Does Genocide Require Malice?,' *University of New South Wales Law Journal* 21, p. 224.

Sundiata, I.K. (1990), *Equatorial Guinea: Colonialism, State Terror, and the Search for Stability*, Westview Press, Boulder.

Toland, J. (1977), *Adolf Hitler*, Ballantine, New York.

Toynbee, A.J. (1915), *Armenian Atrocities: The Murder of a Nation*, Hodder & Stoughton, London and New York.

Triffterer, O. (2001), 'Genocide, Its Particular Intent to Destroy in Whole or in Part the Group as Such,' *Leiden Journal of International Law* 14, p. 399.

van der Vyver, J.D. (1999), 'Prosecution and Punishment of the Crime of Genocide,' *Fordham International Law Journal* 23, p. 286.

Van Schaack, B. (1997), 'The Crime of Political Genocide: Repairing the Genocide Convention's Blind Spot,' *Yale Law Journal* 106, p. 2259.

Verhoeven, J. (1991), 'Le crime de génocide: originalité et ambiguïté,' *Revue belge de droit international* 24, no. 1, p. 5.

Walker, C. (1992), *The Prevention of Terrorism in British Law*, Manchester University Press, Manchester and New York.

White, A.A. (1949), 'Tomorrow One May Be Guilty of Genocide,' *Texas Bar Journal* 12, p. 203.

Whiteman, M. (1937), *Damages in International Law*, vol. 1, p. 275, US Government Printing Office, Washington.

Ziemele, I. (1999), 'Questions Concerning Genocide: A Note on the Supreme Court Judgements in Cases #PAK-269 of 4 November 1996 and #K-38 of 13 December 1995,' *Latvian Human Rights Quarterly* 7-10, p. 327.

Ziemele, I. (1997), 'The Application of International Law in the Baltic States,' *German Yearbook of International Law* 40, p. 261.

Zimmerman, A. (2003), 'Main Features of the New German Code of Crimes against International Law (*Völkerstrafgesetzbuch*),' in M. Neuner (ed.), *National Legislation Incorporating International Crimes: Approaches of Civil and Common Law Countries*, p. 137, Berliner Wissengeschafts Verlag, Berlin.

Zimmermann, A. (1998), 'The Creation of a Permanent International Criminal Court,' *Max Planck Yearbook of United Nations Law* 2, p. 169.

Index

Made in United States
North Haven, CT
29 January 2024

48055621R00176